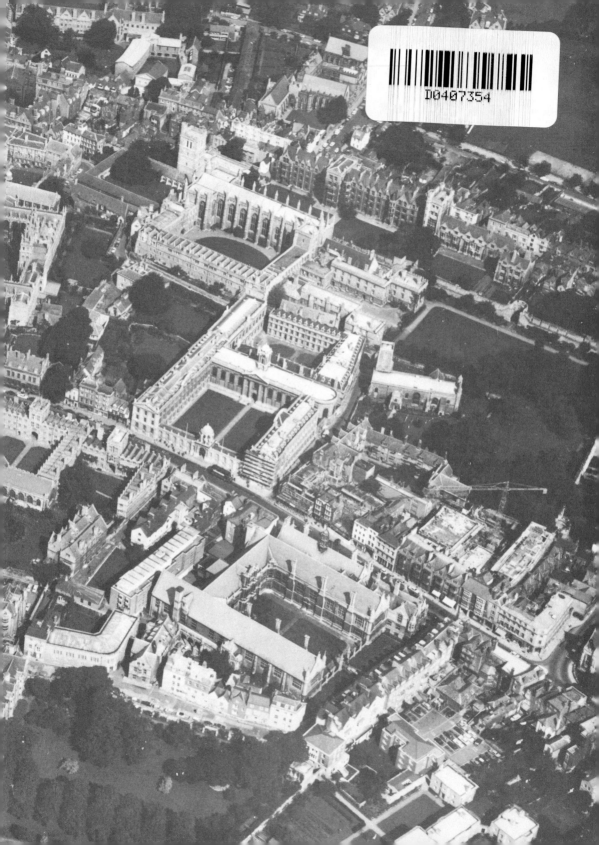

THE REGIONS OF BRITAIN

The Upper Thames

THE REGIONS OF BRITAIN
Previous and forthcoming titles include:

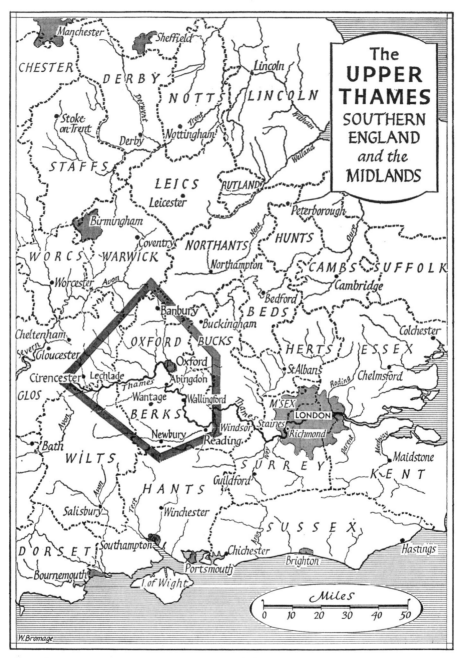

Map 1   *The Upper Thames, Southern England and the Midlands.*

J. R. L. ANDERSON

The
Upper
Thames

EYRE & SPOTTISWOODE · LONDON

First published 1970
© *1970 J. R. L. Anderson*
Printed in Great Britain for
Eyre & Spottiswoode (Publishers) Ltd
11, New Fetter Lane, London E.C.4
by Cox & Wyman Ltd,
Fakenham and London
S.B.N. 413 27400 4

Contents

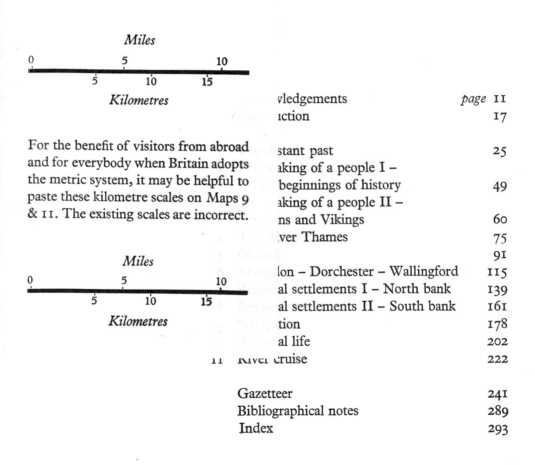

Metric Conversion

Miles

For the benefit of visitors from abroad and for everybody when Britain adopts the metric system, it may be helpful to paste these kilometre scales on Maps 9 & 11. The existing scales are incorrect.

Miles

Kilometres

Illustrations

Acknowledgements

This book is about my home, in a part of England where my mother's family has lived for something like 1,000 years. I have drawn facts (and, perhaps, a few fancies) from so many sources that I cannot hope to acknowledge them all fairly. And I have, I fear, a magpie mind which stores trinkets from a lifetime of reading and listening in the corners of memory without always instructing the brain's computer to recall where they came from. If I have drawn on anyone's work without saying so, I am sorry.

My conscious debt is so great that I can hardly hope to pay it. In common with all who care for the Thames, I am overwhelmingly indebted to F. S. Thacker, who spent every spare moment of his life in compiling an immense history of the river. He lived, it may be, in a more leisured age, for most of his work was done before the First World War. Advantage or not, his industry would shame most of us. And if there were fewer harassments in life then, he walked where we go by car, and he explored the river without benefit (or curse) of outboard motor. What he did have above all was passion. He knew and loved almost every reed in the river, explored physically every yard of it, and explored, too, in a hundred documentary sources, from the *Chronicon Monasterii* of Abingdon Abbey through the dusty files of endless Parliamentary Proceedings, spread over centuries. I doubt if his work could be repeated, but he did it so well, and his scholarship is so meticulous, that he did it for all time. It was nearly lost, or all but lost. He published his books privately, at his own expense, Volume I of his General History in 1914, and Volume II of his detailed study of every lock, weir and bridge on the river, in 1920. Inevitably, these works went out of print and became extremely rare. In 1968 they were rescued and restored in photo-litho

11

copies of the original texts by David & Charles of Newton Abbot, a fine piece of publishing enterprise. In my own sketch of the history of navigation on the Thames I owe almost everything to Thacker, and I can but hope that he would approve of the new bridge across the centuries that I have tried to construct with the stones he hewed. I must thank, too, Mr G. E. Walker, for many years Secretary to the Thames Conservancy, who replied patiently and good-humouredly to my many letters, and who gave me much valuable information; and Mr Kingsley Belsten, who put at my disposal much original work based on researches by him and Mr H. Compton relating to the Thames at Oxford and Eynsham.

Mrs Ruth Parsons lent me a fascinating *History of Shipton-under-Wychwood*, compiled by her mother, Mrs Muriel Groves, for a Women's Institute competition in 1935 (and deservedly winning a prize). Major R. A. Colvile lent me a rare copy of the Rev. J. A. Giles's *History of the Town and Parish of Bampton*, published privately in 1848, and a number of other valuable documents. Mr R. D'O. Aplin gave me particularly helpful information about Bloxham, and Mr C. A. Butler lent me a copy of his address on the Bloxham Feoffees to Banbury Historical Society in 1961. Mr Thomas M. Eyston, who lives at Hendred House, East Hendred, held by his family in unbroken succession through five centuries, generously gave up time to let me talk to him.

I owe a particular debt to my mother Mrs G. M. L. Anderson for her care in preserving family records through the upheavals of two world wars. And I must acknowledge a special, though posthumous, debt to my kinsman, Sir Alexander Croke, of Studley, for his immense labour in compiling *The Genealogical History of the Croke Family, originally named Le Blount*, published by John Murray in two quarto volumes in 1823. Sir Alexander carries the family back to a Danish Viking who flourished around A.D. 700 . . . a pleasing thought, but they were confused times. With the ninth century marriage of another ancestor, Baldwin II, count of Flanders, to Elstrude, daughter of King Alfred, the genealogy has more of the substance of history. Their granddaughter married a Danish Viking, and the great-grandsons of this marriage came back to the Upper Thames with Duke William in 1066. This is particularly interesting in showing how mixed-up Saxon and Viking families were before the Conquest which established the Norman Vikings in England.

Mr Charles Birdsall and other officers of the Department of Employment and Productivity went to much trouble on my behalf in preparing a statistical survey of livelihoods and jobs in the region. The Meteorological Office at Bracknell provided me with invaluable records of regional rainfall and climate, and the

Ministry of Transport gave me generous help with details of road schemes and planned motorway routes. Many officials of local authorities in the region were equally generous with their time in answering my questions. They include Messrs D. Murray John (Town Clerk of Swindon), A. A. Crabtree (Town Clerk of Cheltenham) F. G. E. Boys (Town Clerk of Banbury), Leslie Southern (Town Clerk of Newbury), R. A. Ingram (Town Clerk of Chipping Norton), E. W. J. Nicholson (Town Clerk of Abingdon), D. Waring (Clerk to Cirencester U.D.C.), R. Hopcraft (Clerk to Thame U.D.C.), Wilfrid C. Wigney (Clerk to Ploughley R.D.C.), A. F. Barrett (Clerk to Northleach R.D.C.), L. F. Radford (Clerk to Abingdon R.D.C.), L. C. Wort (Clerk to Bullingdon R.D.C.), M. G. Knapman (Clerk to Chipping Norton R.D.C.), E. Francis (Surveyor to Bradfield R.D.C.), C. D. Read (Clerk to Faringdon R.D.C.), Ernest Rowles (Clerk to Witney R.D.C.), L. Woodgate (Clerk to Wantage R.D.C.), H. F. Daw (Clerk to Cheltenham R.D.C.), and D. J. Brittain (Clerk to Hungerford R.D.C.).

Canon R. G. Gibbon, vicar of Somerford Keynes, ignored rain to show me the wonderful Saxon door of his church, and gave me a copy of his scholarly history of the parish. Mr G. R. Starr, of the Atomic Energy Research Establishment at Harwell gave me much help, as did Mr Richard Early, of Charles Early and Marriott, the Witney blanket company which celebrated its tercentenary in 1969, Mr W. L. Murdock, Land Agent to the Duke of Marlborough at Woodstock, Mr J. P. Honeywill, of Smiths Industries, Witney, Mr B. W. Hanning and Mr B. Dray, of General Foods, Banbury, Alcan Industries, Banbury, Mr R. H. G. Ring, of Dent, Allcroft and Company, Miss Helen Anderson, warden of Denham College of the National Federation of Women's Institutes, Miss Jean Cook, then director of the Oxfordshire Museum at Woodstock, Mr Roye England, of the Pendon Museum at Long Wittenham, Mr D. J. Kinnersley, General Manager of the British Waterways Board, Mr Richard Winter, of Town Bridge Antiques, Fairford. I am grateful for letters and kindly suggestions from the Rev. W. H. Cox, Minister of Abingdon Baptist Church, Mr William Breakspear, Mrs Marjorie Boyles, Mr W. Tynan, and Mr J. W. Eborn.

I owe very much to Professor W. G. Hoskins both for many practical suggestions and for his generous encouragement, and to my publishers. They have saved me from many infelicities, and those that remain are wholly my own fault. The book owes its existence to a suggestion by Miss Tessa Harrow that I should write it.

Acknowledgements and thanks for permission to reproduce photographs are due to the Ashmolean Museum, Oxford, for plates 1, 5, 6, 9, 11a, 11b, 11c, 15, 17, 21a, and 21b; to Pix Photos for plates 3, 7, and 12; to the Estate Office, Blenheim Palace for plate 8; to *The Oxford Mail and Times* for plates 10a, 16a, 16b, 26a, 26b,

30a, 30b, 36a, and 36b; to *The Architect & Building News* for plate 10b; to the United Kingdom Atomic Energy Authority for plate 13; to Mr Ivor Fields for plate 35b; and to Aerofilms for plate 33 and the picture that appears on the endpapers. All the maps were drawn by W. Bromage.

To say this is one thing: to convey my sense of gratitude to those who gave up hours of their time to help in finding and selecting pictures for me is more difficult. Mr Bromage combined his skill as a cartographer with endless patience. Mr P. D. C. Brown, Assistant Keeper of the Ashmolean, not only explored in the files of the museum to find precisely what I needed, but gave generously of his own deep scholarship to explain and to interpret photographs. Mr Alec Russell, librarian of *The Oxford Mail*, gave me similar help. Photographs not otherwise acknowledged are my own, and they owe everything but the taking to Mr Ivor Fields. He helped with advice on cameras and film, did all the processing for me, and lent me prints from his own expert collection.

Finally, I must offer a brief explanation of the Persian *tamām shōd* which appears on p. 240. Where a latin scribe would write *finis* at the end of a manuscript and an English author (of an older generation) put *"The End"*, medieval Persian literature was accustomed to use *tamām shōd*. I came across this many years ago, and it has always pleased me, for it does not mean *"The End"* but *"it is become complete, or whole"*. I owe the beautiful calligraphy of the phrase in Persian to Mr Salah Morsey.

A Note on Town Plans

The preparation of town plans for this book has involved a number of rather special difficulties, for the pace of physical change in many old towns is swifter than at any time in the region's history. And it is not necessarily lasting change, for plans may be modified almost as soon as they are made, planned development is not always carried out, and today's link-road to serve the motor-car may be tomorrow's pedestrian precinct. In places the printing-press is hard put to it to keep up with the bulldozer. Yet the medieval framework of old towns, the bony structure, as it were, for the changing body, still conditions change as the shape of the human skull conditions facial expression. I have tried, therefore, to present town plans in their formative structure rather than in a peripheral and perhaps transitory dress. In this there is both gain and loss. The town plan of Oxford, for instance, shows Castle Street in its formative shape, although with its old neighbour Church Street it has been transformed in the redevelopment of St Ebbe's. I hope the gain outweighs the loss, for historical setting is preserved through transitory change to meet traffic and other modern needs that are themselves constantly changing.   J.R.L.A.

For
Helen Elizabeth
who did most of the driving

Upper Thames

Introduction

The oldest man, or woman rather, whose bones have yet been found in Britain lived in the Thames Valley, and left her skull in the gravel at Swanscombe perhaps a quarter of a million years ago. Swanscombe woman was a true member of the species *homo sapiens*, and it makes (or should make) for humility to know that the size of her brain was about the average of that for English women now. Her father, her husband, her son, gathered enough from the river and its marshes to survive, to enable her to survive, to be one of our ten-thousand times great-grandmothers.

Swanscombe is not on the Upper Thames but in the valley of the lower river, nearer the sea, or, more probably when Swanscombe woman lived, nearer the Rhine to which the Thames was a tributary before the North Sea surged over the low-lying land around the Dogger Bank and gave the Thames an estuary of its own. Traces of man 250,000 years ago are few, and it is interesting that one of those few traces points to the habitation of the Thames Valley. Man is a wanderer, and when he had to move from place to place in search of food, he must have wandered up and down river valleys. Water gives life, and the Thames has sustained life since the people of the Swanscombe period, and perhaps their unknown ancestors, coming whence no one knows, first wandered to its banks. In those first chapters of the human story man could not always stay, even by the banks of a kindly river. Swanscombe woman left her bones in the gravel and we lose sight of her race, for intense cold came back with renewed glaciation farther north, and the *sapiens* branch of mankind wandered away – Britain was still joined by land to the Continent – in search of warmth. Our Neanderthal cousins seem to have been better fitted to survive cold, but this

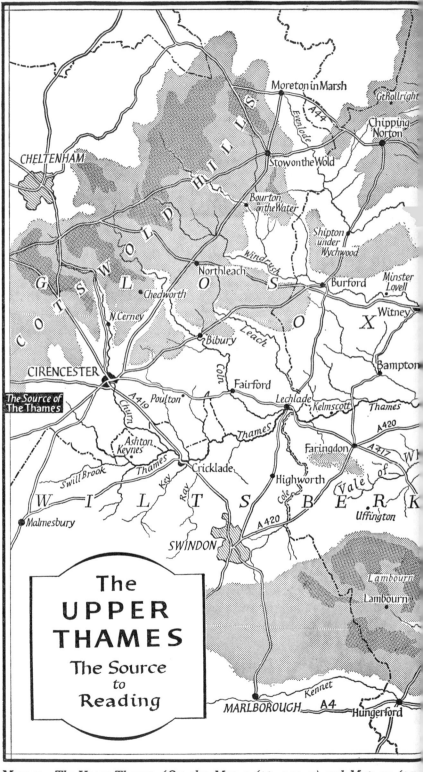

Map 2 *The Upper Thames. (See also Map 9 (pp. 140–1) and Map 11 (pp.*

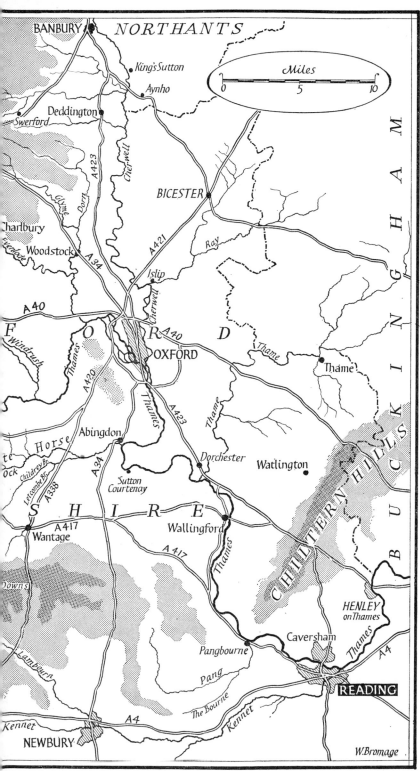

BANBURY • NORTHANTS

King's Sutton

Aynho

Miles

0   5   10

Swerford

Deddington

Charlbury

Cherwell

A423

Dorn

Glyme

BICESTER

Woodstock

A421

Ray

Evenlode

A40

A34

Islip

F   O   R   D

A40

Cherwell

Windrush

Thames

OXFORD

Thame

A420

A423

Thame

Thame

Horse

Abingdon

A34

Thames

Dorchester

Watlington

Ock

Childrey Br.

Letcombe Br.

A338

Sutton Courtenay

S   H   I   R   E

C H I L T E R N   H I L L S

B   U   C   K   I   N   G   H   A   M

A417

Wantage

Wallingford

A417

Thames

HENLEY on Thames

Downs

Thames

A4

Lambourn

Caversham

Pangbourne

Pang

READING

The Bourne

Kennet

Kennet

A4

NEWBURY

W. Bromage

162–3) for detailed maps of the Northern and Southern Tributaries respectively.

was not Neanderthal country. Neanderthal man wanted caves, not frozen river marshes.

The climate grew warmer again and our nearer ancestors came back to the Thames, making their way up river to a countryside that had the shape if not the surface cover of much that we know still. The time band moves through pre-history, to nearly recorded history, to written history. Neolithic farmers, Iberians, Celts and Gauls, Romans, Saxons, Danes and Normans came, passed and stayed. The region of the Upper Thames and its tributaries was the meeting-place of cultures, the battleground of competing invaders, the heartland of the Saxon people of Wessex whose kings became kings of England and knit the Anglo-Saxon people into the English nation. The Norman Vikings succeeded them, but county and even most parish boundaries as we know them still were fixed by the Saxons, Saxon mothers bore Norman sons, and soon that invasion like the rest was but an incident in the continuum of life along the Thames.

> Then 'twas before my time, the Roman
> At yonder heaving hill would stare:
> The blood that warms an English yeoman,
> The thoughts that hurt him, they were there.
> (A. E. Housman)

It is comforting to contemplate our remote forbears. Could they envisage us, their descendants, across a few thousand years? Can we envisage our descendants in the fourth or fifth millennium A.D.? There must have been many times when our ancestors doubted whether human life could go on: yet we are here. A regional study is a good lesson in the wonderful persistence of man.

I am concerned in this book with the region of the Upper Thames, roughly from the hill-country of its source, near Cirencester, in the west, to Banbury in the north, Thame in the east, Newbury and the Kennet in the south. It is an awkward shape on the map, because of our conventions of map-making. If you could look down from a satellite, say, and see it whole, its unity as a region would be apparent.

Save when dealing with nice, isolated islands, all boundaries of geographical study must to some extent be arbitrary: a book is finite, it must begin and end. Why include Newbury and leave out Reading? Why bring in Thame and not Aylesbury? Partly, but only a little partly, for convenience. Landscape and social setting really do change at Reading: there is not much in common between the heaths of Ascot and the chalk downs of north Berkshire; the downs are Thames country, their rivers flowing to the Thames, the heaths are not. The river itself

20

is more difficult to define, because of its meandering course and the continuity of its own nature. Below Reading, at Henley, say, the riverscape is not much different from the physical setting of Abingdon or Wallingford. But there are differences, and they are real. Below Reading the Thames begins to feel London. Although Henley is still in Oxfordshire and Marlow is in Buckinghamshire, both now look more to London as their capital than to Oxford or Aylesbury; both draw their major economic sustenance from London. Where the Kennet joins the Thames at Reading is a true regional boundary. So with Thame and Aylesbury. The Thame is a tributary of the Thames, and the lower valley of the Thame belongs to Thames-side. But above Thame it is a subtly different country. The Cherwell presents a similar problem. To think of the Cherwell is to think of Oxford, and of course the Cherwell belongs to Oxford and the Thames. But for the early part of its course the Cherwell flows through Northamptonshire, and one could not properly hold much of Northamptonshire to be part of an Upper Thames region. Banbury is another true border town.

Oxford presents a problem of another sort, and of peculiar difficulty. It is the natural capital of the region, and by far – by very far – its largest town. But Oxford is also unique, with a history that is international rather than regional, or even national. To have attempted to write fully about Oxford would have meant writing a book on Oxford. And there have been many books, whole libraries of books, on Oxford. This is not to say that Oxford does not merit yet another book, or many books: there is always room for a book which can find something new to say, however old the subject, and Oxford is of perennial interest. But it could not be this book. Oxford has a life and a history of its own, but just as the greatest men are yet part of their families, so Oxford, for all its individual greatness, is part of its region. I have tried to show the development of Oxford in its regional setting. This has meant omitting much of special interest to Oxford, but such a treasure-house of Western civilization has long been well-catalogued, and the proper way to enjoy the Ashmolean is to go there.

I hope, indeed, that this excellent principle may be applied generally. The gazetteer that forms the last part of the book has been designed to this end: every place listed has a six-figure reference to locate it precisely on the one-inch Ordnance map, and the reader with a car or a liking for country walks can plan private explorations for anything from an afternoon to a leisurely tour lasting several weeks. And he can travel in time as well as in space, to little churches whose stones were laid by Saxon hands, to earthworks far older than the Saxons, to fords and river-places where men and women walked when there were mammoths on the Berkshire Downs.

The particular theme of my book is the geo-social unity of the Upper Thames Region. This has been clouded by political history, for the region has always been border country and the unifying river has also been a boundary. In pre-Roman Britain it came between the main tribal areas of the Atrebates in the south, the Dobunni to the north-west, the Catuvellauni to the north and the Trinovantes in the east. Later it was on the boundaries of Wessex and Mercia, then between Saxon England and the Danelaw. After the Norman conquest the region came between the main centres of Norman power along the line of the Thames – London, Windsor, Reading, Oxford – and the unsettled Midlands and South-west. In our own period it is the borderland between the intense industrial development of the Midlands, the 'motor belt' from Birmingham to Oxford and Abingdon and the industrial-suburban spread of London along the Great West Road. North of A4, and the line of the new motorway M4, and west of the 'motor belt', the region is still almost wholly agricultural, a mixture of arable and pasture land supporting villages and little country-market towns. I should write 'that used to support', for agriculture has become capital-intensive and the land which once found work for everybody provides fewer and fewer jobs for people as tractors and machinery take on the tasks of human hands. I show in later chapters how other livelihoods have come into the region, and new ways of life. But prosperity is fragile, and a single Government decision – to curtail, say, the work of the Atomic Energy Authority at Harwell – or some development in the motor industry that might demand the concentration of production in an area away from Oxford and Abingdon, would bring severe economic hardship quickly. It would bring suffering to the region as a whole, but present concepts of regional planning offer next to no defences. Until the promised reforms in Local Government are carried out administration in the region will continue to reflect its border history, dividing it among four counties, Wiltshire, Gloucestershire, Oxfordshire and Berkshire, with salients in two more, Northamptonshire and Buckinghamshire. The establishment of a coherent regional administration based on Oxford is a social necessity. This is recognized in the Redcliffe–Maud report on local government, which recommends a new administrative area covering almost exactly the region outlined in this book. (It goes a few miles farther into Northamptonshire than I do, but is essentially the Upper Thames region depicted here.) It is encouraging that the geophysical entity of the region has at last been recognized so powerfully.

But in this era of central national planning that alone is not enough. Because the Upper Thames region had no nineteenth-century factory industry it is fortunate in having no industrial slums where such industry has decayed.

Present economic life can decay as well as past. It is right that national policy should be concerned with the rehabilitation of worn-out old industrial areas, but wrong that it should ignore the future problems of areas that are not worn-out: that is simply to condemn an unborn generation. Several people in the Upper Thames region have urged that to secure a healthy future the region should be developed as an area of science-based industry, employing the special skills that have been created in two decades of work at Harwell, and making the fullest use of proximity to the universities of Oxford and Reading. Such new industry, light, clean, capital-and-skill intensive and individually small in scale, could be spread among the villages and small towns without hurting the landscape or the quality of regional life, with benefit both to the region and to the nation. But such new industry needs to be planned coherently, and it cannot come at all if central national planning continues to restrict industrial development in the late twentieth century to areas that were industrialized early in the nineteenth. The quality of life in the countryside is worth preserving: let science help to preserve it.

By world standards, the Thames is not much of a river. Its length can be variously computed, but you cannot make it more than just over 200 miles, with an optimistic pair of dividers perhaps about 209 miles. Beside the Amazon, Yangtze, Mississippi, Volga, Danube, Rhine and many others, this is small beer. But size is not everything. David's place in history is more notable than Goliath's.

I

The distant past

The source of the Thames is disputed. The Thames Conservancy, the Ordnance Survey, and most authorities nowadays accept the source as a spring in a clump of trees at Trewsbury Mead, about $3\frac{1}{2}$ miles south-west of Cirencester, and just to the north of the old Roman road (Fosse Way) between Cirencester and Tetbury. This spring is marked on the One-inch Ordnance Map as 'Source of the River Thames'. But others hold that the true source of the Thames is not at Trewsbury Mead, but some eleven miles farther north, at Seven Springs, near Coberley, a little to the south of Cheltenham. On 26 February, 1937, the supporters of Seven Springs made an attempt to get their locality officially recognized when the Member of Parliament for Stroud put a question to the Minister of Agriculture in the Commons, asking that Seven Springs should be marked as the true source in the next edition of the Ordnance Survey. The attempt failed, the Minister accepting the conservators' view that Seven Springs is the source not of the Thames but of the Churn, a tributary that joins the Thames at Cricklade.

It is an argument that can never be wholly settled. If the ultimate source of a river is the source farthest from the sea of the waters it carries, then Seven Springs has a good case. But which is tributary, which main river? The stream that flows from Trewsbury Mead has been called the Thames throughout recorded history, and the rivulet from Seven Springs undoubtedly is called the Churn, giving its name to the villages of North and South Cerney, and to Cirencester (Corinium) itself. To promote the Churn to be the Thames would be against all history; moreover, it would be unfair to the Churn, which has a place on the map of its own, and has held it for near two thousand years. Certainly the

Churn feeds the Thames, and with Cole, Ray, Cherwell, Evenlode, Windrush, Ock, Thame, Kennet, Pang and a host of other streams is part of the Thames river system. It must be left at that.

On leaving Trewsbury Mead the Thames flows more or less due east, as one would expect for a river draining to the North Sea. A glance at the map without studying the contours would suggest an outlet for the Thames somewhere around Clacton: had the Thames flowed thus, Colchester would probably have been the capital of Britain, and London a small market town serving an agricultural district of Kent or Essex. The path of the Thames made history differently. Having flowed docilely east for thirty miles or so, the Thames comes up against a ridge of hard high ground at Cumnor and makes a right-angled turn to the north. It sweeps in a semi-circle round Wytham to turn almost due south to create Oxford, a meeting-place of land and water trackways between the high ground of Berkshire and the Chilterns. From Oxford it continues to flow generally southwards until it meets the greatest challenge to its course in the ridge of chalk downs standing across southern England from Hampshire to the Wash. At Goring the Thames cuts through this ridge, turns east again, gathers the Kennet at Reading and flows on unhindered to London, the estuary and the sea. The remarkable cut at Goring – the Goring Gap – has been one of the physical determinants of English life from pre-history through all of history. It opens a path for invasion or commerce from the coast of Kent, the nearest shore to the Continent, into the heart of England. The Thames itself is a highway to and from the sea. It has always been navigable (though sometimes with difficulty) to Oxford and, for smaller boats or barges, to Lechlade, and even to Cricklade. The tidal limit of its estuary is the natural site for a port, with the river to serve its hinterland and, at need, to be defensive. So London came into being.

In terms of geological time, the countryside of the Thames is young; for most of the past 200 million years it has been beneath the sea. The vast earth movements of earlier periods that hurled up the ancient rocks that form the Scottish Highlands, and the less ancient, but still very old, landscape of the Pennines and the Mendip Hills, have left no mark in the Thames valley, although, since they brought in the waters that did shape it, they obviously influenced its formation, as they have influenced the physical form of the whole world. The story of the Thames may reasonably be said to begin between 170 million and 140 million years ago, with the seas of the geological period called the Jurassic. The lives and death of incalculable millions of marine organisms laid down the oolitic limestone that forms the Cotswolds, and the ooze of the Jurassic seas, brought down by

HUMAN TIME SCALE (BRITAIN)　　　MAN'S ANCESTRY　　　GEOLOGICAL TIME SCALE

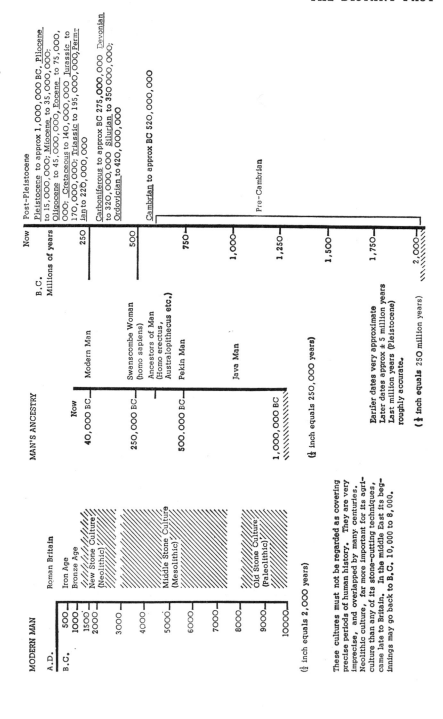

GEOLOGICAL TIME SCALE

Now　Post-Pleistocene

Pleistocene to approx 1,000,000 BC. Pliocene to 15,000,000; Miocene to 35,000,000: Oligocene to 45,000,000, Eocene to 75,000,000; Cretaceous to 140,000,000 Jurassic to 170,000,000; Triassic to 195,000,000, Permian to 220,000,000

Carboniferous to approx BC 275,000,000 Devonian to 320,000,000 Silurian to 350,000,000; Ordovician to 420,000,000

Cambrian to approx BC 520,000,000

Pre-Cambrian

B.C.
Millions of years
250
500
750
1,000
1,250
1,500
1,750
2,000

MAN'S ANCESTRY

Now

40,000 BC　Modern Man

250,000 BC　Swanscombe Woman (homo sapiens)
Ancestors of Man (Homo erectus, Australopithecus etc.)

500,000 BC　Pekin Man

Java Man

1,000,000 BC

(½ inch equals 250,000 years)

Earlier dates very approximate
Later dates approx ± 5 million years
Last million years (Pleistocene) roughly accurate.

(¼ inch equals 250 million years)

HUMAN TIME SCALE (BRITAIN)

MODERN MAN

A.D.　500
B.C.　1000
1500
2000
3000
4000
5000
6000
7000
8000
9000
10000

Roman Britain
Iron Age
Bronze Age
New Stone Culture (Neolithic)

Middle Stone Culture (Mesolithic)

Old Stone Culture (Paleolithic)

(½ inch equals 2,000 years)

These cultures must not be regarded as covering precise periods of human history. They are very imprecise, and overlapped by many centuries. Neolithic culture, far more important for its agriculture than any of its stone-cutting techniques, came late to Britain. In the middle East its beginnings may go back to B.C. 10,000 to 8,000.

rivers from the older land masses to the north and west, formed the clays that today make the soil of the Thames Valley itself, and of its tributary Vale of the White Horse. The earlier Jurassic seas seem to have been muddy waters. Later, they cleared a little, and corals grew, to form the Corallian limestones that crop up as the hills round Faringdon and Cumnor – the North Berkshire Ridge – which force the Thames to its remarkable turn north and then south to get round them above Oxford.

As the Jurassic period ended, about 140 million years ago, the seas that covered most of Southern England became exquisitely clear, perhaps because the older highlands had been drained of most of their mud, and a hot, dry climate kept them mud-free. In those clear waters, the shells of marine creatures and the fossilized remains of seaweeds were deposited as pure white chalk, forming the ridge of chalk uplands that has done so much to influence human development in the region. It was a slow process: it took about 2,500 years to form one inch of chalk rock. The bed of chalk lying across Berkshire is about 700–850 ft thick, which means that some twenty-five million years went to its making.

Those clear Cretaceous seas were important to later humanity in other ways than by forming the bare chalk downs that made for easy travel and fairly safe living, free from the dangers and ambushes of the marshy jungles in the vales. Beautiful glass-like sponges – siliceous creatures – grew in the clean water, and their remains made the flints, deposited with the chalk, that gave man the best of his early cutting tools and which were, for Southern England, perhaps the first commodity of international trade.

About thirty million years ago, after the bones of the Thames landscape had been largely formed, came the last of the great earth-spasms that shaped the world around us. This is known as the Alpine Folding because it threw up the Alps – and also the Himalayas. The area that is now Britain was well to the west of the epicentre of this tremendous earthquake, and as the tremors spread westward their force was gradually spent. They had little effect on Southern England, though they tipped the hills a little, and thrust up that curious steeple of chalk on the south bank of the Thames that the Normans, with an eye for such things, quickly chose as the site for Windsor Castle.*

Throughout the formative period of the region – in the modern counties of

---

* Although the Alpine folding had little effect on the relatively soft rocks of Southern England, it had a marked influence on the landscape farther north. The soft southern rock simply tilted a little, but older, harder rock resisted the earth movement and tended to crack, releasing lava from volcanic activity in other parts of Britain.

Gloucestershire, Oxfordshire and Berkshire – the land mass that is now Britain was as much a part of the North American continent as of Europe, or rather, it was part of a vast North Atlantic land area stretching from Greenland across Canada and the northern United States. Fairly late in geological time, in the Pliocene period that began about fifteen million years ago, the sea made the decisive inrush that separated Greenland from Europe, and the North Atlantic made Britain a peninsular jutting out from Europe. South-East England was connected to Europe by a land bridge across the Channel until almost historical times: the chalk ridge lying across the Channel from Kent to the Pas de Calais was not finally cut until about 6,000 B.C. long after the coming of man.

As the aeons of geological time passed, the hot dry climate of the Cretaceous period slowly changed to a supposedly temperate climate, no doubt influenced by the spreading Atlantic ocean, of the Pliocene period, and then, because of changes in the ice-cap that are little understood, to the intense cold of the so-called Ice Age. This brings us to the almost recent Pleistocene period, from about one million to perhaps ten thousand years ago. 'Ice Age' is a bad term, because there were several glaciations as the ice-cap advanced, with warmer, inter-glacial periods between them as the ice temporarily receded. We are presumably living in an inter-glacial period today, and the ice may one day return, though the time scale of tens of thousands of years over which these major climatic changes happen may offer us no immediate threat. But past glaciations have influenced human history by determining the landscape in which our ancestors had to survive. By the time the Pleistocene ice came south, the hill and river system of the Thames region was formed, and the effect of glaciations was to modify rather than to create physical land shapes. Southern England escaped relatively lightly in the severe cold periods. There were no great glaciers south of the Thames, and although North Berkshire once lay under ice, it was not a very thick ice cap. Its main effect was to mould the downs to the lovely rounded slopes they show today, and to grind exposed rocks to gravels, to drift downhill and mix with the clays in the valley soils. Perhaps the ice had one major influence in helping the Thames to cut the Goring Gap. Precisely how and when the river made its dramatic break through the imprisoning chalk ridge is uncertain. The very ancient Thames, as land was formed and there were hills to be drained, may have lost itself in marshes, seeping rather than flowing to the sea. Some hold that the river was once dammed by the chalk to form a considerable lake, and that in one period of melting ice the waters rose to surge over a natural dip in the chalk at Goring, afterwards gouging a channel through the ridge. Alternatively, a small

29

channel through some fissure in the chalk may have been enlarged by the grinding force of icebergs in the river: there are quite formidable masses of floating ice in the Thames in any hard winter, and in the various ice-ages there must have been bergs of awesome size and weight.

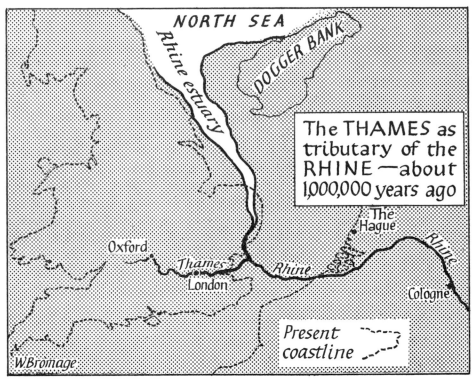

Map 3   *The Thames as a Tributary of the Rhine.*

The ebb and flow of ice affected the relationship of land and sea around the coasts of Britain. Such enormous quantities of water are held in ice that in periods of severe glaciation the level of the sea would fall materially, to rise again when the ice melted. For a long part – indeed for most – of its existence, the Thames had no estuary of its own, but was a tributary of the Rhine, meeting the Rhine as it flowed over land now drowned in the shallows of the North Sea. The final break with the Rhine, as England's final break with Continental Europe, is relatively recent.

The last severe glaciation came between 50,000 and 100,000 years ago, and lasted until perhaps 20,000 years ago, when the climate began a slow but steady improvement. Man was certainly in the Thames Valley before that last ice age. Swanscombe Woman lived at least a quarter of a million years ago, and near her in the Thames gravels have been found primitive stone implements of the culture called Acheulian, which may go back to 300,000 B.C. or so.

There is evidence that some of the very earliest of all more or less human creatures knew the Thames, wandering into Britain across Europe from Africa about half a million years ago; they could cross from Africa to Spain by a land bridge that then spanned the Straits of Gibraltar. These were people who used the earliest of shaped human tools, mostly a sort of prototype hand axe formed of a flintstone chipped to a rather jagged edge, following whatever might be the natural contour of the stone. Their culture is called Chellean, from a site at Chelles, on the river Maine in France. Chellean man lived in small communities, probably in trees in river valleys, or in caves by the seashore. He fed on what he could get from the woods or gather by beachcombing, turning, it is thought, to hunting animals for food as one of the 'ice ages' set in bringing winters when edible roots and berries grew sparse. Chellean axes have been found in the valley of the Wey, one of the lower tributaries of the Thames, and presumably Chellean man wandered in the Thames Valley, too. His epoch, by far the longest in the human story, is judged to have lasted from somewhere between 600,000–500,000 B.C. to around 300,000 B.C. He was succeeded by Acheulian Man (called after another French site, St Acheul, near Amiens), who was a better craftsman in flint. Acheulian man gave his flint axes a straight cutting edge, which made them more efficient.

Hand axes of this Acheulian culture of the Early Old Stone Age have been found scattered about the Upper Thames region, mostly in gravels along the line of the Thames, but also in the valleys of the Thame and Evenlode. This dim period of our human past, though shorter than the Chellean, covers an enormous span, from around 300,000 B.C. or so to 235,000 B.C. or thereabouts, an era of at least 65,000 years. Hand axes believed to date from early or fairly early in the Acheulian period have been found near Woodstock, at Wolvercote, near Oxford, near Sutton Courtenay, on the Thames below Abingdon, and in gravels about two miles to the east of Crowmarsh Gifford, on the Oxfordshire bank of the Thames across the river from Wallingford.

Stone tools of the Middle Acheulian period have been found at Abingdon, and near Oxford, Radley, Crowmarsh and Wallingford. A more advanced type of hand axe, attributed towards the end of the Acheulian period (c. 235,000 B.C.), has been found at Lechlade.

These relics of very early man prove beyond doubt the existence of human settlements in the Upper Thames Region before the onset of the last severe glaciation, but they are not enough to provide any clear pattern of settlement: moreover, such finds are the outcome neither of random chance nor of anything approaching a controlled search of the whole area; they come about partly because there happen to be gravel workings or excavations in a particular locality, partly because someone with archaeological leanings happens to be around at the right time. In a sense, they may be said almost to reflect the pattern of settlement in our own times, because they occur in places where man is now most active. Nevertheless, the distribution of Early Old Stone Age finds is interesting, for it suggests – if it cannot prove – that very early man chose for his settlements riverside or near-river places along the Thames and its tributaries that are still attractive as dwelling places today; that always have been attractive to mankind, giving rise to the villages and towns of our own period, most of which have geophysical roots going back to the distant past. The roots of some thriving Thames-side communities – Lechlade, Oxford, Abingdon and Wallingford among them – indeed go back far into pre-history.

Acheulian man must have wandered into the Thames valley from somewhere on what is now the Continent of Europe, crossing the Channel by land, for he came long before the land link across the Channel was severed; or perhaps he entered the Thames from what were then the marshes of the Rhine estuary, as later prehistoric peoples certainly did. Nothing but his stone axes has survived, but this is not to say that chipping stone axeheads was the limit of his culture. He must have used the axes for something: mere stones would have done almost as well for killing. Did he know anything of rafts or boats? It seems nearly inconceivable to carry knowledge of even the most rudimentary navigation to that remote stage of human development, but everything that we learn of primitive man carries back knowledge of human devices farther and farther into the past. Man is ingenious, and has always used ingenuity to save himself trouble. One of his first observations must have been that wood floats, and it is not a far step from there to sit astride a log and float with it, and then to lash two or three logs together to make a more or less manageable raft. There would be strong incentive to do this, for it would not have taken long to discover that it is often easier to move by water than by land. So perhaps some of those early men made their way up the Thames by raft. They would have had to work upstream, but when the river is low the current is not formidable, and to pole and haul a raft upstream would still have been easier than to hack and tear a way through the jungles of the river valleys.

Primitive man had few possessions, but he had skins and bits of bone and stick that he valued; and he had women and children. A raft load would keep his family and whatever were their household goods together; moreover, as long as he kept to the river he was sure of water, fish, and a fair supply of the birds and animals that he hunted. So I think it almost certain that some of the earliest settlers on the Upper Thames made their way there by the river itself, using the river for transport as it has been used throughout its history.

Primitive man chose the river for settlement because the river and its marshes and jungles could supply his needs better than the chalk downs which attracted later peoples. He was neither agricultural nor pastoral; he was simply a hunter and food-gatherer, collecting berries and edible roots where he could find them, and killing such animals as he could. The pattern of Old Stone Age finds suggests that primitive man penetrated the Thames as far as Oxford very early in his story, and from settlements around Abingdon and Oxford adventured west-ward from time to time, perhaps on hunting expeditions after the bigger game that roamed the more open country of the Cotswolds and North Berkshire. In warmer periods bison roamed this countryside (with the accompanying danger of lions that were as eager as man to feed on the bison). As the climate grew colder, reindeer, mammoths and the musk-ox replaced the bison and the lions. The onset of glaciation changed the countryside to something approaching the tundra of the Canadian Arctic, and man was hard put to it to survive. When he could kill nothing better he fell back on lemmings, small rat-like creatures that still inhabit Northern Scandinavia, whose ancestors have left their bones in parts of Southern England.

As glaciation grew more severe, primitive man did not survive in the Thames Region: he went away. There was still a land route to Continental Europe and a better climate in the South. Ice did not spread dramatically, like a forest fire: the climate worsened slowly, over thousands of years. As life in the Thames Region became harder and harsher, man simply retraced his steps, wandering back whence he came.

The British climate began to change for the better again after the last severe glaciation perhaps 20,000 years ago. At first it was not much of a change: a flicker of a slightly warmer summer one year and a little less ice on winter hill-sides. No doubt there were backslidings, a renewed harsh winter after a decade of slightly milder ones. Over centuries, however, there was a gradual shift to more liveable conditions. Cave refuges like Kent's Cavern, Torquay, and the Creswell Crags in Derbyshire where man was able to exist in a still sub-Arctic Britain are not to be found in the Upper Thames Region, and human remains of the later

c

periods of the Old Stone Age before 10,000 B.C. or so, when life in Britain was cold but not impossible, are few. Flakes of flint produced by techniques attributed to the Late Old Stone Age have been found near Reading and at Sutton Courtenay near Abingdon, but these traces of Late Old Stone Age people do not suggest long residence: they could easily derive from hunting expeditions. Moreover, dates and classifications of periods of human culture are all pretty wildly approximate, particularly when they extend into tens of thousands of years B.C. Habits and traditions overlap generations, even today. In my own village coal grates and oil-fired central heating exist side by side; I know a cottage lit by candles less than a hundred yards from one with television. And this is an age of swift technical change: when techniques and ways of doing things changed slowly, perhaps over thousands of years, men of one tribe might carry on with an accustomed way of making a flint tool long after a neighbouring group had adopted some more 'modern' method. Archaeological finds indicate that men and women of roughly (very roughly) this or that level of cultural development lived or passed here and there, but, particularly for the remoter periods of mankind, they cannot give any exact information of who they were, or why they left tools where they did. This is a necessary caveat to all attempts to interpret the remote past.

With improvement of the climate after about 10,000 B.C. the river valleys and wildfowl-rich marshes that had been attractive to very early man again became attractive to settlers. About this time a considerable migration was taking place in Northern Europe of a fair-haired people who seem to have started from Western Asia and penetrated into Sweden, Norway and Denmark. They are called Maglemosian, from 'Maglemose' ('Great Marsh'), the name of a marshy lake region where they settled in Denmark. They appear to have been primarily marsh or lake-dwellers, and they were skilled with boats, for on their migrations they had to make many river crossings. Offshoots of this folk made their way into Britain across the Rhine and the marshes of the Rhine estuary that were still more land than sea between the Netherlands and East Anglia. They worked their way up the Thames and into the Kennet valley, where they found a site greatly to their liking on what was then a small lake at Thatcham, near Newbury. They probably came up the Kennet (having entered the river from the Thames at what is now Reading) by boat, and when they found their lake near the north bank of the stream they made a clearing in the trees (then mostly birch and pine) for a settlement. The site seems to have been continuously in use, though not necessarily continuously lived in, for nearly 1,000 years, from 8,400 B.C. to about

7,500 B.C. Dates here are more reliable than the approximations of the Old Stone Age, for they can be checked against the archaeological evidence by the system known as 'carbon dating'. This is based on the known rate of 'decay' of a radioactive isotope of carbon known as 'Carbon 14'. It is present in all living matter, and although unstable and constantly decaying in life, it is as constantly renewed by inhalation (in plants as well as animals) of radioactive carbon from the atmosphere. This process of renewal ceases at death, and 'decay' sets in at a rate that can be calculated. The mathematics is not simple, because the process of radioactive decay continues theoretically to infinity; it can be considered most easily in terms of what is called 'half life'. The calculated 'half life' of Carbon 14 is 5,760 years – that is, any given quantity of Carbon 14, not subject to renewal, will have diminished by half in 5,760 years. The remaining half will then have a 'half life' of 5,760 years, after which the remaining quarter will have a similar 'half life', and so on to infinity. The quantity of Carbon 14 present in living matter is known, and by measuring the amount remaining in dead organic substances – bone or wood, for instance – the time that has elapsed since death can be computed. After very long periods the Carbon 14 content remaining to be measured becomes infinitesimal, but advanced techniques of measurement have been devised which are said to give accurate results to ages of 50,000 years, or even more. Perhaps one may be a little sceptical of the degree of accuracy at these extreme ranges, but carbon-dating is an invaluable tool of modern archaeology, and for the first few millennia after death the degree of accuracy is considered to be high.

The Thatcham site has provided a good deal of evidence of the way of life of those early lake dwellers, from whose stock some authorities consider that many fair-haired Britons today may be descended.★ Continuous work at cutting back trees and undergrowth to keep their dwelling place clear is suggested by the quantity of flint tools found on the site – seventeen axes, and numerous other worked flints, including interesting little blades called 'microliths', sharp flakes of flint about half an inch long, which apparently were set in sticks to make a saw-edge (and a most efficient one). No doubt these sharp little flakes were also used to tip spears and arrows, for the bow was in use by then. There seems to have been almost a factory for making flint tools at Thatcham, for the quantity of cores and chippings found there shows that implements were made on the spot, though the raw flints for working were not local. These were brought from the

---

★ 'When you see fair-haired men and women in the British Isles you may as reasonably reckon them descended from this remote Maglemose stock as Angles, Saxons and Vikings.' S. E. Winbolt, *Britain B.C.*

chalk downs to the North West. The distance is not great, a round trip of ten miles or so would have kept the 'factory' supplied with flints; but the organization of supply of the right quality of flints is evidence of a considerable degree of foremanship or leadership, even if this were exercised only within some family group.

The Thatcham people probably lived mainly on fish and birds, but other bones found on the site indicate that they enjoyed – at any rate after successful hunting trips – a pretty varied diet. Bones found there include wild pig, red deer and roe deer, wild ox and horse (an early form of horse, the size of a small pony, hunted for food.) Bones of beaver, fox, badger, pine-marten and wild cat indicate a fair supply of animals to be hunted or trapped for fur: the flint 'scrapers' made in the factory on the site were clearly for dressing skins. Most interesting of all, perhaps, bones of dogs have been found at Thatcham, suggesting that dogs were domesticated and trained for help in hunting. The dog may have been useful for defence, too, for the bones of wolves show that man had to compete for his food, and the dog would be an ally worth having.

There were other settlements of similar people in the valley of the Kennet, and another 'factory' for making flint tools was found during excavation at the sewage outfall works just outside Newbury itself. Probably there were similar settlements on the Upper Thames and in the marshes of the Ock (the Vale of the White Horse). The Thatcham and Newbury finds were fortunate, for the size of these Mesolithic (Middle Stone Age) communities was tiny, often a single family, probably never more than a few related families of cousins and near kin. Life was hard, infant mortality must have been appalling, and to survive to forty was to reach old age. All the evidence suggests a population very thin on the ground, and probably migrant: a place would be inhabited while the hunting and fishing was good, and then abandoned for a time, to be returned to later (as at Thatcham, where occupation, though probably at intervals, went on for nearly 1,000 years). Where land has been dug and re-dug for centuries it is remarkable that any traces of human settlement thousands of years ago should remain: one cannot expect many.

The Thatcham settlement appears to have been abandoned about 7,500 B.C., after severe flooding. Later Mesolithic sites have been found outside the Upper Thames Region, near Selborne in Hampshire, and at Downton, Wiltshire. It is reasonable to suppose that the descendants of settlers who came up the Thames into the Kennet valley migrated South and West. The site near Selborne is believed to have been occupied between 4,470 B.C. and 4,230 B.C., showing that this Mesolithic culture lasted a long time. The Hampshire site is also interesting for indicating the enormous labour that went into making flint tools: of 186,000 pieces of flint counted there, only some four bits in every hundred were usable as blades; the rest was waste.

Around 6,000 B.C. Britain was finally severed from the Continent. For a long time before this final break the low-lying lands of the Rhine estuary in what is now the North Sea had been sinking slowly, and gradually the sea engulfed them, leaving at first a series of small, marshy islands, and a low ridge of more or less firm ground where now the Dogger Bank lies submerged. At last this went too, and then in some raging gale the sea broke through the remaining ridge of chalk between Kent and the Pas de Calais, and Britain was an island. It is believed that this complete encirclement of sea brought some further improvement in the British climate, the insulating waters modifying Continental extremes of cold, and enabling currents of relatively warm water emanating from the Gulf Stream to assist in maintaining conditions more or less equable and temperate.

The great event of Britain's final assumption of insularity is unrecorded, and it may be doubted if it meant anything at all to the scattered families of hunters and fisherfolk living in the neighbourhood of the Upper Thames. In the long run it influenced their history profoundly.

How the next wave of settlers reached the region is unknown, but it was by far the most important influx of people yet to have taken place, for the newcomers brought conceptions of agriculture and of flock-keeping that begin the story of modern Britain. The newcomers brought much else as well: improved techniques for making flint implements to assist their agriculture, pottery, and the domestic skills that enable man to make a settlement a home.

Between the fairly precise dating of the Mesolithic (Middle Stone Age) Hampshire settlements around 4,230 B.C. and the earliest finds of the new culture, dated at about 3,500 B.C., there is a gap of nearly 1,000 years. There is no reason to suppose that the old culture suddenly died out – indeed, there is strong evidence that it didn't, for traces of an older pattern of life remain in archaeological finds from after 3,000 B.C. Populations at various stages of cultural development may have known little of one another: the new farmers sought the cultivable soil on the slopes of the chalk downs, and on the gravel terraces of the rivers, while the older inhabitants kept to the marshes and thick woods of the valley bottoms. Ultimately the peoples must have met: perhaps the older race was enslaved by the technically more efficient newcomers, who needed labour for their farms and flocks. No doubt the older race could teach the newcomers a thing or two about hunting. The races must have merged in the end, perhaps by captivity, perhaps by more pacific mingling – with what were then vast open spaces of virgin land to be had for the taking there was no economic competition to lead to hostility, and no need for the newcomers to kill off the older race, who did not want their farmland, anyway.

Because these new immigrants brought improved techniques of flint working, their culture has been called Neolithic (New Stone), continuing the nomenclature of cultures from the Palaeolithic (Old Stone) Age, through Mesolithic (Middle Stone) to the New. It is not a good name, for the agriculture and ideas of trade that these people brought with them are vastly more significant than mere techniques of stoneworking. But 'Neolithic' is so rooted in archaeological study that it remains a general label. What is important is to remember that whatever labels are used for cultural stages – Bronze Age and Iron Age equally – they do not imply any *sudden* transition from one period to the next. Carpenters still saw by hand, in spite of power tools. Men and women at different stages of development must continue to live side by side – a fact which is at the core of some of the bitterest political problems of our own time.

The first immigrants bringing a Neolithic culture to the region apparently came into it from the Bristol Channel, or the Westerly beaches of the English Channel. They were a Mediterranean people, perhaps originally from Crete, who had acquired knowledge of the agricultural civilizations of the Middle East, and, as they multiplied, sent offshoots to find new land to the West. Over centuries they spread across the Mediterranean to Spain and into the Biscay areas of France, learning seamanship on the way, or rather, becoming master seamen, for they had probably known boats as far back as their folk memories went. Whether they crossed to England from France or the Atlantic coast of Spain is not known: the prevailing south-westerly wind would have helped them on their way to landings on the Bristol Channel coast, or on the beaches of the English Channel. People of the same stock also reached Ireland, apparently from Spain, for the old name for Ireland – Hibernia – derives from its settlement by people from Iberia.

The newcomers found good upland routes inland, to the kind of country that they were looking for to farm. From the Cotswolds* into the valley of the Upper Thames, or along the chalk downs through Dorset and Wiltshire into Berkshire,

---

* The chines and valleys of the Cotswolds were much more densely wooded then than they are now. The name Cotswold is derived from the OE Cod's weald, meaning Cod's (a personal name) forest, so that there must have been thick woods still in Saxon times (as in some of the chines there are today). The exposed summits and upper slopes of the hills were more sparsely wooded, and prehistoric travellers followed open country where they could.

they could travel in relatively open country, finding game to feed themselves. The chalk downs, with their overlay of light soil, almost naturally terraced on their gentler slopes, and the good gravelly earth of the old terraces cut by the Thames, were much to the liking of these farmers. They began to plant crops, and to assemble herds. They also began a process that has not ceased, of changing the whole landscape by the activities of man.

The landscape as these Neolithic farmers found it was mostly damp oak forest in the lower valleys, with a dense undergrowth of thorn and bramble. Much of the floor of the river valleys was waterlogged and marshy, though the Thames itself, particularly round Abingdon, and in its upper reaches above Oxford, offered good stretches of fairly open country. On higher ground, the trees – for the most part oak and ash, with some birch and yew, but few beeches then – tended to thin, and on the chalk of the downs woodland was sparser still. On the ridge of the downs, which formed the high road of these ancient peoples – a green track still called The Ridge Way – there were no woods to bar the way. There were occasional trees – the lone thorn is typical of the high downs still – and perhaps some scrub, but nothing that a man could not walk round easily, nothing that required the hacking of a path.

Nothing remains of very early settlements on the downs themselves, for being so bare of vegetation the chalk has weathered, and the surface is believed to be about two feet lower now than it was when the first settlers came. Traces of ancient cultivation that show in photographs from the air, as marks that still shadow modern grass, probably date from a period considerably later – 2,000–1,000 B.C. or so.

A picture of the general life of the region in the early period of agricultural settlement can be pieced together, however, from a remarkable group of finds at Abingdon, and from what is known of related cultures elsewhere. And although we may not have much direct evidence of how these early inhabitants of the region lived, we do know what elaborate care they took of their dead, at any rate of their dead chieftains, for they built impressive tombs for them called Long Barrows. These great earthworks have survived millennia, and survive still, a present, visible link between ourselves and our remote ancestors. One of the greatest of these works of Neolithic man, 200 ft long and with a portico of huge stones, looks down on the Ock valley – the Vale of the White Horse – from the ridge of the downs about a mile from White Horse Hill. It is called Wayland's Smithy, though the legend of the Teutonic God, Wayland the Smith, from which it gets its present name, was brought by the Saxons more than three thousand years after the time of the men who built it.

The settlement at Abingdon, which seems to have come fairly early in the Neolithic period, although it continued in use long after it, was on good gravel ground on a sort of peninsula between two brooks draining into the Thames. The main stream of the Thames at Abingdon now was originally an artificial channel cut by the monks of Abingdon Abbey, and the behaviour of the river has been much modified by locks and weirs; it is hard to visualize the riverside of 4,000 years ago. The settlement would seem to have been well chosen, surrounded on three sides by water or marsh. Its landward flank was protected by a causewayed ditch, that is, a ditch with a section left undug to form an entrance, a feature typical of prehistoric camps or enclosures, mostly on high ground, and mostly constructed a good deal later, that are numerous in the region.

In the settlement there were a number of storage pits for grain, and traces of cooking hearths have been found, with bones and broken pots around them. The early pottery (there was later pottery, too, from the Bronze Age) is mostly of a type that archaeologists call Neolithic A, from the first wave of Neolithic immigration. Flints found there show mastery of advanced flint working techniques: they include a beautiful leaf-shaped arrowhead, polished axes, knives, scrapers, and the blades of a flint sickle. More interesting than anything else, perhaps, were stone axes made from Langdale rock from Westmorland, proving the existence of Neolithic trade. The trade route from the North West no doubt entered the region via the Cotswolds. Langdale axes have been found by the Thames below Abingdon at Sutton Courtenay, near Dorchester, where the Thame joins the Thames, and scattered about the region in North Berkshire, near Bampton in Oxfordshire, and in the Windrush valley. Abingdon may have been a centre for this very early trade.

Those first Berkshire farmers grew a primitive form of wheat known as *emmer*, and a little barley: the grains have been identified by the odd chance of grains on unswept potting floors leaving impressions in clay pots before they were fired – good examples of this are to be seen in the museum at Avebury, Wiltshire. Flint arrowheads prove the use of bows, and some Neolithic bows have actually been found preserved in the Somerset marshes: in the right conditions of wetness without access to air, wood can survive for what seems an incredible time. The Neolithic bow was much like the famous English longbow of the Middle Ages, and was made from yew, a tradition that survived in England for at least 4,000 years.

Impressions of food grains in fragments of pottery prove that Neolithic settlers in the region tilled land to some extent, although at first not in fields as we understand fields now. They planted in clearings where they could, turning first to places where nature had done some of the work for them, as where trees had been uprooted in a storm. But they set out to clear land for themselves, too, making extensive use of fire. There is evidence from the Choukoutien caves in China* that man's distant ancestors understood the use of fire some 350,000 years ago, and the Swanscombe woman who lived in the Lower Thames valley about a quarter of a million years ago had a fire to warm herself by. Whether she could light a fire for herself is another matter – mankind's first fires were gifts from heaven, started by lightning, and kept going as sacred fires, perhaps for generations. Archaeological evidence from Krapina, in Yugoslavia, however, suggests that European man could make fire by rubbing sticks something like 100,000 years ago. Neolithic settlers coming to the Upper Thames knew about rubbing sticks, and their flint-working must have taught them how to strike sparks from flint. So they could clear land of trees and scrub by burning. But they had little in the way of tools to work the land: digging sticks, with points hardened in fire, picks or hoes of a sort fashioned from antlers. They could not have done much more than scratch the soil, but there was plenty of soil to go round for a population that may not have been more than a few hundreds. They planted somehow, and they reaped, for the flint blades of their sickles still show traces of the polish they acquired in cutting straw. But although they farmed where they could, these people were primarily pastoral, grazing animals on the Downs and in the thinner woodlands. This was another aspect of the great Neolithic revolution in human culture – the domestication of animals. Middle Stone Age hunters seem to have domesticated the dog: it was their Neolithic successors who tamed the cow, the pig and the sheep. At first they kept mainly pigs, but they had some sheep and long-horned oxen (bos primigenius).† As time went on man's animals as well as man himself materially changed the country-side. Pigs rooting in the woods ate acorns and destroyed saplings; so the woods were gradually thinned. Oxen and sheep pasturing on the downs cropped grass and kept it short; they also manured the downland, helping it to grow a better pasture, leading to that wonderful turf sward that stretches for mile after mile on the downs today. The famous Berkshire pig and the downland sheep have a long ancestry.

Stock-raising and farming produced a sufficient surplus to support trade. Westmorland axes, as we have seen, came into the region in fair quantity, and there was an export trade in flint for arrowheads and knives. Flint from seams in

* Carlton S. Coon, *The History of Man.*
† Peter Fowler, *Archaeology of Wessex.*

the chalk downs flakes admirably, making razor-sharp blades, and flints of this quality were keenly sought. There was certainly some organized flint mining on the downs, though not on the scale of the Norfolk workings at Grime's Graves (at least, nothing on this scale has yet been found in the region). It is significant that Abingdon seems to have been one early market or trade centre, for it suggests that water transport on the Thames influenced the pattern of economic life from the first beginnings of mercantile activity in Britain. Abingdon was a useful centre, for it had easy access both to the river and to the cross-country routes running along the chalk downs to the South, South West and East, and to the Jurassic belt providing a good route over the Cotswolds to Wales and the North West. By about 2,500 B.C. there were recognized trade routes into and across the region from the Channel, Cornwall, Wales, the North West and East Anglia. Seaborne trade followed the Neolithic settlers from early in the period – they had themselves come by sea. As the Neolithic period merged into the Early Bronze Age around 2,000 B.C. the region became a market of growing importance, for wares from Brittany and Ireland as well as other regions of Britain; probably, too, its merchants built up a considerable entrepot trade, for they were well-placed to do so. The existence of these trading activities is the best evidence there could be of prosperity in the region: communities can support merchants and specialists only when they can produce a surplus of food sufficient to maintain men who do not themselves spend their lives hunting or growing food. The Neolithic farmers of Berkshire and Oxfordshire were prosperous men of their day, with goods to barter for the particular stone axes they wanted, and for whatever in the way of luxuries the pedlar had to offer. Population, although still trivial by modern standards, must have multiplied substantially as the age progressed.

The next great wave of immigration to the region came about 2,000 B.C., when a new stock, round-headed compared with the long-headed Neolithic settlers, made their way up the Thames. They were a virile, tough folk, called the 'Beaker' people, from the distinctive form of pottery they brought with them. These Beaker folk appear to have originated in Spain, although whether they made their way into Spain from North Africa, or ultimately from the Middle East, is a matter for conjecture. They certainly came from Spain, crossed Europe to the Low Countries, and came on by sea to the Thames Estuary. Later they came into the region also from the Channel coast. Their coming was enormously important, for they brought with them if not the end at least the beginning of the end of the Stone Age in Britain: they brought bronze and gold, and knowledge of how to work them.

Again it must be stressed that there was no swift transition: stone tools continued in use for many centuries; indeed, they have not yet been abandoned wholly. Flint was used in England for muskets and fowling pieces well into the last century, and there is still a small export trade in flints for flintlocks, primarily to clubs in the United States. With the coming of bronze, and later iron, stone axes and knives were superseded gradually, but for a long time metal tools and weapons were only for the rich, and the implements commonly in use remained of stone. But the immigration of the Beaker folk changed society decisively, if slowly, for the knowledge of metals that they brought increased the range both of human skills and of trade.

Trade gave the region an importance new in kind as well as in degree. Chalk downs for stock raising, rivers for fish, and good riverside land to be cleared for pasture and fairly easy tillage acquired an additional importance in that they could provide not mere subsistence, but a sufficient surplus to make men rich enough to make long journeys profitable for merchants. Trade grew up to some extent in Neolithic times, with recognized routes to and from North, South, East and West. Metal working created new demands, and with the coming of the Beaker folk these trade routes began both to be used more regularly, and to be greatly extended. No ores for either copper or tin occur in the Upper Thames region, so that all bronze wares had to be imported. Copper came mostly from Ireland and Anglesey, tin from Cornwall. Ireland itself was a main manufacturing centre in the early Bronze Age, but bronze-making industries supplied with raw materials by sea developed in Scotland, Northern England and North Wales. Bronze implements were first brought to the Upper Thames as finished goods from the manufacturing centres, but as bronze-smiths became more numerous a trade in ingots of copper and tin developed, and bronze wares were made on the spot. There is evidence of journeymen smiths who went from settlement to settlement, setting up shop, as it were, to meet local needs. An early bronze-smith's working equipment came to light at Burgess's Meadow, Oxford, and a piece of raw copper has been found beside a Bronze Age axehead near Banbury. Gold from Ireland also came into the region, and this is direct evidence of economic prosperity, for only a rich farmer or tribal leader could afford gold ornaments for himself or for his womenfolk. Money was not yet in use: metal wares were bartered for skins, grain, worked flints and sometimes, no doubt, for land, or for the supply of labour for porterage on the travel routes. The Beaker people certainly used, if they did not settle in, the Neolithic encampment at Abingdon, and they have left many traces of themselves in the neck of land between Abingdon and Stanton Harcourt enclosed by the Thames where it

43

makes its great bend to the North to get round the Cumnor heights to Oxford. This area grew steadily in importance as the meeting place of trade routes and river transport, and archaeologists consider that a large part of the Beaker people's prosperity – indeed, their economic dominance of the region – derived from their activities as merchants and forwarding agents in Bronze Age trade.

From the Beaker immigration until almost historical times – in the last few centuries B.C. – there is nothing to suggest any large-scale invasion of the region by new settlers. There was probably a fairly steady influx from the Continent of the kinsmen of existing settlers; there was land to accommodate them without any need to fight over it and probably they came peacefully. There was steady cultural development of Bronze Age British society, but no major change until the invasion by powerful Belgic tribes from Gaul in the centuries just before the Roman Conquest. The transition from bronze to iron was gradual, not abrupt. The smiths who worked in bronze took to forging iron, and their craft became more general as iron bars, providing raw material for sword and sickle and hoe, came into use as a primitive form of currency, replacing straight barter in the region's trade. Probably flint working continued through the ages called Bronze and Iron: flint was cheaper, and while the skills remained few knives of early bronze or iron could match for sharpness those murderous little razor blades that could be flaked from flint. Certainly bronze went on long into the Iron Age: some of the British fighting-men who opposed the Roman legions had only bronze swords to match against the iron of Rome.

For some 2,500 years, from about 3,000 B.C. to around 500 B.C., the downs and river country of the Upper Thames and its tributaries enjoyed a period of cultural development that seems to have been almost all peaceful – an immense span of peaceful change not again matched in history. Jacquetta Hawkes considers that this was when a female principle giving primacy to worship of the Earth as Mother prevailed over the male principle of worshipping warrior Gods. We have no means of knowing whether Neolithic society was matriarchal in any particular way, though there is some evidence of religious cults based on a Mother Goddess and fertility rites. And there is little to suggest warfare: weapons are not numerous in the finds on Neolithic sites, and although the causewayed camps that dot the region were used later for tribal defences, their original purpose seems to have been for herding cattle. Where there is no written record and all evidence is circumstantial, speculation can be wrong. 'Weapon' is a dubious term: an axe can kill a man as well as fell a tree. But the benefit of doubt here is on the side of peace: there is little evidence of the violent disruption of settlements, little to suggest any special effort to design man-killing tools, little to imply the construction of military earthworks. And on the positive side there is strong evidence that the region contrived a consistently rising standard of living during century after century, and found resources in manpower for the building of immense burial mounds and magnificent stone temples or monuments, of which Stonehenge and Avebury, on the outskirts of the region, are the greatest and best known examples. These things could not have been achieved if the region's social capital had been exhausted generation after generation to pay for war.

There must have been troubles, of course. When the Beaker folk found earlier inhabitants occupying a particularly attractive stretch of downs or riverside those wickedly sharp flint arrowheads must have been loosed with intent by covetors and those in possession alike. But the evidence is against long periods of struggle, and much more in keeping with live and let live, trade, and the assimilation of peoples to enjoy a common prosperity. There was land enough for all, and no pressing need for aggression. Miss Hawkes's theory of the pacific influence of women is nice to contemplate, though history is against it. Agriculturists with enough to go round are not ferocious, and can worship an Earth Mother with the gentleness that derives from security: the warrior Gods came in to inspire peoples whose birth-rate outstripped their means of livelihood, and the women of such races were as keen on conquest as their men. The Thames of 5,000 years ago enfolded a countryside where security could be taken almost for granted. There were plenty of natural hazards and some dangerous animals, but few men who needed to be dangerous to other men.

Of the daily life of that Golden Age we know tantalizingly little: the men and women who lived it have slipped into oblivion, leaving nothing but fragments of their hardest possessions, and here and there scraps of their own bones. They built of wood, wattle and mud, and nothing of their dwellings has survived, save occasional traces of holes where posts must have stood to support the branches of thatch that sheltered them. Loom weights of stone tell us that they had cloth as well as skins, woollen garments from their sheep and linen from flax that they could grow and ret in the Thames and its tributary streams: as the millennia wore on, skins became less necessary for daily wear and woven garments commoner; with the coming of bronze there was soon a considerable manufacture of pins to secure clothing. The earliest oxen, *bos primigenius*, disappeared from the herds as stock breeding from animals brought from the Continent with the Beaker people produced the smaller and more versatile *bos longifrons*. This was a good general-purpose ox, useful for haulage as well as food. With the clearance of woodland, and, no doubt, increasing demand for wool, sheep outnumbered pigs, though

45

both continued – as they have continued to this day – to be important staples of farming prosperity. There were salmon as well as trout in the Thames and its tributaries, freshwater mussels and eels, all valuable food. The aurochs, a wild ox sometimes called the European bison, which had been hunted on the Berkshire downs in early Neolithic times, died out between 2,000–1,000 B.C., but deer were plentiful to add variety to diet and the excitement of the chase to the more hum-drum tasks of agricultural life. The horse, a rather smaller animal than the modern horse, was certainly ridden over what are now the training gallops of the downs well before 1,000 B.C.

If we have no more than a dim, imagined picture of ordinary life in the region 4,000–5,000 years ago, these remote ancestors have left abundant evidence of a ceremonial life whose grandeur still inspires awe. Wayland's Smithy, the im-mense barrow overlooking the Ock valley, was built as a tomb about 2,800 B.C. The first edifice was a mound 54 ft long, enclosing a grave room formed of huge stones and baulks of wood. It seems to have been used like a family vault over a long period, for excavation showed fourteen burials in it, and the mound was later extended to some 200 ft in length, with three more funeral vaults added – eight burials took place there. At the entrance to the vaults a majestic portico of stone still stands; gigantic single blocks of stone form the portals and the passage to the tombs is walled with unmortared stones, as carefully matched as in the best dry stone walling of recent times. This impressive barrow was carefully recon-structed after excavation under the Ministry of Works in 1963–4.

The stones used for this great tomb and other monuments or temples in the region are called Sarsens. They are relics of the Ice Age, left scattered on the chalk downs, and have inspired both building and legend as long as man has known the region. Their very name – Sarsen – indicates the mystery that local people have always felt about them, for it derives from the Saracens who em-bodied the mystery and magic of the East at the time of the Crusades: some for-midable magic must have produced the stones, and foreign magic at that, for they seem (and, indeed, geologically are) alien to the chalk landscape. To the medieval mind, not having the benefit of modern knowledge of ice-sheets, the Saracens were as good an agency as any. The stones are sometimes called locally Grey Wethers, for a distant group of Sarsens can look much like a flock of sheep. They are supposed to grow, and perhaps to move, by themselves. The myth that gives the Sarsen-lined barrow at Ashbury its name of Wayland's Smithy derives from (relatively) modern times: it is that if you leave your horse and a coin at the entrance to the tomb you may come back to find your horse shod by the magic of the Saxon deity Wayland Smith, the Smith of the Gods.

Did the stones inspire the ancient cult, or the cult seize on the great stones to express itself? The Neolithic immigrants who brought agriculture, ultimately from the Middle East, may have brought folk memories, or active religious beliefs, associated with the temples and stone monuments of Mesopotamia, Egypt, or Crete. Whatever the inspiration that called or drove men to the vast labour – and remarkable engineering – that moved stones weighing many tons about a roadless countryside, and set them up in finely modulated circles, or to mark monumental tombs, the work remains to excite wonder and to demand humility.

The cult of great stones, or at least the skill of moving them and setting them up, was brought to the region by Neolithic immigrants before the Beaker folk, but it seems to have been the Beaker people, with their superior technology, who developed it to its final magnificence. The greatest remaining examples of the cult, at Avebury and Stonehenge, are just outside the region, though they must have drawn on the prosperity of the region, as Canterbury Cathedral reflects the wealth of London as well as Kent. And although there can scarcely have been structures to rival Avebury and Stonehenge, there were other 'henge monuments' in the region, now lost under the plough. Mr Peter Fowler, in his *Archaeology of Wessex*, reasonably observes that if the 'henge monuments' of Wessex appear mostly in the west of the area, this 'may be due to lack of sufficient archaeological work in Hampshire and Berkshire'. The earlier part of Wayland's Smithy is perhaps 1,000 years older than Avebury, and nearly 1,000 years older than the earliest part of Stonehenge. The skills, and, perhaps, the social organization, that contrived the noble tomb overlooking the Ock surely contributed to the development of man's capacity to build Avebury and Stonehenge. They may be seen as the flowering of a Wessex Culture that had its roots in the region of the Upper Thames, just as the later Saxon Kingdom of Wessex had its roots along the Thames. The Rollright Stones, at Little Rollright, Oxfordshire, on the Beaker trade route over the Cotswolds from the Thames Valley to the North West, offer further evidence of the cultural force that spread outwards from settlements around the Thames.

A Golden Age – perhaps: for whom? If wars were rare, the orgy of stone-moving, and the raising of huge barrows to house the dead, suggest that an aristocratic upper class kept the mass of people hard at work in gruelling forms of labour. Almost certainly Bronze Age society was based on slavery: almost all human societies until very recent times have been based on slavery. But it was not necessarily a particularly cruel slavery. The late Sir John Clapham argues this point in discussing the building of the Wessex 'henges' and barrows:

47

Was it in fact servile labour from some relatively dense population that did this – like pyramid building in imaginative pictures? Second thoughts pass to medieval cathedrals, often built leisurely over long years, with a comparatively small labour force. A cathedral of some kind Stonehenge certainly was; it may have been built slowly; and it may not have been necessary to set up more than a couple of uprights and a single carefully worked cross lintel in a year – a great feat of skill, but a job that need not have employed sweating crowds.

(*A Concise Economic History of Britain*)

The barrows, of which Wayland's Smithy was but one huge example, and the encampments with their causewayed ditches, look more like slavery: even so, one must beware of the impatient modern habit of foreshortening time. There is evidence that Wayland's Smithy was not built all at one time: its final form may have been reached over centuries. The field of barrows near Lambourn called Seven Barrows (though in fact there are at least twenty-six) looks like gigantic labour – but so does the gravedigging in a well-filled churchyard. Again, the work may have been done over centuries. The great ditches of the causewayed camps must have been dug, one would think, for a specific purpose at a specific time, but they may have been deepened over many years. We plan a building and expect to see it occupied next year: Neolithic and Bronze Age men may have thought differently. We have no means of knowing what their social system was, but that is no reason for guessing at it in the harshest light. It may have been a society of cruel slavery, but it may have rewarded hard work with a generally fair share of the good things of life. Hard work there must have been, but work is the lot of man, and work in itself is not cruelty.

1. *Linch Hill corner at Stanton Harcourt (Oxon.). The marks are Bronze Age ring ditches, Iron Age rectangular enclosures and clusters of storage pits.*

2. *Two very old village churches, probably on Saxon foundations.*

a. *At Inglesham, near Lechlade, Glos.*

b. *At Charney Bassett, Berkshire.*

3. *Cleeve Mill, Oxfordshire.*

4a. *The navigable channel of the Thames under Abingdon Bridge.*
4b. *Clifton Hampden Bridge across the Thames.*

2

The making of a people
I-The beginnings of history

From about 500 B.C. the by-then ancient way of life on the Thames Valley began to be increasingly disturbed. Iron tools promoted a more efficient agriculture, enabling populations to grow, and as populations grew there was pressure to find new land. There was much tribal movement on the Continent, and fresh groups of immigrants began to cross the Channel, peoples from Gaul of so-called Celtic stock. They came to take, they had iron swords, and they did not come peacefully. They came early to the Thames: traces of settlements marking an abrupt change from the old Beaker culture, and dating from the fourth century B.C. have been found at Long Wittenham, and in the old Beaker homeland in the great bend of the Thames between Stanton Harcourt and Abingdon. The old trade routes were used, and the importance of places where the Thames could be forded became more marked. Wallingford and Shillingford, a couple of miles upstream, were two such places, with convenient access to the Ridgeway route over the chalk downs. A mile or so above Shillingford the Thame joins the Thames, with the valley of the Thame offering a useful route northwards towards the Dunstable Downs and the ancient trackway to the East coast. A settlement at the junction of Thame and Thames (Dorchester), which had been in use from Neolithic times – which had, indeed, been known to Paleolithic man – grew in importance, becoming more important still to the Romans and later to the Saxons.

The Iron Age Celts from Gaul brought new weapons, and new ploughs, and seem to have brought a new religion. The Great Stone Cult of the Beaker and the Neolithic peoples had its chief places of worship in open spaces on high ground, where the arch of the sky could be seen, and the sun's path across it traced: it was a religion of light and air. The Celts brought Druids who worshipped in sombre woodland groves, practising a cult of darker mystery. Here, perhaps, is Jacquetta Hawkes's contrast between the 'female' principle of worshipping the life-giving force of earth and sun, and the opposite principle of calling on the dark Gods of war. Popular superstition is still inclined to people the Great Stone monuments of the region with Druids, but these structures were already old a thousand years before anyone in the area had heard of Druids. Their day was later: by the time the Roman legions came, Druidical worship was the religion of Britain.

In the last century B.C. unrest and war in Gaul sent powerful Belgic tribes across the Channel, whose leaders carved kingdoms for themselves in Britain. The Catuvellauni established themselves on the North bank of the Thames as far as the Cherwell, and by conquering the Trinovantes in what is now Essex won control of the North bank to the estuary, and over much of what later became East Anglia. Another Belgic tribe, the Atrebates, pushed up from the South Coast and secured a tribal homeland South and West of the Thames, covering most of what is now Berkshire and extending over North Wiltshire.

But the Belgic tribes did not have things all their own way. West of the Cherwell, and in the valley of the Upper Thames above Oxford, a non-Belgic people, the Dobunni, managed to hold on to their territory, successfully resisting expansion by the Atrebates and the Catuvellanni. Indeed they seem to have been able to maintain salients into Atrebatic territory, for the Ock valley was Dobunni country up to Roman times; the figure of a White Horse cut into the chalk at Uffington, which gives its name to the Vale of the White Horse, was a tribal symbol of the Dobunni. Their headquarters was on the Churn, near Cirencester and the Roman town founded there was called *Corinium* (after the Churn) *Dubonnorum* (of the Dobunni).

Julius Caesar's invasion of Britain in 55 B.C. was in no real sense a conquest, though it led to increasing Roman influence, and paved the way to the serious conquest of Britain by Claudius in A.D. 43. For the next 300 years the region, with the rest of Southern England, was effectively ruled by Rome. That is historically certain; what it meant in terms of everyday life for the inhabitants is less clear. The Romans occupied Britain at first with four, later with three, regular legions, augmented from time to time by levies of locally raised auxiliaries. The regulars were quartered at various garrison towns, none of which was in the Upper Thames region. There was no need for such garrisons, for although there were tribal boundaries in the region, manned, no doubt, by police posts, there was no frontier with perennially hostile tribes, as on the Welsh border, or with restless and uneasy alliances, as in the North. The occupation of the Upper Thames and its surrounding countryside was no great military task for soldiers as efficient as the Romans: there were no powerful centres of resistance, nothing but farmsteads and scattered settlements to defend; moreover, the Romans seem to

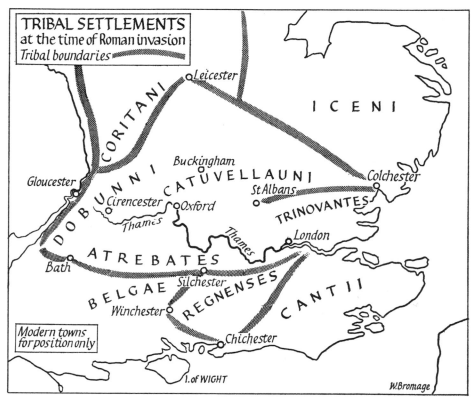

Map 4   *Tribal settlements at the time of the Roman Invasion.*

have been able to count almost from the start on the active assistance of the Dobunni. The profound changes brought by the Roman occupation were not here in the building of towns and in the creation of urban life, but derived from the Roman road system, from the development of a money economy, and from the efficiency of Roman administration and its tax-farmers.

Politically the Dobunni seem to have done well out of the Roman conquest. They were non-Belgic, hostile to the Atrebates and Catuvellauni anyway, and although they may have resisted Roman invasion of their territory in the very early days, they soon came to terms with Rome, accepting the Romans as allies rather than conquerors. The Twentieth Legion (Valeria Victrix) at Gloucester gave them security from the wilder tribes farther West, and the Dobunni soon became among the most civilized of Romano-British subjects. To the Romans this was a useful alliance. Dobunni country was brought as firmly under Roman administration as anywhere in Britain, but no great garrisons were needed to subdue it, and the Dobunni seem to have been left to run their domestic affairs in much the same relationship to Rome as that of a State friendly to Britain in the old Indian Empire.

If the Romans stationed no large bodies of troops in the region, they still needed to be able to move troops across it quickly, and with their accustomed skill in such matters they at once set about roadmaking, conscripting local inhabitants for the job. Cirencester, one of the great Roman foundations in Britain, is on the extreme North-Western edge of the region, its hinterland more Cotswold country than Upper Thames. In the main body of the region only two towns of any importance were established, Dorchester-on-Thames and Alchester, near the modern Bicester. Both seem to have been primarily staging posts or road centres, later becoming local markets. The main Roman road from South to North across the region ran from Silchester, on the Hampshire--Berkshire border, the capital of the Atrebatic country, to Dorchester, where it crossed the Thames, and then straight on, keeping a little east of Oxford, to Alchester. The most formidable obstacle on this route was the great marsh at Otmoor, in the low-lying country through which the River Ray flows to join the Cherwell just above Oxford. Roman engineers drove their road straight across Otmoor on a causeway. At Alchester the Roman road connected with an ancient trackway running West to East from the Cotswolds to the Chilterns. The Romans made this trackway into a proper road (later known as Akeman Street) and used it as a link with Watling Street, the great road from London to the North-West. To the West, near Cirencester, the improved trackway from Alchester met the Fosse Way, the great road running across Britain from Exeter to Lincoln.

Unlike Dorchester, which is a natural site for a village or small town and sustains to this day a thriving local life, Alchester had nothing but proximity to Akeman Street to recommend it. There are fertile fields there now, but in Roman times the site was marshy, and to build on it at all required the laying down of huge loads of gravel. It appears to have been lived in until Roman power declined at the end of the fourth century, but the place then seems to have been abandoned and over the centuries what remained of its buildings were pulled down and carted off for building stone elsewhere. Alchester was known to have existed, but its site disappeared from the map until excavation in the nineteenth and twentieth centuries revealed the foundations of its houses and the plan of its streets extending over an area of some 25 acres.

Within the ring of Roman roads, with minor trackways serving them, pastoral and farming life in the region seems at first to have continued much as it was before the Romans came. By the second century A.D. life began to show important differences. The local landowners were becoming romanized: some, perhaps, were Romans, if not from Rome itself, at least made Roman by years of service in the Roman Army. These married with the equivalent of what used to be called 'county families', and a Romano-British upper class developed, speaking Latin, and demanding the comforts of Roman living. With better roads to take its agricultural produce to market, and so to earn more from its crops, the region could provide them. Homesteads of wattle and daub, where even the richer farmers lived side by side with their beasts before the Romans came, were re-placed by comfortable villas, with paved floors, baths and heating systems – a standard of plumbing not reached again in Britain for nearly two thousand years. Such villas were not simply 'gentlemen's residences', but the working centres of considerable estates, equipped with workshops and granaries, and with huts or lodgings for their farm labourers. The dimensions of the granary belonging to a Roman villa excavated at Ditchley suggest that it was built to store the grain from about 500 acres.* There were many such villas in the region, in the valleys of the Evenlode, Windrush, Glyme, Cherwell, Ock and other tributaries of the Thames, as well as by the Thames itself.

Traces of Romano-British settlements, single farms or groups of farms more often than villas, are fairly numerous along the Thames from Lechlade to Dor-chester, particularly in the old areas of Beaker and Iron Age habitation, where the Thames makes its great bend to the North, by Standlake on the Windrush just before it joins the Thames, Northmoor, Stanton Harcourt and Eynsham. Between two and three miles above its junction with the Windrush, the Thames can be forded at Duxford, where a patch of shallows provides a crossing that was in use long before there were any bridges. There is no road to the river at Dux-ford – the tiniest of hamlets – today, but a track still leads to the ford, and in Roman times, indeed for centuries before the Romans, it must have been an im-portant place. Although dangerous when the river is in flood, the crossing here must always have been safer than at fords lower down the Thames, and it offered

* I. A. Richmond, *Roman Britain*.

a route from the Windrush valley and the Standlake–Stanton Harcourt settlements eastwards to Abingdon and south-west across the Ock Valley to the Berkshire Downs and the Ridgeway.

The larger villa-estates were mostly north of the Thames, along the east-west route to the Fosse Way and Cirencester. This is what one would expect, for Cirencester, on the edge of the region, was by far its most important market.

The villas were the estates of gentry, not princely holdings, but good solid property, providing a comfortable life and the means for occasional trips to Cirencester or Bath. There is evidence, too, of smaller holdings, where peasant farmers worked the little fields that seem to have been in existence since Beaker times; there were several such settlements on the Lambourn Downs, around Lambourn and Letcombe Bassett, and perhaps also in the Standlake–Stanton Harcourt area. These little fields, of which traces can still be identified, are called, rather misleadingly, 'Celtic fields'. They are almost certainly older than the Celtic invasions, and are probably among the improvements to Neolithic agriculture introduced by the Beaker folk. They continued in use through Roman times.

Next to nothing is known of systems of land tenure in the region in the Roman period. There were no colonies of ex-soldiers as there were no garrison towns to provide pensioners for settlement. Possibly the more senior ex-Army men could get grants of land in an area of their choice: much of the region is attractive countryside, and an officer who had brought a detachment of troops through it may have marked a particular place in his mind for his eventual retirement. Records of land transactions have been lost in the chaos that followed the collapse of Roman rule, but the obvious prosperity of villa life suggests that landowners, whether of Roman or of romanized British stock, enjoyed long security of tenure. How the land was worked we can but guess: a landlord may have owned slaves, or there may have been half-free peasants attached to an estate, bound to work their lord's land in return for the right to cultivate plots to feed themselves; or both. The smallholders of the Lambourn Downs seem to have been peasant proprietors rather than servile labourers, but in practice there may not have been much difference between the two; indeed, a labourer on a well-managed estate may often have been better off than a peasant proprietor working a holding of his own without capital, and perhaps in debt. Taxes, which often had to be paid in kind, in skins, or grain, or horses, were heavy, and there must have been much conscripted labour for the upkeep of roads. Gibbon's famous observation

If a man were called to fix the period in the history of the world during which the condition of the human race was most happy and prosperous, he would, without hesitation, name that which elapsed from the death of Domitian to the accession of Commodus.

may apply to the upper classes rather than to labourers. Nevertheless, Roman justice was real, there was security of life and goods, and for most people in the region life under the Romans for the best part of three centuries was possibly better than anything their descendants were to know for at least 1,000 years.

Where they did not actively conflict with Roman policy, Rome was tolerant of native institutions, and seldom interfered with local religious cults: rather, local deities were adopted into the Roman pantheon. An exception was the Roman attitude to Druidism: here no mercy was shown, and the Romans did their utmost to destroy the cult. A policy so out of keeping with the Roman character raises many questions. It has been suggested that the Druids were the focus of political hostility to Roman occupation and that the Romans persecuted Druidism as later rulers have persecuted Protestants or Catholics or Communists, primarily for political reasons. It may be so. But there seems also to have been something in Druidism, perhaps its cult of human sacrifice, that was repugnant to Roman feeling. One may perhaps see a later analogy in the attitude of the British towards *suttee* – the practice of widows burning themselves to death on their husbands' funeral pyres – in India. The British on the whole are also tolerant of other people's religions, but *suttee* in India was stamped out relentlessly. We do not know to what extent Druidism was practised in the Upper Thames region: perhaps it never took much root, for the region was almost the headquarters of the earlier Great Stone cult. It is significant that the Romans made no effort to destroy the Great Stone monuments, apparently accepting them as religious places to be respected. The region took no part in revolts against Rome, so it may be that Druidical power here was never particularly strong and soon forgotten.

Nothing is known about the religious beliefs of the Great Stone cult (and little enough about the religious beliefs of Druidism). The burial with the dead of grave-goods in Neolithic and Beaker barrows suggests belief in some form of after-life, but beyond this we can only guess. There is a moving example of the continuity of human reverence in the Ock Valley, a few miles from where the Ock joins the Thames at Abingdon. Near Frilford, on the north bank of the Ock, a Roman temple has been excavated, and within the Roman work are traces of an earlier shrine to some unknown deity, dating from the early Iron Age. Later, the

Roman temple, or its ruins, was regarded as a holy place by the Anglo-Saxons, who buried their dead in a field nearby. This graveyard was in use for centuries, alike for the cremations of the earliest Anglo-Saxon invaders as for the burials of later – perhaps Christian – times. There was similar lasting reverence for a particular place on the Thames itself, at Long Wittenham, though here without an identifiable temple. At Long Wittenham Christian burials definitely took place on a site that had seen cremations and burials from early in the Iron Age through the Roman period, and on through the coming of pagan Anglo-Saxons to their conversion to Christianity. The certain evidence of Christian burial here was the finding in a boy's grave of a basin or stoup with panels illustrating scenes from the New Testament.

Another Roman temple has been found at Woodeaton on the Cherwell, a little south of Islip, and doubtless there were others. A statuette, reputedly of Venus, came to light at Woodeaton, and a carving of an unknown goddess, apparently Roman or Romano-British, was found during dredging in the bed of the Thames at Bablockhythe. In the eighteenth century an altar inscribed to Jupiter Optimus Maximus was found on the bank of the Thames at Little Wittenham, below the two strange hills known as Wittenham Clumps, across the river from Dorchester. On the east-lying hill of the pair of 'clumps' is a prehistoric (probably early Iron Age) hill camp, fortified by a deep ditch: it may have been used as a Roman post to guard the crossing to Dorchester of the Silchester–Dorchester–Alchester highway. This altar was taken to the grounds of a house at Canterbury, but was removed when the house was sold before the First World War, and its whereabouts are not now known.

In the fourth century A.D. Roman power collapsed as the legions were withdrawn to assist competing generals in military takeover bids at home, and to provide troops for the defence of Rome itself. With the weakening of Roman power invaders from the Continent again began to make their way to Britain, at first as pirates rather than as settlers. In the third century raids by Germanic tribes loosely called 'Saxons' became so serious that a network of coast defences was constructed against them under an officer known as the Count of the Saxon Shore. The invaders were good seamen from the North Sea coast of Germany, around the mouth of the Elbe and from the Friesian Islands. Rivers and estuaries they understood and they were soon in the Thames. Early Saxon finds at Dorchester suggest that they were raiding from the river there while Rome was still more or less in control of the region. In the fifth century they came in earnest, no longer pirates merely, but invaders determined to conquer and to settle.

Records of regional life over the next three centuries, the Dark Age of British history, are obscure and few. Writing all but disappeared with the Romans, and although the early Christian Church in Britain tried to guard such scraps of knowledge as it had, practically all records perished in the chaos of Anglo-Saxon wars and the later Danish invasions. Archaeology is less help than might be expected for a period relatively so recent in human history, for the Anglo-Saxons built in wood, and first cremated, later buried, their dead in graves unmarked by mound or monument. Where Anglo-Saxon cemeteries have been discovered, as at Frilford and Long Wittenham, information of great interest has come to light, but discoveries of unmarked graves and settlements are mostly accidental, brought about by the chance of the plough or gravel working. Nevertheless, there is some physical evidence of Anglo-Saxon settlement on the Upper Thames from very early times, and the period is not quite without written sources, though most of these record events that happened long before they were written down. The chief written sources are *The Destruction and Conquest of Britain* (*De Excidio et Conquestu Britanniae*) by the monk Gildas, himself a Briton, who wrote in Wales about the middle of the sixth century (*c.* 540–45), Bede's great *Ecclesiastical History of the English Nation*, completed in 731, and the *Anglo-Saxon Chronicle*, that remarkable attempt to maintain a running series of *Contemporary Archives* long before print was heard of. The *Chronicle*, however, although it purports to record events from the beginning of the Anglo-Saxon period, consists of manuscripts compiled between the ninth and the eleventh centuries: the earliest text that has come down to us was written – at Abingdon – about the period 891–900. This is itself a copy of an older document, and no doubt incorporates material from older documents still: but here one must return to conjecture. What is certain is that the early kings of Wessex established their kingdom on the south or Berkshire bank of the Upper Thames from Reading to Faringdon and the borders of Gloucestershire and Wiltshire, and that it was from this heartland of his kingdom that Alfred the Great (849–99), who was born at Wantage, extended his power to make the Kings of Wessex Kings of England. This early Kingdom of Wessex was mainly on the south bank of the Thames, but it included Dorchester on the north bank in what is now Oxfordshire, probably as a frontier post, and controlled the crossing of the Thames at Hinksey – the ford that gave its name to Oxford. So much is certain, but the early kingdom is a somewhat shadowy realm. Later Saxon genealogists trace the ancestry of the Royal House of Wessex through a continuous succession of kings going back to one Cerdic or Cynric who brought his band up Southampton Water and landed in Hampshire about the year 495, but there is some mystery about these early ancestors. Bede, discussing the origins of the English, distinguishes between Saxons, Angles and Jutes, peopling Essex, Sussex and Wessex with Saxons, Northumbria, Mercia and East Anglia with Angles, and Kent, the Isle of Wight and the Hampshire mainland opposite the Isle of Wight with Jutes. There is nothing to suggest that the Saxon House of Wessex was of Jutish descent, and the persistent claim that its founders landed in Hampshire is puzzling: the Thames was penetrated very early, and it seems more probable that the early Saxon Kingdom on the Upper Thames was won by invasion from the river. This does not rule out the possibility that some band of Saxons landed in Jutish territory in Hampshire and made its way by the ancient route over the chalk downs to its kinsmen established, or fighting, on the Thames; and the leaders of this band may have become dominant in the Wessex Group. Written records are so sparse that it is easy to attach too much precision to the few there are. Bede was writing some 300 years after these events, and he had the historian's instinct to classify. Saxons, Angles and Jutes were different tribes, coming from different territories around the Elbe, but they were much the same sort of people, and in invading England there must have been all sorts of temporary alliances among them. Distinctions disappeared with the early kingdoms: the Angles gave their name to England and the English language, and a fusion of the three groups produced the Anglo-Saxon English people.

Gildas, writing in Wales at least 100 and perhaps nearer 150 years after the event, says that a British ruler, whom he does not name but describes as 'superbus tyrannus', recruited certain Saxons as mercenaries to repel other invaders, and that these mercenaries then rebelled and seized the country. This appears to have been early in the fifth century. The British – that is, the Romano-British families in power at the end of the Roman occupation – gradually regrouped their forces and some years later won a resounding victory over the Saxons at a place called Mons Badonicus, under a Romano-British leader, Ambrosius Aurelianus. Bede, writing nearly 200 years after Gildas, tells much the same story, though with more detail, naming the British chieftain who recruited Saxons as mercenaries as Vortigern, and the leaders of the mercenary rebellion as the brothers Hengist and Horsa. It is hard to disentangle history from folk-myth, and as hard to attempt dates. Hengist is an early Saxon name, in a form which seems to have gone out of fashion in the fifth or sixth century: it is of particular interest to the Upper Thames for it occurs in the place name Hinksey, meaning 'Hengist's Island', denoting the island of firm gravel which made it practicable to ford the Thames at Oxford. No one knows where 'Mons Badonicus' was, but there is some evidence that the Saxons were temporarily driven out of the Upper Thames valley around the year 500, retreating along the Icknield Way across South Oxfordshire, Buckinghamshire and Bedfordshire towards the East Coast: earth-works across the Icknield Way that appear to be post-Roman suggest Saxon defences to resist pursuit. A battle of some sort was fought about this time on the slopes of White Horse Hill, for a group of skeletons, some with objects that appear to be late Roman, others Saxon, has been unearthed there, apparently buried hurriedly, as might have happened after a fight. It is conceivable that this was a Romano-British victory, though whether it relates in any way to the battle of Mons Badonicus must be pure speculation. The Arthurian legends that arose out of this Romano-British victory are not traditionally associated with the Thames, but it is certainly possible that a major success for British arms some-where in the West was followed by local actions to drive Saxons from the Thames Valley.

3

The making of a people
II - Saxons and Vikings

The Saxons were not driven out for long, and by the end of the sixth century they were back in secure occupation of the Upper Thames. The *Anglo-Saxon Chronicle* records that in 571 Cuthwulf of Wessex won a major victory at Biedcanford (possibly Bedford), which gave him control of South Bedfordshire, North Buckinghamshire and the Thames from Bensington (now Benson) to Eynsham (Oxfordshire) – Aylesbury (Bucks), Benson and Eynsham are recorded identifiably. This is in keeping with a Saxon counter-attack in force back to the Thames along the Icknield Way. Having returned to the Thames the Saxons stayed, extending the dominion of Wessex westwards through the Vale of the White Horse to Swindon and North Wiltshire, and southwards over the Berkshire Downs to Salisbury Plain and Hampshire. By A.D. 600 Wessex was a powerful kingdom, mostly south of the Thames, though continuing to hold the important crossings at Dorchester and Hinksey (Oxford). North of the Thames was Mercia. From Gloucester and Cirencester to the Windrush, and at one time extending into Worcestershire and Warwickshire was the kingdom of the Hwicce, whose name survives in Wychwood Forest (Oxfordshire).

To the end of the sixth century the Saxons in England were pagan, and they have left the names of pagan gods in several of our days of the week Tuesday (Tiu, the god of war), Wednesday (Woden), Thursday (Thor) and Friday (Freya.) They have also left some of them on the map, in the Grim's Ditches (Grim was another name for Woden) to denote the earthworks (most pre-Saxon) that occur on the Downs and elsewhere, and perhaps in the Oxfordshire Tews (Great Tew, Little Tew and Dun's Tew). Christianity came to Britain in late Roman times, and there was an early British church, though it seems to have had next to no success in converting Saxon invaders. Through the first two centuries of Saxon occupation paganism undoubtedly triumphed, though the British church survived in Wales and Cornwall. In 597, St Augustine, sent by Pope Gregory, converted Ethelbert King of Kent, and founded the See of Canterbury.

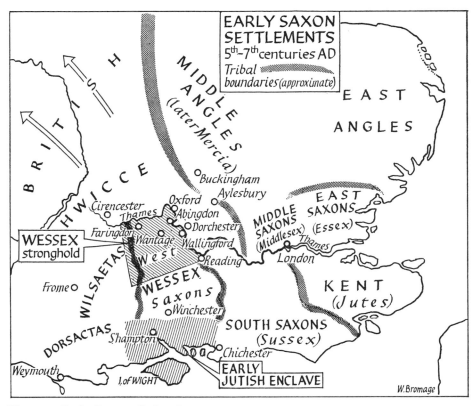

Map 5 *Early Saxon tribal settlements.*

Wessex remained pagan, but in 635 St Birinus was sent from Rome on a special mission to Wessex, apparently a more or less private enterprise, independent of Canterbury. St Birinus met Cynegils, King of Wessex, at Dorchester and baptized him in the Thames, or, more probably, in the Thame, thus bringing Christianity to Wessex. Cynegils endowed a bishopric for St Birinus, and he established his see at Dorchester, building a cathedral there. Nothing of this Saxon cathedral remains, but the Norman abbey-church that succeeded it remains one of the glories of the Thames.

The first capital of Wessex was at Faringdon, strategically well placed to command the upper reaches of the Thames above Oxford and the flank of the Ridgeway on the high downs at Uffington. As the kingdom was extended south of the downs and into Hampshire, the capital was transferred to Winchester. 'Capital' is not, however, a good term, for the administrative centre of the kingdom in those early days was where the king with his thanes and chief officers happened to be, and with war or the threat of war almost endemic, the court was perpetually on the move. Late in the ninth century we learn of King Alfred's settling a law suit as he was 'in his chamber washing his hands'. There were a number of royal residences to which the court returned from time to time. Faringdon remained one of them until the end of the Saxon dynasty, and another was at Wantage. King's house like peasant's hut was built of wattle and daub, and nothing of either Faringdon or Wantage 'palace' remains, though the sites of both are known, at least by tradition. Alfred was born at Wantage in 849 and his son, Edward the Elder, died at Faringdon in 924. The hold of the House of Wessex on the Upper Thames was shaken at times, but never broken until the end of the dynasty. The last of his House to rule in England, Edward the Confessor, was born at Islip, near Oxford, in 1004.

Under the vigorous rule of Ine (688–726) the boundaries of Wessex were pushed far to the south-west, but after Ine's death the fortunes of Wessex declined with the rise of Mercian power. Under Aethelbald (716–57) Mercia absorbed or subjected most of the other Saxon kingdoms south of the Humber. The westward expansion of Wessex was halted by Mercian invasion, and defeat at the battle of Somerton in 733. The men of Wessex fell back to their old strongholds on the Thames. These held, and although Wessex was forced to acknowledge Mercian supremacy, the kingdom remained intact. Mercia had absorbed the kingdom of the Hwicce in the Oxfordshire Cotswolds, but an attempt in 752 to invade the heartland of Wessex from the Windrush valley failed. The Mercian army was met by the West Saxons at Burford, and defeated. Three years later another Mercian force again attacked Wessex but was decisively defeated on the Berkshire Downs. In this battle Aethelbald of Mercia was killed.

Wessex remained independent, but Mercian power was not broken. Aethelbald's successor Offa (757–95) maintained Mercian supremacy over most of the rest of England, but his policy towards Wessex differed from Aethelbald's: he was content to hold the North bank of the Thames and to exercise what in modern terms would be called diplomatic control over Wessex rather than attempt annexation. Control of the crossings of the Thames at Wallingford, Dorchester, and Hinksey, and of the upper reaches of the river from Faringdon, had always been a first principle of the West Saxons: the river was their main line of defence, and they were determined to resist to the last all Mercian attempts to cross the Thames. Offa, wisely, did not embark on what would inevitably have been a costly military operation. He inflicted a sharp lesson on Wessex by destroying an outpost at Benson, on the Oxfordshire bank of the Thames and achieved political domination of the kingdom by recognizing a rival to the established House of Wessex, one Brihtric, and marrying him to a Mercian princess. The leader of the older line, Egbert, went into exile at the court of Charlemagne. Wessex could no longer expand, but the core of the kingdom on the Upper Thames remained intact. That was to exercise a decisive influence on the later course of English history.

Offa died in 795, and his puppet king of Wessex died in 802. Egbert at once returned from exile, was accepted by the West Saxons as their ruler, and took the offensive. Mercia was distracted by civil war and by Danish invasions on the east coast. Egbert renewed the old drive to the west, re-established the authority of Wessex in Somerset and Dorset, and occupied Devon, pushing the boundary of his kingdom to the Tamar. He also struck north, routed Mercian forces in the Midlands, and was recognized as overlord by the Northumbrians. By 829 his influence was supreme from the Forth to the Channel, and he could rightly style himself 'King of the English'.

The title lasted, but the supremacy did not. Within a generation Wessex was forced back to its old corner on the Upper Thames, and was sorely pressed to hold that. The enemy now was not any rival Saxon Kingdom, but the Danish invader.

The Danish or Viking invasions of England, Scotland, Ireland, Flanders and Normandy in the ninth century were the outcome of what we should now call a population explosion in Scandinavia. Offshoots of the same tough race which produced the Angles, Saxons and Jutes to raid England in the fourth, fifth and sixth centuries had settled in Scandinavia, developing into some of the finest seamen that the world has known. As they outgrew the land resources of their rocky fjords, they turned to the sea for survival. It is rather misleading to think in terms of the modern nations of Norway, Sweden and Denmark, for there were no hard and fast frontiers in the ninth century, and people of much the same stock, under different tribal leaders, occupied the whole area. It is better to think of them all as Norsemen or Vikings. They expanded in three main directions. Those living in the south and east of the Scandinavian peninsula crossed the Baltic and drove up the Dvina, Volga, and other rivers to occupy or subjugate much of ancient European Russia – indeed, the name Russia derives from them,

63

for they were called Rus. Vikings from what is now Norway went into the North Sea and the Atlantic, to reach Scotland, Ireland, Iceland, the Faeroes, Shetlands and Orkneys. Later waves of these Vikings discovered Greenland and went on to cross the North Atlantic to discover America. The Danish Vikings concentrated on Flanders, Normandy, and the east and south coasts of England. These were general spheres of influence, not hard and fast divisions: Danes and Norsemen from Norway in particular were a good deal mixed up. In England the invaders were called generically 'The Danes'.

They were consummate seamen, and formidable warriors, and they wanted land. The English Saxons had largely abandoned seafaring, and at first they were no match for the savage men who sailed and rowed up rivers and creeks in their long black ships. By the middle of the ninth century the Danes could come and go as they pleased almost anywhere on the East Coast, had occupied much of Mercia and Northumbria, and turned ferociously on Wessex.

The attack came mostly from the Thames, though there were Danish landings on the South Coast as well. By 870 the Danes had got up the Thames as far as Reading, where they established a fortified post. From Reading they attacked in force up the valley of the Kennet. The men of Wessex, under Aethelred I, grandson of Egbert, and his brother Alfred, fell back to the Berkshire Downs, where they rallied, and somewhere in the open country of the Downs at a place called 'Ashdown' they succeeded in routing the Danes. 'Ashdown' has never been satisfactorily identified: identification is made difficult by the habit of the Anglo-Saxon chroniclers of using the general name 'Ashdown' for the whole area of the Berkshire Downs. King Alfred's biographer, Asser, gives an account of the battle and identifies the place by a stunted thorn tree, which, apparently, was a conspicuous mark in the open downland where the fighting was. That is not much help 1,000 years later – except that stunted thorn trees are still conspicuous on the downs above Wantage and Lambourn.

The Battle of Ashdown figures in contemporary records as a great victory: it was an important moral victory, proving that West Saxons could beat Vikings, but in a military sense it did not achieve much, for a few weeks later Aethelred and Alfred were on the run. Viking reinforcements reached Reading, and an ill-judged attempt to take Reading led to a West Saxon defeat. The West Saxons had learned, however, that the Vikings were not invincible: fighting from their ships, or from stockaded camps, they could nearly always win, but if they could be induced into open country they were much less formidable. Knowledge of this Viking weakness, though bought at a price, was an important factor in King Alfred's later triumphs. But for most of the decade 870–79 it was touch and go.

5. *The site of a Roman villa at Ditchley, Oxon. The granary could store grain produced from some 500 acres.*

6. *Roman iron tools found in the Upper Thames Region. A brooch, knives, billhooks, sickles and hoes.*

7. *Whitchurch, Oxfordshire.*

8. *Blenheim Palace – aerial view from the West.*

Early in 871 King Aethelred died, and although he left children, he was at once succeeded by his brother Alfred: an interesting example of the pragmatic elective principle in the early English monarchy. It was no time for a boy king and a long regency. There followed twelve months of incessant fighting, tersely recorded in the *Anglo-Saxon Chronicle*:

> In the course of the year (870–1) nine general engagements were fought against the (Danish) host in the Kingdom to the South of the Thames, besides those innumerable forays in which Alfred the King's brother and a single ealdorman and King's thanes rode on, which were never counted. And in the course of this year were slain nine jarls and one King, and this year the West Saxons made peace with the host.*

It was not a lasting peace, but it gave Alfred time to regroup his forces, and, above all, to build ships to engage the Vikings *at sea*: the King and his naval architects experimented with designs on the broad reaches of the Thames near Oxford. In 875–6 the Danish Vikings, having occupied or subdued much of Mercia and Northumbria, and established themselves strongly in Ireland, again attacked Wessex. Their plan was to assemble a fleet in the Channel, join with another fleet from Ireland, and mount a powerful invasion of the South Coast. The plan miscarried. King Alfred's ships managed to defeat a Danish fleet off Poole, and the expected reinforcements from Ireland never came because they were scattered by a storm. Again the Danes made a truce undertaking to leave Wessex, but in 878 they were back in force, attacking in the West from Gloucester. Alfred took refuge in the Somerset marshes, built a fort at Athelney, and went in for guerrilla tactics against the Danes. The core of Wessex on the Upper Thames was still intact, and while he kept the Danes occupied with guerrilla warfare in the west the King gradually assembled an army in Berkshire and Hampshire. In May 878 he was ready to strike: he marched out of Athelney with a force of men from Somerset, linked up with his levies from Berkshire, Hampshire and Wiltshire on the Wiltshire Downs and met the Danish host at Edington, about 15 miles south of Chippenham. This time the West Saxon victory was decisive: not only were the Danes driven out of Wessex, but their King, Guthrun, agreed to accept Christianity, and he and some thirty of his nobles were baptized in Alfred's presence. The Danes withdrew to East Anglia and agreed by treaty to stay north of the Thames – and out of London. To make sure that they did Alfred strengthened his defences in London and at the main fords up-river,

---

* *Anglo-Saxon Chronicle*, translated by G. N. Garmondsway.

including Wallingford, Hinksey (Oxford) and Cricklade. Manpower for the earthworks and fortifications at these places was assured by allotting to each fortress a special holding of land, each hide (about 120 acres) of which had to provide one man in time of need. Wallingford, with 2,400 hides, ranked with Winchester, the capital, also with 2,400 hides, a significant indication of the continuing importance that the king attached to his own homeland of the Upper Thames. The crossing at Hinksey, becoming known as the 'oxen-ford' or cattle-crossing,* and growing in importance as a route across the river, was allotted 1,500 hides to maintain men for its defences, Cricklade 1,400 hides.† The theory behind this allocation of manpower was to provide four men to every pole ($5\frac{1}{2}$ yards) of bank or earthwork, so that one man's outstretched arm could touch his comrade's. At Wallingford, where the plan of Anglo-Saxon defence works can still be traced, this allocation was met almost precisely. The earthworks on three sides of a rectangle fronting the river extend for just over 3,000 yards: the 'hidage' providing 2,400 men would permit 3,300 yards of bank to be manned at four men to a pole. By this reckoning the defences covering the ford at Oxford ran to just over 2,000 yards of bank, and at Cricklade to about 1,900 yards.

This is not the place to write King Alfred's contribution to the life, learning and development of England: by any standards he is among the greatest of European rulers, perhaps the greatest of all dynasties of English monarchs. His hold on the Upper Thames, and the loyalty of Thames-side to him, were decisive in enabling him to preserve the political integrity of his kingdom, the kernel that was to grow into the English nation. Not least among Alfred's achievements was his encouragement of the English language. It is primarily because of him and the group of scholars he inspired that the ninth century speech of Wallingford, of Faringdon, of Wantage, has lived to grow into the richest and most flexible tongue on earth.

Alfred the Great died in 899. He left the Kingdom of England a reality, though its strength was still mainly regional, and it had still to endure and absorb more waves of invasion. They did not come at once, for Alfred had strong successors, and his impetus lasted. He himself had established his rule from the Channel to the Thames. His son Edward (the Elder) and daughter

* The first known reference to the ford at Hinksey as Oxnaford occurs in the *Anglo-Saxon Chronicle* about 911–12, but the name must have been used in speech, perhaps for a long time before it got written down.

† P. H. Blair, *An Introduction to Anglo-Saxon England.*

Aelthelflaed, who married the ealdorman to whom Alfred had entrusted the defences of London, and who continued to give spirited assistance to her brother after her husband's death, extended English control into Oxfordshire and through the Eastern midlands to the Humber. King Alfred's grandsons, Athelstan, Edmund and Eadred, who all reigned, harried the Danes north-westward, incorporating Lancashire and Westmorland into the Kingdom of England. Eadred, the last of the grandsons, who reigned from 946–55, drove Eric Bloodaxe, son of the King of Norway, from York – a decisive action, which determined that there was not going to be an independent Viking Kingdom in Yorkshire.

But the population explosion in Scandinavia was not yet over, and in time its effects on the seaboard of Western Europe were irresistible. Strong kings might succeed in holding most of England, but the population could not provide man-power to garrison the whole East Coast, and the Thames and its estuary remained an open invitation to raiders from the North Sea. Viking pressure was relentless, and weak rulers attempted to buy it off by payments of 'Danegeld', to raise the money for which they imposed ever-increasing taxation. This put a grievous burden on their subjects, and further weakened their rule. And paying blackmail did not work. Towards the close of the tenth and at the beginning of the eleventh centuries there were incessant Danish attacks on England. In 1010 a Danish force under Thorkell the Tall came up the Thames and burned Oxford, which was becoming an important place since the fortifying of its ford by King Alfred and his successors, and was acquiring something of the character of a small regional capital. But the spirit that might have held Oxford a century earlier was lacking in 1010. Aethelred II, who has gone down to history as 'The Unready', inspired no one. The nickname is, perhaps, unfair, and it means 'unwise' rather than unprepared: Aethelred II might have been a reasonable country squire, but he was hopelessly unfitted to be a king. A monk, writing at Abingdon in 1010, with Viking pirates ravaging round Abingdon and Oxford, was scathing:

> When the enemy was to the East, our Army was kept to the West, and when the enemy was to the South, then was our Army kept in the North ... At last there was not a leader who was willing to assemble an Army, but each fled as best he could.*

A yet more formidable invasion came in 1013, under Svein Forkbeard, King

---

* *Anglo-Saxon Chronicle*, translated by G. N. Garmondsway.

of Denmark. Svein took Oxford, Winchester and London, and Aethelred fled to Normandy. Svein was then recognized as King of England, but in 1014 he died. His elder son Harold went back to Denmark, and the Danish Army in England accepted his younger son, Cnut, as King of England. Cnut, however, was by no means secure. Aethelred, with his powerful son Edmund Ironside, came back from Normandy and Cnut was temporarily driven off to Denmark. He collected reinforcements and was back a year later (1015). In 1016 Aethelred II died. London recognized Edmund Ironside as king, but Cnut was strong on the Thames, and parts of Wessex recognized him. Loyalty to the House of Alfred, however, remained a powerful force, and Wessex as a whole went over to Edmund. But Cnut had his fleet, and he controlled the Thames estuary. After much fighting a treaty was drawn up acknowledging Edmund Ironside as King of Wessex and leaving the rest of England to Cnut. The clock was set back 150 years, but still the old Wessex was intact, and the Upper Thames again enclosed the core of England.

In November 1016 Edmund Ironside died, and Cnut, who had married Emma of Normandy, the widow of Aethelred II, became King of England.

The confused next period of history, culminating in the last successful invasion of England in 1066, is best understood in terms of a domestic struggle for power among the ruling Viking families. Cnut and his Danes, the Counts of Flanders and the Dukes of Normandy were all of the same Viking stock, and so by this time were many of the leading families in England. The Anglo-Saxons themselves were the offshoot of an earlier expansion by much the same people. They had developed differently from the Vikings: with good land in England to settle they had largely given up seafaring, they had accepted Christianity earlier, and because of their more settled way of life and the longer influence of the Church they had adopted somewhat different institutions. But it was not difficult for Anglo-Saxons, Danes, and later Normans (Norsemen, not Frenchmen) to live together. One of Cnut's first acts on becoming unchallenged king in England was to hold an assembly at Oxford, where it was agreed that the laws and customs of the Anglo-Saxons should be recognized generally south of the Thames, and Danish laws and customs north of the river. Cnut was clearly conscious of the strategical and political importance of the Upper Thames: he wanted to win friends there, not to provoke hostility. For as long as he could he kept Wessex under his personal rule – and he ruled well. But he became more and more involved with affairs in Scandinavia, and later he put Wessex under an Earl, one of his particular comrades, Godwin. It is another thread of Upper Thames in the tapestry of English history that Harold Godwinson, who claimed the throne of England on the death of Edward the Confessor in 1066 and who was killed at Hastings, derived the substance of his power from his earldom of Wessex.

Cnut was certainly at Oxford, and there are persistent traditions giving him a palace at Cherbury Camp, an Iron Age earthwork about a mile from Charney Bassett, lying between the river Ock and the ancient ford across the Thames at Duxford. The manor of Pusey, near Cherbury Camp, is said to have been granted by King Cnut to one Wyllyam Pewse to hold by virtue of 'horn service', a most ancient form of tenure requiring the holder to blow a horn for his lord. The horn (or at least a horn) about 2 ft 6 ins long, and made of ox horn, was produced in Court in a Chancery action in 1681, and the grant accepted by the court as genuine. Just across the Ock, a manor at Denchworth is also supposed to have been held by a grant from King Cnut. Doubt has been cast on these traditions on the ground that such forms of tenure by knight-service are Norman, not Anglo-Saxon or Danish. That is essentially a nineteenth-century view of history: later research has shown that various forms of feudal tenure were well established in the Anglo-Saxon period, and that the Norman system was grafted so easily into English life largely because it brought no abrupt change in customs that were generally understood. This is not to say that the Cnut traditions in the Vale of the White Horse are historically accurate: what one can say is that they are not inconsistent with history. Cnut is known to have taken a close personal interest in the Upper Thames, and it is at least not improbable that he understood the strategical value of the ford at Duxford and was at pains to keep its hinterland in friendly hands. Where local tradition has endured persistently for centuries, there is commonly something in it.

The conquest that brought William of Normandy to England in 1066 was more a change of dynasty at the top than an upheaval of the local life of land and river. The Danish Viking rulers of Normandy and Flanders were already much mixed by marriage with the Anglo-Saxon dynasty in England. Aethelred II had married Emma, daughter of Richard of Normandy, and great-aunt of William the Conqueror; she was later married to Cnut. Baldwin II of Flanders had married Elstrude, a daughter of King Alfred, and his great-great-granddaughter Matilda married William the Conqueror. Flanders and Normandy were fairly closely linked and a number of Viking knights from Flanders accompanied William on his expedition to England. Normandy had given refuge to Aethelred and Edmund Ironside in their troubles with Svein Forkbeard, and Aethelred's youngest son Edward (by Emma of Normandy) was brought up in exile there while Cnut and his sons reigned in England. Edward, the last of the Anglo-Saxon House of Wessex to rule in England, was called to the throne on the death of Cnut's son Harthaknut in 1042. The piety which led him to be called Edward the Confessor was admirable, but no match for the rapacity of the Viking lords on both sides of the Channel. He died childless, and although the young grandson of Edmund Ironside was formally elected king he had no chance against Harold Godwinson, Earl of Wessex, and William of Normandy. Harold seized power, but his brother Tostig, in alliance with Harold Hardrada, King of Norway, and William of Normandy were both out to take England if they could. The Viking force from Norway arrived first and Harold succeeded in defeating it at Stamford Bridge. A few days later William landed in Sussex, and Harold was killed.

The land enfolded by the Upper Thames remained a very English part of England. Norman lords replaced Saxon lords, but not everywhere. Many Saxon landowning families were dispossessed, but the family feuds of warring dynasties had left loyalties mixed. On the Thames itself, a great Saxon landowner, Wigod of Wallingford, had supported William against Harold. He was left undisturbed, and on his death his daughter Aldith inherited his estates. She married a Norman knight, Robert de Oyley (later D'Oyley), securing both continuity and a natural transition from Saxon to Norman succession. Some of the Saxon noblemen who had fought with Harold went into exile abroad; several took service with the Emperor in Constantinople, who was glad to recruit Saxons into his Varangian (originally 'Viking') Guard. They left sisters and daughters. Most of the adventurers who fought with William and who expected land as a reward did not bring wives, and many of them married into the old Saxon ruling class: the grandson of a Saxon landowner might thus inherit an estate of which his uncle or his cousin had been dispossessed. The influx of new blood was not great. Estimates of the size of William's army vary from 12,000 to 6,000 men and the smaller figure is probably more nearly correct. Many of them would have gone home, with such loot as they could collect. Relations and hangers-on of the first generation Norman barons certainly followed them to England in the hope of pickings, but the opportunities of land-grabbing grew less as a stable Norman-Saxon stock emerged, resentful of newcomers. The church was a great landowner from the Saxon period: Saxon Abbots were replaced, and much Church land in England was granted to foundations on the Continent. It is doubtful if this made much difference to those who worked the land.

By 1066 the region of the Upper Thames was the most settled and civilized part of England, the Thames itself a unifying bond as well as a protection. This part of England was in many ways more civilized than the Normandy and Flanders from which its conquerors came, and it civilized its conquerors. Though the conquest gradually changed much, it left much unchanged. The boundaries of shire, of many parishes even, are still unchanged from Saxon days; the churches that stand today, built and rebuilt by Norman knights, eighteenth-century squires and Victorian businessmen, often stand on Saxon foundations. Towns, villages and hamlets were all settlements when the Normans came, their names Saxon or Roman, occasionally older than either. The conquest added a few place names to the map, but mostly tacked on to older names – thus Charney Bassett and Letcombe Bassett, linking Ralf Basset, a great Norman officer (Justiciar) in the establishment of Henry I with two ancient villages in the countryside where his father had been granted land; Kingston Blount, preserving the name of a family that sprang from the brothers Robert and William Le Blount, two knights from Flanders who accompanied William of Normandy; Stanton Harcourt, Kingston Lisle, Compton Beauchamp, and the like.

Society in the region was relatively stable by late Saxon times, but the class gradations of English life always have been subtle and complex. The Saxon invaders followed their leaders as free men, and as they settled to agricultural life the original families retained their freedom, subject to certain obligations. But men varied in importance, and in the days before there was much king's justice it was necessary to know the importance of a man, because somebody might kill him, and his relations would then want compensation as the alternative to a tiresome blood-feud. Custom, therefore, assessed social importance in the simplest of all ways, by setting a money value on it. This was called 'Wergild'. There were two main classes of free men, thanes (originally *gesithas*, companions of the leader) and churls – roughly, gentlemen and players. In the region, and in Wessex generally, the *wergild* of a thane was set at 1,200 shillings, a price which seems to have originated in the value of 300 oxen. A churl was worth 200 shillings, or 50 oxen. Both were free, entitled to own, to bequeath and to inherit land, and the difference in their money values was not as unfair as it sounds, for from the greater, more was expected: if a thane committed an offence he was punished on a higher scale of fines; it was common practice to fine a man the amount of his own *wergild*. As time went on and thanes' sons lost some of their land a class of gentry not belonging to the highest class was recognized, at least in Wessex: these had a *wergild* of 600 shillings, three times a churl's value, but only half a thane's. Below the churl there were slaves, who did not count. A slave could be killed without any payment of *wergild*, though his owner could demand his value, commonly regarded as around 20 shillings, from the killer. Slaves might be remnants of the original population, or prisoners from other Saxon tribes taken in war. They could be bought or sold like cattle, but in Wessex an English slave could not be sold abroad. (In Kent he could be sold to the Continent, or to any slave dealer.) There was movement up and down society. A slave could be freed; a churl could become a thane by acquiring more land; a trader who owned his own ship and had made not fewer than three voyages in her could become a thane. The churls, broadly speaking, were our present middle class, providing not only the farmers of a predominantly agricultural society, but the merchants, traders and craftsmen – for the skilled man then was a journeyman, his own master, and not an employee. But, as in the great English middle class, there were gradations in the degree of churl, though we do not know much about them: some were prosperous yeoman farmers, others drifted downwards, as some slaves drifted upwards, to become peasants nominally free but in practice bound more or less to the land from which they got a living. The Normans inherited this social system, and gradually debased it. Their French clerks could not, or did not try to, unravel the complexities of churldom, and tended to list all who were not gentry and tenants-in-chief as 'villanus' (villein), which conveyed no status, and did not mean much more than 'villager'. A villein was not a serf or slave, and he might have certain local rights, but he was not free. With the gradual hardening of latin feudalism introduced from France, a system more rigid and more absolute than feudalism in its Saxon or Danish forms, the social position of the poorer people deteriorated, and they were bound more firmly to their lord and to the land. The Norman church did, however, put a stop to the commercial traffic in slaves: the slave market at Bristol, which continued into Norman times, was abolished by a Norman bishop.

The status of women also declined after the conquest. The Saxon, and still more the Viking, attitude to women was almost modern: they could dispose of their own property after marriage, and if they were unhappy with their husbands they could divorce them, and any dowry they had brought on marriage had to be paid back. Divorce naturally became more complicated as Christian rules became more generally accepted, but a Saxon woman was never the chattel that she became under the influence of Norman-French law. The Viking woman was always a person in her own right, and Viking genealogies attach as much importance to mothers and grandmothers as they do to males. A Viking woman kept her name after marriage: if she were Herjolfsdotter she remained so, although her husband might be Andersson. The women of Wessex who married into early Norman families were a spirited lot, and did much to preserve the continuity of society in the region.

So, by the end of the eleventh century, was formed the people whose descendants inhabit this region of England to this day, predominantly Saxon, mixed with some Danish Viking, and with the blood of unremembered older stocks: the Romanized Britons whom the Saxons conquered, the Beaker folk, and the misty Neolithic, Mesolithic and Palaeolithic, overrun by one another in the migrations of the distant past. Blood is indestructible: slave's blood and thane's blood course in the myriad great-grandchildren of which both slave and thane are common ancestors. After the eleventh century there was no major immigration into the region, and with no large towns save Oxford there was not much coming and going of merchants to bring the blood of far countries to the native stock. There were no settlements of refugees from religious persecution, like the Huguenots in London and the South East. For seven centuries Oxford has attracted men from every corner of the world, but Oxford gives out rather than absorbs. Large-scale industry, drawing people from other parts of Britain, did not come into the region until after the First World War.

For centuries until the war of 1914–18 probably four-fifths of the regional population lived and died within ten miles of where they were born: even today there are old people in the villages who have never been to London, never seen the sea, never travelled farther than to Oxford or to Reading. Until the upheaval of the First World War and the coming of the motor car, the population of the region was exceptionally stable, a good stock, slow-speaking, perhaps a bit slow-thinking, but even slower to abandon a cause or a conviction, staunch friends and stubborn enemies. In *fyrd* (the Saxon call-up), militia, and county regiments they have fought for their land whenever they have felt it threatened.

There has been more fundamental change in the region in the past fifty years than in as many generations. A Roman official riding at dusk into a Thames-side village in my childhood would not have noticed much to cause him surprise. (I write 'at dusk', because in daylight he would have wondered at the glass in cottage windows.) At the inn a man would have taken his horse; inside a candle would have lighted him to his room. Social organization would not have bewildered him: the squire, the tenant farmers, the farm labourers, all would have seemed to him quite natural; so would have seemed the gamekeeper and the poachers. Two world wars and the motor car have brought an avalanche of social change. But much is unchanged. It needs only mist from the water

73

meadows to hide the television aerials and the hedgerows. The Thames and its tributaries still enrich some of the finest pastureland in the world, men and women still draw their livelihood directly from the land. That there are other livelihoods now from the factories at Cowley, Banbury and Witney, from atomic energy at Harwell and Culham, has widened life, not removed its nearness to the river-bounded land.

4

The River Thames

The loads men carry
are soon set down,
and soon untrodden
the paths of man.
Before man was
the river ran,
and the river will run
when man is gone.

We know nothing of the tongue that our Neolithic ancestors spoke, but something of it may be preserved in the name Thames. It was in use when the Romans came, but the root does not appear to be Celtic. The phonetic spelling is *Tems*, which the Romans latinized to *Tamesis*. The *h* in the modern spelling is an addition as unjustifiable as it is unnecessary. It appears occasionally in the *Chronicon Monasterii* of Abingdon as 'Thamisa', a variant of Tamisa, Tamasa and Tamesis in latinized versions of the Saxon Temese. It was dug out to please an antiquarian fancy in the seventeenth century, and has been fashionable ever since – to make things harder for schoolchildren, perhaps. Isis, which mapmakers continue obediently to give as an alternative name for the upper river, is equally factitious. There is *no* record of its use in any early charter: it was never used by either Romans or Saxons, and does not occur anywhere before the fourteenth century, when it appears as 'Isa'. It is a made-up name from confusion between the Thames and its tributary the Thame: apparently it struck some medieval scribe as neat to take the Latinized ending 'isa' from Tamisa and add it to the Thame to marry the two rivers below Dorchester. No countryman living by the Upper Thames ever uses, or has ever used, the word Isis. It is a purely literary conceit, and the schoolboy who writes 'Tems' is nearer truth than the grammarians.

The modern chart of the Thames follows the navigable river to Lechlade, but before there were roads the river provided transport far more nearly to the source. It was not easy transport: barges had to be towed and pushed and shoved over the shallows by gangs of men called 'scufflehunters', with such help as they could get from horses floundering in the meadows before there were any towpaths. But river transport was possible, capable of taking much greater loads than either human porters or pack animals. And it was used: the Thames was once navigable, after a fashion, well above Cricklade, as far as Waterhay Bridge just below Ashton Keynes. Had railways not come when they did, the Thames and Severn Canal in the north, the Wilts and Berks Canal through the middle of the region, and the Kennet and Avon Canal in the south could have been developed to make the Thames and its feeders the main east-west highway across England, from London and the estuary to the Bristol Channel.

The Thames has always been navigable for most of its length, though often with difficulty. The Kennet was made navigable from Reading to Newbury between 1715 and 1723. In 1789 the Upper Thames was linked with the Severn by a canal that ran from Inglesham near Lechlade, to Stroud, burrowing under the Cotswolds through a tunnel at Sapperton on the way: at Stroud it met the Stroudwater canal, to join the Severn at Framilode. In 1810 two links with the Avon were completed, the Wilts and Berks canal from Abingdon through the Vale of the White Horse to Semington, near Bradford-on-Avon, and the Kennet and Avon canal from Newbury to Bath. There was talk of turning the Kennet and Avon into a ship canal, so that ocean-going ships could sail from Bristol to London.

All this was in keeping with history, for the Thames had peopled its region and created the communities which needed it to transport their goods. The energy that went into canal building in the late eighteenth and early nineteenth centuries was not misplaced. It was wasted because a generation later came the railways, and in the mania for trying to make money out of railways nobody bothered to preserve the older systems of water transport. They competed with railways – and the railwaymen had the money and the power. So the navigations were bought out and killed, or deliberately allowed to die. Now that railways have been largely made obsolete by road transport the value of our lost system of waterways, capable of carrying all the heavy things we need without noise, without danger to other traffic, without wear and tear of either nerves or road surface, is perhaps beginning to be understood.

The Thames could not be destroyed. It has lost its goods traffic, but the upper river remains the greatest stretch of inland water in Britain on which to take pleasure in boats. Its use has been diverted from commerce to recreation, but recreation is also commerce: meeting the needs of tourists and holidaymakers is one of Britain's most important industries. The Thames continues to give livelihoods as well as life to its region.

There was little fighting anywhere near the Thames after the conquest of 1066, and with brief interludes of misery during the Wars of the Roses and the Civil War, and some bombs during the war of 1939–45, the region has known nearly 1,000 years of peace. It has developed as quietly as its river flows, moving imperceptibly from the medieval to the modern without violent change. The churls who lost status after the conquest gradually recovered it. The half-free condition of villeinage and the bonds of serfdom were eroded as it became more profitable for landlords to draw rents and pay wages than to maintain estates by services in kind: forced labour is always reluctant labour. By the end of the fourteenth century, and particularly after the dreadful mortality in 1348–9 of the plague called the Black Death, men might be poor, but they were mostly free: the plague assisted freedom by reducing the population to a point at which labour was so scarce that a landlord was not inclined to ask questions if a man from another village came asking for a job. A subsistence economy, in which every hamlet had to be more or less self-supporting, changed to a market economy. The Thames helped to promote the change, for it provided transport to markets, partly directly, but more importantly by the links of its fords and (later) bridges with the road routes that developed from prehistoric trackways. Food was the chief wealth of the region, grain and cheese and meat. Away from the river, particularly on the lias soils to the north of Oxford, and on the lower slopes of the chalk downs in Berkshire there is good land for wheat and barley, and the water meadows of the Thames and Cherwell and in the Vale of the White Horse give some of the finest pasture in the world. Andersey Island, lying between the main river and a backwater at Abingdon was coveted throughout the Middle Ages by both Church and Crown for the richness of its grazing. The Vale of the White Horse was noted for its cheese at the time of the Domesday Survey in 1086 and remained so until cheesemaking left the dairy for the mass production factory. Most of the Vale's cheese was carted to Buscot and shipped from there to Oxford and London. There was a wharf at Buscot known for centuries as 'The Cheese

Wharf', and huge quantities of cheese were sent to market from it: in 1809 nearly 3,000 tons of cheese was shipped from Buscot, by that time mostly to London. Reckoning 10 cheeses to the hundredweight, about the average weight, this is around a quarter of a million cheeses in one year.

The region had wealth in other forms. The sheep which Neolithic farmers introduced to the Berkshire Downs and Oxfordshire Cotswolds thrived through Roman and Saxon times, and by the twelfth century were producing large quantities of the wool which was England's main export throughout the Middle Ages. The wool trade grew through the next three centuries, creating rich men in the wool towns that grew with it, among them Witney, Fairford, Chipping Campden, Northleach and Newbury. With the wool trade grew a trade in skins and fine leather: Abingdon and Woodstock specialized in gloves, Witney in leather breeches. There was also stone, the lovely Cotswold stone to be quarried round Burford and Taynton, good stone, too, from Headington, and stone slates from many places in Oxfordshire, notably from Stonesfield, which gets its name from them. Professor Hoskins has examined the tax quotas of 1334 which show Oxford as the richest county in England and Berkshire the third richest (second place went to Norfolk).

Until the 1920s, when the motor industry began to be important in Oxford, the region was predominantly agricultural, with its traditional trades continuing to supplement agricultural life, quarrying in the stone districts, blanketmaking at Witney, leatherworking at Woodstock, Charlbury and Abingdon, clothmaking at Newbury, withy-cutting along the Thames and its tributaries for basket work and hurdlemaking (an important craft in a sheep country) and rushcutting, particularly in the Windrush, for sealing beer barrels. The rush seal used to be vital for wooden barrels, but has departed with the advent of the metal drum. Small towns, most of which have remained small, grew up as local markets, and as collecting centres for the outwork done in cottage industries – outworking is still important in the glove trade. All Upper Thames towns are on the sites of ancient settlements, brought into being by the geophysical conditions that provided sustenance and shelter, created fords or made a meeting for trackways. There is a modern theory that Governments can will New Towns, decreeing that human settlements of such and such a size and shape shall come into being at a given place. Such towns can be built, of course, but the evidence of 2,000 years is against their ever taking root: if man is to come to terms with his environment he must plan with humility and decree with a compassionate sense of history.

The Upper Thames countryside is a wonderful example of an environment with which man has come to terms, and kept on good terms. Its towns and villages seem to grow from the soil – as, indeed, most of them have, for until the concrete and glass of our present generation men mostly had to build with what they could get locally.

Early man settled by the river partly to be sure of water, with a bonus of fish, partly for protection: a moat makes for security. It is not chance that all the riverside towns of the Upper Thames are where tributaries join in, or where there are fords to be guarded. Cricklade is at the meeting place of Churn and Thames, Lechlade is on the north bank of the river on a peninsula between the Leach and the Thames, protected to the south by the Coln and the Cole. Oxford, the greatest of all Thames towns above London, is an island fortress of firm gravel between the Thames and Cherwell, still more protected by a network of backwaters and little streams. These ancient defences served Oxford well against bombing in the Second World War. Enemy pilots who thought that they could find Oxford by following the Thames were confused by the patchwork of waterways, and their bombs did much less damage than they might. Abingdon, Dorchester, and Reading are all peninsular towns, at the junctions of Ock, Thame and Kennet. Wallingford grew up to protect its ford, and the track from the south to what was probably a better crossing at Shillingford: it is itself protected to the south and west by a number of brooks and runnels which would once have made a considerable area of marsh – the best of all natural defences. From very early times Wallingford had a bridge, probably the first bridge across the Thames. A charter of 957 calls the track from Wallingford to Shillingford the *Brycwege*, which means Bridgeway. Nothing is known of this bridge, but the place was so important to the Saxon Kingdom of Wessex that it is quite possible that a timber bridge was built to improve the crossing of the ford. Streatley is another ford settlement, once, perhaps, the most important of all, for it is here that the prehistoric Ridgeway from the Berkshire Downs descended to the river to meet the Eastern section of the Icknield Way at the Goring Gap.

All these Thames-side towns were in origin defensive, settlements to take advantage of the natural protection afforded by the river and its tributaries, or to guard the precious fords. Commerce went with defence. A Beaker merchant with a pack of valuable Westmorland axes would naturally take his wares to a secure settlement, where both he and his customers could feel reasonably safe from molestation. Trade came naturally to the river crossings: they were keypoints in the trade routes, and from the earliest times must have offered rudimentary inns or caravanserais where travellers and pack animals could find rest and food before going farther. Such places were the first markets, where good flints or bronze wares were exchanged for food and, as trade developed, for flocks and herds. Such places went on to become medieval market towns, the more important of them accommodating moneyers granted a royal licence to mint coin: in late Saxon times there were such mints at Wallingford, Oxford and Cricklade.*

Inland from the river the sites of towns and the larger villages were determined by the meeting of trackways, partly for convenience, partly again for defence, for to hold a crossroads may protect a considerable hinterland. Faringdon and Wantage are good examples of this. Both are nodal points for routes running north, south, east and west, ancient tracks which have become modern roads.

The towns, formed by the river, its tributaries, and the trackways leading to fords, have helped in turn to form the life of the region. None, save Oxford, and Reading on the southern edge, has grown to any size. Dorchester was a bishopric a thousand years ago, but it lost its bishop to Lincoln in the eleventh century and has remained a village since. Oxford has the sole cathedral in the region. Abingdon nearly became a mixture of Swindon and Didcot, for Brunel's original plans for the Great Western Railway envisaged Abingdon as a major junction and site for railway workshops, but the town would have none of his railway and stuck loyally to its river and canal. Later it had to petition for a branch line, and was given a single-track route from the main line to Oxford at Radley, remaining a footnote in railway history. That Abingdon branch had its eccentric charm but was closed in 1956. Didcot became an important railway junction, but the workshops went to Swindon, and although Didcot has now added an immense power station to its railway activities it has remained in a strange administrative backwater – no more than a parish in the Wallingford Rural District.

But the towns, though small, are adult places, combining dignity with distinction, each sharply conscious of its local importance. There are hazards both to dignity and distinction, which I shall discuss later. For the moment let us consider the urbanity – I use the word in its original sense – that the Thames has given to its countryside.

It does not start urbanely: it would be hard to imagine a more inconspicuous source, timid, even, for a river with such a place in history. Without the Ordnance map, the source is not easy to find, and the map suggests only roughly where it is. Go eastwards from Cirencester by the old Fosse Way, here A429. Ignore the turn to Malmesbury and continue along the Fosse Way, which has now become A433. About $3\frac{1}{2}$ miles out of Cirencester, just before you go under a railway bridge, and before you reach the Thames Head Inn, there is a layby

* Professor W. G. Hoskins.

80

9. Sutton Courtenay, Berks — parallel ditches of a 'cursus', a strange prehistoric enclosure, the purpose of which is unknown. The ring ditches are Bronze Age barrows. An Anglo-Saxon village was in the rough ground bottom left – continuous habitation of a site for thousands of years.

10a. *New buildings in Blue Boar Quad, Christ Church, Oxford.*

10b. *St Catherine's College, Oxford.*

11a. *Roman pottery from Shotover, Oxford. These little faces were used to decorate jugs. 3rd–4th centuries A.D.*

11b. *From an early Anglo-Saxon grave (approximately 6th century) at Standlake, near Witney.*

11c. *Early Saxon pottery (6th–7th centuries) from the village at Sutton Courtenay.*

12. *The Thames at Lechlade, Gloucestershire.*

where you can pull off the road. There is nothing to direct you to the source of the Thames, but walk downhill a hundred yards or so, towards the railway bridge, and to the north of the road you will find a five-barred gate. Go through it, cross a wide field, and go through another gate in a stone wall. Two or three hundred yards beyond this gate you enter a clump of trees, and there, in a small railed enclosure, is a statue, somewhat chipped, of Old Father Thames. He adorned the Crystal Palace in London until its owners, the (then) London County Council, included him in a sale, and he was bought by the Hon. Michael Berry, son of the first Lord Camrose, as a garden ornament. Mr Berry sold him in 1957 to Mr H. Scott Freeman, a member of the Thames Conservancy, who presented him to the Conservancy to commemorate the centenary of that body. He weighs three tons. Father Thames is bearded and reclining, and somebody has given him a wooden paddle to hold. He was put in his pen at Thames Head in 1958. An iron notice board, rather like those cast-iron affairs by which the old Great Western Railway used to instruct passengers not to cross the line, records:

Conservators of the
River Thames
1958
This statue was placed here
By the Conservators
To mark the source of the River Thames
The statue was given by
H. Scott Freeman, Esq.
Conservator
Sir Jocelyn Bray, D.L., J.P.
Chairman

This statue puts one in mind a little of Shelley's Ozymandias, for 'nothing beside remains'. A jumble of broken stones in a depression in the ground suggests a spring, but in summer there is seldom any water in it, for the Thames here is a *winterbourne*, coming to the surface normally in winter only. Yet there is always water underground, and in substantial quantity: in the late eighteenth and early nineteenth centuries a well at Thames Head to tap the spring was a vital source of water for the Thames and Severn Canal. Water was pumped originally by windmill, later by a Boulton and Watt steam engine into a large stone pound to feed the canal: a print of 1793 in my possession shows an overflow from the enclosed well gushing most satisfactorily into Trewsbury Mead. All these works are now gone, and the canal itself departed. The unseen Thames crosses the

Fosse Way by a culvert under the road, becoming a proper rivulet in the fields above Kemble and Ewen and a beautiful young river by Somerford and Ashton Keynes. Here it begins to nourish if not exactly urban at least built-up life: the two Keyneses, beautiful villages today, have known gracious buildings since Saxon times. The church at Somerford Keynes contains a rare example of surviving Saxon stone work in an arched doorway in the North Wall, unblocked in 1967. Among the treasures of this church is a Saxon, or possibly Viking, carving of the heads of two dragon-like animals, either biting each other, or (as it is pleasanter to think) playing with a ball.

County boundaries are much involved here, the lines on the modern map reflecting long-forgotten struggles for power in what was always border country. Having begun its life in Gloucestershire the Thames has a brief course in Wiltshire before returning to Gloucestershire. Its first town, Cricklade, is in Wiltshire. The Thames here, though it can be spanned by a telegraph pole, is deep enough for a ford to be important, and the ford at Cricklade was one of Alfred the Great's frontier posts. The Cirencester–Swindon road (A419), once Roman and running straight as a die for miles, no longer needs the ford, for it crosses the Thames at Cricklade by a bridge, a neat stone bridge with the river channelled through a single arch and with a notice beside it to tell you that it is the River Thames. A nice contrast is the footbridge made from a telegraph pole that crosses the river to a cottage a few yards from the roadbridge. Although physically no larger than many a village Cricklade (pop c. 2,000) is a town, and could be called nothing else: its wide main street and tall stone houses are both urban and urbane. Its fortresses are gone, its river now undefended, but you can feel that some Saxon C-in-C Cricklade was once proud of his job. It is a tiny metropolis still.

Lechlade, eight miles north-east as the crow flies, but some three miles farther as the river wanders, is another true frontier town. Here four counties meet – Wiltshire, Gloucestershire, Oxfordshire and Berkshire. Lechlade itself is in Gloucestershire, but its two bridges over the Thames lead to two different counties: the upper one, Halfpenny Bridge, once a toll bridge that cost a halfpenny to cross, leads into Wiltshire, and the lower, St John's, goes into Berkshire. The Leach joins the Thames near St John's bridge, and across the Leach is Oxfordshire. The chart of the Thames takes navigation to Lechlade, 146 miles above the tidal Thames at Teddington. A note on the chart warns navigators, 'Upstream from Lechlade the river is not easily navigable even for a launch drawing only 2 ft 6 ins.' The chart is optimistic. Small launches can go a couple of miles upstream, almost to Inglesham, but above Inglesham the safest boat to use is a canoe. Navigation is, however, coming back to these upper reaches of the Thames. The growth of cruiser traffic on the river has encouraged the Conservancy to reopen to navigation more of the Thames above Lechlade. Dredging has started, and in a few years it may be possible for modern cruisers, like the barges of a hundred years ago, to get up to Cricklade.

But Lechlade has long been the effective head of navigation, and St John's Lock, just below Lechlade, is the highest on the navigable river. Up to Lechlade the Conservancy maintains a buoyed channel with a summer depth of 3 ft, enough for most river cruisers of a normal size (though there are hazards to navigation that I shall touch on later). The Conservancy at present is more cautious than the chart. It says in its cruising guidebook, 'Above Lechlade navigation is only possible at times for the smallest class of pleasure boats.' As the channel is reopened cruisers will be able to explore some particularly lovely stretches of the river.

As the effective Head of Navigation for a long period, Lechlade has a special place on the Thames. It is a beautiful old town, its church spire crowning the gentle landscape – a magic picture looking upstream from St John's Bridge, especially when a light mist lies over the water meadows and the soaring spire pierces the mist. Two main roads cross in the town, A361 crossing the Thames by Halfpenny Bridge to go north, A417 crossing by St John's Bridge on its way west. The church (St Lawrence) stands back from the roaring crossroads, in a corner screened by buildings making two sides of a square that was once a market place. There is still peace to be found in the churchyard, and in the church some beautiful glass and fifteenth-century brasses. Lechlade has lost its market, but it is a thriving little place, with some pleasant old inns, in spite of Thomas Baskervile's recommendation to travellers in 1692 to avail themselves of the 'strong march beer' to be had in bottles at an inn by St John's Bridge 'for as far as I remember in Lechlad [sic] there is no tavern'.* The old docks, once busy with barge traffic to and from the Thames and Severn Canal, are still there, hard by Halfpenny Bridge: they are now a boatyard.

Halfpenny Bridge was built in 1789, primarily to serve the barge dock. St John's Bridge is far older, having some claim to be considered the oldest bridge, or at least the site of the oldest bridge, across the Thames. It is a claim that can never be settled. A bridge was built across the Thames here by the monks of St John's Priory at Lechlade in 1229, and in 1341 the prior was granted 'pontage' (a medieval tax for the upkeep of bridges) for repairing it. The crossing is said to

---

* Quoted by F. S. Thacker, *The Thames Highway*, Vol. II.

be on the line of an ancient ford. At some time during the troubles of the four-teenth century the bridge was apparently destroyed, being rebuilt about 1387. It had a thriving traffic from then on, with a five-day fair of its own (St John's Bridge Fair, established by a charter of 1234) which brought people thronging to the meadows to sell their cheeses and farm produce to barge merchants from Oxford and beyond, and to buy the little luxuries that before the days of shops were only to be had at fairs. Baskervile reports in 1692 seeing 'six or eight boats together' loading and unloading goods. This river traffic was sometimes piratical. In 1677 the people of Cricklade, to which barges then went on from Lechlade, complained of a certain Captain Cutler who held barges to ransom at St John's Bridge, and would not let them pass without paying a levy to him. In 1790 a pound lock was built at St John's, to improve navigation and primarily to serve traffic from the Thames and Severn Canal. This required an addition to the bridge over the lock cut. It was nothing like as good a job as the medieval bridge, for by 1795 it was falling down. It was patched up several times, and wholly rebuilt in 1879. The old bridge was extensively restored and rebuilt in 1820, after some 500 years of service, and carries the ever increasing traffic of twentieth-century roads without noticeable complaint.

Of St John's Priory next to nothing remains, though some of its stones went into the porch of the parish church and, no doubt, into other buildings in Lech-lade. The order was hospitable, and in addition to its pious work of bridge build-ing maintained a hospital or hospice on the Gloucestershire side of its bridge. This is now the Trout Inn. Whether it was the inn where seventeenth-century travellers could get their 'strong march beer' I do not know, but it remains a pleasant hostelry for our own century.

From Lechlade to Oxford – some 31 miles of river – the Thames is townless, or rather its market towns Bampton on the north bank and Faringdon to the south lie a couple of miles inland. Both are road centres, both of great antiquity, controlling trackways to the river long before there were roads. Radcot Bridge, another claimant to the title of the oldest bridge on the Thames, serves both. In terms of medieval masonry still surviving Radcot now probably is the oldest of the Thames bridges, but the monks at Lechlade may have got their bridge across the river first. Radcot Bridge was built some time before 1312, perhaps quite a long time, for a grant of 'pontage' made in 1312 was for the 'repair' of the bridge, which suggests that it had then been in use for a good many years. The bridge today is much as it was in the fourteenth century, with very steep 'humpbacks' over its main arches. It is of great length, as much a causeway as a bridge, for it crosses what were originally three streams, the main river, and two backwaters

84

where the river forks to form a small island, reuniting a few hundred yards downstream. It is difficult to trace the pattern of the medieval river, for there was an artificial diversion to feed a millstream, and the navigable channel today is not the original main river but an eighteenth-century side-cut. There was further tidying up of streams and streamlets between 1878–86 to remove 'obstructions', which were reported then to be 'extensive'.* The cut was dug in 1787. It required an extension to the old bridge, and this was built in the same year. F. S. Thacker, writing around 1910, did not consider the new channel an improvement. 'Why the navigation was diverted,' he wrote, 'I cannot determine, except that just then people were mad on alterations, whether for better or worse.'

In 1387 one arch of the old bridge was destroyed by the supporters of Henry of Lancaster (later Henry IV) during his revolt against Richard II. Henry's strength was in the west midlands and the Welsh Marches in the territories of his father, John of Gaunt. A force of some 5,000 men, probably mostly raised in Oxfordshire and Berkshire, was sent to meet him and marched to cross the Thames at Radcot. Henry's friends got news of this, and the King's men, under the Earl of Oxford, reached Radcot to find the bridge down and the crossing strongly defended. In the engagement that followed the King's force was routed, many men losing their lives in the river. This Battle of Radcot was not decisive, but it played its part in Henry's later victory over Richard.

Radcot Bridge saw fighting again in the Civil War, when Charles I had his headquarters at Oxford. The bridge, an important outpost for Oxford, was held for the Royalists, who also held Faringdon: one of their strongpoints there was Faringdon House, which then belonged to Sir Robert Pye, whose son, also Sir Robert, had married John Hampden's sister and was a prominent Parliament man. In 1645 Cromwell attacked Faringdon and sent a detachment of cavalry to take Radcot Bridge. Both attacks failed. Faringdon House was so gallantly defended that the Parliament troops had to withdraw, and a cavalry charge by Prince Rupert scattered the force sent to seize Radcot Bridge. These Royalist victories achieved no more than a breathing space for the king; in the following year Cromwell sent Sir Robert Pye (the younger) to invest his own home at Faringdon. Radcot Bridge was forced and fell to Parliament, and after a siege of seven weeks the defenders of Faringdon House surrendered to Sir Robert Pye.

Radcot was a river port on the Upper Thames for centuries, serving a large

* Thames Conservancy Report, 1879.

area of North Berkshire and Oxfordshire. Building stone from Burford was carted to Radcot for shipment to London. Burford stone is reputed to have been used for the original St Paul's Cathedral in London, and it was certainly used in the building of Wren's St Paul's. Most of the present St Paul's is Portland stone, brought to London cheaply by sea, but Wren specified Burford stone for parts of the building and all this went by river from Radcot. Three of Wren's master masons, Christopher Kempster, Ephraim Beauchamp and Edward Strong, were Burford men. Berkshire cheese is believed to have been shipped downriver from Radcot for export to the Low Countries even before the Norman conquest. Towards the end of the eighteenth century the cheese trade went mainly to Buscot, a few miles upstream from Radcot, largely through the enterprise of the then owner of Buscot Park, who built special warehouses for cheese at Buscot Wharf. Radcot, however, remained important in the Thames carrying trade, particularly for coal, until the coming of railways; and in spite of railways its coal trade lasted to some extent to the turn of the present century.

At some time in the eighteenth century, probably for the convenience of Bampton, a new bridge was built three miles downstream from Radcot by a weir called Tadpole weir. The bridge became known as Tadpole Bridge. The original Tadpole Bridge was possibly of wood: the present stone bridge was built in 1802. Although now apparently in the middle of nowhere, Tadpole Bridge also had a wharf, and a quite important coal trade in the early nineteenth century.

Bampton is of great antiquity. Saxon invaders coming up the Thames had a settlement in the neighbourhood early in the seventh century. The fords at Duxford, on the Berkshire bank of the Thames, and Shifford, on the Oxfordshire bank nearly opposite (perhaps originally a continuous stretch of shallows) gave Bampton a strategical importance on the north bank of the river similar to that of Faringdon to the south. Alfred the Great held a parliament or council at Shifford* in 890, recorded thus in a more or less contemporary Anglo-Saxon poem

> At sifford seten thaines manie
> Fele biscopes and fele woclered
> Erles prude cnihtes eglochet†

---

* Upper Thames patriotism naturally inclines me to give this famous assembly to Shifford, though I have always doubted whether what in the ninth century must have been mainly marsh could have accommodated such an assembly. It is also claimed for Shefford, in the Lambourn valley, and for Seaford in Sussex.

† This Anglo Saxon MS was at one time in the Cottonian collection at Oxford, but is believed to have been lost in a fire. It is quoted by the Rev J. A. Giles in his *History of the Parish and Town of Bampton,* printed privately in 1848.

At shifford many Thanes sat
Many bishops, and many men learned in books,
Wise earls and awe-inspiring knights . . .

Bampton had a market before the Norman conquest, granted in the reign of Edward the Confessor. Land at Bampton was held by Leofric, chaplain to Edward the Confessor, who became the first Bishop of Exeter, and in 1046 he gave his Bampton lands to Exeter Cathedral. Bampton market is recorded in the Domesday Survey of 1086 as being worth 50s. a year. The ecclesiastical history of the place is fascinating. The magnificent church is mostly thirteenth century, though some of the stone work is considerably older, certainly early Norman and perhaps Saxon. Its early connection with the Bishops of Exeter gave the parish a number of peculiar privileges. Until the middle of the last century it was an enormous parish of some 10,000 acres, and it had three vicars, with three vicarages in the church close. They were not, however, rival vicars, for this was a means of sharing out preferment to the considerable revenues of the parish – the three vicars were termed 'portionists'. Normally there would be only one incumbent, the other two 'portions' going to absentee clerics: occasionally the revenues from two 'portions' might be combined. This arrangement came to an end in the nineteenth century with the splitting of the huge medieval parish into three separate parishes – Bampton, Lew and Aston. Two of the charming vicarages in Bampton itself are now private houses. Another beautiful old house is the Elizabethan Deanery, originally used by the Deans of Exeter when they came to Bampton to collect tithes.

Bampton gradually lost importance as a market to Witney, Faringdon and Oxford. In the seventeenth and eighteenth centuries it had a substantial cottage industry in the making of leather breeches and jackets, from skins dressed at Witney, but a factory industry never developed there. Bampton today is a dignified old town in a well-farmed countryside, enjoying a comfortable present in the architectural framework of its remarkable past. And one branch of almost medieval life is vigorously alive in the Bampton Morris Dancers. They are probably the oldest troupe of Morris dancers in Britain, with a continuous history going back for at least 350 years. Whit Monday is their great day, and a visit to Bampton on Whit Monday is a reminder of the natural gaiety that sprang from the countryside when people had to make their own entertainment.

Faringdon is a settlement as old as Bampton, perhaps even older, though the two go naturally together on the approaches from the south and from the north to one of the earliest crossing places on the Thames. It was one of the key points in the triangle Faringdon–Hinksey (Oxford)–Wallingford in the defence of the original Kingdom of the West Saxons. Nothing of King Alfred's palace at Faringdon remains, but it is traditionally supposed to have been on the site of the Salutation Inn, opposite the parish church. The Thames was the ancient frontier between Wessex and Mercia, and later between Saxon England and the Danelaw. But in the great days of Wessex march territory to the north of the river was held, too, and the West Saxons always tried to maintain at least strong bridge-heads on the north bank at vulnerable crossing points. King Alfred's parliament at Shifford on the north bank (if it was at Shifford) might have been a political demonstration that his power extended to both sides of the Duxford–Shifford crossings.

Alfred's son, Edward the Elder, the first Saxon ruler to be called King of England, died at Faringdon in 924. The town remained royal property, and was so recorded in the Domesday Survey. In 1204 King John gave the manor to the newly-founded Abbey of Beaulieu, and granted the Abbey a weekly market right. Faringdon is thus a younger market town than Bampton, which got its market from Edward the Confessor, but Faringdon was an important place for centuries before its market was formally approved. Whatever buildings the monks of Beaulieu had at Faringdon are gone, but their magnificent barn at Great Coxwell, a mile and a half to the south-west of the town, stands as solidly as when its thirteenth-century builders left it. William Morris called this barn 'as noble as a cathedral', and it is built rather like a cathedral, with a vast nave and transepts: it is just over 152 ft long and 51 ft high. Its size is evidence of the fertility of this stretch of the Vale of the White Horse: it could hold grain to feed a city, and shows how richly these Faringdon lands added to the revenues of Beaulieu.

Faringdon House, the home of the Parliamentary Pyes but a Royalist stronghold in the Civil War, has already been mentioned. It stands in fine grounds near the church, but the present Faringdon House is not the one besieged in the Civil War. That was much damaged in the siege, and finally destroyed by a fire in the eighteenth century. The present house was built around 1780 by Henry James Pye, who achieved the somewhat surprising distinction of becoming Poet Laureate. He is one of the less remembered of Poets Laureate, and perhaps it is as well: Sir Walter Scott thought his poetry 'contemptible'. He produced an Ode to George III (a difficult subject for an Ode) which at least earned an eighteenth century chuckle with the pun:

> When the Pye was opened
> The birds began to sing.

Whatever the merits of his poetry, Pye seems to have been otherwise a worthy citizen, and he built himself a most pleasing house.

A family of older distinction than the Pyes lived at Wadley House, still partly Elizabethan, a mile to the east of Faringdon. Queen Elizabeth really did stay there in 1574, when she was entertained by Sir Edward Unton. His son, Henry Unton, fought beside Sir Philip Sidney at Zutphen, and was knighted in the field by the Earl of Leicester. Queen Elizabeth sent him as her ambassador to France, where he created something of a diplomatic stir by challenging the Duke of Guise to a duel for speaking 'impudently' of the Queen of England. This interesting precedent ended, I fear, rather unheroically, for the Duke was apparently persuaded not to accept the challenge, and the duel was never fought: Unton, however, was undoubtedly the winner on points. There are descendants of the Untons still living within a few miles of Faringdon: the author of this present work is one of them.

All Saints Church at Faringdon is one of the glories of Berkshire. It has a setting as near perfect as could be devised, at the top of a slight hill leading from the Market Place, shaded by trees but open fully to the view of passers-by. Its building reflects the love of centuries, from early Norman to late Victorian, but there has been no awful rebuilding and the church remains whole and wholesome. The thirteenth-century South Door has some lovely medieval scrollwork, with dragons' heads, and there is more beautiful stone carving on the capitals to the nave and tower arches. The church once had a spire, but this was destroyed by cannon fire during the siege of nearby Faringdon House in the Civil War. The rather low tower that remains, repaired after the fighting, is perhaps more beautiful than a spire: it leaves the church looking as if the whole building had grown naturally from the ground. Inside are Pye and Unton chapels, with brasses and memorials to various members of both families. There are some good earlier brasses, too, going back to the fourteenth century.

Brabant's *Berkshire*, published in 1911, described Faringdon as 'a town of dwindling importance on a branch line of the Great Western Railway'. The railway did severely affect the economic life of towns that lay off the track of its main routes, particularly so for Faringdon by killing the barge trade on the Thames. But it has been a brief interference in Faringdon's long history. It has been the railway line that has dwindled. The branch line is now a ghost on the Ordnance map, labelled 'track of old railway', and Faringdon, at the meeting place of roads leading to bridges across the Thames, has regained its old importance as the little capital of the Western part of the Vale of the White Horse. The ridge of high ground that sends the Thames on its great bend to the north a few miles east of Faringdon gives the town a splendid hill from which to survey the Vale. It used to be known as Faringdon Clump, but it is now more commonly called Faringdon Folly, from a brick tower, 140 ft high, with a look-out room and battlemented top. It ought to have been built in the eighteenth century, but in fact was built in 1936 – 'it must,' writes Professor Nikolaus Pevsner in his *Buildings of England*, 'be the last of the follies'. I wonder.

5

Oxford

Abingdon, Dorchester and Wallingford were all old before Oxford was heard of. The geophysical causes which promoted human settlement on the Upper Thames make this understandable. Oxford lies off the prehistoric trackways of the chalk downs, and the natural river crossings were at Streatley and Walling-ford. For early settlers coming upriver, the downland countryside of Berkshire, to be reached by the Kennet and Ock valleys, was more attractive than the hinter-land from the Oxfordshire bank. Dorchester is the only one of these very ancient towns in Oxfordshire, and for that there are special reasons.

For much of its history the Thames has been a frontier, and its more advanced peoples settled to the south and (where the river turns north to continue south-wards) west. The Berkshire bank was therefore the bank to be defended, and the defences of the early crossing places were mainly on the Berkshire side. These became steadily more important in the Saxon period, after the West Saxons had established their kingdom.

Wallingford and Dorchester go together. The Romans, always sound strate-gists, saw that if their south–north road from Silchester to Alchester was to be defended at its crossing of the Thames, the peninsula between the Thame and Thames was the place to hold. So they chose this site for a small fortified town or frontier post, and built Dorchester. The Saxons always tried to hold Dorchester as well as Wallingford, and it is not chance that St Birinus, bringing Christianity to Wessex early in the seventh century, was given Dorchester for his see: King Cynegils obviously reasoned that the establishment of a Christian bishopric here would stabilize things in what was then the most sensitive area of his kingdom. His political instinct was sound, but like so many political initiatives it was over-

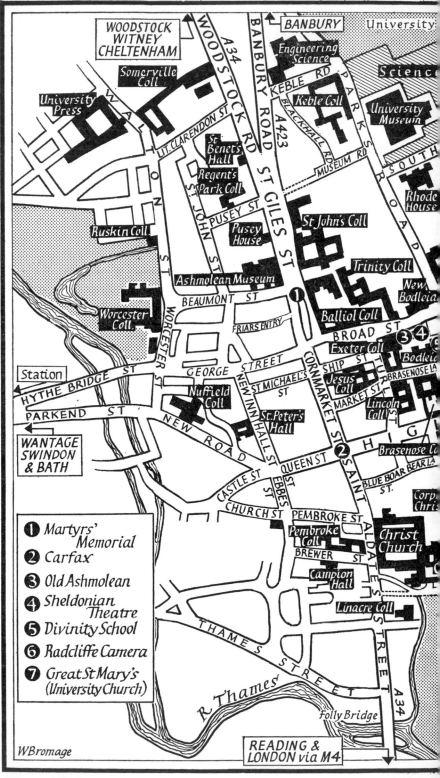

Map 6 *Plan of Oxford.*

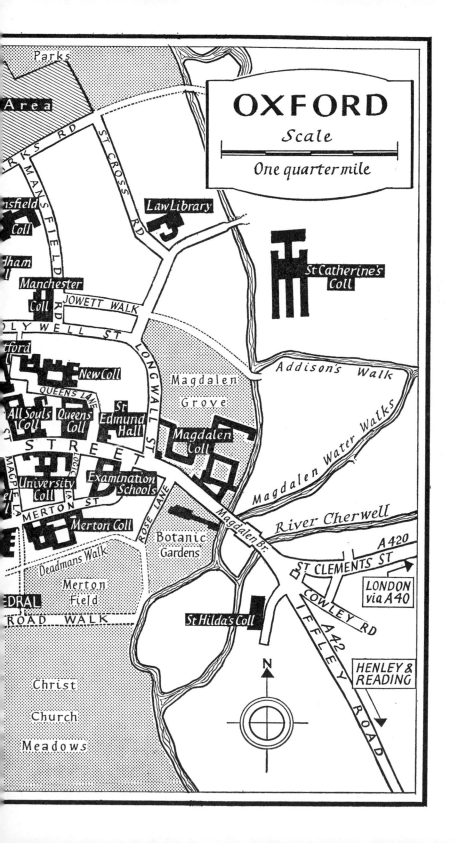

taken by a new situation: the aggressive expansionist policy of Mercia. Dorchester was too exposed a frontier for a bishopric to create the stability for which the West Saxons hoped, and the see had to be moved to Winchester. The recovery of Wessex and its ultimate defeat of Mercia restored the security of the frontier, and in the ninth century, when Mercia was over-run by the then pagan Danes, the Mercian bishopric of Leicester was transferred to Dorchester, which remained for the rest of the Anglo-Saxon period the ecclesiastical centre of a vast diocese reaching from the Thames to the Humber. William of Normandy gave the whole lot to the Bishop of Lincoln, making his an even more enormous diocese, most of which Lincoln kept until Oxford was given a bishop of its own by Henry VIII.

Abingdon, well placed at the confluence of Ock and Thames, was a settlement and trading centre in Neolithic times, and another early centre of Saxon Christianity. Cissa, a prominent West Saxon thane or sub-king in the Abingdon area, founded an Abbey there in 675. It had cells to accommodate twelve monks and a church, all or mostly of wood, recorded as having been 120 ft long. The original Abbey was sacked and burned by the Danes in 870, restored after King Alfred's victories over the Danes, but sacked and burned again in 944. It was refounded by King Eadred, grandson of Alfred the Great, and remained an extremely important religious house until the Dissolution. Abingdon was a seat of learning before Oxford existed.

Probably there were religious foundations of some sort at Oxford soon after the seventh century establishment of Abingdon Abbey. It is impossible now to disentangle myth from history, but the priory at Christ Church (on the site of the cathedral) and the nunnery at Godstow were both early foundations. They are attributed to St Frideswide, one of the most attractive of medieval saints, who is held by tradition to have died in 735. She was the daughter of a king or sub-king on the Wessex–Mercian border, and of exceptional beauty. Her father's name is given variously as Didan, Duddo and Deddo, and one tradition has it that she was born at Didcot – an improbable birthplace, suggested by the presumed derivation of 'Didcot' from 'Duddo' or 'Deddo'. It is more likely, I think, that her father's house was at Bampton or Abingdon – Didcot might, of course, have been in his territory. The Mercian Algar of Leicester sought her in marriage, and sent an embassy to arrange the match, with instructions, apparently, to abduct the lady by force if she were reluctant. St Frideswide did not wish to marry Algar, and the abduction plan miscarried, for the abductors were stricken with blindness. Algar then pursued St Frideswide himself, and nearly captured her. But she escaped by night and fled to the river, where she found a boat awaiting her, with an angel at the oars. The angel rowed her to Abingdon, and the pursuing Algar was himself punished by blindness. St Frideswide founded her nunnery and priory in gratitude for her escape, and her father endowed them with land. Another version of the legend has St Frideswide hiding from Algar in woods around Bampton. She was surely a saintly woman, for having escaped Algar's clutches she declared her forgiveness of him, and he and his men had their sight miraculously restored.

St Frideswide's Saxon church at Oxford was destroyed in the troubled times of Aethelred the Unready, but rebuilt with a gift from him, and the priory was firmly established at the time of the Norman Conquest. It was given a charter by Henry I. St Frideswide's bones rest in Christ Church cathedral on the site of her priory, and her shrine, a thirteenth-century work of great beauty, is still there.

Although less important then than Wallingford and Abingdon, Oxford began to have a recognized place in the region towards the end of the ninth century, with the formal allocation of a 'hideage' for its defence. Alfred's eldest grandson Aethelstan, who reigned from 924 to 939, had coins minted there. Cnut, who attached much importance to the region and who seems to have had a personal liking for the Upper Thames, had some sort of coronation ceremony at Oxford, followed by an assembly of Saxon and Danish notables at which he attempted – with considerable success – to institute a policy of pacification of the two halves of his realm. One of the more fascinating 'ifs' of history is to contemplate what might have happened if Cnut had had abler successors. England would have become the principal state of a powerful Scandinavian empire. There would have been no Norman conquest and the Anglo-Norse people, following Leif Eriksson to North America (Vinland) in the eleventh century, might have populated America five hundred years before Columbus sailed.

Having made a late start, Oxford began rapidly to dominate the region. Again the map shows why. In the days of petty kingdoms, with the Thames a frontier, the land enclosed by the river's bend towards Oxford could be defended for itself: it was a rich pasture, capable in those days of miniature economies of almost indefinite self-support; and who held the river crossings at Wallingford and Duxford, could hold the district. With the imposition of political unity on England, and the development of a larger-scale economy, the strategical situation changed. There was much more to defend. From being a frontier the Thames became more important as a highway; and Oxford, from being an outpost on a frontier, became a nodal point in *national* communications. Its rivers, Thames and Cherwell, gave it physical defences, and its position commanded important routes westwards to the Cotswolds and South Wales, northwards to Banbury, Coventry and the Midlands, east through the Vale of Aylesbury and south-east to London. The bend of the Thames, which diminished Oxford's importance in primitive times by making it a crossing-place only to a sort of island almost surrounded by river, now added to its strategical significance. Across the neck of land from Oxford to Eynsham is only about four miles: a relatively small body of troops from Oxford could be sent quickly to cut off the whole area. The coming of bridges added at once to Oxford's importance: who held Oxford not only held the Upper Thames but controlled the route from London to the West Midlands, and could dominate much of Buckinghamshire, Bedfordshire and Northamptonshire as well. The site of Oxford makes it a capital city. It has been a regional capital for close on 1,000 years, and served Charles I as a national capital during the Civil War. Had London become untenable during the war of 1939–45 Oxford might have become again the nation's capital.

The physical foundation of Oxford is a plateau of firm gravel, roughly two miles long and about three-quarters of a mile wide, between the Thames and Cherwell. It is nowhere more than some 25 ft above the river, but this is enough to stand clear of water when the river floods; and being of no great height above the river, the plateau readily provided wells for medieval builders. Around the plateau is a *glacis* of the river's flood plain terrace, useful for defence – and useful too, alas, for the mean, cheap houses that were flung up for working-class people in the nineteenth century. Old Oxford, the old, walled city, is all but an island, with the Thames and its network of backwaters and brooks to the south and west, the Cherwell to the east. When the rivers flood, the old city is an island still.

With the gradual emergence of something approaching a Kingdom of England in the late ninth and tenth centuries the physical advantages of Oxford attracted political attention. The Cherwell was bridged, on the site of the present Magdalen bridge, in 1004, enabling men garrisoned at Oxford to move quickly south and east. The ancient cattle ford at Hinksey, the 'Oxen-ford' from which Oxford took its name, gave access to the Berkshire bank of the Thames, and this was supplemented by ferries. Cnut recognized the importance of Oxford, but did not live long enough to develop it. William the Conqueror sensed its strategic value quickly, and in 1071 sent one of his principal knights – Robert D'Oyley, who married the Saxon heiress of Wigod of Wallingford – to hold the place. D'Oyley built the castle at Oxford, taking two years over it: it was finished in 1073. Almost certainly he built it on the site of an earlier Saxon stronghold, and the mound that survives probably began as a Saxon earthwork. The site is a natural fortress, protected by the Thames itself and by a honeycomb of branch streams

96

13. *Atomic Energy Research Establishment, Harwell, Berks – view from the East.*

14a. *Once the main stream of the Thames, now a backwater at Sutton Courtenay.*

14b. *A new reach opens up to the river voyager.*

15. *Dorchester, Oxon. Crop marks, probably traces of ditches surrounding late Iron Age huts.*

16a. *New College Chapel, Oxford.*

16b. *Christ Church Library, Oxford.*

and rivulets forming Osney island. The Thames here is a palimpsest of rivers, impossible now to decipher, for a thousand years of man's channel-cutting are imposed on the streams of the eleventh century. Once off firm ground then the whole district must have been a marsh, adding to the defences of the gravel plateau on which Oxford stands. The present navigable channel of the Thames through Osney lock, rejoining the main river at Medley above Fiddler's Island, is not the old navigation, which went east of Osney island under what is now Hythe bridge. The Osney cut, though perhaps always a sidestream, was an eighteenth-century 'improvement' of a millstream made by the monks of Osney Abbey to serve their mill: perhaps that was a twelfth-century 'improvement'.

An Abbey at Osney followed the building of Oxford Castle. It was endowed by Robert D'Oyley, or, it might be said more accurately, by his wife, for it was built at her request and doubtless he used part of the fortune she brought him for the endowment. The story goes that when she and her husband lived at the castle she used to enjoy walking by the river. One day she was attracted by a chatter of magpies, which made such a clamour that she felt they were trying to talk to her. She told her confessor of the incident, and he observed that the birds she had seen were not magpies, but the souls of those in purgatory who were asking her help. Osney Abbey was then founded to ensure prayers for them. It was linked closely to the Castle, and the canons of Osney were required to attend daily at the church or chapel of St George-in-the-Castle. To get there they built a bridge across the stream – their millstream, or the branch of the river that they turned into a millstream.

Nothing remains of Osney Abbey, and little of the castle. The castle mound is there to dominate the traffic pouring through Oxford to the railway station and the Eynsham road, and a squat Norman tower still stands. Below ground, the crypt of St George-in-the-Castle exists. That is all. What looks like a castle, or a Victorian replica of a castle, is the crenellated entrance to Oxford Prison. There was a curious renewal of the link between Castle and Osney in 1789, when prison labour from the castle was used to build Osney lock. The keeper of the prison was paid £50 for the job, hopelessly undercutting a contractor's estimate of £750. How much of the £50 the prisoners got one does not know. Still, a bit of navvying in the open air was probably a welcome change from being shut up in an eighteenth-century gaol.

The Cherwell was bridged before the Conquest: when the Thames at Oxford was first bridged is unknown. The first historical record of a Thames bridge is in or about 1085, when Robert D'Oyley bridged the river at the site of the present Folly Bridge. There is a tradition that there was an earlier Saxon bridge here, and

G

it seems probable, for the ford at Hinksey was really a crossing of the marshes between South Hinksey and the Thames, and although the main river may sometimes have been fordable it must always have been a difficult and dangerous job. Perhaps it got the special name of Oxen-ford from the need to swim beasts over the deeper stretches: it may have been safer to go with the beasts, to have a good sturdy ox to hang on to. As Oxford grew in importance a Thames bridge was certainly needed. But the crossing at Folly Bridge needs more than a bridge: it requires a long causeway across the streams and marshes. D'Oyley's bridge was originally called Grand Pont, and soon afterwards a second bridge, known as South Bridge, was added to it. The causeway that carries the road towards the present Folly Bridge was built at intervals during the twelfth century. The proper name of the whole structure is Grand Pont. It seems to have got its name of Folly Bridge from a house at one end of it where that strange and brilliant Franciscan scholar Roger Bacon lodged in the thirteenth century. His was one of the most original minds of the Middle Ages and he was one of the first to apply physical experiment to the theoretical conclusions of natural philosophy. He was in and out of favour with his ecclesiastical superiors, and his scientific experiments inevitably earned him the reputation of practising magic. He died (at Oxford) in 1294 and became a popular legend as a magician. In the seventeenth century a man named Welcome acquired the house where Roger Bacon lodged, and added a rather crazy upper storey to it. This became known as Welcome's Folly, and the bridge as Folly Bridge. The Folly is long gone, but the name sticks.

By the end of the twelfth century Old Oxford, the original walled town, had taken much the shape that the heart of the city retains today. The walled area covered about 95 acres, its longer axis running east to west from the Cherwell to the Thames. At the western end was the castle and a gate leading to wharves along the Thames, whilst at the eastern end giving on to the Cherwell bridge (Magdalen bridge) was a chapel (Holy Trinity) and another gate. The walled town, roughly rectangular, was crossed by east-west and north-south roads, meeting at St Martin's church (of which only the tower stands) at the crossroads now called Carfax, supposedly derived from the latin *quatuor furcas*, 'four forks'. These roads are the present High street and Queen street, Cornmarket street and St Aldate's. These are not the medieval names. High Street appears always to have been High Street, but Queen Street was originally the Great Bailey (outside the castle), Cornmarket was North Gate Street, and St Aldate's Fish Street. Between these four main streets was a congeries of alleys, the forerunners of the little narrow streets that gave central Oxford such charm before the days of the motor-car.

98

The street-plan of old Oxford, efficient still though grossly overloaded for taking traffic across two rivers, is a remarkable example of medieval town planning. It suggests that the town *was* planned by someone as a whole, and that it did not just grow from a huddle of huts that sprang up around the ford in the shelter of its fortifications. It may have been Saxon planning rather than Norman, for although the Normans built the castle and built (or re-built) bridges, they built on what the Saxons had left. Oxford comes late into written history, appearing rather suddenly in the *Anglo-Saxon Chronicle* (as Oxnaford) in 911 or 912, which further suggests that it rather suddenly acquired importance as a new place. The planning is admirable, turning every natural feature to advantage. The concept is to defend the river crossing, and, within the same defences, to create a river-port, to enable the garrison to be supplied and reinforced. The castle, or earlier Saxon earthwork, was the strongpoint of the defences, but the whole island site between Cherwell and Thames was itself a natural fortress. The main roads crossing the site provide quick access to any particularly threatened point of the perimeter, and, in case of really desperate need, any one quarter could be sealed off. Was this King Alfred's planning? It has a touch of his imagination. The place was sufficiently important in his son's reign to have a substantial 'hideage' of land officially allotted to maintain men for its defence, and the conception may well have been Alfred's.

What was originally a military plan also served commerce. Medieval trade needed protection, which the fortifications gave, and the logistical needs of trade in transport and communications are much the same as those of armies. Good physical planning can promote both trade and defence, and Oxford's town plan helped soldier and shopkeeper alike to go about his business. Oxford's twentieth-century traffic problems, appalling as they are, would be many times worse if her streets had not been planned so well to serve her river-crossings in the tenth (or perhaps late ninth) century.

In the troubles between Matilda, daughter of Henry I, and Stephen of Blois, grandson of William the Conqueror, Oxford was held for Matilda and besieged by Stephen. In the winter of 1142 Matilda escaped by one of the earliest recorded tricks of camouflage. The Thames was frozen, the fields snow-covered; it was a white landscape. Putting on a white cloak Matilda walked, invisible, through Stephen's lines, to the safety of friends at Abingdon, who conducted her to Wallingford, where the castle was also held for her. The struggle for Thames castles in the wars between Stephen and Matilda bears out the strategical importance of the river. Matilda's escape from Stephen restored the blood of the old House of Wessex to the Angevin Kings of England, who succeeded Stephen, for Matilda's mother was the great-granddaughter of Edmund Ironside. Matilda's son by Geoffrey of Anjou, who became king as Henry II, was thus a lineal descendant of King Alfred and the ancient Saxon House of Cerdic.

At this time, as, indeed, for three centuries more, Oxford was in the diocese of Lincoln. It had a powerful ecclesiastical life of its own, and its remoteness from its ruling bishop may have helped in the development of the remarkable independence which came with the establishment of the university in the thirteenth century. It is a curious reflection that the Viking invasion of Mercia which sent the Bishop of Leicester to Dorchester, and enabled the Conqueror to reward the Norman Bishop of Lincoln with a ready-made gigantic see, helped to safeguard the independence of learning at Oxford.

There were four major religious foundations in medieval Oxford: St Frideswide's Priory at Christ Church and her nunnery at Godstow, Osney Abbey, and the Cistercian Rewley Abbey, which was on the site of the London and North Western, later London Midland and Scottish station that once tried to rival the Great Western at Oxford. The LMS station, next door to its Great Western rival, has joined the Abbeys in history.

St Frideswide's foundations particularly enjoyed royal favour and her nunnery at Godstow enshrines the romantic legend of Rosamund Clifford – 'Fair Rosamund' – and her lover, Henry II. The Norman kings had a hunting lodge at Woodstock, and were fond of visiting the place. Henry II is said to have met Rosamund, the daughter of Lord Clifford, on a royal visit to the nunnery at Godstow: she was not a nun, but a girl of about fifteen, being educated by the nuns. The King fell violently in love with her and she became his mistress. His wife, Eleanor, was considerably jealous, and in order to meet Rosamund in secret the King built a 'bower' at Woodstock concealed in a sort of maze, so cunningly contrived that no one without secret knowledge was supposed to be able to find the entrance. The suspicious queen, profiting by classical learning, arranged for a skein of silken thread to be attached in some way to Rosamund's dress, so that as she left the 'bower' one day the thread unwound after her, leaving a silken trail which led from the bower to the nunnery. The triumphant queen pursued Rosamund to the nunnery where she is said to have invited her to choose between poison and a dagger for her mode of death – the wretched girl's preference being for poison. So much for the legend. There is no doubt of the King's attachment to Rosamund Clifford, for she had two sons by him, but the facts, such as can be unravelled, would seem to acquit Queen Eleanor of bringing about her death. No doubt the queen's attitude made things difficult for the lovers, and the affair seems to have come to an end with Rosamund's retirement

100

to the nunnery, an end which all concerned would have considered wholly proper. She seems to have died of natural causes at Godstow some considerable time afterwards, and she was buried in the nuns' church, in a magnificent tomb, inscribed, according to the sixteenth-century antiquarian, John Stow:

> Hic iacet in tomba Rosa mundi, non Rosamunda
> (Here lies not Rosamund, but the Rose of the World).

Rosamund Clifford's tomb at Godstow seems to have been venerated almost as a shrine, so much so that the Bishop of Lincoln, visiting the nunnery in 1191, two years after Henry II was safely dead, ordered Rosamund's coffin to be taken out of the church and re-buried in a less conspicuous chapel. This was done, but the nuns were deeply attached to their Rosamund, and with the Bishop out of the way at Lincoln, her coffin was dug up again and put back in the church. They seem to have had at least tacit approval of this from King John, who re-endowed the nunnery so that prayers might be said for the souls of his father and Rosamund. One of Rosamund's sons by Henry II is believed to have become a later Bishop of Lincoln. Her bones do not seem again to have been disturbed until the dissolution, when Henry VIII gave the property to the physician, Dr George Owen. As a private house the nunnery was held for the King in the Civil War, and burned down after a siege in 1646. Many coffins – but whether Rosamund's among them I do not know – were dug up when Godstow lock was cut through what had been the grounds of the nunnery in 1790. The stone coffins were used to make a footpath to the neighbouring village of Wytham.

The university derived in the thirteenth century from Oxford's religious houses. All education was then in the hands of the church, as was much of the King's government, and literate clerks were needed both by the church itself and to administer estates for the Crown and great landowners. Teaching – as it has remained in many religious orders – was part of the function of monasticism. Monasteries attracted students, and because Oxford was compact with religious foundations, it attracted an unusual number: and such students could come to Oxford because the surrounding countryside was rich enough to feed them. Those cheeses from the Vale of the White Horse, with fish and eels from the river, played a not unimportant part in the establishment of the university. The 'degree' for which men studied was an ecclesiastical licence to teach, and it was obtained in much the same way as the right to practise any other craft by a system of apprenticeship – in this case to learning. Undergraduate students were concerned with three subjects only: Latin grammar, logic, and philosophy. They had to attend lectures for five years, and to take part in the 'disputations' – almost physical exercises in learning – that accompanied the lectures. After putting in five years of this, serving his time, as it were, the student was recognized as a 'bachelor' of arts – the word is obscure, but crops up in various medieval uses to imply a definitive stage in the acquirement of skill or status: a young knight learning the trade of arms under the banner of an established knight was a 'bachelor'; some hold that its academic sense derives from the laurel ('bacia lauri', laurel berry) as the ancient symbol of achievement in art and learning. After three more years of attendance at lectures and disputations the bachelor became a 'master' and received his licence to teach. The higher studies of theology, law and medicine were all post-graduate schools, attended by men who had taken their master's degree. There were no colleges in the modern sense, and the students did not live in the religious houses. Lectures were given publicly by established scholars, and the students lived where they could, originally with friends or families, later in lodging houses run privately by townspeople who began to make a business of providing lodgings for students. As the learning of the Church attracted students, so the existence of a body of students attracted teachers, and in the first quarter of the thirteenth century two great orders of teaching friars, the Dominicans and the Franciscans, sent men specially to work at Oxford. By the middle of the century there were perhaps 1,500 students living and studying in Oxford.

This was a considerable population by medieval standards, and of men, most of them young, not subject to the normal disciplines of lord or trade. The university as such came into being as a system of civil administration. In other centres of learning that grew up around the church in Western Christendom there was usually a bishop at the head of things, to preside over a system of episcopal administration. Oxford's bishop was far away at Lincoln, and there was no central ecclesiastical authority to maintain discipline. Rows between students and townspeople were frequent, and there was a serious incident in 1209 when two clerks were hanged by a mob of angry townsfolk. There was a period of some confusion when it looked as if the schools might be compelled to break up and the students go elsewhere, but in 1214 the Papal Legate intervened with a charter setting out rules for the settlement of disputes and appointing a Chancellor to supervise things. Many of the early quarrels in Oxford were about rents – the rents charged to students, which were often considered too high, and students who were bad payers of rent, which naturally provoked resentment. In the dispensation of 1214 there was a rent-restriction clause.

There was serious trouble again in 1238, when a Papal Legate visited Osney

Abbey. The townspeople had various grievances and sent a deputation to present a petition to the Legate. Either he declined to receive the deputation, or the deputation felt that it was being fobbed off, for the next thing was an assault on the Abbey door in an attempt to force admission. To repel the attackers one of the Abbey cooks flung a pan of hot soup at them, and in the commotion that followed he was killed. There was then general tumult round the Abbey, and men-at-arms had to be brought from Abingdon to deal with it. The worst riot of all occurred in the next century, on St Scholastica's Day (10 February) 1355, when a complaint by scholars over the wine served to them at an inn led to furious fighting in the town. The disturbance lasted for two days, six students were killed, and many people hurt.

These various troubles showed the need for central authority in Oxford, and it was met by giving greater and greater powers to the Chancellor and representative bodies of the schools. The dispensation of 1214 creating an office of Chancellor gave a sort of corporate status to the *studium generale*, or recognized group of faculties for all studies, which was the forerunner of the university. It must be understood that in the thirteenth century there was a distinction between 'clerks', and all who were more or less professionally attached to the Church, and the rest of the community: and the Church was jealous in looking after its rights and privileges. In 1244 Henry III gave Oxford a charter by which the Chancellor of the university obtained jurisdiction over practically all disputes with townspeople in which 'clerks' might be involved, including quarrels provoking breaches of the peace and cases concerning debt, rents, the hiring of horses and the buying of food and clothing. These formidable powers were strengthened after every major new dispute: the university always won in the end. After the St Scholastica's Day riots in the fourteenth century the Chancellor was given powers to control almost every aspect of life in Oxford: he could make and unmake tradesmen, promulgate rules for the conduct of all business. The university was supreme. Nominally, the Chancellor of the university was subject to the bishop: but, as we have seen, Oxford's bishop was remote in Lincoln. This gave *de facto* power to the Chancellor, strengthening his independence, and so strengthening the independence of the university he represented.

A medieval university, as such, had no need of colleges: it was much more like the supposedly modern concept of an 'open' university, a continuing series of Adult Education lectures, open (originally) to all who cared to attend them. But students must eat, and the colleges which have given such a special character to Oxford came into being as 'societies' to sustain the housekeeping needs of scholars.

University College has a shadowy claim to have been founded by Alfred the Great. The Victorians, whose romantic attachment to the past was less inhibited than ours, duly celebrated the millenary in 1872. It is a claim that cannot be disproved, and, as I have suggested earlier, Alfred may have played a considerable part in the original planning of Oxford. But a legendary foundation by King Arthur would be as valid. The historical foundation of University College was in 1249, when a legacy from William of Durham was used to establish a society for the support of four masters of arts in the study of theology. Balliol, endowed originally with a grant of land by John of Bal(l)iol, a power in the Border country, whose son, also John, became King of Scotland, was founded in 1263 as a similar 'society' to support masters in the pursuit of higher learning. The first John, who died in 1269, left further endowments to his society by will, and his widow worked devotedly to get his wishes carried out. University and Balliol were both originally 'support' foundations, providing common rooms and libraries for their students, and grants for their support, but not living accommodation: the men lived, as all other students lived, in rented lodgings in the town. Merton, founded at Malden, Surrey, in 1264 and transferred to Oxford in 1274 was the first college to come into being essentially to enable students to live together. This is the foundation of Walter de Merton, Lord Chancellor to Henry III and later Bishop of Rochester, who died in 1277. He provided for the establishment of a college not merely to support but also to house students, setting a residential pattern for collegiate life, soon followed by existing 'societies' and adopted by all later college foundations. Merton can thus claim fairly to be the oldest of Oxford's colleges as we understand them today.

The fourteenth and fifteenth centuries brought several more great foundations. William of Wykeham's New College in 1379 was important in itself and had a lasting influence on university architecture – not only in Oxford – for it established the grouping of quadrangle, hall and chapel that are now traditional for college buildings. These, and all other early foundations, were exclusively, or almost so, for what we should now call post-graduate study: they enabled their fellows (*socii*) to stay on at Oxford to continue learning after having taken a first degree. William of Wykeham's successor as Bishop of Winchester, William of Wayneflete, brought nearer the modern idea of a university by his foundation of Magdalen College in 1458. His foundation provided not only for the now usual 'fellows', but also for the support of 30 younger students, who were called '*demisocii*' (demies). The acceptance by colleges of undergraduate commoners became fairly general during the next century. Two major administrative steps towards the modern university were also taken during this century. In 1552 the

Chancellor instituted a register requiring the names of all those living in colleges and halls, and in 1565 a Matriculation Register was compiled.

Until nearly the middle of the sixteenth century Oxford remained an ecclesiastical dependency of the See of Lincoln. The creation of a Bishopric of Oxford, imperative as it now seems to church administration, was in fact a by-product of the dissolution of the monasteries. That event, or rather, course of events, was not always the savage driving out of the inhabitants of religious houses that it sounds. Some devoted members of monastic orders chose death rather than surrender to the King the land and property that they considered held in trust for God, but in other cases dissolution was more in the nature of tactful acquiescence in a takeover bid. It saved trouble and unpleasantness if an abbey could be persuaded to surrender voluntarily, and in such cases its chief officers and often its monks were normally well rewarded or quite generously pensioned off: there were all sorts of benefices in the Crown's gift. This is not to imply that voluntary surrender was necessarily corrupt: the Reformation in England had in it genuine idealism as well as politics, and within as well as outside monasteries there were men who believed it right, and who preferred the authority of a King of England to that of a Pope in Rome. In 1539 the last Abbot of Osney surrendered the Abbey to Henry VIII, and in consequence, if not in return, was made a bishop – not, at first, of Oxford, for a See of Osney was created, with a palace for the bishop in Oxford. This was Gloucester Hall, an early Benedictine foundation related to the Abbey of Gloucester, now forming part of Worcester College.

In 1525, some years before the surrender of Osney Abbey, Cardinal Wolsey had founded and begun to build a college to eclipse all others in magnificence. This was on a site that had been part of the Priory of St Frideswide, and it was to be called Cardinal College: the church of St Frideswide was to form the college chapel. Wolsey's work, however, remained unfinished, for he met political disaster and in 1529 he died, his wonderful college, with his other enterprises, falling into the hands of Henry VIII. That curious monarch has many stains on his memory, but in his youth he had been well tutored, and a respect for learning never left him. Oxford owes him its Regius Professorships of Divinity, Hebrew, Greek, Civil Law and Medicine, its Bishop, its Cathedral, and the unique relationship between its cathedral and the college once called Cardinal College, renamed Christ Church. In 1546, the last year of his life, Henry VIII set about tidying up Cardinal Wolsey's unfinished business in Oxford. He transferred the See of Osney to Oxford, giving the Bishop of Oxford (ex-Osney) the priory church of St Frideswide for his cathedral. This had been intended by Wolsey to be the magnificent chapel of his magnificent college. And so it remains to this day, the chapel of Christ Church, and the cathedral of Oxford.

Wolsey's great hall, his gateway, the kitchen and some of his other building remains. Much of the present glory of Christ Church, however, derives from the seventeenth century and the initiative of two Deans who were father and son, Samuel and John Fell, whose name (most unfairly) is remembered chiefly now (outside Christ Church) for the lampoon:

> I do not love thee Dr Fell
> The reason why I cannot tell,
> But this I know, and know full well
> I do not love thee Dr Fell.

It is supposed to be an on-the-spot translation of an epigram of Martial by an undergraduate rebuked by the Dean. If so, it is a brilliant piece of work, though hard on Dr Fell that it should accompany him to eternity.

Samuel Fell was Dean of Christ Church in the reign of Charles I and he built the staircase to the Great Hall just before the Civil War. Christ Church was deeply loyal to the King, and its plate was melted down to provide money for the Royalist cause. Samuel Fell's plans for the college could not be carried out because of the war, but they were taken up by his son John, who became Dean in 1660. John Fell called in Christopher Wren, who built the fine tower – Tom Tower – which surmounts Wolsey's original gateway. Here is another link with the Abbey of Osney, for the great bell, Old Tom, which gives its name to the tower, came from Osney, although it was recast in 1680. John Fell became Bishop of Oxford as well as Dean of Christ Church, and he did much other work for college, university and diocese. He gave new plate to the cathedral to replace that melted down for Charles I and re-built (at his own expense) the Bishop's Palace at Cuddesdon, partly a gift from Charles I, which was burned down during the Civil War. The Bishop's house at Cuddesdon now is not Dr Fell's, for that in turn was destroyed by fire, and the present building is modern.

The cathedral chapel of Christ Church more than fulfils Cardinal Wolsey's most ambitious intentions for his college: it must be the noblest chapel in the world. Not much of Saxon work remains visible, though the foundations are still St Frideswide's, and no doubt Saxon hands hewed some of its stones. The nave and choir are mainly Norman, though the superb vaulting in the roof over the choir was done in the fifteenth century. Wolsey's rebuilding involved demolition of the west end of the nave, and the present west entrance is modern, being the work of Gilbert Scott. The lovely eight-sided spire, rising 144 ft above the Norman tower, was built quite early in the thirteenth century, a remarkable architectural achievement in the setting of its time. Through the centuries a succession of benefactors has enriched the church and there is material for a lifetime's study in its monuments, glass and traces of early wall paintings.

This cannot be a history of Oxford, nor of the university. Christopher Wren's epitaph in St Paul's – *Si monumentum requiris circumspice* – sums up the story of Oxford, though you must look not at one great building, nor ten thousand, but at every facet of British life, and at much beyond Britain. I am concerned here with Oxford's place in the region of which it is the natural capital.

The geographical advantages, so ably exploited by Saxon and Norman military engineers, encouraged the development of medieval Oxford. A large wharf under the castle walls was in use from very early times. Barges brought food and building-stone from Lechlade, Radcot and the upper river to Oxford, and went on downstream to pick up wool and leather goods at Abingdon, and local produce of one sort and another at many points on the Thames for transport to London. Upstream they brought whatever goods the London merchants hoped to sell in the region. Fish was a staple of medieval diet, and fishing was an established trade on the river from unrecorded times. Abbeys and lay landowners jealously guarded fishing rights, to the rage of the boatmen who naturally resented fish weirs that interfered with the passage of their barges. Mill streams, and weirs serving them, which directed water from the navigable river, and made dangerous shallows for the boatmen, were another cause of friction. The history of the river itself for most of the past eight centuries is a record of struggle between navigators and riparian owners for the use of water. Throughout these centuries, however, boatmen, fishermen and millers had to share the river for their livelihoods. Somehow they contrived to do so, for, in spite of quarrels, those livelihoods were interdependent: the millers needed barges to bring their grain and to help to shift their flour, and everybody needed salt and firewood and the goods the barges brought. Much of the Upper Thames region has been short of fuel from very early times. The chalk downs of North Berkshire are largely bare, and wood cutting in the royal forests of Woodstock and Wychwood was a right strictly reserved: in any case, the forested areas could never have supplied the whole region. When sea-coal – that is, coal from the Tyne – began coming to London it was an important cargo up-river, but always scarce and expensive. The eighteenth-century canals brought coal to Oxford and the Thames-side towns in something approaching reasonable quantity for the first time in the region's history, and in the brief heyday of the canals competition did something to reduce prices, for the Oxford canal brought coal from the Midlands, the Wilts and Berks from the Somerset coalfield, and the Thames and Severn from the Forest of Dean and South Wales.

Long before there were any canals, the river was the main trade route for heavy goods, and its ferries and bridges determined the routes for land transport. Oxford grew from its river. The Merton College Rolls have many entries about building stones being brought by river, as far back as 1310. Stone from the Taynton quarries, near Burford, was carted by road to Eynsham, and there embarked for Oxford. Eynsham was an early river port: in the middle of the thirteenth century a certain Robert Navigator was living there, and in 1342 the records of Eynsham Abbey list one Robert le Rower as the tenant of a dwelling owned by the abbey. The name 'Fisher' also occurred at Eynsham from at least the thirteenth century – and 'fisherman' is still listed as a trade at Eynsham six hundred years later in a nineteenth-century directory.

Fifty years ago Oxford was one of the most beautiful cities in Europe: even its too prominent Victorian gasworks merged at a little distance into the cool grey calm of Oxford's stone, and its towers and spires rose serenely above everything. The towers and spires still rise serenely, and can still be a breathtaking vision from the Abingdon road where it descends Hinksey hill. But it is a vision best seen nowadays when the kindly Thames provides a slight mist to veil the sprawl of the modern suburbs. Oxford's development in the past fifty years – much of it in the past twenty years – has been a complete break with its past. From being a university town grafted naturally on to the market capital of an almost wholly agricultural region, Oxford has become, in historical terms suddenly, a major centre of modern industry.

At the turn of the century Oxford had a population of not quite 50,000. Today it numbers over 110,000, and this is a statistical abstraction, for it represents only the population within the formal boundaries of the borough. Oxford is now the centre of an urban area, spreading over many miles of what not long ago was Oxfordshire countryside, and across the Thames into Berkshire. The population of the urban area is at least twice and probably nearer three times that of the place formally called Oxford. None of this is out of keeping with the geophysical factors that brought Oxford into being: its location as the hub of a road system with crossings of the Thames and Cherwell giving access to good routes linking London and the Midlands made some such development inevitable in the setting of modern industrial life. Oxford's development is sometimes put down to the chance that W. R. Morris, the late Lord Nuffield, was an Oxford man, who began assembling motor cars at Oxford because he lived there. This is only partly so. It may be chance that particular Morris bits of what is now the vast British Leyland Motor Company are in Oxford, but if it had not been Morris it would have been someone else. Oxford could not escape being drawn into modern industry: many might ask, Why should it want to? The problem, in some sense the tragedy, of Oxford is that its inevitable industrial development conflicts with its unique human history. That history has real meaning only to a small minority of people: most of us would rather have high wages, a car, and access to a supermarket than live on bread and scrape in a gem of a thirteenth-century courtyard surrounded by quiet books. Perhaps it is a pity that this should be the choice: perhaps it *need* not be the choice. But care for the beauty of the past is a passion in individuals rather than of majority concern. Much of the beauty of Oxford has been saved by the care of individuals, and more could be saved if the community can ever come to terms with the motor car.

History has made Oxford into a national treasure house, but geography has helped to determine history, and shapes it still. Oxford presents on a large scale the problem that may arise at home if you possess a few pieces of valuable china: do you use them as they were made to be used, risking breakage, or do you lock them away in a safe? The old city is in one sense a museum, a wonderful collection of architecture assembled through the centuries, in what was, and could be again, a nearly perfect setting. But a city is built to be lived in, and Oxford is also a living city, full of bustling, thriving people, wanting all the things their contemporaries want, wanting them with no more, but equally no less, of the tastelessness that afflicts so much of contemporary life. One may be saddened by the needless ugliness that so often goes with modern industrial and commercial development, but not by the fact of such development, for that would be to deny life.

In a planning report made after the last war it was recommended that the whole of the (then) Nuffield works at Oxford 'should be removed to some other part of the country'. This was an understandable feeling, but it would not do. The motor industry at Oxford pumps livelihoods into every town and village in the region: short of directing people to leave their houses to go and live somewhere else, there has *got* to be industry at Oxford. The economics of large-scale industry – another aspect of geography – may one day suggest that the whole of the British motor industry should be concentrated on the lower Thames at Dagenham, or on Merseyside, or perhaps between Birmingham and Coventry. It would then become a political task to find Oxford something else, or – if a Government were ruthless enough – to permit houses to fall empty and Oxford to decline because technology could make better use of geographical assets else-where. That has happened often enough in the past when the balance of geo-graphical advantage has tilted – by the building of ships too big to use a once-flourishing port, for instance. But it is a cruel process. Industry could be planned into Oxford, but it cannot now be planned out of it without a cost in human misery that no democratic community is ever likely to want to pay.

Until the First World War Oxford had only one major industry of its own, the rather special activity of printing. That derives directly from the university, which was licensed to use a press towards the end of the fifteenth century, soon after Caxton brought printing into England. Books were printed occasionally at Oxford over the next hundred years or so, but there was no permanent University Press until 1585. That began with the establishment of a printing house by Joseph Barnes, a bookseller in Oxford, and the university was a partner in the enterprise from the start, lending Barnes the £100 he needed to set up his press. In 1632 Charles I gave the university a charter authorizing it to possess two presses and to print any book not banned. This included the right to print bibles and prayer books, but the immense value of this right was not at once appreciated, and the university foolishly traded it to the Stationers' Company for an annual licence fee of £2. The university was rescued from this folly by that same Dr Fell who was such a good friend to Christ Church and to the diocese. He renegotiated the right to print bibles and prayer books with the Stationers' Company and, with a great deal of trouble, recovered it for the university. He took a close interest in the management of the press and spent his own money on buying founts of type for it.

Dr Fell arranged for the press to be installed in the Sheldonian Theatre, a gift to the university by Gilbert Sheldon, Warden of All Souls and Archbishop of Canterbury. It was designed by Wren to provide a dignified setting for great assemblies of the university, and at Dr Fell's practical suggestion a home for the press was incorporated in the building. It was opened in 1669 and the press – in fact two presses, one for bibles and one for other books – worked there until 1688. Then it began to be feared that vibration from the presses was damaging the building so they were taken out. No existing building capable of accommo-dating both of them could be found, so they had to be dispersed, and for the next 25 years the Bible Press and its companion, called the Learned Press, had to work from different premises. Print itself enabled them to come together again. Edward Hyde, Lord Clarendon, who had been Lord Chancellor to Charles II and later became Chancellor of the University of Oxford, wrote his celebrated *True Historical Narrative of the Rebellion and Civil Wars in England,* and he gave the profits from the book to the university. By 1713 these had accumulated sufficiently to finance a new home for the University Press and the Clarendon Printing House, designed by Sir John Vanbrugh, was built for it. The presses worked here until 1830, by which time the work of the printing house had out-grown its building and the University Press was transferred to new premises at Walton Street. Lord Clarendon's *History* brought further benefit to Oxford. It continued to earn money, and this was invested. By 1870 there was a con-siderable sum in hand, and this was used to establish the Clarendon Laboratory, the university's department of physics, in 1872.

Having set the Oxford University Press on its feet, Dr Fell turned next to paper. He was dissatisfied with the quality of the printing paper that the press was able to buy, so he arranged for the university to make its own paper at a mill on the Thames at Wolvercote. The mill flourished: it is still in business, turning out high-grade papers, and it is still owned by the university.

The Oxford University Press is an industry in itself, but Oxford is a good place for printers and there are several other printing works in the city. The related industry of bookbinding is also long established there. Until the coming of the Morris car, printing and bookbinding was Oxford's only industrial activity on any scale. The town lived by the university, and by fulfilling its age-old func-tions as a regional capital – county town, assize town, administrative centre, market and shopping centre. In terms of regional economics university education has always been a major 'export' industry, students from all over Britain – indeed, from all over the world – bringing in money in return for local services. The considerable staff of the university, paid for by endowments and money provided from outside the area in fees and university grants, also in a sense 'export' their services. The balance of trade is, therefore, very much in Oxford's favour, sustaining shops of a standard far higher than that normally to be found in provincial towns.

University and the provision of regional services, however, provide a reason-able living for a relatively small and stable population: the expansion of both university and administration over the past fifty years, considerable as it has been, could not support the economy of the area as it exists now. When Mr Morris produced his first car in 1912 an old economic order was on the brink of dissolution: a stable population, drawing its livelihood mostly from land worked by labour-intensive systems of agriculture was shortly to emerge from the upheaval of war into a period of swiftly dwindling employment on the land. The motor industry and the ancillary industries it brought with it came to Oxford when they were needed. Industrial development after the Second World War met an even greater need for alternative employment: farms which in my boyhood employed a dozen men are now highly mechanized, employing one or two. Men from villages throughout the Upper Thames region, with no hope of the jobs that supported their father and grandfathers, earn wages in Oxford's factories. Without Oxford's industry many of these villages would have died, and much of the social capital invested in the region over a thousand years would have been wasted. That is the background against which Oxford's industrial expansion must be seen: it created factory jobs at a period when men without other means of livelihood were there to do them. If there has been much loss in terms of an older quality of life (a quality, perhaps, that was chiefly of value to a few) there has been much gain in terms of real wealth to the community. A capital-intensive agriculture produces a surplus of food for the industrial areas of Britain with a labour force that would have seemed inconceivably small a generation ago: and the men displaced from the land by machines create wealth in Oxford's factories.

One's anger is at the ugliness – the needless ugliness – that has accompanied the change. It is not this generation alone that is at fault. The Victorians built railways and gasworks and rows of mean houses for their workers: they chose to site their dirtier works at Oxford along the banks of the incomparable Thames. The Thames at Oxford is a more beautiful river than the Seine in Paris: contemplate the noble buildings on the Seine, consider Oxford's debasement of the Thames, and realize what might have been. It is happier to imagine what Oxford may yet make of the Thames, for the river will be there when its mean environment has decayed, and time will give Oxford a chance to redeem its treatment of its river.

There seems less hope of redemption from ugly suburbs. The community that Old Oxford grew to house had to be largely self-sufficient: a man lived next to his work; his church, his tavern, his market stall had all to be close at hand. The division of modern life into housing 'estate', factory 'area', shopping 'centre', with recreational 'facilities' tacked on here and there may make for some sort of efficiency, but it makes for dreary living. Modern brick boxes may have better plumbing, but emotionally they are a poor exchange for little friendly alleyways of Headington or Burford stone. But this is a national, not merely an Oxford, problem. If homes in our society must be reduced to 'housing', Oxford can scarcely hope to contract out.

But how much, how very much, remains. The museum aspect of Oxford may be brutalized by traffic and some of the shopfronts of chain stores, yet the heart of Oxford is still the finest living medieval town in Britain. In a walk of a few

18a. *The rival source of the Thames at Seven Springs, near Cheltenham. The river that rises here is actually the Churn, a tributary of the Thames.*

18b. *Inscription at Seven Springs to mark what some regard as the source of the Thames.*

HIC TUUS
O TAMESINE PATER
SEPTEMGEMINUS FONS.

19. *Thatch is still a common roofing material in villages in the region.*
Two contrasting styles at (a) Kingston Lisle and (b) Let-combe Regis.

20a. *The Ampney Brook, a tributary of the Thames, near Ampney Crucis, Glos.*

20b. *The Letcombe Brook, a tributary of the Thames, at Grove, near Wantage.*

yards you can cross centuries, moving from the contemplation of transistor radios in a shop window to study stones that Norman masons set in a wall. You have only to step through a gateway to be out of the twentieth century and in the quiet loveliness of a quadrangle or courtyard in which medieval scholars discussed the weight of angels – or perhaps the poor cooking of the fish they had for dinner. You cannot walk at all in Oxford without treading in the footsteps of half the men in the *Dictionary of National Biography,* poets, princes, prime ministers, empire builders and the winders-up of empire, scientists, financiers, bishops, men who have written history, and men who have made it. Shakespeare was often in Oxford, and stood godfather to the son of his friend John Davenant in the church whose tower stands at Carfax (though the rest of the church is gone). Beaumont Street retains the name and crosses the site of Beaumont Palace, where Richard Coeur de Lion was born. The savagery of men is in the streets of Oxford, too. In Broad Street you pass the place where the Protestant Bishops Hugh Latimer and Nicholas Ridley were tied to a post and burned with faggots of wood in October 1555, and where Archbishop Thomas Cranmer suffered the same death in March 1556. Their visible memorial is the Martyrs Memorial by Sir Gilbert Scott in St Giles: their better memorial is in the Oxford air, and wherever Church of England prayers are said.

The lawns of Oxford are unmatched this side of the Elysian Fields. This is partly due to the peculiar virtues of Thames Water and Thames light, partly to generations of care. There is an Oxford story of a college gardener who was asked by a visitor how a lawn so perfect as that he tended could be made. He is said to have scratched his head doubtfully, and then to have replied with conviction, 'Well, Sir, you start about three hundred years ago.'

Industry is not the only expansion that the twentieth century has brought to Oxford. The foundation of colleges has never stopped. Across the road from the mound of Robert D'Oyley's castle is Nuffield College, endowed by Lord Nuffield in 1937 and built after the war, on what was once the main wharf at the terminal basin of the Oxford Canal. Lord Nuffield also gave a generous endowment to help the establishment of St Peter's College, founded in 1929 as St Peter's Hall to commemorate Dr Francis Chavasse, sometime rector of St Peter-le-Bailey in Oxford and later Bishop of Liverpool. He retired from his bishopric at the advanced age of 77, and returned to Oxford, where he set about trying to raise funds to establish a college, primarily to train young men as Evangelical clergy. He died before his college could be founded, but his work was carried on by his son, Christopher Chavasse, and St Peter's Hall (now college) came into being. Lord Nuffield's endowment paid off a mortgage on its buildings and set it on its feet. It is not limited to candidates for ordination, but is a normal college of the university, open to undergraduates for any course of study.

St Antony's College was founded in 1948. That returns almost to the tradition of the oldest of the medieval colleges in being mainly for post-graduate work. St Catherine's College is more recent still. It has always been possible, though not particularly easy, for people to work for degrees at Oxford without being members of any college. Such non-collegiate students joined a society – again in the medieval tradition – called St Catherine's Society. Now the society has become St Catherine's College, with modern buildings of its own. Grants from the Wolfson and Ford Foundations were accepted by the university to establish Wolfson College in 1966.

Women were formally admitted to degrees at Oxford in 1920, a date that seems astonishingly recent, though much in the general enfranchisement of women that is nowadays taken for granted really goes back only to the First World War. Women have been studying at Oxford, however, since long before 1920, for they were permitted to take examinations without the formal award of degrees. Lady Margaret Hall was founded as a college for women in 1878, and Somerville in 1879. St Hugh's was added to the establishment for women in 1886 and St Hilda's in 1893. St Anne's became a college in 1952, but it is among the older of Oxford institutions providing university education for women. It was founded as the Society of Oxford Home Students in 1879, to enable women to study at Oxford without being members of a college.

So Oxford lives and grows, the motor works at Cowley replacing ancient trades in providing livelihoods, the State largely replacing parents in financing under-graduates, and both the livelihoods and the undergraduates more numerous than at any other time in history.

6

Abingdon – Dorchester – Wallingford

The Thames at Abingdon does not follow its original course, although the river has flowed there much as it does today for the past 1,000 years. The natural course of the main stream is half a mile or so to the south of the present navigable channel, at the foot of a low ridge rising away from the Oxfordshire bank and ending at Culham. This stream, though choked with weeds, still runs, leaving the present river about a mile above Abingdon, and rejoining it at Culham. It is called – improbably in relation to its present state – the Swift Ditch. This is a very old name, and although it has been suggested that it may derive from the Saxon personal name Swaefe, as Swaefe's Ditch, it is more reasonable to accept that it denotes just what it says, a narrow stretch of river running fast.

The character of the Thames in its original course explains the early history of Abingdon. There was no good crossing of the river here. It could be forded at Culham, a mile downstream, but upstream not before Sandford, on the outskirts of Oxford, and there often with danger. The Culham crossing, too, although long used, was also a dangerous one. Thus for most of its early history Abingdon was rather isolated by the river, a situation good for defence and encouraging early settlement, but leaving it a little apart from the social and political developments that promoted the growth of Oxford.

Isolation no doubt attracted the monks who built the first Abbey at Abingdon in 675. Next to nothing is known of this early foundation, and little survived its two sackings by the Danes in 870 and again in 944. A few years after the second sacking King Alfred's grandson, Eadred, persuaded Athelwold, then a monk at Glastonbury, later canonized as St Athelwold, to go to Abingdon as Abbot to restore the Abbey.

115

The shape of Abingdon still reflects the dominance of the medieval Abbey. The original town was simply a collection of hutments outside the Abbey's gate, where the little tradesmen and craftsmen who hoped to do business of one sort and another with the Abbey's purchasing officers, made their homes. The Abbey

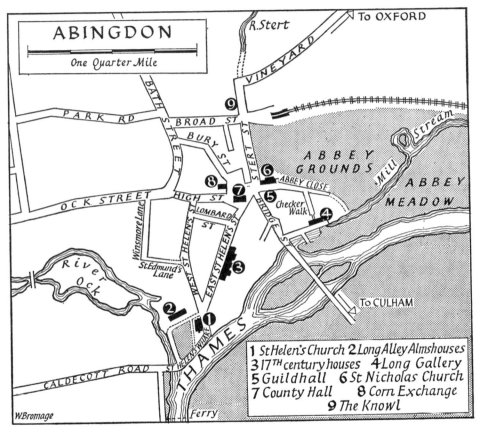

Map 7 *Town plan of Abingdon.**

controlled everything, held all market rights, fishing rights, mill rights, and everything else. Without licence from the Abbey nobody could trade. The market was outside the walls, at the main entrance to the Abbey: the market place is still there today, and a weekly market is still held. Across the road is the area (now blocks of flats) still called The Vineyard, where the monks grew

* In 1970 a new road, not shown here, was made to link Ock Street with the Oxford road via the Vineyard corner.

116

grapes. Contrary to general belief, the English climate is not wholly inimical to viticulture, and in the tenth, eleventh and twelfth centuries there was a considerable production of wine in the Upper Thames valley. There could be still – I have drunk an admirable light wine from grapes grown at Pangbourne. The abolition of English viticulture was more a matter of politics than of climate: the Angevin kings wanted the revenues from wines produced in their own dominions in France, and frowned on wine-making by their English subjects. The Vineyard at Abingdon is a nice reminder that the grape can grow in England.

The curiously hunched plan of old Abingdon, the medieval huddle of old buildings that gave, and here and there still gives, the town such charm, is explained by the Abbey's occupancy of most of the land in the shallow triangle of riverside between the Thames and its tributary the Ock: the site of the Abbey and its private grounds (now made into an attractive park) covers about three times the area of the medieval town. What became the town was in essence much like the crowded bazaar quarter outside some spacious cantonment in what was once British India. The main streets – Bridge Street, leading to the Thames, the road to Oxford, East St Helen Street, leading to the parish church, and High Street, serving the market place – all radiate from the Abbey's gatehouse, still standing (although of course rebuilt from its earlier days) on its original site. After the Abbey had gone, the independent merchants of Abingdon went on using these streets for their houses and shops. It is this cramping of streets from the original huddle of the homes of those whom the Abbey permitted to dwell outside its gate that makes the motor-car such a harsh intruder in Abingdon now.

St Aethelwold was a noble man and a fine scholar, but he was concerned with the practical business of living as well as scholarship. At some time before his translation from Abingdon to Winchester in 963 he arranged for his monks at Abingdon to divert the main stream of the Thames from its course along the Swift Ditch to the channel it now follows, almost washing the walls of the Abbey. There was further engineering work on the river in the next century,

> Beyond the precinct of the Church at a place called Barton next the hamlet of Thrup the wide bed of the river used to cause rowers no little difficulty, for the land below, being steeper than that above, often made the said channel slack of water. The citizens of Oxford, therefore, having most traffic there, petitioned that the course of the river might be diverted through the church's meadow farther south, so that ever after by all their vessels a hundred *allecia* should be paid as toll to the cellarer of the monastery.*

* F. S. Thacker, *The Thames Highway*, Vol. I.

just before the Norman conquest. The chronicles of the Abbey record that under Abbot Ordric (1054–66) a new or improved channel was cut. The scribe explains '*Allecia*' is usually translated 'herrings'. At first sight this seems rather a puzzle, for one would not expect herrings to be come by easily on the Thames. But there was a considerable medieval trade in salted herrings, and no doubt these were meant. The toll seems to have been collected only in Lent.

A thousand years after Abbot Athelwold's civil engineering works, and nine centuries after Abbot Ordric's, it is impossible to determine precisely what was done when. The river system is complex, for not only have the Thames and its various branches, man-made and natural, to be considered, but two other streams as well. The Ock, a considerable river in its own right, draining the Vale of the White Horse, joins the Thames here, and so does the Stert. The course of this stream, now culverted through Abingdon under Stert Street, is relatively short, for it rises at Boar's Hill. But it is also relatively steep, and after heavy rain or snow it brings a swift inrush of water to the Thames.

There are some clues to the hydraulic detective story. An important one is the name of the land between the old course of the Thames – the Swift Ditch – and its present channel at Abingdon. This is Andersey, which means 'Anders's (or Andrew's) Island'. The -ey termination is a common Saxon (also Norse) word for 'island', and it occurs in many British place names (Anglesey, Bardsey) and frequently in the Upper Thames region to denote places that are or were islands in river or marsh. The name Andersey is an old one, in use before St Athelwold's time, and it suggests that there was always a stream of some sort close to the Abingdon settlement, to make an island of the land between the settlement and the ancient main stream of the Thames. This seems probable, for the Thames has a habit of branching into side-streams, making little islands, and joining up again below them. So I think that there always was a branch of the main river following the course of what is now called the Abbey Stream, and that the Ock and Stert flowed into this, meeting the main river at Culham. It would have been far easier for the monks to enlarge and improve an existing stream than to dig a wholly new channel, and I am pretty sure that this is what they did.

The history of the Thames at Abingdon, however, is further complicated by the fact that the old course of the river along the Swift Ditch was restored as the navigable channel in the seventeenth century. The passage from Burcot, just below Clifton Hampden to Oxford, had become so difficult from silting and the resultant shallows that goods for Oxford had to be unloaded at Burcot, and sometimes even at Henley, and carted overland. An Act of James I in 1605, re-enacted with more effective powers in 1623, established a body of Commissioners, known as the Oxford-Burcot Commission, to improve this stretch of river. The Commissioners built the first modern locks on the Thames at Iffley, Sandford and Abingdon. The lock at Abingdon was not where the present lock is, but higher upstream at the entrance to the Swift Ditch, thus providing water to restore the old course as the navigable channel. Abingdon by this time had an important river trade, with wharves just above and just below St Helen's Church. One would have thought that there would be strong objections from the citizens to the diversion of the navigation away from the town, but nobody seems to have been worried by it. There appears to have been a good channel from Culham to the Abingdon wharves, and this, though it became, as it were, a branch stream, was not interfered with. Some citizens of Abingdon then were substantial barge-owners, and they would naturally benefit from the improved passage to Oxford. The present channel, Abbot Ordric's old 'improvement' of 1054–66 was re-opened in 1790, and the Swift Ditch fell again into disuse.

Crossing the Thames in the vicinity of Abingdon remained a dangerous under-taking throughout the Middle Ages. The ford at Culham was always tricky and to get to the Abbey or town from the Oxfordshire side of the river required a ferry, which plied where Abingdon bridge now stands. Moreover the route from Abingdon to Culham, now the main road to Henley and London, was itself liable to be dangerous, for the Swift Ditch and the various streams around it flooded readily, and in times of flood man and pack animals could be swept off their feet into pools that were deep enough to drown them. In 1316 the then Abbot of Abingdon and a number of his monks tried to cross by ferry when the river was in flood. Their boat upset, and they were all drowned. To make the route from Abingdon to Culham safer the monks laid a cause-way along the path, still in use as a raised pavement along the side of the main road.

In 1416 the Thames was bridged at both Abingdon and Culham. Both bridges still stand, although the Abingdon bridge was much restored and rebuilt, its navigation arch widened, in 1927, and the bridge at Culham is no longer used (save as part of an enchanting walk) since the main road was realigned and a modern bridge built over the Swift Ditch. The causeway between the two bridges remains a blessing to travellers on foot, providing sanctuary from the heavy traffic of the London roads. In severe floods it can still serve its ancient purpose.

The Abbey appears to have contributed nothing to the beneficient work of building the two bridges. It is sometimes supposed that they were the gift of Henry V, for a more or less contemporary poem written by one Richard Farman, an ironmonger, records:

King Herry the fyft in his fourthe yere
He hath i-founde for his folk a brige in Berkshire
For cartes with carriage may goe and come clere
That many winters afore were marred in the myre

In fact, the monarch probably provided no more than a charter or licence authorizing construction. Stone for both bridges was the gift of Sir Peter Besils or Bessels, of Besselsleigh, a village near Abingdon, and the labour was paid for by Geoffrey Barbour, a Bristol merchant with Abingdon connections, and a great benefactor to the town. John Hachyns and William and Maud Hales also provided money for the upkeep of the bridges.

This bridgework was, indeed, an important example of lay determination to be independent of the almost all-dominant Abbey. One of the ways in which resistance to the Abbey expressed itself was the coming together of citizens in Parish Guilds. These were essentially charitable institutions, but at a time when there was no local government whatever except the Abbot's *fiat*, they were also a means of acquiring some administrative control over the things that mattered to people in their daily lives. A Guild of Our Lady was in existence at Abingdon from early in the fourteenth century, and this was succeeded by the Fraternity of the Holy Cross, which erected a magnificent cross in the market square. The Fraternity took on the job of maintaining the bridge and in 1441 it was granted a charter of incorporation. It built almshouses, and undertook a number of other charitable – but also administrative – activities, meeting for business in a chamber known as the Exchequer Room in the parish church. In the course of time, by gifts and legacies, the Fraternity acquired a good deal of property. It was rich enough to be suppressed by Henry VIII, but in 1553 various members of the old Fraternity, with some newcomers, succeeded in getting a new charter from Edward VI, tactfully changing their name and becoming Christ's Hospital. This achievement was assisted by the good offices of Sir John Mason, the son of a cowherd at Abingdon who got his schooling at the Abbey and, showing great ability, was sent on to the universities of Oxford and Paris. He served as Ambassador to France for Henry VIII and became Clerk of the Privy Council and also Chancellor of Oxford. He is reputed to have played a considerable part in enabling the University of Oxford to preserve its funds from the grasping hands of his royal master. Mason must have been a diplomatist of a high order, for he contrived to remain in service under Edward VI, Mary and Elizabeth, as well as Henry VIII. He managed also to be Dean of Winchester, although apparently he never took full Holy Orders. He was a lifelong friend to his native town, and after securing the incorporation of Christ's Hospital from Edward VI he went on to secure a charter of incorporation for Abingdon from Philip and Mary in 1556. Christ's Hospital continues in existence beside the Borough Council, and continues to play an important part in the life of Abingdon, administering considerable revenues from its properties. It has a Master and eleven governors, of whom the Borough Council now elects four. In addition to almshouses and several centuries of looking after the bridge, Christ's Hospital has provided Abingdon with tennis courts, a bowling green, a 14-acre park, and a free library in the days before such things came out of the rates. It has also contributed large sums to the maintenance of schools.

The drivers of the cars and lorries that pour over Abingdon bridge now are still in debt to Christ's Hospital. When the county councils of Berkshire and Oxfordshire, the modern road authorities, rebuilt the bridge in 1926 they tried to get Christ's Hospital to pay for it, on the ground that having looked after the bridge as an act of charity for centuries the Guild had acquired a legal obligation to make it fit for motor traffic. It was a harsh demand, but after a long dispute the county councils agreed to a settlement whereby Christ's Hospital contributed about one tenth of the cost of rebuilding the bridge. The public, most of whom have never heard of Christ's Hospital at Abingdon, have done pretty well out of this survival of a medieval charity.

The early history of Abingdon is mostly guesswork based on legend, the legends assisted by a deliberate bonfire of records in the nineteenth century for the practical reason that their storage was becoming a problem. A committee selected some for survival, but since one does not know what went on the fire there is no means of assessing the value of what was lost, though it was certainly great. Mercifully, the *Chronicles* of the Abbey, a priceless collection of medieval records, were safely in the hands of the Master of the Rolls. Legends making Abingdon the site of a great British city before the coming of the Romans are simply myths, though like most such myths they probably embody folk memories of some sort, in this case perhaps the thriving trade centre of the shadowy Beaker folk. Another legend derives the name Abingdon from one Aben, who is said to have survived slaughter by the early Saxon leader, Hengist, to become revered as a hermit. The name 'Aben' does not fit the period, though the recurrence of Hengist is interesting, for the near-by Hinksey certainly derives from Hengist. At one time historians were inclined to dismiss the whole Hengist and Horsa story as mythical, but an early Saxon leader called Hengist undoubtedly left his name on the Upper Thames. Professor Kenneth Cameron, in *English Place Names*, derives the name Abingdon from the personal name Aebba (or the female Aebbe) combined with *dun*, meaning a slope or hill. Since the site is river plain, the 'hill' seems rather improbable, but some early spellings call the place Abing*ton*, and the original suffix may have been *tun* (enclosure or village) rather than *dun*. But the site of the first Abbey, before it was moved nearer the Thames, may have been at Sunningwell, which is on a hillside on the rising ground between Abingdon and Oxford.

Although the Saxon Abbey, and the settlement that grew around it, were unquestionably on the Wessex bank of the Thames, the whole district was border country in the period of Wessex–Mercian wars. In the days of Mercian supremacy Wessex was confined strictly to the south bank of the river, and Offa of Mercia appears to have held that this was the south bank of the stream or streamlet running by the Abbey, and not of the main course of the river along the Swift Ditch. Probably he was not greatly concerned with legalistic arguments. In any case, he took from the Abbey all the land of Andersey, lying between the settlement and the old course of the Thames, a considerable area of rich pasture. He is reputed to have given the Abbey land at Goosey in exchange, though whether this was Goosey, now Goose Acre, between Abingdon and Radley, or Goosey in the Vale of the White Horse, is unclear. Neither was his to give, for both were certainly in Wessex, but the Mercian kings seem to have been generous with grants of Wessex land. Offa's successor in Mercia, Cynwulf, granted Charney (Bassett) to Abingdon Abbey. Some of these grants, however, are distinctly suspect, for the later monks were not above forging charters to give themselves a better title to land. And it may have seemed politic to forge Mercian charters from a period of known confusion.

The Abbey got back Andersey. Offa is said to have built himself a palace there, and to have used it as a hunting lodge, but the baying of the royal hounds disturbed the monks at their devotions, and the loss of some of the finest pasture in England was perhaps almost equally disturbing. In the reign of Cynwulf of Mercia the Abbey suggested Sutton (Courtenay), a couple of miles downstream, as an alternative site for the hunting lodge, where the baying of hounds would be less distracting. The suggestion was tactfully accompanied by a gift of 120 pounds of silver, and Cynwulf agreed to accept the silver and the manor of Sutton in exchange for Andersey. So the Abbey recovered its best pastureland.

Alfred the Great was dubious of the Abbey's somewhat grasping practices, and tried to reduce the power of the Abbot by retaining for the Crown a number of properties that the Abbey said it owned. This was but a temporary clipping of wings, for the Abbey got back most of them from his successors, and went on getting richer. Whether Offa's palace on Andersey survived, or whether the Saxon Kings of England built a new one for themselves, is obscure, but there certainly seems to have been a palace of some sort there in the reign of Alfred's grandson, Athelstan. The King spent Easter at Abingdon in 926 and there received an embassy from Hugh, duke of the Franks, who sought to marry Athelstan's sister. It must have been one of the most splendid occasions of the Saxon court, for the Franks brought a fantastic array of gifts, including 'perfumes such as never before had been seen in England', the sword of Constantine the Great, a spear used by Charlemagne and said to be invincible, and many priceless religious relics, among them fragments of the True Cross and of the Crown of Thorns. Professor Dorothy Whitelock, in *The Beginnings of English Society*, comments, 'The suitor had taken the trouble to study Athelstan's tastes; this King was a great collector of relics, and apparently not very critical of what he was told about them.'

Eadred, another of Alfred's grandsons, and Edgar, his great-grandson, raised the Abbey to real greatness by their support of St Athelwold and his reforms. Cnut is said to have presented the Abbey with a reliquary and two bells. Edward the Confessor was naturally attracted to the Abbey and appears to have had a liking for Abingdon, for he seems to have been a fairly frequent visitor. There is a touching story in the *Chronicle* that his queen, Edith, was so distressed to learn that the novices had only bread for supper that she gave the Abbey an estate to provide meat for them.

By the time of the Conquest Abingdon Abbey was one of the richest institutions in England: in the Domesday Survey of 1086 it figures as the largest landowner in Berkshire, holding some 40 manors in the county, as well as lands in Oxfordshire and other properties. And the Domesday list must be taken as an understatement, like some later tax returns. No tact in compiling tax returns, however, could disguise the Abbey's wealth, and it was considerably mulcted under the early Normans. With the accession of Henry I in 1100 things took a turn for the better. In the last years of William Rufus the monks had suffered under an unpopular Norman Prior, and complained that the King kept the Abbacy vacant. According to the *Chronicle* the monks prayed constantly for help, and one night the Virgin appeared to a novice keeping vigil at the altar and told him:

> Fear not, tell the Prior and the Convent that they shall receive my chaplain, the cellarer of Malmesbury, Faritius by name, and he shall provide well for you, for I shall be with him.

The novice reported his vision, and a request was sent to the new King that Faritius should be appointed Abbot. This was done.

Next to St Athelwold, Abbot Faritius was the greatest Abbot in the Abbey's history. He was born in Italy, and had lived in Rome before coming to Malmesbury, where his appointment as cellarer was an important one. He was a man of deep piety, and also a scholar and able administrator. His bent in scholarship was towards what we should now call science, and he made a particular study of medicine. Henry I's marriage to Matilda of Scotland, great-granddaughter of Edmund Ironside, brought a queen of the old Saxon line to share his throne. She was immensely popular, particularly in what had been Wessex, and she appears to have loved the Upper Thames countryside. She chose Sutton Courtenay, which had remained a royal residence since the obscure period of Cynwulf's hunting lodge, for her lying-in at the birth of her first child. Abbot Faritius attended her, and in gratitude for his skill the queen gave new endowments to the Abbey. Like others who have been physicians to monarchs, Faritius became a fashionable doctor. One of his patients was the heir – Geoffrey – of one of the most powerful of Norman lords, Alberic (or Aubrey) de Vere, who held among other manors that of Kensington, now in the heart of London. Aubrey de Vere seems to have made over to Geoffrey this manor of Kensington for his maintenance as heir.

Abbot Faritius treated Geoffrey de Vere at first successfully, but his condition deteriorated and he died at Abingdon. On his deathbed he gave to the Abbey his church and some 270 acres of land at Kensington. No one seems to have thought that this gift was due to any unfair pressure by the monks, for it was confirmed by Geoffrey's father. Moreover, both father and mother felt so grateful to Faritius for looking after their son that they founded a priory at Colne in Essex, where they lived, to be administered as a subordinate community of Abingdon Abbey. Kensington remained in the possession of the Abbey until the Dissolution. The 'Abbot' in the name of the church known as St Mary Abbot's in Kensington is the Abbot of Abingdon. Colne Priory remained subordinate to Abingdon until the fourteenth century, when it became an independent community.

Faritius was Abbot of Abingdon until his death in 1117. His rule restored the Abbey's reputation for scholarship to something approaching its greatness under St Athelwold, and he increased vastly its material possessions. He carried through a big building programme, raising the community of monks from 28 to 80. He left the Abbey a major power in the realm.

Abingdon may claim at least a part – and quite a big part – in St Athelwold. Half a century or so after the death of Abbot Faritius it was the birthplace of another saint – St Edmund. Abingdon's very own saint, Edmund Rich, was born in 1170 in a narrow lane, St Edmund's Lane, in the heart of the town. His father retired to the Abbey at Eynsham, and at the age of 12 the boy went with his mother to live in Oxford at an inn that belonged to Eynsham Abbey. Young as he was he began attending lectures at the university, often, perhaps, begging the money to give the lecturer his fee, for in spite of their name the family was far from well-to-do. His mother did manage to equip him with a hair-shirt, which he promised to wear on Wednesdays. He was a brilliant child, and after some years at Oxford he begged his way to Paris, where he was quickly recognized as an out-standing scholar. Begging in this context implies no disgrace, for in medieval times poverty and scholarship were expected to go together: it was proper to beg alms to study, and virtuous to give them. After studying at Paris Edmund Rich returned to Oxford as a lecturer. He was the greatest teacher that Oxford had so far known, and men flocked to him. Among his pupils was Roger Bacon and to the end of his life he remembered Edmund Rich with love and gratitude. Mindful of his own poverty when attending lectures, Rich asked no fee for his own and was content to accept what anyone chose to give. The story goes that when handed money after a lecture he would then throw it on to a window ledge, observing 'Dust to dust'. And he would leave it there, sometimes to be stolen. One wonders if 'stolen' is the right word, or if he hinted to penniless students who had not been successful in their begging that they were welcome to what they could find in the dust of his window sill. With scholarship, Edmund Rich combined an extreme ascetic piety, spending whole nights in prayer and vigil, and sometimes collapsing at a lecture from sheer weariness. In 1222 he was appointed Treasurer of Salisbury and in 1233 he became Archbishop of Canter-bury. His was not an easy Primacy. Henry III was eager to recover what he re-garded as his possessions in France, and England was torn between the King and his French party and the English party which was opposed to wasting lives and money in an apparently endless series of French wars. The King tried to streng-then his own position by calling in aid from the Pope, and this led to increasing demands from Rome and heavy exactions on the English church. Edmund Rich supported the English party and resisted what he felt was overbearing inter-ference with the Church. In the end he went into exile at Pontigny, where he died in 1240. He was canonized in 1246. There was considerable political opposi-tion to his canonization but the saintliness of his whole life could not be gainsaid and the devotion he had inspired won the day. His shrine is at Pontigny. St Edmund of Abingdon has always been a popular saint. If there was an element of English nationalism in his canonization he also stands for a tradition of scholarship that knows no national frontiers. He was one of the founding fathers of the greatness of Oxford as a university. In 1288 a chapel was built in his memory on the site of his birthplace in Abingdon, but the chapel, alas, has disappeared, and with it exact knowledge of the site in St Edmund's Lane.

Abbot Faritius had left Abingdon Abbey a power in the realms of learning and piety as well as in the terrestrial realm. Some of his successors in the Abbey were pious and good men, but others were more concerned with their state as temporal peers than as spiritual fathers. The Abbey dominated medieval life in Abingdon and, indeed, in North Berkshire, and it became exceedingly unpopular as a land-lord. There was much trouble over markets. Market rights were property rights in the Middle Ages (and vestigially so still). In communities without shops, with cottage industries dependent on locally bought materials, the market town was the hub of the universe, and resort to it an economic necessity for the buying and selling of livestock, produce, wool, skins, and other staples of life. Control of a market brought an income in market tolls, and it also meant control over much of rural life in the area served by the market. The Abbey held market rights at Abingdon, and tried to monopolize trade by excluding merchants from Oxford and Wallingford – the market was limited strictly to the Abbey itself and its own tenants. This did not please the tenants, for it meant that they had only one customer – the Abbey – and only one supplier of goods from the outside world – again the Abbey. And it did not please the men of Wallingford and Oxford, for they were denied access to an important area of local trade. Petitions for free trade at Abingdon were all rejected, and in 1327 there was an armed rising against the Abbey. This was a well-planned affair. Allies from Oxford and the country-side assembled quietly in the neighbourhood of Abingdon, and it was arranged that on a signal given by a peal of bells from St Helen's Church there should be a concerted attack on the Abbey. St Helen's, the parish church and the home of the medieval parish guilds, was always 'our' church as distinct from 'their' Abbey.

Security was not as good as it might have been, for when the bells rang and the attack was made the Abbey was ready for it and had disposed its lay members for defence. Two of the attackers were killed, and the first assault failed. Reinforce-ments for the free traders, however, poured into the town and a second assault next day took the Abbey by storm. Some buildings were set on fire and the whole place was looted. In the confusion the Abbot and most of the monks managed to escape, but the Prior, who was sick, was left behind. The free traders compelled the Prior to sign a deed declaring that the Abbey had given up its rights over the town. This did not do much good. For the best part of six months the free trade party controlled both Abbey and town, but the Abbot got the ear of the King and came back with a force of soldiers and archers sufficient to make further resistance futile. A number of those who had taken part in the revolt were captured and tried summarily at Wallingford Castle. At least four of them, possibly as many as twelve, were hanged. In the next century, in 1431, there was another rising against the Abbey, led by William Mandeville, a weaver, who declared that they 'would make the heads of the clergy as cheap as sheep's heads'. This also was put down.

A bitter comment on the Abbey at Abingdon occurs in *Piers Plowman*. The writer of that great poem, William Langland, was born, probably near Ledbury, in Herefordshire, about 1330, and there is some evidence suggesting that he may have been an illegitimate son of Eustace de Rokayle, who lived at Shipton-under-Wychwood, near Oxford. If so, and if he spent any part of his youth at Shipton, he could well have known Abingdon. He was contemptuous of the worldliness of the monk of his day, whom he described as

> A leader of lovedays and a land buyer
> A pricker on a palfrey from manor to manor
> An heap of hounds at his arse as he a lord were.

He went on to prophesy

> Ac there shall come a kyng and confess yow
> religiouses,
> And beat you as the Bible telleth for brekynge
> of your rule.
> And than shal the Abbot of Abyngdone, and al
> his issue forever
> Have a knock of a kyng, and incurable the wounde.

Langland's prophecy was fulfilled. In 1538 Abingdon was the first of the major abbeys to make a 'voluntary' surrender to the crown of all its possessions. The last Abbot (one Thomas Rowland) did not do badly. In return for his voluntary surrender he had a pension of £200 a year for life (a fine income in Tudor pounds) and the manor of Cumnor. The monks also got pensions. This was in marked contrast to the treatment of the last Abbot of Reading, Hugh Faringdon. He refused to make a 'voluntary' surrender of property that he felt he did not own, and he was hanged.

If the traditional date of 675 be accepted for the Saxon foundation of Abingdon Abbey, it had a continuous history of 863 years. Little remains. The Saxon church is recorded in the Abbey's *Chronicle* as having been 120 ft long, and having rounded apses at both East and West ends. The Norman church that succeeded it was huge and of great richness, on a wonderful site on the bank of a branch stream of the Thames. Nothing of the church remains: it was utterly destroyed, even its foundations being dug out and removed; for generations it must have been a quarry of building stone for the citizens of Abingdon. The site of the church, now called the Abbey Park, is beautifully maintained as lawns and gardens by the Town Council. Of remarkable interest near the site of the great church is a fine collection of ruins – *built as ruins* as a nineteenth-century folly!

The splendour is gone, but something of the Abbey compound is left to indicate what a vast place it was – a small walled town in itself – in the days of its glory. The fifteenth-century arched gateway, with a gatehouse over it, stands, and next it is a lovely congeries of old buildings, part of them once the Abbey's Hospital of St John, now mixed with seventeenth- and eighteenth-century work to make a most attractive whole, housing among other things a council chamber and a court. Fronting Thames Street, not actually on the river, but on the outlet from the millstream, now a charming backwater, are parts of the Abbey's granary, and next to them the counting house or exchequer still called The Chequer. Most of this is thirteenth century, and rising from a splendid fireplace that once warmed the monastic accountants a thirteenth-century chimney crowns the roof like a miniature church tower: Professor Pevsner considers it 'the most interesting of its date in England'. Running on from The Chequer is the late-fifteenth-century Long Gallery, a fine timbered cloister. The original roof still covers what were once a series of little rooms opening from the cloister. It has been suggested that this was once the Abbey's guest house, but it seems unlikely that guests would have been mixed with what were essentially the Abbey's offices. It is more probable that the Long Gallery's rooms housed the monks attached to the Treasurer's staff. Within this group of buildings is now the Unicorn Theatre, a beautiful little reproduction of an Elizabethan theatre, seating about 90. It was constructed after the war, when the buildings were acquired by the Friends of Abingdon, who maintain them admirably.

Although Abingdon Abbey ceased to exist over 400 years ago, there is still – in spite of Langland – an Abbot of Abingdon. The papacy has never accepted the dissolution, and there is a titular Abbot of Abingdon in Rome. The title is conferred on the vicar of the Church of St Paul in Rome.

A desire to feel independent of the Abbey, and, after the Dissolution, relief

21a. *The White Horse and Uffington Castle. Bottom Left is Dragon Hill, where St George killed the Dragon.*

21b. *The White Horse at Uffington.*

22. 'Ride a cock horse
To Banbury Cross . . .'
The present Banbury Cross is a Victorian replica.

23a. *In the glades, a majestic avenue of beech trees at Kingston Lisle.*

23b. *The Blowing Stone at Kingston Lisle. King Alfred is said to have summoned his Saxon Warriors to battle with the Danes by blowing through the stone, but it is far older than King Alfred's day.*

24. *Wayland's Smithy, a burial chamber of 3–4,000 years ago on the Berkshire Downs near White Horse Hill*

from its dominance, led the townspeople of Abingdon to lavish particular devotion on their parish church of St Helen. It has an incomparable setting on the Thames, and its spire apparently rising from the water makes a memorable approach to Abingdon by river. It stands on or near the site of a nunnery traditionally founded by St Helena, the mother, as some hold, of Constantine the Great. If so, the nunnery would have been far older than the Abbey. But all trace of the nunnery is lost, and there remains only the hope that archaeology may one day cast some light on it.*

The present church, with five aisles, is broader than it is long. Parts of it are thirteenth-century, but the work of every century since has gone into it. Its chief treasure, unique in England, is the panelled and painted roof of the Lady Chapel. The chapel was constructed at some time after 1350, and the roof repaired in 1390–91: an indulgence was granted by Pope Boniface IX in 1391 to those contributing to the repairs. The church once had much medieval stained glass, but this was smashed by Parliament men in the Civil War, who are said to have stabled horses in the church. Grouped round the churchyard, on three sides of a square of which the church is the fourth, are three rows of almshouses, the newest built in 1748. The oldest, the Long Alley Almshouses, date from 1446, the third row from 1718. There is nothing comparable in England: the quiet river a few yards away, the quiet churchyard, and the quiet, beautiful old almshouses enclosing what can sometimes be the peace that comes with age. On the river end of the oldest row of almshouses is a rather crude painting of what was once Abingdon's market cross, also destroyed by the Parliament men.

The cross is gone, but the market place holds yet another architectural glory unique in England. This is the Town Hall (once the County Hall, for when it was built Abingdon was the county town of Berkshire). It was built over four years from 1678–82 by Christopher Kempster, one of Wren's masons in the building of St Paul's, and although Wren's name does not occur in the accounts, the design, or at least the conception of it, almost certainly derives from him. The ground floor is open to form a covered market, and over it rises a tall and magnificent chamber, much used in the eighteenth and early nineteenth centuries for County balls. From the parapet round the roof the Mayor of Abingdon throws buns – plain buns, a bit like hot-cross-buns – to the crowds assembled in the square on State occasions. This is an established Abingdon ceremony, apparently

* Some people have doubted whether the nunnery existed, regarding the stories about it in the later *Chronicles* of Abingdon Abbey as medieval myths. On the other hand the connection of St Helena with Abingdon, although no doubt partly mythical, is very old, and belief in the nunnery is deeply rooted in tradition.

started for the Coronation of George IV, still kept up: there was a bun-throwing for the Coronation of Queen Elizabeth II. The excuse for a bun-throwing does not have to be a Coronation; it may celebrate any important national or municipal occasion. It is considered lucky to catch a bun, and when caught they are sometimes taken home and varnished. Properly varnished, a bun will keep indefinitely, though it gets a little wizened.

In 1642 when Charles I decided to move his court to Oxford, Abingdon was occupied by an advance party under Prince Rupert. The King himself was for a time at Abingdon, and held councils in the inn now known as the King's Head and Bell. Abingdon was held for the Royalists until early in 1644, and it was at Abingdon that the King saw his Queen Henrietta Maria for the last time, when he said farewell on sending her to safety in France. By this time the Royalist cause was failing, and soon after the departure of the Queen Abingdon was abandoned to a Parliamentary force under General Waller. This was a serious reverse, for Abingdon in Parliamentary hands was a constant threat to the Royalists at Oxford. A counter-attack was made in January 1645. The Royalists succeeded in crossing Culham Bridge but were defeated in a sharp battle on the causeway before they could reach Abingdon Bridge. It was Waller's troops who destroyed the Cross and did such damage in St Helen's Church: presumably they thought the Cross and stained glass windows idolatrous. It was a harsh time. Abingdon had been a Royalist town and Cromwell's men may have wanted to make the inhabitants know who were their masters. Many Irish prisoners captured fighting for the Royalists were brought to Abingdon and hanged: so many that the hangings gave rise to the bitter saying about 'The old Abingdon law, where execution precedeth trial.' Charles II got a rapturous welcome when he visited Abingdon after the restoration, and the corporation's silver gilt mace, presented in 1661, has a nice Royalist touch: it is dated 'in the twelfth year of Charles II', ignoring the Commonwealth altogether. Abingdon played a moving if unconscious part in the final drama of James II. William of Orange rested in the town on his way to London, staying at a house in East St Helen Street (now a private house) used as the Judge's Lodgings when Abingdon was an assize town. It was here that he was brought a message telling him that James had fled, and that London was his without a fight.

Abingdon Market, won in the end by the free traders, is still held on Mondays. There is a 'statute fair' still held at Michaelmas – a 'statute fair' because the rate of wages for the ensuing year fixed under the fourteenth-century Statute of Labourers was customarily proclaimed at Michaelmas. This fair is called the Hiring Fair, and certainly as late as 1905 farm workers would assemble to be engaged by farmers. A week after the Hiring Fair there is a smaller fair called the Runaway Fair. At this, labourers who for one reason or another did not like the jobs they had taken were given a second chance to present themselves for employment. It was to Abingdon Fair in 1560 that the unhappy Amy Robsart, who was staying at Cumnor, let her servants go on the day she met her mysterious and lonely death. Queen Elizabeth was in love (or apparently in love) with her husband, Robert Dudley, Earl of Leicester, and it must have seemed to Dudley that Amy's existence was the only thing that stopped his hope of being Prince Consort. Amy was staying at Cumnor Hall, which had been leased by Anthony Forster, her husband's steward. The servants spent the day at Abingdon Fair, and when they got back they found her lying dead at the foot of the stairs. Accident? Suicide? Murder? Leicester's enemies said murder: a coroner's jury (possibly bribed) said accident. Suicide, though the method seems unlikely, is not impossible. No one can know. Her death did her ambitious husband no good, and the hall where she met her death, however it came, was demolished early in the nineteenth century.

Perhaps in reaction to the Abbey, there has long been a strong non-conformist vein in Abingdon, and there are some exceptionally fine Free Churches in the town. The Congregational Church, built about 1700 and rebuilt in 1862 (not at all in the style of Victorian Nonconformist architecture) is reputed to include in its timbers the masts of the *Mayflower*. Certainly they are ships' masts of about the right period. Another story is that they are the masts of a ship wrecked on the East Coast, whose sole survivor was a minister who had the masts salvaged and built into the church. There is a handsome Baptist Church from the early nineteenth century, and a Methodist Church of 1845.

The Abbey owned much sheep land in Berkshire, and in the Middle Ages Abingdon had a considerable trade in wool and cloth. That ended with the Middle Ages, but a leather trade, deriving from the sheepskins that came with the wool, flourishes still – water in the Thames at Abingdon is supposed to have peculiar properties that favour leatherworking. The town remains the market centre for the north-eastern end of the Vale of the White Horse, and has prospered from the spread of the motor industry from Oxford. The M.G. car works were moved from Oxford to Abingdon in 1929 and since the war instrument making and light engineering have come too. The economy of the ancient town has also benefited from the newest of industries – nuclear energy. Many employees of the Atomic Energy Research Establishment at Harwell and at the Culham Laboratory live in Abingdon, and a number of new houses for A E R E people have been built there.

Rather poorly served by public lavatories nowadays, Abingdon was one of the first towns in Britain to maintain a 'public privy'. It was built directly over the Stert stream, before it was culverted, with a private dwelling for the keeper above the privy. The corporation let it out on lease in 1584, and it appears to have been in existence long before then. In terms of medieval sewage, this direct use of a river draining into the Thames was probably to be considered advanced. It would not be approved now, and it is long departed.

Abingdon has suffered more than Oxford from the twentieth century: it is much smaller, and more easily hurt. Almost until 1950 it remained a medieval town; now it is a town with medieval buildings sandwiched between housing estates and modern shopping centre. Its river front is still the most beautiful on the Thames, and its approach by river remains as magical as when St Frideswide was rowed there by her angelic boatman. The motor industry and nuclear energy have pumped economic life into arteries that were becoming hard. New life is good, but one feels sadly here as in Oxford: why must so much of modern life be so ugly?

Abingdon, though an older town than Oxford, could never have become the capital of the Upper Thames as Oxford did. It is on the wrong side of the Thames, isolated by the river rather than enlarged by it, and with no good river crossing before its bridge was built. But for the politics of the eleventh century it is conceivable that Dorchester, ten miles downstream, might have become the region's capital. The Romans, with a good eye for sites, built Dorchester as their one town on the Upper Thames. The river was fordable nearby, and, like Oxford, Dorchester commands routes north-east through Buckinghamshire and Bedfordshire and south-east to Wycombe and London, as well as commanding an important crossing of the Thames. On a peninsula between the Thames and Thame it is a good defensive site. But it was of no particular importance to the Normans. The South and South-East of England were firmly in Norman hands soon after the Conquest, and with castles at Windsor and Wallingford strongly held there was no need for another castle at Dorchester. It was different at Oxford. Danger to the Normans was in the North and West, and it was imperative to create strong points to extend the conquest from the Midlands. Thus a castle at Oxford was necessary and William I was quick to send Robert D'Oyley to build and garrison one. The whole flank of the Thames could be turned at Oxford, and this was a hazard not to be risked. Moreover there was fine hunting at Woodstock and Wychwood, better than anything to be had between Oxford and Reading. So Oxford grew, and Dorchester did not.

Dorchester now seems far too little for its history, like a boy wearing the clothes of a tall man. Yet this imbalance between past and present gives the village – it is really no more – an extraordinary brooding charm. Dorchester is nearly as important in the early history of Christianity in Britain as Canterbury. St Birinus converted heathen Wessex from Dorchester as St Augustine converted Kent from Canterbury. Of the Saxon cathedral of St Birinus nothing remains. The cathedral-like church in its lovely setting by the Thame (not Thames) served Dorchester Abbey, founded by the Bishop of Lincoln for a community of Austin (Augustinian) canons after the Normans had transferred the Bishopric of Dorchester to Lincoln. Fortunately for the church, Dorchester Abbey never became as powerful as Abingdon: it aroused no particular hostility, and since Dorchester remained a village there were fewer people around at the Dissolution eager to quarry stone from the Abbey for their own buildings. The church was bought intact by one Richard Beaufort, who preserved it as a church. It is a noble legacy. The early Norman church was small, but it was rebuilt and added to over the thirteenth, fourteenth and fifteenth centuries. It has some of the finest thirteenth-century glass in Europe, and treasures of sculpture and painting. In the days of the Abbey the church was shared by monks and villagers, the monks having the chancel and the villagers the use of the nave. What now seems rather a blank wall divides the two, but this wall was once a glorious display of fourteenth-century wall paintings. The traces of these that remain are rare examples of a medieval art that time and the climate have almost lost to Britain. Although chancel and nave are seldom walled off, as at Dorchester, where there was a practical reason for it since the church was also the chapel of the Abbey, the principle of chancel for priests, nave for people follows a very early tradition: indeed, the priestliness of the chancel is commonly marked by a rood screen. The principle was also financial – the repair and upkeep of the chancel was considered the incumbent's responsibility in parish churches, repair or restoration of the nave the job of the parishioners. If you find an old church with a beautified nave and a rather bare chancel it nearly always points to a period of absentee-incumbency in its history, when some well-to-do parson held it as one of several livings, appointing a curate, often on a low wage, to serve the parish. Devout parishioners would look after the nave, but leave the chancel, and if an absentee rector ignored his responsibility the chancel would fare badly.

The final resting place of St Birinus is unknown. He was almost certainly buried at Dorchester, but when the See was transferred to Winchester (before Dorchester became the great Mercian bishopric transferred to Lincoln by

William I) his bones are reputed to have been moved there. They may, however, have been brought back to Dorchester. In the thirteenth century Dorchester Abbey claimed to possess his relics, and the shrine of St Birinus in the Abbey church was an important place of pilgrimage in the Middle Ages. His shrine is still in the church.

The bridge which the Oxford–Henley road crosses at Dorchester is over the Thame, not the Thames: the crossing of the Thames is at Shillingford, just over a mile to the south-east, after the Thame has joined the Thames. Thame and Thames unite about a quarter of a mile south of the present village of Dorchester. Between the village and the Thames are the prehistoric ramparts of Dyke Hills, two enormous ditches dug between Thames and Thame, making a formidable fortress of the place. Across the river, on the Berkshire bank, is the equally formidable fortress of the Wittenham Clumps or Sinodun Hills. These fortifications must relate to one another, but of their origin little is known. They are far older than the Romans, though the Romans used them: their existence as ready-made strongpoints was no doubt one of the reasons for the Roman selection of Dorchester as the site for a Thames-side town. These great earthworks go back to late Neolithic or early Bronze Age times, although they were improved and probably added to by later builders of hill forts, perhaps in the last century or so before the coming of the Romans. Dorchester was a sanctuary or holy place 1,000 years or more before it became the see of a Christian bishop. There are traces of a cursus – a long enclosure between banks of earth, presumably for some ceremonial purpose – and of henge monuments that would seem to relate to the Great Stone culture of Avebury and Stonehenge.

Wallingford, on the Berkshire bank of the Thames three-and-a-half miles downstream from Dorchester, was by far the most important Saxon settlement on the upper river. Its key place in Alfred the Great's system of river forts has been described. It was captured and burned by Svein Forkbeard in 1006, in the wars that brought his son Cnut to the throne, and rebuilt by Edward the Confessor. The Saxon monarchs had a mint at Wallingford, and coins went on being minted there until 1270, a dignity that survives in the name Goldsmiths Lane. Its last Saxon lord, Wigod, submitted to William the Conqueror, and allowed his troops to cross the Thames freely. This is not to be equated with treachery. There was reason enough to regard Harold Godwinson who seized the throne on the death of Edward the Confessor as a usurper, and loyalties were sadly confused. In recognition of Wallingford's welcome, William I permitted the town an hour's extension from the curfew generally imposed.

The Saxon embankment enclosing the town on three sides, with the river guarding the fourth, can still be traced. In origin these are perhaps much older earthworks, coeval with those at Dorchester. Wigod seems to have had a castle of some sort, and this was rebuilt and added to by the Norman Robert D'Oyley who married Wigod's daughter. There was a priory at Wallingford, traditionally

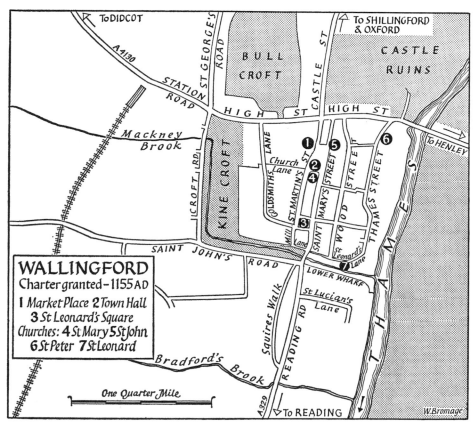

Map 8 *Town plan of Wallingford.*

founded by D'Oyley, but in fact established as a daughter house of the Abbey of St Albans. D'Oyley, or his wife, who were active in founding Osney Abbey at Oxford, may have helped in the establishment of Wallingford Priory. As a foundation subject to St Albans it never achieved the territorial grandeur of the great Abbeys of the region, and it was suppressed, with other minor foundations, in 1525, before Henry VIII tackled the major religious institutions. Its property

135

was used by Cardinal Wolsey towards the establishment of his Cardinal College at Oxford.

Like Oxford, Wallingford owes much to the Saxon army engineers – an interesting contrast with Abingdon. As a town, Wallingford is much better laid out than Abingdon, with neat military thinking in its rectangular plan. The forgotten general who paced out its lines had to accommodate men who were to fight for him: he wanted them fit, and, if possible, happy, an attitude markedly different from that of the Abbey at Abingdon, which regarded the dwellers outside its gate simply as hangers-on. Moreover, he had to look beyond Wallingford itself to his communications. The Romans gave the place its main road north (A439), running roughly parallel with the river and a couple of hundred yards away from it. The east-west road (now A4130) is older: it was once a prehistoric trackway leading from the river-crossing to the Downs and the Ridgeway. The Saxon fortifications, making use, perhaps, of far older earthworks, guarded both the crossroads and the river-crossing, and the settlement that grew up round them was kept a tidy place. As at Oxford, military planning also served trade, and Wallingford developed as a market town. It suffered a crippling economic blow from the building of Abingdon bridge in 1416. Until then the main route from London to Gloucester and South Wales crossed the Thames at Wallingford, and the town had thriving inns and all the general activity of an important staging post. When Abingdon had a bridge the traffic went by Abingdon, and Wallingford's fortunes declined. Its castle, however, remained of military importance, and its tenacious defence by the Royalists in the Civil War made it a thorn in the side of the Parliamentary forces operating against the King at Oxford. Wallingford Castle was never taken. It was the last stronghold of the Royalists on the Thames after everything else was gone, and surrendered only after King Charles had himself surrendered in July 1646. Cromwell was so irritated by its defence that he had the castle blown up and demolished.

That was Wallingford Castle's last appearance in the history of England, a history that it had played no small part in shaping. In the wars between Stephen and Matilda it was held for Matilda. By then it was in the hands of Wigod's half-Norman (but equally half-Saxon) grandson, and it is a pleasant reflection on Wigod's acceptance of the Norman conquest that it was to be his grandson who did perhaps more than anyone else to ensure that the blood of the ancient Saxon house of Wessex should return to the throne of England in Matilda's son, Henry II. Oxford also stood for Matilda, and when she had to flee from Oxford, Wallingford was her last hope. Wallingford did not fail her. It was besieged by Stephen but held out against all assaults. It was their final failure to take Wallingford that convinced Stephen and his supporters that they could not win, and that the long struggle against Matilda was to be ended only by agreement. It was at Wallingford that the treaty between Stephen and Matilda – the Treaty of Wallingford – was signed, giving Stephen the crown of England for life and the succession to Matilda's son, afterwards Henry II. On his accession Henry held a parliament at Wallingford, and in gratitude to the town granted the burgesses a charter conferring various privileges. In 1955 Queen Elizabeth II visited Wallingford to celebrate the eighth centenary of its charter.

In the tangled chronology of Thames bridges one thing is scarcely to be questioned: that Wallingford was the first major crossing of the river to have a fixed bridge, the first anywhere on the river. There was a Saxon bridge at the time of the Conquest, and a good solid bridge a century later, for in his siege of Wallingford Castle Stephen built a tower on the Oxfordshire bank of the Thames to overawe the bridge. It is not known whether this was a bridge of wood or stone: probably it was a mixture of both. From 1231 to 1271 Wallingford was held by Richard Earl of Cornwall (brother of Henry III) who was elected King of the Romans. He is reputed to have built a bridge of stone, and the earliest arches of the present bridge date from about his period. Three of the existing arches are of thirteenth-century masonry, but the bridge as a whole has been much restored and rebuilt. When Wallingford Castle was held for Charles I in the Civil War the defenders cut the bridge in four places, constructing wooden drawbridges, which could be hauled up, over the gaps. These remained in use until the middle of the eighteenth century: the gaps were not restored with masonry until 1751. In 1809 the bridge was badly damaged in a flood and more or less rebuilt, the old narrow carriageway being widened by some seven feet.

Wallingford suffered severely from the Black Death in 1349, and its inhabitants were reduced to a handful. A century later only 44 houses are said to have been occupied – but this would take account of the decline in trade that came with the building of Abingdon Bridge. Wallingford Bridge, having lost both traffic and citizens to see to its upkeep seems to have fallen into a deplorable state of ricketyness. The demolition of the Priory in 1525 provided a cheap source of materials with which it was repaired to some extent. Both before and after the Civil War it seems generally to have been in rather poor condition, and there were frequent complaints in the seventeenth century about its interference with barge-traffic on the Thames. The Admiralty, which used the Thames for bringing timber to its yards at Deptford, complained particularly that its arches were too narrow for the timber barges.

In the great Plague of 1665 Wallingford remembered its bitter experience during the Black Death, and men were stationed on the bridge to keep out any-one coming from the London road. In spite of these precautions sixteen people in Wallingford died of the plague, a heavy death roll for a small community. But the effort to keep out strangers seems to have worked to some extent, for the pestilence of 1665 was not the calamity of that of 1349. Perhaps hygiene generally was better.

In its great day in the Middle Ages, Wallingford supported fourteen churches. Now it has seven – three Anglican, one each for Roman Catholic, Baptists and Methodists, and a charming cottage meeting house for the Society of Friends, built in 1724. The spire of St Peter's Church, a slender thing rising in tiers much like a wedding cake, gives Wallingford a curiously fairy story look as one ap-proaches either by the Henley road or by river. It was designed by Sir Robert Taylor in 1777. Not everyone admires this spire, but I think it charming. In his book on Berkshire in 1911, F. G. Brabant condemns it, observing 'The curious stone spire is far too prominent, and spoils most views of the town.' Professor Pevsner says 'It is rather cheeky, but entirely convincing.' Of what it 'convinces' I have no idea, but it adds a lovely little grace note to the rather sombre score of Wallingford's long history.

7

Regional settlements I – North bank

Human settlement spread from the Thames up its tributary valleys, which extended the growth of the region and in turn fertilized growth. The earliest settlements – transitory resting-places, rather – were in the marshy jungles of the valley floors, where crayfish were to be had from the streams, berries from the woods. As man devised better weapons and techniques for hunting, the uplands, where larger game was to be found, became attractive, and men began to roam the chalk downs of Berkshire and the Cotswold hills about the headwaters of the Thames and its western tributaries.

The Romans found the Cotswolds delectable country, and because of the readiness of the Dobunni to become Romanized they did not have to do much fighting: they could civilize instead. They built a splendid city at Cirencester, and established rich villa estates around it. The museum of Roman antiquities at Cirencester (the Corinium Museum), beautifully kept up, is a wonderful place to contemplate the continuity of life. Roman women used make-up, and one may see the little mirrors they held when they were putting on their faces. At Chedworth, in the Coln valley, seven miles to the north-north-east, you can see a rich man's villa of about A.D. 180–350 on the spot; at least, you can see the remains of it, with another beautifully kept museum, and it does not need much imagination to people it.*

This is on the western edge of the upper Thames region, but still part of it, for the Coln and its neighbour the Churn feed the Thames. Seven Springs, the source of the Churn and a disputed source of the Thames is a couple of miles south of Cheltenham, and you get there by taking the A435 out of Cirencester to

---

* But do not go on a Monday unless it happens to be a Bank Holiday, for the place is closed.

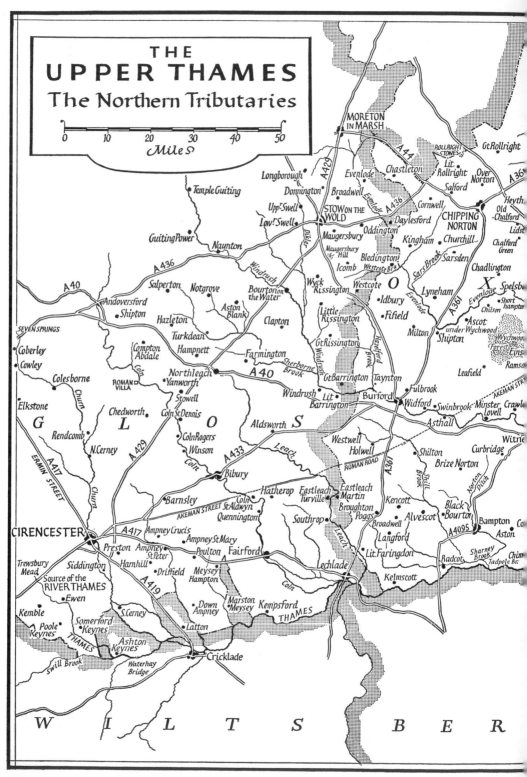

Map 9 *The Upper Thames: Northern Tributaries.*

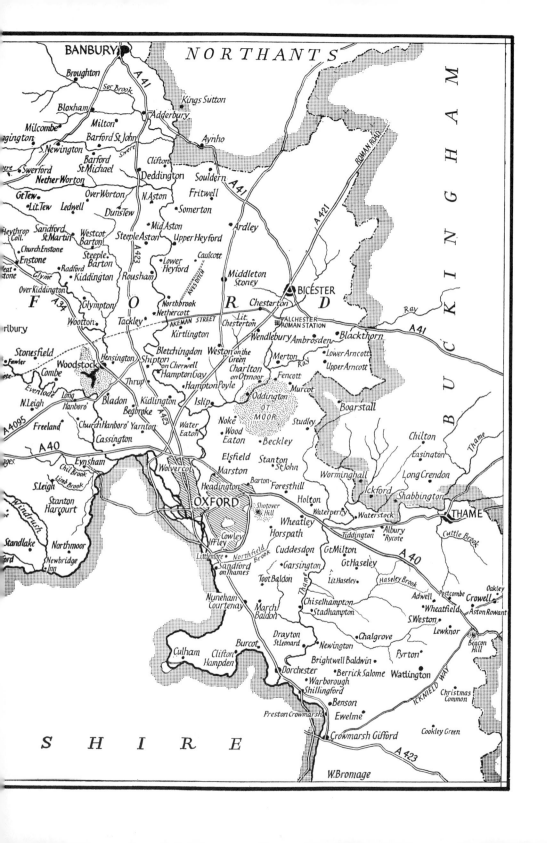

Coberley, and then turning left at the junction with the A436. Seven Springs is an island site in the main road (A436) almost at the junction. It is considerably more dramatic than Thames Head. There is a carved name post informing you that this is Seven Springs, a steep dell, with water in it, and a Latin inscription cut into stone:

Hic Tuus
O Tamesine Pater
Septemgeminus Fons

Immediately on leaving his septemgeminal source, Father Thames (or Churn) plunges into a drain under the main road to emerge into a little lake or, rather, large duck pond, on the other side. Then he makes his way towards his other self (the Thames at Cricklade) through steeply wooded chines, collecting the Hilcot Brook at Colesborne Park on the way. Once you leave the main road it is romantic, lonely, lovely country. The water at Colesborne is a deep turquoise in the pools; you would not be surprised to see the white arm of the Lady of the Lake emerge to grasp Excalibur (if this were Arthur-country, which it is not). The Churn gives its name to Cirencester itself (rather awkwardly for the school which would call Churn Thames) and to the beautiful villages of North and South Cerney. The Coln, flowing a few miles east of the Churn, joins the Thames just above Lechlade. It has two settlements of enchanting loveliness, Bibury and Fairford. Both go back to the dawn of English history, and have known in turn wandering Old Stone hunters, tribesmen of pre-Roman Britain, Roman, Saxon, Viking, Norman and the English folk who come from all these forbears. In the late Middle Ages both prospered exceedingly from the wool and woollen cloth trades, and the substantial citizens those trades created have left enduring monuments in the buildings where they lived and worked and worshipped. William Morris declared Bibury to be the most beautiful village in England – a claim hard to refute, equally hard to sustain. It is an exquisite village of old cottages, stream, church and immemorial trees, grouped together by time and chance and the native taste of their builders into a whole as near perfection as one can hope to find. Fairford is more of a small town, with its particular glory in its church. This church, which replaced an earlier church, was started and mainly built in 1490–93 by John Tame, a wealthy wool merchant, and finished by his son Edmund. Both, perhaps, felt that they had sufficient treasure on earth, and they spared no expense to lay up treasure in heaven. The *surety* of medieval faith is infinitely moving here. The cynical may say that the Tames built to impress the neighbours, but I

142

am quite certain they did not: they built for the glory of God, in absolute conviction that to build for the glory of God was to atone for the sins of being man. There are ignobler convictions – at least it implies consciousness of sin. The particular splendour of the Tames' church at Fairford is its glass, a series of 28 windows presenting a vivid strip cartoon of the story of mankind from the Garden of Eden, through the Old Testament to the coming of Christ and on to the Last Judgment, with the physical weighing of souls and pictures of the really horrible fate awaiting those who are found wanting. This glass is the work, or mostly the work, of Bernard Flower, who has windows in the chapel of King's College, Cambridge, and at Westminster. He was a supreme master of stained glass, and the windows at Fairford are perhaps his masterpiece, expressing the boldness, simplicity and richness of a still-medieval imagination with absolute confidence. John Keble was born here – a nice continuity of faith.

East of the Coln are two of the loveliest tributaries of the Thames, lovely both in themselves and in their names, the Windrush and the Evenlode. Both, like the Thames itself, are Cotswold streams. Temple Guiting, near the headwaters of the Windrush, offers another example of the mingling of Saxon and Norman after the Conquest. It was a royal manor, held by Edward the Confessor, who leased it to one of his nobles, a man called Alwyn. His widow married a Norman knight. Guiting was not then called Temple Guiting: it acquired that name later when the manor was held by the Knights Templar. The Bishops of Oxford had a summer palace there.

At Bourton-on-the-Water the Windrush has become a sizeable river, but it has widened rather than deepened, and the toy-like bridges that give such charm to the village on both banks of the wide stream have no need to be much more: stepping stones would serve as well. The bridges are in fact toys, the first built in the eighteenth century when it was fashionable to build in the Italian manner. It is among the most pleasing of follies, and the little brood of bridges that have followed it make Bourton perhaps the most photographed village in Britain. The latest Bourton bridge was built to commemorate the coronation of Queen Elizabeth II. The Fosse Way crosses the Windrush at Bourton, and the modern road bridge – the Romans were content to use a ford – has a plaque that fittingly commemorates the 2nd Legion (Augusta), whose engineers built the road. Two tributary streams, the Dikler and the Sherborne, join the Windrush below Bourton, and in the days when men were prepared to haul and shove barges anywhere a barge could float, the river was more or less navigable up to Windrush village, halfway between Bourton and Burford.

Burford, the first town on the Windrush, is one of the oldest settlements in the region. The river (now bridged) could be forded here, and Burford grew up to guard the ford and the crossing of the east-west route that followed the valley of the Windrush from Oxford and Witney to Gloucester, and the north-south route from Coventry and the Midlands to Wiltshire that crossed the river by the ford. It was a frontier post of the minor Saxon Kingdom of Hwicce, and, when that was overrun by Mercia, Burford became a frontier post of Wessex. In the struggle between Mercia and Wessex a Mercian invasion was halted here in 752. The emblem of Wessex was a golden dragon, and for centuries the victory of Wessex in the Battle of Burford was commemorated on midsummer eve by a procession carrying the figure of a dragon through the town. In the Middle Ages Burford grew rich from wool and stone, wool from Cotswold sheep and stone from quarries in the neighbouring hamlets of Upton and Taynton. Burford stone is among the finest building stone to be found in Britain, some would say the finest without peer. It is less harsh than Portland stone, warmer than Aberdeen granite, and it has wonderful wearing qualities: after weathering on the surface to the colour of dark honey it retains its hardness more or less for ever. A building of Burford stone laid by a good mason has an enchanting quality of seeming to have grown out of the ground. And Burford has produced masons to match its stone. Christopher Kempster, one of Wren's master-masons in the building of St Paul's, was a Burford man, and Wren had a high regard for him, recommending him to Dr Fell for work at Christ Church, Oxford, and employing him himself whenever he could. The splendid Town Hall at Abingdon is Kempster's work. He loved his stone, and went on working until he died at eighty. He lived by his quarry at Upton, and his home there, known as Kit's Quarry, was later the home of C. E. Montague. Christopher's son, William, was also an outstanding mason, and a sculptor of something approaching genius. He, too, worked at St Paul's and a lovely cherub's head by him earned the particular praise of Wren and a bonus of £20 for his 'extraordinary diligence and care'.[*] He carved the beautiful memorial to his father in Burford church. Several other Burford men worked for Wren at St Paul's and the tradition of fine craftsmanship in stone lives on. The Groves of Milton-under-Wychwood, three miles north of Burford, carry on a business as stonemasons and builders that has been in their family without a break for over 300 years.

The Kingdom of Hwicce has left its name on the map in Wychwood, once an enormous forest covering the countryside from Woodstock to the Windrush

[*] T. A. Ryder, *Portrait of Gloucestershire*.

25. This view of Didcot Power Station is taken from the site of an Anglo-Saxon settlement at Sutton Courtenay.

26a. *Thatcher working at Appleton, Oxfordshire.*

26b. *The fine old art of thatching as demonstrated by a Master Thatcher at Wantage.*

valley. Most of it is now gone, though woods that were part of the great forest still stand here and there. Wychwood was a royal game forest under the Saxon monarchy, and Cnut, in the Danish interlude, issued an edict reserving hunting to the King, to maintain the crown's privilege. The Norman kings naturally took over all the royal hunting rights, and enforced even stricter game laws. The importance of hunting in the early history of England – in places, indeed, almost to this day– reflects more than a passion for sport. Venison and other game was a necessary source of the vast quantities of meat required to feed the army of officials and retainers that accompanied the King wherever he went, and similarly to supply the households of the feudal nobility: game remained a valuable, sometimes a necessary, supplement to the housekeeping of many country families for centuries – as rabbits were to the nation in the last war. If the King and his nobles wanted game, so did their lesser tenants: for many cottage folk even in my boyhood poaching was not fun but part of the business of living. The early game laws expressed not merely the landowner's wish to preserve shooting rights but a firm, often cruel, determination to ensure that the food to be got by hunting was kept for his own family and friends. The crown was harshest of all in maintaining hunting rights. It used to be said with bitterness that Oxford Gaol was built to house men sentenced for hunting for themselves in Wychwood.

The wars between Stephen and Matilda at least made life easier in Wychwood, because the rival claimants to the throne were too much occupied in fighting each other to bother about enforcing forest laws. This freedom ended under Henry II. He was particularly fond of Wychwood (partly because it was at Woodstock that he used to meet Fair Rosamond) and at the Assize of Woodstock in 1184 he imposed a new code of forest laws. His code was slightly milder than the savagery of the earlier laws, but in some ways bore more hardly on the men of Burford, Shipton, Milton, Ascott and the other Wychwood settlements because his administration was more efficient than his predecessors' and poachers were more likely to be caught. A man whom the King's officers were after for illegal hunting would sometimes succeed in getting away. He was then liable to be declared an outlaw, and his village had to pay a collective fine.

The forest laws were complicated by the fact that the villagers of Wychwood possessed rights of common in certain areas, rights far older than the forest laws, going back to the time when Wychwood was the wood for all the Hwicce, who gave the forest its name. There were frequent disputes over which places were royal forest and which were not. The crown's interest was to extend the forest – that is, the area subject to the forest laws – and the inhabitants' to reduce it. The crown did well under Henry II, but King John, compelled to be more sensitive to public opinion, undertook to reduce the forest to its former size. Not much seems to have been done, however, for an official 'perambulation' of the forest in the reign of Henry III brought to light several encroachments on land that was held to be outside the afforested area. Woodcutting was an offence as well as hunting, and the penalties for both could be severe. The forest had its own courts, but they could be kindly as well as harsh: it was not uncommon for an accused man to be excused punishment because the court was touched by his story of poverty. Nevertheless, the road to gaol at Oxford was well trodden. An awkward situation arose in the reign of Edward I. In 1303 the King's own coroner for Oxfordshire, one Robert of Ascott, was put in prison for offences against the forest laws of Wychwood. The Sheriff of Oxford was ordered to find a new coroner.

With the end of the Middle Ages the royal need of hunting for food declined. It was easier to get land declared 'disafforested', and although deer stealing remained an offence liable to severe punishment many of the forest laws gradually fell into disuse. Charles I tried to revise them as a means of raising money by fines, and in 1638 proposed bringing back within the scope of forest laws all land that had been royal forest in Norman times. This would have 'reafforested' a huge area, including districts that had been free of the laws since the fourteenth century. The Civil War put an end to this proposal, and the suggestion was not revived. The forest laws did not finally lapse, however, until 1856, when the last parts of Wychwood remaining royal forest were formally disafforested. (The *game laws*, protecting game on private property, and requiring a licence to hunt game, are, of course, another matter.)

The forest conditioned life in this part of Oxfordshire for centuries. Deer stealing – if stealing is a fair word – was naturally practised until it became almost a fine art, and the Wychwood communities were in collective alliance against the royal keepers. There were many ingenious hiding places for venison waiting to be cooked – sawpits, a room over the church porch at Shipton church, hiding places among the tombs in Bursford churchyard were all used. The townspeople of Bursford early acquired the right to one day's hunting in the forest, and the capture of two bucks. The hunt was traditionally on Whit Sunday after church, and the townsfolk elected a Lord and Lady of the Feast for the feast that followed the hunt. The hunt itself was abandoned in 1593, when there was a pestilence in Burford and it was feared that crowds of Burford people roaming the forest might spread it to other villages. The brace of buck, however, were presented by the keepers without the hunt, and this custom continued until the final disafforestation in 1856. The election of a Lord and Lady to preside over a general saturnalia also continued, but early in the (outwardly) more respectable nineteenth century this, too, was abandoned 'in consequence of the gross improprieties to which it led'.★ A dinner given by the churchwardens was substituted.

The houses of the well-to-do wool and stone merchants, built and rebuilt from the fifteenth to seventeenth centuries, make Burford a gracious old town, with a wide, steep main street running down to the Windrush. There are some fine old inns from the days when it was a coaching town on the Gloucester road. The coaches used to descend to Burford from Witney, and then climb the hill out of it again. In the eighteenth century the 'top road', the present A40, was made, cutting out the descent into Burford, and the town lost its coaching trade. In the nineteenth century it was not prosperous. Robert Gardner's *Oxfordshire* of 1852 describes Burford as 'a quiet insignificant country town, becoming yearly of less importance. . . . The sign of this decline is visible everywhere; it is to be seen in the once large and handsome mansion now apportioned into small tenements. . . .' Those 'small tenements' a century later are coveted residences, often commanding rich men's prices. Industry at Oxford and Witney has made Burford highly desirable as a dormitory town, and the loss of its main road has added to its attractions as a place to live in.

Its thirteenth-century Priory or Hospital of St John the Evangelist was acquired on the Dissolution by one Edward Harman, whose memorial, commemorating also his sixteen children, is in the church. It passed next to Sir Lawrence Tanfield, Lord Chief Justice in the closing years of Elizabeth's reign. He built the imposing mansion still called the Priory, and entertained James I there. His daughter married the first Viscount Falkland, whose son, Lucius Cary, second Lord Falkland, died at Newbury fighting for King Charles I. Before the outbreak of the Civil War, Cary sold the Priory to William Lenthall, who became famous as the Speaker of the Long Parliament – the Speaker who told Charles I, when he came to the Commons with an armed guard to arrest five members, that he had 'neither eyes to see nor tongue to speak but as the House is pleased to direct me'. Burford Priory has now returned to the church: it is an Anglican convent.

Burford changed hands several times in skirmishes during the Civil War, when the Parliamentary Army was trying to encircle Charles I at Oxford. After the execution of the King, Cromwell had much trouble with what would nowadays

★ *Oxfordshire*, Robert Gardner 1852.

be called his political left wing, the Levellers. Some months after the King's execution the Levellers organized a revolt at Banbury. This was a serious matter for Cromwell, for they attracted many discontented soldiers from the Parliamentary Army. General Fairfax met a force of some 400 of the rebels at Burford and defeated them. Prisoners were put in the church to await the arrival of Cromwell. Four days later he came, held a court martial, and ordered three men to be shot. The executions were carried out in the churchyard.

In the Windrush valley two miles below Burford is the small village of Swinbrook, for some 300 years the home of the Oxfordshire branch of the Fettiplace family. The Fettiplaces were a curious clan, originally a Berkshire family. The first of whom anything much is known was Thomas Fettiplace, of Shefford in the Lambourn valley, who married (as her fourth husband) Beatrice, the illegitimate daughter of King John I of Portugal by his mistress Agnes Perez. John I came to the throne in 1385. His family was considerably mixed up with England, for his wife (but not Beatrice's mother) was a daughter of John of Gaunt. Beatrice married well, her first three husbands being the Earl of Arundel, the Earl of Shrewsbury and the Earl of Huntingdon. She was still young enough to have two sons by Thomas Fettiplace, William and John, and brought them considerable possessions. The family flourished, went on marrying profitably, and acquired land in fifteen counties, giving rise to the old Berkshire saying

> The Tracys, the Laceys and the Fettiplaces
> Own all the manors, the parks and the chases.

This saying was also current in Oxfordshire. A branch of the family moved to Swinbrook about 1500 and stayed until 1806: Anthony, the first of the Swinbrook Fettiplaces, is commemorated by a brass in Swinbrook church dated 1510.

Through the Wars of the Roses, the Civil War, and all the other upheavals of English life, the Fettiplaces kept out of the way, acquiring neither peerage nor national prominence, marrying well, and living as country gentlemen. Marrying heiresses, however, was self-defeating in the end, for towards the middle of the eighteenth century the family reached a point at which it seemed able only to produce daughters. The last male Fettiplace, George, died in 1743, and with him died the baronetcy that the family had achieved as its solitary title. The estates went, through George's sister Diana, to her son, Thomas Bushell, who took the name Fettiplace by Act of Parliament (he could not, of course, take the baronetcy). By 1806 there were again only daughters to succeed, and the estates were split up and sold. So the name goes from history. But through the daughters there are still Fettiplace descendants living in Berkshire. There are two Fettiplace daughters among my own ancestresses, and my home is within a few miles of the first Fettiplace home at Shefford.

There is a fine collection of monuments to sixteenth-, seventeenth- and eighteenth-century Fettiplaces at Swinbrook, their effigies accommodated in tiers, as if they were lying in bunk beds. To the last they – we – remain a curious clan. Their house at Swinbrook had a curious end. Shortly before the estates were broken up the old house at Swinbrook was let to an apparently hospitable gentleman, who entertained lavishly. His guests, however, were paying guests in an exact sense, for this last occupant of the Fettiplace house was in fact a highwayman, and on their way home from his parties the guests were waylaid and robbed. This occupancy ended with the arrest of the tenant by Bow Street Runners. The house was left empty, fell into ruin, and has now disappeared.

Swinbrook Church has a memorial more moving than that to any of the Fetti-places in a window commemorating both a wartime vicar and the church's escape from major damage when a German land mine fell on the parish in September 1940. The mine shattered windows containing some beautiful fourteenth-century glass. The Vicar, the Rev. William Grenville Boyd, searched for and recovered almost every fragment, and the glass is reassembled in his memorial window.

Between Burford and Swinbrook is the tiny hamlet of Widford. You need good map reading to find it, but it is worth finding because a walk across its meadows takes you to one of the most remarkable churches in Britain. It is the church of St Oswald, and it is built actually on the site of a Roman villa. This was discovered in 1904, when the isolated church was all but falling down. During repairs bits of the tesselated pavement of the villa, still intact, were found under the floor. There are also some fourteenth-century wall paintings.

Some six miles below Burford is the Windrush's largest settlement, Witney. This is another Saxon settlement, originally an island in the marshes between the Windrush and the Thames – its name means Witta's Island. Unlike other towns in the region it has a long industrial history: for centuries Witney has had a world trade in blankets, and more recently it has acquired an important place in the motor industry as well, making instruments and components for cars. But Witney has somehow absorbed industry rather than been absorbed by industry: it is living proof that an industrial town need not be ugly. The heart of the place is an immense green, more like a cathedral close than the centre of most industrial towns, with the great parish church built and adorned by generations of pious

149

wool merchants, looking down on it. Witney prospered with the Cotswolds' sheep, making cloth from their wool and leather breeches from their skins. And Witney kept its prosperity when the rest of the early wool trade moved away from Oxfordshire: it went on making blankets and horse cloths, and Witney merchants went on selling them against all competition. The rise of the huge Yorkshire woollen industry, with access to cheap coal from nearby coalfields, might have been expected to put Witney, far from any coalfields, out of business. It did not: Witney's traditional skill in blanket weaving gave its wares a quality that the world went on buying. And Witney men showed great ingenuity in selling: they were quick to see, for instance, a new outlet for their blankets among the Red Indians of North America, and built up a useful trade in supplying them through the Hudson's Bay Company.

This survival of a local medieval craft through the changing industrial pattern of six centuries is a remarkable achievement. It has been put down to many causes, among them the nature of water in the Windrush, which is said to be of unique virtue in the treatment of wool, giving it a surpassing whiteness – writing in 1677 in his *Natural History of Oxfordshire*, Dr Plot observed that Windrush water ensured 'that no place yields blanketing so notoriously white as is made at Witney'. Certainly the Windrush helped to establish the blanket industry at Witney, though its provision of water power for mills was probably more important than the qualities of the water itself, valuable as these may have been. But many other early industries, now vanished, had water power. Why did blanket weaving stay, and thrive, in Witney?

Wool is a very old industry in England, and Governments have always wanted to 'regulate' it. So have the wool men themselves: the instinct to form 'closed shops', to keep up prices and to restrict competition is also very old. The woollen industry at Witney could not escape from statutory controls, but Witney seems to have been remarkably free from all local restraints on trade. Until the eighteenth century, when the Company of Blanket Weavers was formed to enforce general rates for the trade, Witney weavers seem to have been content with a policy of live and let live. Dr Alfred Plummer, the modern historian of the blanket industry, thinks that this may have had something to do with the survival of the industry in Witney. Until the formation of their 'Company' in 1711 (this was a trade association, not a company in the financial sense) the weavers of Witney apparently preferred to look after themselves without asking the State for charters for Guilds, and Dr Plummer suggests 'that in consequence many weavers were attracted to Witney in preference to towns where guild regulations were more irksome, and probably more exclusive. . . . Apart from general laws, the Witney weavers were, as far as we know, almost, if not entirely, untrammeled by local regulations prior to the eighteenth century'.

Other factors were the collective common sense of Witney people in sticking to the weaving of coarse yarns, thereby developing special skills and earning a good name for Witney broadcloths, and the close family relationships between weavers and merchants. The community seems to have developed and maintained an astonishingly wise collective attitude to blanket weaving, deciding that what was good for blankets was good for Witney, and acting on the principle. Again unlike most other British industries, blanket weaving in Witney does not seem to have owed much to the immigration of skills from abroad. Dr Plummer writes, 'Occasionally such names as John Brabant and Thomas Franchsteer, woolstapler, are encountered, but they fade into insignificance in the crowd of Earlys, Marriotts, Duttons, Townsends, Whites, Redgates, Greenways, Birds, Colliers, Bowmans, Boultons, and so forth, all engaged in the woollen manufacture in Witney.' These men were apprenticed to one another, learned their trade thoroughly, and found their own capital. The Witney masters were almost all journeymen, who could work a loom as well as anyone they employed. Modern mills, techniques and company structures have come to Witney, but blanket weaving there retains a wonderful continuity with the past. The firm of Charles Early and Marriott celebrated its tercentenary in 1969, and Richard Early (b. 1908) is the eighth generation of his family to direct its fortunes. He maintains the Witney tradition: put him at a loom, and he will weave a first-class blanket.

Witney itself seems to reflect the corporate goodwill of its most famous industry. The manor of Witney was given by Edward the Confessor to the Bishop of Winchester, but since the medieval jurisdiction of its bishops no great lord has ever dominated the town: its weavers have been its aristocracy, and are still. They built their houses beside their mills and preserved the qualities of their town as they preserved the good name of their blankets. Witney has grown *with*, not *from*, its blanket industry. And although distance from the coalfields may have worried its nineteenth-century blanket manufacturers, geography has been kind to Witney here. When coal came to the Witney mills it was relatively expensive, and could not be used in the prodigal fashion that poured grime over industrial towns in the North and Midlands. It had to be burned well, and the thrifty Witney men saw to it that it was, to their own economic advantage and the great benefit of their town.

The Windrush at Witney is near the end of its course, for six miles on it joins the Thames at Newbridge. Between Witney and Newbridge are the pleasant villages of Ducklington and Standlake, but for the rest the Windrush country here is quiet and remote, islanded by branching arms of the river, which unite again just before the end. At Newbridge there is nothing but the bridge, and two inns, the *Maybush* at the Berkshire end of the bridge, and on the Oxfordshire bank the pleasingly named *Rose Revived*. For all its title, Newbridge is of great antiquity. Little is known of its origins, but it seems to have been built towards the end of the thirteenth century, and was 'new', perhaps, soon after the building of the ancient bridge at Radcot. It is hard to say which is in fact the older, but Radcot bridge is generally given precedence by a few years. Like St John's bridge at Lechlade and Radcot, Newbridge is approached by long causeways on both banks, indicating the formidable engineering that the medieval builders had to undertake to bridge not merely the stream of the river but to carry their roads across difficult marsh country to reach the river at all. The first arches of Newbridge on the Oxfordshire bank bridge the Windrush rather than the Thames for they carry the road across both rivers at their confluence.

Newbridge stands today much as it stood 600 years ago, its narrow, pointed arches giving it immense strength. On the upstream side V-shaped buttresses stand against the current, providing neat recesses on the roadway for foot passengers to take refuge from traffic. The navigation arch has been smoothed a bit over the centuries, but for the rest the bridge presents the same picture to our eyes as it did to wayfarers through the dynasties of Lancaster, York, Tudor, Stuart and Hanover.

On 27 May 1644, the Royalists repulsed an assault on the bridge by Parliamentary troops under General Waller who were trying to encircle Oxford. A week later – on 2 June – Waller's force crossed unopposed, but rejoicing at the Royalist withdrawal was premature, for the Parliamentary Army marched on into a trap, to be met and given a severe mauling at Cropredy, on the Cherwell.

In the Middle Ages Wychwood Forest covered almost the whole area between the Windrush and the Evenlode, the next major easterly tributary of the Thames. Both are magical rivers, their villages, their valleys and their flanking wolds the very picture book of England, the England that exiles dream about. The Windrush belongs almost wholly to the Gloucestershire Cotswolds, the Evenlode more to the Oxfordshire Cotswolds. There are subtle differences, but I am a Berkshire man, and must let those who contend for the surpassing loveliness of one or the other contend as they will.

The Evenlode rises near the village of Evenlode, a couple of miles south-south-east of Moreton-in-Marsh. Geological ages ago it is conceivable that the Severn basin once drained into the Thames through the Evenlode valley, for glacier-borne rocks that more properly belong to the Severn's side of the Cotswolds are scattered about the Evenlode's country: some of them have been used to construct the mysterious monument of the Great Stone culture known as the Rollright Stones. The upheavals of geological time, however, kept Thames and Severn apart – until man joined them by the Thames and Severn Canal. The Evenlode belongs now wholly to the Thames, but it may not be entirely fanciful to feel that there is a touch of mystery about Evenlode country, as if the Evenlode is a little apart from the other rivers of the Thames.

A mile-and-a-half below the village of Evenlode, the river meets a pair of lovely little villages, both with a particular place in history. They are Adlestrop and Daylesford. Adlestrop was where a train carrying Edward Thomas stopped unexpectedly one summer afternoon before the war of 1914–18 in which he was killed, prompting him to the haunting poem

> Yes, I remember Adlestrop –
> The name, because one afternoon
> Of heat the express train drew up there
> Unwontedly . . .

Daylesford is the scene of one of the most touching of local-boy-makes-good stories. Daylesford belonged to the powerful medieval family of Hastings, but they supported Charles I in the Civil War, were impoverished, and lost their land. A thin connection, however, remained, because an eighteenth-century Hastings in Holy Orders was presented to a living nearby. His son was Warren Hastings (1762–1818), who as a boy is said to have determined to buy back the home of his ancestors. This he achieved by taking service with the East India Company, becoming the first British Governor-General of India, and acquiring an immense fortune. On his return to England he did buy Daylesford, built Daylesford House, and a new church (later pulled down and replaced, for what reason goodness only knows). The story, however, does not go quite as it should. With retirement by the great proconsul to dignified squirearchy, Warren Hastings was impeached for alleged corruption in his administration in India, and his trial, the longest State trial in English history, lasted seven years. In the end he was acquitted – and also ruined, by the legal costs of defending himself. But the East India Company stood by him, and he was able to keep Daylesford until he died. Through the tortured years of his trial thoughts of Daylesford must largely have kept him going: he went on gamely building Daylesford House while his trial proceeded. And how often he must have thought of the Evenlode during his years of power by the Ganges! His life covers an immense span of British Imperial history: in rather moving contrast barely three miles of Evenlode country come between his birthplace and his grave. The house where he was born can still be seen at Churchill, a charming small village between Daylesford and Chipping Norton, and he is buried at Daylesford.

The Windrush was the southern boundary of Wychwood Forest: the Evenlode is that once-great forest's own river. The woodlands of Bruern Abbey and of Cornbury remain to show what it was like. There are no towns to speak of on the Evenlode. Chipping Norton, not on the river, but on the Cotswold ridge forming the northern rim of the Evenlode valley, is its metropolis, a border town between Oxfordshire and Gloucestershire. The 'Chipping' reflects its status as a market – the same root meaning trading place is met in London's Cheapside. Chipping Norton is another wool town, and a tweed mill still flourishes there. The place was given a charter for a fair by King John in 1205 and incorporated as a borough in 1606. Its Wednesday market, having existed (according to the Charter of Incorporation) 'from the time whereof the memory of man is not to the contrary', went into abeyance in the nineteenth century but was revived with great enthusiasm in 1958, and the fine old market place is again bright with trader's stalls on Wednesdays.

The largest settlement on the Evenlode itself is Charlbury, some five miles south of Chipping Norton. For most of its history Charlbury was a forest village, and it has remained a biggish village rather than a town. It is an attractive old place, clinging to its hillside above the river a bit like a cliff-hanging Cornish village. It was once an important centre of the glove-making industry, and still has glovers doing out-work for factories in Somerset. Cornbury Park, with its surviving woods of Wychwood Forest, is just across the river. Appropriately, perhaps, it has strong Royalist connections. Its great house was the home of Edward Hyde, Lord Clarendon, faithful friend of Charles I and Charles II, father-in-law of James II (who married his daughter Anne), historian of the Civil War, and great benefactor of the University of Oxford. The Stuart connection went on after the abdication of James II, and the woodlands of Cornbury hid much pathetic and futile Jacobite plotting: the Young Pretender is said to have visited there in disguise.

Perhaps because their masters were such staunch Royalists, the people of Charlbury developed a strongly Puritanical streak. Anne Downer, a notable early Quaker, and said to have been the first woman to preach publicly in London, was born there in 1624. The Society of Friends is still vigorously alive in Charlbury, and its meetings are a direct link with an important chapter in the history of religious conviction. The present Meeting House, however, was not there in Anne Downer's day, but it is nearing its second century – it was built in 1779.

The Evenlode skirts Blenheim Great Park, but can claim neither Blenheim nor the town of Woodstock: they belong to its tributary, the Glyme. They join on the edge of Blenheim Park at Bladon, the little village where Sir Winston Churchill is buried. Churchill was born at Blenheim Palace, in a small ground-floor room that is shown to visitors – apart from having a bed, it is not unlike a dentist's waiting room. For all the tremendous scale of his life, barely a mile separates Churchill's birthplace from his grave. Like Warren Hastings, he came home.

Blenheim Palace draws tourists by the tens of thousands, and they get their money's worth, for the place is rich in historical treasures, and the gardens are a delight. Even when confronted by its stupendous presence, Blenheim Palace is a little hard really to believe in. The house – if you can call it a house – alone covers some three acres and everything about it, except for the homely little bedroom where Winston Churchill was born, is several sizes larger than life. The arrangements for visitors are good, and the guides who take you round know what they are talking about. But it is something of a relief to return to the everyday world.

Woodstock, huddling round the gates of Blenheim (they weigh something like 17 tons) is a beautiful little world to come out to. The Glyme runs almost in a ravine here, and Woodstock's narrow old streets tumble to the river in a cascade of grey stone and (in summer) creeper-covered walls. The church, with a thirteenth-century nave rising to an eighteenth-century tower, is neither grand nor grandiose, but fits perfectly into its niche in the old town. Across the road from the church, in what was once a biggish private house, is Oxfordshire's County Museum. This is a splendid place, a record of life, not of the dead past, with pleasant rooms set out to illustrate the crafts – gloving, thatching, wheel-making – that were the country's livelihood. It is entirely in keeping that next door to a display of wheelwright's tools is a cut-out model showing the assembly of a motor-car at Cowley. In the kitchen, not in glass cases but in their proper place, are the spits and jugs and ladles that our great-grandmothers used. Outside is a walled garden, with a lawn that has been cared for through two or three centuries. It is a place to sit and reflect – on Fair Rosamund, the Black Prince (who was born at Woodstock), the first Duke of Marlborough, Sarah Jennings and Queen Anne, Sir Winston Churchill – the procession of the great who have passed through Woodstock while the glovers and the housewives kept life going behind their cottage walls.

The Evenlode, having collected the Glyme at Bladon, meets the Thames a couple of miles to the south between Cassington and Eynsham. The next considerable tributary is the Cherwell. Although it belongs to the Thames, the Cherwell also belongs to the Midlands. It rises at Charwelton, in Northamptonshire, almost on the watershed of Middle England, where the lie of a stone in the path of a rivulet determines whether its water finds a way to the sea via the Bristol Channel, the Wash or the Thames Estuary. Within a mile or two of the headwaters of the Cherwell are the headwaters of the Nene, flowing to the Wash, and the Leam, flowing to the Severn and the Bristol Channel. The Cherwell trends at first southerly, and then south-west to Banbury, its major town. From Banbury to Oxford the Cherwell is almost (but not quite) absorbed in the Oxford Canal, itself a river-like waterway, and of great importance in the navigational history of the Thames.

Banbury is in the Upper Thames Region, but scarcely of it. Banbury's links seem more with Warwick, Coventry and the Midlands than with Oxford: yet, although with its Midland neighbours Banbury has long been a manufacturing town, you could not properly call Banbury a Midland town. It is a place on its own with a strongly individual history.

> Ride a cock horse
> To Banbury Cross
> To see a fine lady
> On a white horse . . .

The cross exists, but regrettably it is not the old cross by which the fine lady (whoever she was) once rode. Perhaps in reaction to the churchmanship of Oxford, Banbury developed early a fanatical streak of Puritanism, and the original cross was destroyed by the townspeople as papistical or idolatrous in 1602. The present cross, in the style of Charing Cross, is a mid-Victorian monument built in 1859 to commemorate the marriage of Queen Victoria's eldest daughter to Prince Frederick of Prussia in 1858. Supporting statues of Queen Victoria herself, of Edward VII and of George V were added in 1914. Banbury's puritanism also blew up (precisely, with gunpowder) its parish church at the end of the eighteenth century, because it had been neglected and it was considered cheaper to blow it up than to attempt repair. The old church was once richly furnished and said to have been very beautiful: the present church is severely plain, with a unique many-sided spire that looks round. Banbury's puritanism has left an uglier legacy in the rhyme about the Banbury man who was seen

> Hanging of his cat on Monday
> For killing of a mouse on Sunday

More pleasantly, Banbury has given its name to Banbury cakes. These are mentioned in town records as far back as 1608 but had no more than local fame until an enterprising woman called Betty White began sending them to London and securing what we should now call 'a national distribution' in 1770. The Original Cake Shop in Parsons Street, where her cakes were baked, stood until 1968, when it joined the old church in destruction because it was considered too far decayed to be repaired. In opposition to Oxford, Banbury supported Parliament in the Civil War. The town and castle, however, were surrendered to a Royalist force under the Earl of Northampton, who commissioned his younger son, aged nineteen, to hold the castle. This the boy did for the rest of the war, resisting siege after siege and declining all suggestions of surrender on the simple ground that he had been instructed to keep the castle 'for His Majesty'. His conduct was so gallant that at the end of the war the half-starving boy and his comrades were given safe-conducts and allowed to depart without interference. In the Banbury tradition, the castle was later pulled down.

For all its rather cantankerous history, Banbury is an attractive town. Industry sits lightly on it, and the honey-coloured stone of its buildings gives the place an almost physical warmth that is unusual in English townscape. Much of North Oxfordshire draws economic sustenance from Banbury's industries. Industrial development has been well planned on open sites to the north of the town and a useful mix of heavy and light industry has been attracted to the area. Alcan Industries has an important aluminium plant at Banbury and a number of engineering firms making components for the motor industry are now established there. In 1965 General Foods Corporation selected Banbury for the establishment of a major new manufacturing centre for food products, and spent some £7 millions on a range of buildings that look more like a garden suburb than a set of factories. This was a particularly important development, for it extended greatly the range of factory jobs available for women in the locality. Agricultural machinery, furniture making and printing are other aspects of Banbury's industrial activity. These industries draw labour from villages within a radius of 20 miles or so from Banbury, providing wages for a host of small rural communities where agricultural employment has fallen off.

Banbury came into being as a market town for the North Oxfordshire and near-Northamptonshire countryside, and it retains all its old importance here. Not far short of half a million beasts a year pass through its cattle market, and its shops like its factories, serve the countryside. The puritan tradition may have less meaning in a secular age than it had once, but it survives in a rugged spirit of independence and self help. The church which replaced the blown-up building is not to everyone's taste, but external severity is relieved by a remarkable use of colour within – quite un-puritanical golden stars shine down from a blue domed ceiling: the whole interior offers space and peace. Like Banbury itself, the church is unusual and interesting.

The Cherwell has no more towns until it gets to Kidlington, on the outskirts of Oxford. At Kidlington it makes a 90–degree turn to the east to Islip, where it collects its tributary the Ray, which joins it after flowing through the strange marsh of Otmoor. Cherwell and Ray flow round Oxford to the east, creating the island on which the medieval city grew. The combined rivers join the Thames after flowing round the eastern and southern flanks of Christ Church Meadow.

Only the western end of the Vale of Aylesbury can properly be considered as part of the Upper Thames region, although the open route provided by the Vale from the Thames through the Chilterns to the Eastern Midlands and the North Sea was integral in the human settlement and historical development of the region. The Thame, which waters the Vale, belongs to the Thames, and the geo-political importance of its junction with the Thames at Dorchester has already been discussed. The town of Thame, which takes its name from the river, 14 miles east of Oxford and just in Oxfordshire, is a regional settlement: westwards and south-westwards from Thame the countryside becomes Thames country. Thame, like Banbury, is a market town that has kept its importance: it has had a weekly market since 1183, and its cattle market is second only to Banbury's in Oxfordshire. The settlement came into being because the river can be forded here, and grew up on rising ground to the south of the river, safely away from floods. Although they have long merged into one, there are really two settlements at Thame, the original settlement directly south of the river and a New Town, planned as such in the thirteenth century, adjoining it to the south-east. Thame was part of the immense medieval bishopric of Lincoln, and the Bishops of Lincoln held the market rights. These were valuable, and the bishops (and their bailiffs) were shrewd in developing them. In 1219 the Oxford–Aylesbury road was diverted to pass through Thame, to bring more traders to the market. The New Town was a bold move to increase the attractions of the market by creating a hinterland free from irritating manorial dues. Some 50 acres of land adjoining the Old Town were taken out of the demesne, divided into acre-strips – called burgages – and offered at a low ground-rent free of all manorial services. Subject to the ground rent, tenants had complete security of tenure: they could sell their strips as they pleased, dispose of them by will, and later were allowed to divide strips into half- and quarter-burgages. This interesting early experiment in freedom was a marked success, for it attracted traders

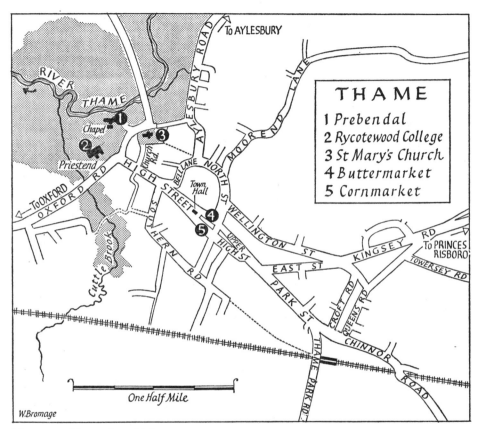

Map 10 *Town plan of Thame.*

and craftsmen to Thame, promoted economic development – and substantially increased the bishops' income. The new town was administered by the bishops as a Manorial Borough. There was a regular fortnightly court, under the bailiff, primarily to try commercial cases. It was called the Portmoot (or Portmanmoot) and took its jurisdiction seriously: traders were prosecuted for throwing offal in the street, for giving bad measure, or for exposing bad meat for sale. This strict control added to the prestige of the market, and benefited bishops and tradesmen alike. The bishops' manor was broken up in the Dissolution and the bishops' court went out of business. By then the traditions of fair-dealing and a well-regulated market were well established.

The results of this far-sighted medieval town planning are still to be seen in Thame's magnificent High Street with its attractive Corn Market and Butter Market in the middle. The exceptionally wide High Street was the original market, and it remained an open space as the surrounding area was built up.

At the Dissolution, the bishops' manor of Thame and other church lands in the region were acquired by Lord John Williams, a curious character who was one of Henry VIII's Commissioners for the Dissolution. He must have been able, for he contrived to serve Henry VIII, Edward VI, Mary Tudor and Elizabeth without losing either his head or the immense fortune he accumulated. At least he gave back some of his fortune to the community, for he re-endowed alms-houses at Thame and founded the Grammar School there. The roll of famous men turned out by Thame Grammar School must be all-but unique for a grammar school in a small country town. They include John Hampden, William Lenthall (Speaker of the Long Parliament), Edmund Waller, Anthony Wood, Thomas Elwood, the Quaker who rescued Milton from London during the Plague, Dr Fell, Dean of Christchurch, Henry King, Bishop of Chichester, Lord Chief Justice Holt, and Sir George Croke, another distinguished judge.

John Hampden, whose stand against Charles I by refusing to pay Ship Money is in all the history books, died at Thame in June 1643. The Royalists then held Oxford, and Thame was held for Parliament by the Earl of Essex. Reinforcements were on the way to him from the south and Prince Rupert came out of Oxford to intercept them. Hampden, with a local levy from Thame, rode out to try to harass Prince Rupert's force on the way. They met at Chalgrove, some six miles to the south-west of Thame, and in a sharp skirmish Hampden was severely wounded. He managed to ride back to Thame. He lingered for six days at the Greyhound Inn, now a shop known as Hampden House, but his wound was mortal and there he died.

27. *Inside the Iron Age fortifications at Segsbury Camp, on the Berkshire Downs.*

28a. *Thatch at Woolstone.*

28b. *Thatch at Long Wittenham.*

8

Regional settlements II – South bank

The Oxfordshire bank of the Thames is the convex rim of the river, thrusting, as it were, into the outer world. Tributaries on the north, or, after Oxford, eastern bank of the river lead to the Thames, but their valleys are as important in leading away from it, to the Gloucestershire Cotswolds, to the Midlands, to Eastern England. The south or Berkshire bank of the Upper Thames is the concave rim, the enclosing bank and original frontier. Settlement and culture extended outwards from this river-enclosed land: even today there is a different feeling about it, a sense of being immeasurably older than other parts of the Upper Thames region.

The Kennet, joining the Thames on the Berkshire bank at Reading, is at once one of the river's most considerable tributaries and itself a boundary, the southern frontier of the region. In its upper reaches the Kennet is a Wiltshire river, rising within a mile or so of Avebury, and giving its name to the strange avenue of standing stones leading from the Great Stone Circle of Avebury to what is called The Sanctuary on Overton Hill. Kennet Avenue is, of course, a modern name, but it is a fitting one, for the bases of the standing stones, set in the chalk, were packed with clay from the banks of the young Kennet to keep them upright. The young river is joined by the Lambourn at Newbury, and this united stream carries the waters of the Berkshire and the Wiltshire Downs to the Thames.

For all the 'New' of its name, Newbury is among the oldest settlements in Britain, this area of the Kennet valley having been more or less continuously inhabited since the Mesolithic lake-dwellers found their way to it some 10,000 years ago. The Romans, who preferred high ground to marsh, had an encampment at Speen, now a suburb of Newbury, on the ridge between the Lambourn

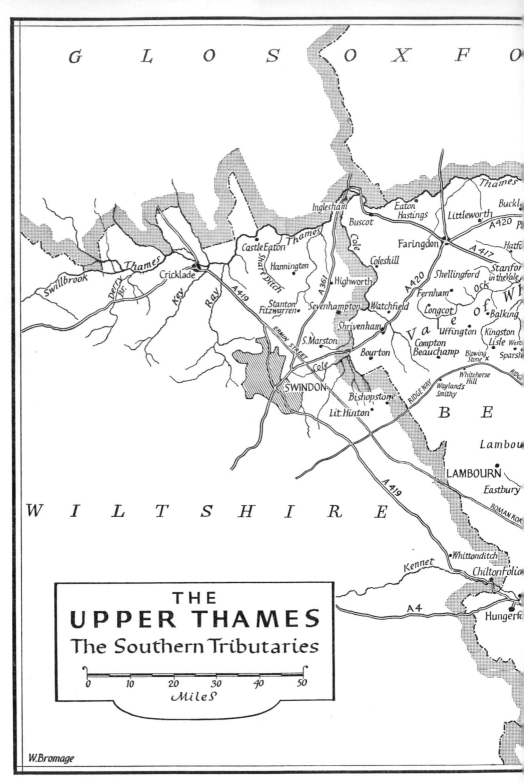

THE
UPPER THAMES
The Southern Tributaries

| 0 | 10 | 20 | 30 | 40 | 50 |

Miles

W.Bromage

Map 11 *The Upper Thames: Southern Tributaries.*

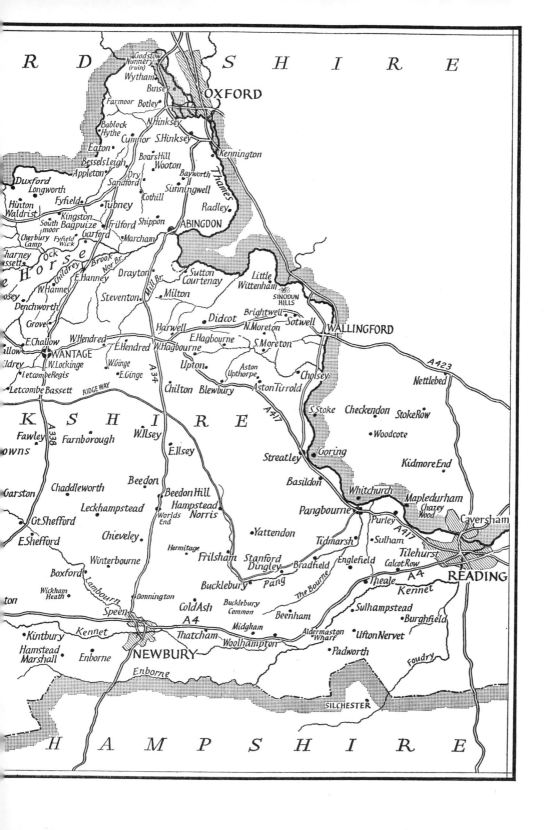

and the Kennet, a mile or so to the north-west of the centre of modern Newbury. This was an important military post on the route from Silchester to Cirencester, and a village grew up around it. Newbury proper, on the Kennet near its junction with the Lambourn, developed as a market and trading centre in late Saxon times, and it probably acquired its 'New' to distinguish it from the older village of Speen. King John granted a charter for a Newbury Fair on St Bartholomew's Day in 1215, and the Bartholomew Fair was held every September for 724 years, up to the outbreak of war in 1939. A Michaelmas Hiring Fair for the recruitment of farm workers was instituted rather later than King John's Fair, and this fair on the Thursday next after 11 October, is still held.

With the sheep of Wiltshire and Berkshire on its doorstep, and good routes to Bristol, Oxford, Reading, London and Southampton, Newbury was of substantial commercial and industrial importance in the Middle Ages. At the end of the Middle Ages the cloth trade produced the town's most famous character, 'Jack of Newbury', who has a reasonable claim to be regarded as the first employer of factory labour on any scale in Britain. Jack was born John Smallwood at Winchcombe in Gloucestershire and his parents apparently wanted him to become a monk. At fourteen he was admitted to Winchcombe Abbey as a boy novice, but he soon realized that this was not his vocation, and he ran away. He turned up in Newbury, where he changed his name to John Winchcombe, and got a job as apprentice to a master weaver. In the tradition of the apprentice who becomes rich he married his master's widow, and extended the cloth-making business to the extent of employing about 1,000 men, women and children in a factory with some 200 looms. Jack became very rich indeed, and raised and equipped a force of 50 pikemen and 50 horsemen, which he is reputed to have led in person to assist King Henry VIII against the Scots at Flodden. Jack was certainly known to Henry VIII, for the King and his first wife, Catherine of Aragon, visited him at Newbury. The story goes that the King offered to make Jack Sir John, but that Jack respectfully declined a knighthood, saying that he was a plain working man and felt it better to remain so. He died in 1519. Parts of his great Tudor house in Northbrook Street still stand. Unlike Witney, which kept its specialized blanket industry, Newbury's cloth trade declined in the eighteenth century as the woollen industry moved to the mills of Yorkshire. In 1811 a fine exercise in public relations was staged in an attempt to revive weaving at Newbury when Sir John Throckmorton of Buckland wagered 1,000 guineas that he would dine in a coat woven and tailored at Newbury from wool that had been on the backs of sheep that same morning. Sir John won his bet: the sheep were sheared at 5 a.m. and the coat was finished by 6.20 p.m., in ample time for dinner at 8 p.m. The sheep from which it was made provided a dinner for the weavers, and the master weaver, one John Coxeter, added 120 gallons of strong ale to go with the mutton.

The Newbury Coat was a splendid piece of textile virtuosity, but Yorkshire with cheap coal could undercut the Newbury weavers and the cloth trade passed into history. There were other activities to replace it, The Kennet was improved and made navigable from Newbury to Reading in 1715, and throughout the eighteenth century shared in the growing prosperity of Reading, sending grain, malt and the produce of the countryside by river. In 1810 the Kennet and Avon canal was opened from Newbury to Bath, providing a through route by water from London to Bristol. Newbury became an inland port of some importance: boat-building yards were established, and with cheap water transport east and west a number of foundries and engineering enterprises flourished. In 1800 a Newbury man, William Plenty, devised a new type of iron plough which became much sought after and found a ready market. Plenty was an ingenious man, for he turned from agricultural engineering to boat building and in 1816 invented a lifeboat that so impressed the Elder Brethren of Trinity House that it was adopted as their standard life-saving vessel, and can fairly be regarded as the prototype of all modern lifeboats. Rather improbably this first of modern life-boats capable of standing up to appalling weather at sea underwent her trials on the gentle Kennet. The firm which William Plenty founded, Plenty and Sons, is still in business as marine engineers. The pioneering spirit of its founder was shown again later in the nineteenth century when it undertook to build engines for Nordenfelt's submarines. Newbury may be an inland town, but its marine enterprise is considerable, and it has been extended to the air. Another of its engineering firms, Elliots of Newbury, builds light aircraft, gliders and sail-planes, and exports them all over the world. The economic stimulus given to the town by the canal has survived the passing of the canal: Newbury's development is a remarkable example of vigorous local enterprise. Horse-racing has helped to make its name known widely. The Downs are racing country, their open slopes and firm chalk turf providing wonderful training gallops. Newbury is the capital of Wessex racing, and for centuries men have met to wager on horses there. The present racecourse was opened in 1905.

Because of its strategical position, Newbury has been fought over more than almost any other town in Britain. An early Norman castle there was held for Matilda in the wars between Stephen and Matilda, but less successfully than Wallingford, for it was taken by Stephen after a siege lasting for two months. Nothing of this castle remains. It was on the river, on the site that later became

Newbury's wharf, and which is now a bus station – its stones have gone into many of the town's older buildings. In the fourteenth and early fifteenth centuries Newbury was held by the Mortimers, but on the death without issue of Edmund Mortimer, Earl of March in 1425, Newbury went to his nephew Richard, Duke of York, the father of Edward IV. This threw Newbury into the Yorkist camp in the Wars of the Roses and in 1460 the town was taken by Lancastrian supporters. Richard was killed at Wakefield, but in 1461 his son Edward came to the throne, and the lordship and manorial rights of Newbury went to the Crown. They remained with the Crown until 1627, when Charles I sold them to the mayor and corporation. While Newbury was a Crown possession, its revenues were often used to provide income for Queens. Henry VIII granted them to Anne Boleyn and Jane Seymour in turn, and James I gave them to Anne of Denmark.

Two major engagements were fought at Newbury during the Civil War. The first battle of Newbury, fought to the south-west of the town between Enborne and Wash Hill on 20 September 1643 embodies one of the 'ifs' of history – it just might have been decisive, winning the war for Charles I. The West of England on the whole was staunchly Royalist, and in the summer of 1643 Charles was doing well there. Essex held Reading for Parliament, but Charles held Oxford and Bristol, and a Royalist force invested Gloucester. Essex moved west from Reading to relieve Gloucester, and Charles had a chance of cutting him off from London. Having reached Cirencester Essex realized his danger, and began to retreat. A Royalist force from Oxford moved quickly, via Faringdon and Wantage. They met at Newbury. A bitter fight began at dawn on 20 September and lasted all day. Casualties were heavy on both sides – all told, some 6,000 men died in this battle. By nightfall neither side had made much progress. Charles held Newbury, but had been unable to break the Parliamentary Army. Essex had been equally unable to break the strength of the Royalists. In fact, Essex was in the worse position: he was without supplies. Most of his men had no food, and a determined Royalist attack at dawn on 21 September would probably have broken him. It never came. Both armies were dispirited by their losses, the Royalists were short of powder, and some excellent rumour-mongering by Parliament men convinced the King that Essex had strong reserves to bring into the struggle (he did not). During the night of 20–21 September the Royalists slipped back to Oxford, and Essex was left with a clear route to London.

There were many tragedies that September day at Newbury. The most poignant, recorded movingly by Clarendon, was the death, almost the suicide, of

Lucius Cary, Viscount Falkland, at the age of thirty-three. Cary, whose home was at Great Tew, where his body was taken after the battle, was the romantic epitome of a cavalier – poet, scholar, handsome, brave. He was one of the ablest men of his generation, and he hated the civil war. Loyalty made it unthinkable for him not to fight for his King, but he had many friends on the Parliamentary side. At Newbury he was depressed and ill, and as he had no particular command he was urged to stay away from the battle. He refused. At a critical moment when a squadron of Royalist cavalry was exposed to merciless fire from a gap in a hedge, he rode into the gap alone and was shot down. There are memorials to him at Newbury and at Great Tew.

The second battle of Newbury was fought on 27 October 1644. The situation then was very different for the Royalists. They had met disaster at Marston Moor in the north, and their cause generally was going badly. The West country was still loyal, and there was a brief renewal of hope when Essex and the Parliamentary Army were trapped in Cornwall. Essex got away by sea, and the army surrendered. Charles was on his way back to Oxford and this time it was the Parliamentary generals who decided to try to cut his route. The Royalists were north-west of Newbury, around Speen and Donnington, and a powerful Parliamentary force, about 20,000 strong, under the Earl of Manchester, Sir William Waters and Cromwell, assembled at Cold Ash and Clay Hill, east of the Newbury–Abingdon road. The Royalists were outnumbered about two to one. Parliamentary tactics were to outflank the Royalists by crossing the Abingdon road to the north at Chieveley and to attack the positions at Speen and Donnington from Bexford and Wickham Heath, in the north-west, as well as from Clay Hill to the east. It didn't work. The Earl of Manchester seems to have been strangely half-hearted, and the outnumbered Royalists fought with such gallantry that although the Roundheads entered Speen, they were unable to dislodge the Royalists from their main positions at Donnington Castle and Shaw House. Charles and his Army got away in the night.

When the Royalist Army escaped, Sir John Boys was left behind to hold Donnington Castle. He ignored alike both threats and inducements to surrender. The Roundheads brought up heavy siege guns, and sent a message to Sir John telling him that unless he gave in, the castle would be blown to bits around him. Sir John sent back a message observing that he felt no obligation to rebuild the castle, but that with God's help he would hold the ground it stood on. He was relieved for a time by a Royalist expedition from Oxford, but again besieged when the expedition withdrew. He held the castle until almost the end of the Civil War, surrendering only when he received direct orders from King Charles to do so, just before the King himself surrendered. That was in April, 1646, a year and a half after he had been left behind to hold Donnington for his King. It is pleasing to record that this tough old Cavalier and the survivors of his band were permitted to march out with all the honours of war.

North of the Kennet, the next considerable tributary of the Thames on the Berkshire bank is the Pang. This delectable chalk river apparently rises at about the 350 ft contour of the Berkshire Downs a little south of Compton, but it is also fed by springs from higher ground to the north-west. Their water mostly flows off underground, but may appear as a brook after heavy rain. The visible Pang flows south of Hampstead Norris and Frilsham, and at this stage of its course it looks like becoming a tributary of the Kennet rather than of the Thames. But within three miles of the Kennet it is stopped by the high ground of Bucklebury Common, and so turns east. Again it meets high ground, and is gradually diverted north to join the Thames at Pangbourne. Its course is thus nearly a circle, enclosing a pretty countryside of wooded hills around Ashampstead, Basildon and Bradfield. It is a maze of lanes, and easy to get lost in.

The Romans knew and liked this countryside, as, indeed, have all settlers to come into the region from prehistoric times. There are ancient earthworks to the north-east of Ashampstead; and between Basildon and Streatley; a Belgic cremation urn turned up at Beenham, and a sword of the Bronze Age at Bucklebury; traces of Roman occupation have been found at Basildon, Upper Bucklebury, and Pangbourne. It is as attractive today, but not so much now for the reasons that brought its earlier settlers – the livelihoods to be won from its woods and sheltered fields. Being near to Reading, and with access to London by the Western Region's main line, it provides country living for people who work in cities. Pangbourne, described as 'a pretty riverside village' when F. G. Brabant wrote of it in 1911, is now a town.

At Pangbourne you can suddenly smell the sea, for the Thames here has sent generations of officers to the Royal Navy and the Merchant Navy. Pangbourne Nautical College was established in 1917 by Sir Thomas Lane Devitt and his son Philip (later Sir Philip) of the great nineteenth-century line of sailing ships known as Devitt and Moore – the firm went on owning sailing ships until 1921. In 1894 their *Harbinger* took part in a famous race from Melbourne against *Parthenope*. They sighted each other off Cape Horn, and after sailing across the world met again at the mouth of the Channel. They raced up-channel together and reached Dungeness pretty well neck and neck. There, tugs were waiting for them. *Harbinger* got her tow rope on board first and was towed past Dover just ahead of *Parthenope* to win. *Harbinger* was the first of two ships (the other was

168

Devitt and Moore's *Hesperus*) to be used for the Ocean Training Scheme for Merchant Navy cadets, started by Sir Thomas Devitt and Lord Brassey in 1890. This scheme was a great improvement on the haphazard system of training Merchant Navy officers by apprenticeship, but it had no land-school for giving boys a preliminary training before going to sea. At the most critical period of the First World War, Sir Thomas and his son bought a big country house at Pangbourne with grounds of about 100 acres for such a school: at such a time, this was an act of great faith in Britain's seapower. In the half-century since 1917 their nautical college has expanded greatly, and now has grounds of some 230 acres around Pangbourne, and a fine frontage on the river, with boathouses, a slipway and a shipwright's workshop. Pangbourne cadets go into the Royal Navy as well as the Merchant Navy, and many distinguished officers of both the Royal and the Merchant Navies first learned boat handling on the Thames. Although specializing in schooling for the sea, Pangbourne has never attempted to force any boy to go to sea – indeed, one of the primary aims of its founders was to ensure as far as possible that no boy should go to sea just because he was bitten by a youthful romance for seafaring, but only if he really wanted to make seafaring his career. From the start the college has maintained a high standard of general education, so that if a boy does not want to go to sea he is well fitted for some other job. So Pangbourne, while giving boys an understanding of the comradeship and discipline of the sea, now launches them on as many different courses in life as any other school. Times change, and many more nowadays than in the past can go to universities if they want to. Standards of education generally are higher than they were when the Nautical College was founded, and shipping companies can draw their future officers from a wider field. To meet changed needs, the name of the school was changed in 1968 from The Nautical College, Pangbourne, to Pangbourne College. The world has changed much since cadets went to school at sea in *Harbinger* and *Hesperus*: but the qualities fostered by their tradition, which Pangbourne College exists to sustain, are not less needed.

Pangbourne has another rather special place in the history of the Thames. Kenneth Grahame, who wrote *The Wind in the Willows*, lived there.

The Ock, which waters a major valley of its own in the Vale of the White Horse, is unusual among rivers in having no town along its whole length. It rises at Little Coxwell, just south of Faringdon, and flows between the Berkshire Downs and the ridge of high land from Faringdon to Cumnor. Its only town is Abingdon, which properly belongs to the Thames, though since it stands at the confluence of Ock and Thames, the Ock may claim a share in it. This river flows through some of the loneliest and loveliest countryside in England. Main roads run north and south of the Vale, and although Brunel chose it for the line of his Great Western Railway from Didcot to Swindon, the expresses go through without stopping: there used to be a few little stations where slow trains stopped, but these have been abandoned, and there is now no halt between Didcot and Swindon.

It is a countryside of villages, and if you look at a good relief map, you will see why: most of the Ock valley is really a marsh, criss-crossed by brooks and streamlets. Villages have sprung up where islands of firm ground reinforced by ledges of local ragstone provide patches of hard standing in the marsh. Their names say precisely what they are – fords or marsh islands. Stanford-in-the-Vale, Lyford, Garford, Frilford and all fording places, Goosey, Pusey, Charney, East and West Hanney are all islands, their names embodying the Saxon -ey suffix that means 'island'. Five thousand years of farming from Neolithic times have changed the matted undergrowth of the marshlands to open fields edged with lines of willows along the streams, with occasional great elms to give shade; as long an effort of digging and clearing drainage ditches has changed the appearance of the marsh to more stable English landscape. But the marsh remains only just under the skin of the land: if you drive from Abingdon or Oxford to Wantage after heavy rain it is wise to be alert for flood warning notices on the roads, and to act on them.

Enriched by the silt of the Ock and its many streamlets, the Vale of the White Horse is rich farming country, once famous for its cheeses and the Berkshire pig, still one of the great food-growing areas of England. The teams of Shire horses pulling Mr Plenty's improved Newbury plough have been replaced by tractors, but it is still horse country, with a mare and foal grazing in most farm paddocks, and someone to give riding lessons in every village. Where the land rises to the Berkshire Downs you meet the racing stables, and see strings of beautiful horses out for exercise.

In the west of the Vale, the north face of the Downs presents the huge escarpment of Whitehorse Hill and Uffington Castle, with the curiously flat-topped Dragon Hill a little below them. Uffington Castle is a magnificent Iron Age hill fort, the earthworks on its summit enclosing some 82 acres in the shape of a gigantic spade-head. The entrance to the fortified enclosure is on the west, and on the north-west slope of the hill the outline of a splendid galloping horse is cut in the chalk. This huge hill figure is some 360 ft long by 130 ft high. It is so big that you need to be some miles away to see it properly: there is a good view from the Swindon–Wantage road (B4507) and a better one from the Great Western main line approaching Swindon. Whitehorse Hill is perhaps the best site in England for flying kites. There is nearly always a wind there, with a grand lift in it, and the bare chalk Downs, with their springy turf, are the best of all places for a boy to run with the string of a kite in his hand.

These Downs are enmeshed in legend. No one knows who cut the White Horse, or even when it was cut. The Ministry of Works, in whose care it now is, has a notice suggesting that it was a tribal emblem of the Dobunni, and that it was cut around the 1st century A.D. It may be so: it may be 1,000 years older; there is nothing in the chalk to tell, nothing in the picture to be carbon-dated. The artistry is astonishing: to conceive the picture as a whole the artist would need to stand miles away, yet the detail of the spirited animal is perfect. Grass encroaches slowly on the outline cut in the chalk, and the horse has survived by periodic 'scouring', when the turf is cut back to a clean edge again. 'The scouring of the White Horse' used to be an occasion of great local festival in the Vale, but nowadays it is a matter for experts of the Ministry. The horse is said to be eating his way slowly uphill – 'scourings' over the centuries, perhaps have sent the line slightly uphill.

Below the horse is a steep chine called The Manger, and on the other side of this is the flat-topped Dragon Hill. Here traditionally St George is said to have killed his dragon.

> For war, for water, or for better grain
> A thousand generations trod this way.
>   Warmed by the sun, shivering in the rain –
> But progress for mankind, or so they say.

The Ridgeway, the oldest trackway in Britain, follows the summit of the Downs here, and a mile or so to the west of Whitehorse Hill is the chambered long barrow of Wayland's Smithy. This has already been described in Chapter 2. It goes back at least 3,000 years before the Saxon Wayland Smith was heard of in Britain, but it is in keeping with the Ridgeway that a divine smith should have a dwelling there to give a hand to travellers: leave your horse, with a coin on the stone at the entrance (the legend goes) and come back to find him shod. The Ridgeway is a strange green road. You cannot walk it without being conscious of the generations of human beings who have walked it from Old Stone Age times, of women carrying whimpering children, of men alert for enemies or dangerous beasts, a trail moving through millennia to inhabit Britain.

A mile and a half to the east of Whitehorse Hill is Blowing Stone Hill. In the garden of a cottage here is the Blowing Stone, a large block of sarsen with holes in it. If you blow through one of the holes (and blow hard enough) you can get a loud trumpet note from it. King Alfred is said to have 'blown' the stone to rally his men in critical encounters with the Danes. Certainly there have been many unrecorded battles on these hillsides, for the skeletons of many men killed in battle have been turned up by the plough. Whether Alfred fought any engagements with Danes here no one can say. The stone is far older than Alfred, and it was here in his time.

The chief settlement of the western vale is Wantage, strategically well-placed where the lower of the ancient trackways, the Icknield Way, crosses the Letcombe Brook. The brook is a tributary of the Ock, and in its upper reaches is distinguished for its watercress.

The first travellers in prehistoric Britain followed the Ridgeway, through the open country of the high downs. It was good walking, with good visibility for approaching enemies, but, being above the spring-line, water was a problem always: there would be puddles in the chalk after rain, perhaps occasional dew-ponds, but mostly you had either the heavy burden of carrying water in skins, or you had to come down from the hills when you needed a drink. If you were driving cattle, this was particularly hard. As time went on, therefore, our remote forbears devised a lower route, roughly parallel with the Ridgeway, but on the lower slopes of the Downs, where there was water to be had. This is the Icknield Way, the second oldest road in Britain, but with a name far older than the descriptive English of the first – the Icknield Way has kept its ancient title, a name so old that it has no known derivation. 'Icknield' is neither Latin nor Saxon, and (like the name Thames) may embody the speech of Beaker or Neolithic folk. The modern Portway leading west from Wantage is part of the Icknield Way: it was paved and improved by the Romans.

The Romans had a post or settlement of some sort at Wantage, though nothing is known of it: Roman coins and pottery have been turned up, there was Roman work on the Portway, and there was a Roman villa between East and West Challow, two miles to the west of the modern town. Roman Wantage is nameless: 'Wantage' is held to be Saxon, said to derive from 'Waneting', meaning a stream that comes and goes, that does not flow all the year round.

Wantage was certainly an early Saxon settlement and of major importance in the original Kingdom of Wessex, for the kings of Wessex had a house or palace there. Alfred the Great was born at Wantage in 849, and his statue, by Count Gleichen, adorns the market place. It is an imposing affair, considerably larger than life, with an inscription:

ALFRED THE GREAT

The West Saxon King, born at Wantage, A.D. 849
Alfred found learning dead,
And he restored it.
Education neglected,
And he revived it.
The laws powerless,
And he gave them force.
The Church debased,
And he raised it.
The land ravaged by a fearful enemy
From which he delivered it.
Alfred's name will live as long as mankind shall respect the past.

The statue, unveiled by Edward, Prince of Wales (later Edward VII) in 1877, was the idea of Colonel Loyd-Lindsay V.C., of Lockinge (later Lord Wantage) who opened a subscription list for it. Money did not exactly flow in, and the bulk of the cost was met by the Colonel himself – fortunately he was a rich man as well as a distinguished soldier. (He won the V.C. at Alma, in the Crimea, and married the daughter of a wealthy banker, who provided the Lockinge Estate as a wedding present. He was a considerable benefactor to Wantage.) The unveiling ceremony, attended by the Princess of Wales (Queen Alexandra) as well as the Prince, was somewhat marred by the fact that it poured with rain – the heavy July rain that the region produced again to make the summer floods of 1968. A more cheerful occasion was the celebration a few decades earlier of the millenary of Alfred's birth in 1849. This was the idea of Martin Tupper, the Victorian poet, who tried to get Queen Victoria to attend, but she declined politely. Large crowds, however, enjoyed an ox-roasting and quantities of free beer, as well as a song, composed for the occasion by Tupper, which went:

Alfred for ever! Today he was born,
Daystar of England, to herald her morn.

Nothing remains of the Saxon palace of Wantage. Tradition (which can probably be respected here) places it at Belmont, on high ground to the north-west of the centre of the present town.

The Great Western Railway never quite got to Wantage, although it did have a station (now closed) called Wantage Road, nearly two miles from the town. This was opened in 1863 and connected to the town by a horse-drawn tram. In 1876 the horse was replaced by a steam locomotive, but the engine was less successful than the horse in tackling the rather steep gradient where the road climbs into Wantage. In 1878 the last of a series of unsatisfactory engines was replaced by the famous Jane (officially named Shannon, but always called Jane), a George England Well Tank Locomotive, bought secondhand. Jane, though not infrequently derailed, pulled the Wantage tram from Wantage Town to Wantage Road until 1946, her last task being to pull up the line itself when it was closed – she pulled up each length of line behind her as she moved forward to the next. After living in a shed for many years she was taken to Didcot for restoration work in 1969, and if the money can be raised she will one day have a permanent home in a small museum of her own at Wantage.

The Wilts and Berks Canal, begun in 1796 and opened for its whole length in 1810, had a far more intimate connection with the life of Wantage than the somewhat stand-offish railway. The canal, linking the Kennet and Avon at Semington, near Bradford-on-Avon, with the Thames at Abingdon, was brought to the Wharf, in the heart of Wantage, by a short branch, three-quarters of a mile long, from the main line of the canal between East Challow and Grove. For half a century it was the main artery of economic life for Wantage, and continued to be important to the end of the nineteenth century. It was closed – not because it had ceased to be of value, but because railway development in Britain was crippling all canals – in 1906. The canal had a number of indirect social effects which were at least as important as its direct economic bearing on the life of the district. In the early part of the last century the unruly behaviour of the 'navigators' (the 'navvies' employed to dig the canal) gave Wantage a bad name: so bad that the place came to be known as Black Wantage, and it was alleged to be the hideout of criminals from London as well as local ne'er-do-wells. Local administration was ill-fitted to deal with the situation. Wantage was not a borough, but still nominally subject to a Lord of the Manor, the income from whose fees and quit-rents had become trivial, and whose courts had passed into history. The vicar – the other source of natural authority – was an absentee: the living of Wantage in the early nineteenth century was a perquisite of the Dean of St George's, Windsor, who enjoyed the (considerable) revenues of the parish and appointed an underling to look after the services. It is scarcely surprising that non-conformity flourished. The people of Wantage achieved their own salvation by self-help. In 1828 a body of citizens, led by a local lawyer, secured the Wantage Improvement Act, authorizing the appointment of 'respectable citizens' as Commissioners to take on many of the duties now performed by local councils as a matter of course – town drainage, street lighting, road improvement, police services (then called 'a watch') and the like. The Commissioners did their job well, and in 1870 bought the manorial rights from the then owner for £1,200. The income from manorial dues at the time of this purchase was £48 15s. 3d., but what was of real importance was that the Commissioners acquired for the town itself all rights over the market and certain residual freeholds which ultimately were of great benefit to the town.

The decline of the Manor was one of the reasons for the ability of so many early Victorian industrialists to get away with what would now be regarded as sheer social robbery, and it is well illustrated at Wantage. When Domesday Book was compiled the Manor of Wantage was a great possession, and the Lord had more or less complete control of the economic life of his tenants; in return, he was responsible for ensuring that the fabric of life was kept in working order. In the twelfth century the Manor of Wantage was granted to the Fitzwarrens, who held it for some 500 years, until the family died out in the seventeenth century. After this the manorial rights passed by purchase to a number of different individuals. By the nineteenth century the rights were an anachronism, and the income vestigial. In 1849 the rights were held by a London merchant, one Sir Henry Martin. When asked by the Town Commissioners to help with improvements to the Town Hall, he replied, 'What I derive from the somewhat pompous-sounding title of Lord of the Manor is too inconsiderable to justify me in involving myself.'*

Although manorial rights had declined in value and the duties that went with them were often ignored, the legal rights remained, to block the emergence of alternative local authority. Boroughs with charters, like Abingdon, Newbury and Wallingford, did not have this problem. Wantage, an important market town and with a number of local industries, began the nineteenth century with no administration but a medieval hangover. The citizens who promoted (at their own expense) the Improvement Act and secured the appointment of Town Commissioners in 1825 acted with foresight and remarkable public spirit.

The Church, which also began the nineteenth century with a number of medieval anachronisms, tidied itself up as the century proceeded. Livings were gradually detached from absentee holders, and the way opened for the devoted parish clergy, whose work meant so much to later Victorian society. In Wantage, the last of the absentee vicars was replaced in 1847 by the saintly William John Butler, who stayed for 33 years until 1880, when he became Dean of Lincoln.

* Kathleen Phillip, *Victorian Wantage*.

Butler found the vicarage all-but uninhabitable, the thirteenth-century parish church in a dreadful state of decay, and much (understandable) hostility in the town to the vicar. He was a High Churchman, and in a community where non-conformity was strong, this did not help – whitewashed notices demanding 'No popery' appeared frequently on walls. By personality and sheer saintliness he overcame all opposition, rebuilt the church, and left his most enduring memorial in the 'Wantage Sisters', now, perhaps, the best known Anglican Sisterhood in the world. The Sisterhood, the Community of St Mary the Virgin, was inspired by Butler, and founded by his disciple, Elizabeth Lockhart. Its first home was a cottage in Newbury Street, Wantage, and the first Sisters made it their job to go round Wantage very early in the morning to clean 'No popery' scribblings off walls. The Convent of the Sisterhood in Faringdon Road was begun in 1855, the chapel built in 1858, and the refectory added in 1866. A home for novices was built in 1878, and another, larger chapel in 1887. The girls' boarding school run by the Sisterhood, St Mary's, Wantage, is mainly housed in a modern building in Newbury Street, put up in 1962, but this incorporates the original school built in 1874, and enlarged at various times since. The Sisterhood now maintains many other schools and missions, in India and Africa as well as in Britain.

Wantage came into being as a settlement commanding cross routes at the western end of the Vale of the White Horse and providing a local market for the produce of the Vale. It remains so, although the motor-car is an uneasy user of its narrow streets, and the mass of traffic, where A338 from Oxford to Salisbury crosses A417 from Cirencester to the Thames at Streatley and the Goring Gap, sometimes seems unendurable. The canal more than the railway widened Wantage's economic hinterland, bringing cheap Somerset coal to local agricultural engineering works, and providing cheap transport for their products. A machine for the manufacture of rotary screening and grading cylinders, used in threshing machines, malthouses and flour mills, was invented by Nalder and Nalder at East Challow in 1870, and gained first a national and then a world market. The machinery was later adapted to the processing of cocoa and coffee beans. At Letcombe Regis on the south-western outskirts of Wantage, the Agricultural Research Council has its radio-biological laboratory, where the effects of atomic fall-out on milk and food plants are kept constantly under review. Just to the south of the two Letcombes (Regis and Bassett) is the Iron Age earthwork of Letcombe Castle or Segsbury Camp, a wonderfully preserved, almost circular fortification enclosing some 26 acres. From the embankment there is a breath-taking view of the pastel-coloured patchwork of the downland countryside. It is a sombre thought that man's preoccupation with defence has

29. *The Ridgeway, among the oldest roads in Europe, still marches across the Downs. You may meet an occasional farm tractor, but it is beautiful walking country.*

30a. *Nuffield College, Oxford.*

30b. *New buildings in the Garden Quad of Balliol College, Oxford.*

31. *Two dovecots.*
a. *at Kelmscott, near Lechlade.*

b. *at Minster Lovell, Oxfordshire.*

32a. '. . . . Maidens who from distant hamlets come
To dance around the Fyfield elm in May.'
Matthew Arnold's elm is actually in Tubney. It was struck by lightning some years ago, but is still growing strongly.

32b. The line of the old Wilts and Berks Canal, filled in and long-disused, near Steventon, Berkshire.

affected this peaceful countryside from the Iron Age fortress to the atomic fears of the late twentieth century.

Wantage is the centre of a covey of 'spring line' villages, settlements that have developed along the spring line of the Downs, where there is water for man and his animals. Away from the main routes of modern commerce, the centuries have used them kindly, and they include some of the loveliest and least-spoiled villages of England. East Hendred is the home of the Eyston family, Roman Catholics who survived all the persecutions of the past and have held the manor for 500 years. The present owner, Mr Thomas More Eyston, is a descendant of St Thomas More. The Chapel of Hendred House, dedicated to St Armand and St John Baptist, has preserved the rites of the Old Catholics in England through the centuries. It has preserved, too, relics of the English Martyrs, St Thomas More and St John Fisher, the staff of St John Fisher and a drinking cup used by St Thomas More. The last Roman Catholic Bishop of Gloucester, James Brook, was rector of East Hendred in 1545. The Letcombes, Regis and Bassett, have been among the pleasanter dwelling places of man from prehistoric times. The Letcombe Brook here is an exquisite chalk stream, producing magnificent watercress: 'Bassett Cress' used to be one of the street cries of London. Thomas Hardy wrote *Jude the Obscure* while staying at Letcombe Regis. Swift wrote his 'Verses on Himself' at the rectory in Letcombe Bassett.

Childrey, lying just below the Icknield Way, now the Wantage–Swindon road (B4507), had a Saxon church early in the tenth century, and still has a beautiful thirteenth-century church built on the Saxon site. It has a rare leaden font, and some splendid brasses. Childrey was one of the early homes of the Fettiplace family, who endowed a chantry there, one of the specific duties of the Chantry priest being to conduct a school for children, and to teach in English. Wisely, the endowment of the Chantry was secured on land given to Queen's College, Oxford, and this preserved the endowment when chantries were dissolved, the priest becoming the village schoolmaster. This Fettiplace school at Childrey is generally considered to have been the first formally established village school in Britain. Childrey also possesses a charming duckpond.

9

Navigation

The Thames is navigable for almost its whole length, and, in theory, rights of navigation supersede all other rights. It is fitting that the first clear statement of rights of navigation on the river that brought the Saxons into the heart of England should have been promulgated by the last of the Saxon kings. In an ordinance on New Year's Day 1066 Edward the Confessor denounced the construction of mills, fish weirs or other works which might hinder navigation, and ordered that if any such hindrances did appear

> let these works be destroyed, the waters repaired, and the forfeit to the King not forgotten

F. S. Thacker, the leading authority on ancient charters relating to the Thames, is doubtful of the authenticity of Edward the Confessor's proclamation, because the King died on 5 January, 1066 and was on his deathbed at the supposed date of the edict. This seems not a particularly good reason for doubt. Kings reign until they are dead, and the King's Government must go on whether the monarch is dying or in the best of health. No king has ever written, or even read, every word that is issued in his name. The promulgation is entirely reasonable. There has been traffic on the Thames from time immemorial, and we know from the chronicles of Abingdon Abbey that commercial barge traffic was important in the eleventh century. The King's edict was a necessary protection, and it related not only to the Thames but to all the so-called 'royal rivers', Thames, Trent, Ouse and Severn, which are the four main navigable rivers of England.

Edward the Confessor's charter, authentic or not, embodied a tradition of the rights of navigation over everything else that has been held always. The Saxon edict was re-enacted in a charter of which there can be no possible doubt by Richard I in 1197. By this the King declared:

> Know ye all that we, for the health of our soul, our father's soul, and all our ancestors' souls, and also for the common weal of our City of London, and of all our realm, have granted and steadfastly commanded that all weirs that are in the Thames be removed, wheresoever they shall be within the Thames.

Richard's charter granted (rather vaguely) the control and supervision of the Thames to the Corporation of the City of London, a supervision which the City exercised in greater or less degree for the next 660 years. After a long dispute with the Crown sparked off by the proposal to build the Victoria Embankment, the City's rights were formally extinguished by an Act of 1857.

The City of London's jurisdiction was originally accepted as covering the whole river, from its source to Yantlet Creek, just above its confluence with the Medway. Until the Act of 1857 the City's claim to rights over the whole river was never formally abandoned, although in practice they were held to extend from Staines to Yantlet Creek. Above Staines there was next to no effective supervision of anything until an Act of James I in 1605 appointed a commission to improve the navigation between Burcot (near Dorchester) and Oxford. Richard's charter was re-enacted by King John in 1215 and rights of navigation, again over the whole river, were written into Magna Carta in a clause (No 23) which states

> All weirs shall be utterly put down by Thames and Medway . . . unless by the sea coasts.

The legal position is, or should be, clear. But it was one thing for medieval monarchs to issue edicts: it was quite another matter to get them carried out. The history of navigation on the Thames is a record of endless struggles between the navigators and local riparian interests, which regarded the river principally as a source of fish, of water-power to drive mills, and as a convenient sewer. Almost until this century, local landowners, being mostly stronger in local matters than any central authority, usually won.

The charters themselves were not precise. What is a 'weir'? There are a dozen different sorts. The Latin clause in Magna Carta reads, *Omnes kidelli deponantur* . . . and 'all weirs shall be put down' is a fair translation. But a kidel ('kiddle' in the modern Oxford dictionary), is also a particular kind of weir: the word is normally used only of fish-weirs, traps of stakes and brushwood set across rivers to catch fish. Such weirs are a great nuisance to boats, but they are not usually very permanent structures, and an energetic barge crew could be expected to demolish them. What about the much more permanent weirs controlling water to drive mills, or those weirs to impound water over shallows which are a necessary assistance to navigation? Bargemen and landowners have argued about the meaning of 'weir' for seven centuries.

The use of rivers as sewers, an appalling problem on the Thames in the nineteenth century, and still a defilement of English life in many places, reflects merely national laziness and corporate selfishness, but fishing and the use of water power are as legitimate demands upon a river as navigation. For most of its history the Thames has been an important source of food for those who dwelt by it: until the defilements of growing population in riverside towns and early industrialization the Thames was rich in salmon, and there were trout, eels, mussels and crayfish to be had in plenty. There are no longer salmon in the Thames, but there are still trout in its upper reaches. Eels, freshwater mussels and crayfish helped to ensure the survival of early man in the Upper Thames region, and were considered delicacies until the wages of the twentieth century turned people's thoughts to imported luxuries from supermarkets. The Fettiplaces, at Swinbrook, had a special pond for fattening freshwater mussels from the Windrush. Crayfish were commonly eaten round Oxford until the First World War. They are like small lobsters, and they still flourish in the Ock at the bottom of my garden. Members of the angling clubs which abound on the Upper Thames and its tributaries no longer fish of necessity, but the fisherman has, and has always had, as proper a place on the river as any man in a boat.

Fishing as such is not necessarily an impediment to navigation, but commercial fishing, unless rigidly controlled, may easily become so. The weirs denounced by the Saxon and Norman kings are an obvious example, and they are more damaging to a river than as hindrance to navigation alone. Fish-weirs on the Thames entrapped enormous quantities of fry, sold by the bushel as pig-food. This was good business for the owner of the weir, but wastefully destructive of fish-life. A petition to Henry IV in 1402 described the taking of small fish for *porcs à manger* (as the Norman French put it) as against the Will of God, as well as to the undoing of the petitioners.

The Crown was usually sympathetic to such pleas, and issued another order against weirs. Henry VI was terse with an edict declaring 'No man shall fasten nets to anything over rivers', and Edward IV made a formidable pronouncement ordering the full observance of Magna Carta's prohibition of weirs, threatening fines of 100 marks on the owner of every weir which was not removed within three months, with an extra 100 marks a month for disobedience after that, and adding for good measure that breakers of the ordinance would also attract an apostolic curse. None of this did much good. The law was occasionally invoked and fish-weirs destroyed, but they seemed always to come back. The trouble was that fishing rights were property rights, the fish were a valuable source of income to the owner, and local magnates were generally too powerful to be interfered with. Still, the principle was maintained, and since men have to live together it became the practice not to put weirs or nets across the whole river, but to leave a gap through which boats could pass.

Millers were a far worse hazard to navigation, because they interfered with the flow of the stream, building weirs to impound the river to keep up a head of water for their mills, and diverting water as they wanted to their own millstreams. And the millers were a powerful group. Mill rights normally belonged to the Lord of the Manor, or to great religious foundations like Abingdon Abbey, and all acted much as they liked. Moreover, mill rights and fishing rights often went together, and the mill-weir might have fish-traps attached to it, making it of still greater value to the owner of the rights and his tenants.

But weirs can assist navigation, as well as impede it. The Thames has a fairly gentle fall, averaging some 1 ft 5 ins a mile, but this is not, of course, an even fall, and there are extensive shallows. When the Saxons took their galleys up the Thames they dealt with shallows as they came, abandoning stranded boats to raid inland, or hauling them over shallows by sheer manpower. Patience, though it might mean waiting for a month or two, would usually bring enough water after heavy rain to negotiate a shallow patch. Man's activities in the way of weirs and diverting water to mills tended to make shallow patches worse, and to keep them permanently shallow. The weirs, however, also offered a means of overcoming shallows. If water was impounded it would increase in depth above the weir, if a considerable head of water were then let loose by drawing the weir, it would surge down the river giving a temporary increase in depth until the surge was spent. Weirs were the forerunners of locks, and the so called 'flash lock' is no more than a weir with a movable paddle or gate which can be opened to let through a 'flash' of water. Boats can go through with a 'flash' – heroic (and dangerous) navigation downstream, a bit like shooting a waterfall; brutal haulage upstream, and also needing careful timing, for the force of the 'flash' to subside, and yet leave enough water to cover shallows and the sill of the weir. The process can be helped by setting rollers in the bed of the stream, and by having a winch above the weir.

As barge-traffic grew with the economic development of the Upper Thames region, the millers came to play a dominant part in it. They controlled the weirs which provided the all important 'flashes', and barges proceeded at their pleasure. Naturally they charged, and sometimes extortionately, for 'making a flash'. As naturally, relations between bargemen and millers were normally hostile.

But the millers did not have things all their own way. The law requiring rights of navigation might be vague and weakly enforced, but it was still the law. To some extent the millers, particularly the bigger millers, needed barges to bring corn and take away their flour. And while the miller might be locally more powerful than the master of a humble barge, the barge provided an essential service for the merchants whose goods it carried, and the merchants might have the ear of King or Parliament.

It was mercantile pressure, partly from London, partly from Oxford, backed by the University of Oxford, which led to the first major attempt to regulate navigation on the upper river. Below Staines, where the London Stone marks the traditional boundary of their active authority, the Lord Mayor and Corporation of London kept a more or less vigilant eye on things, and authority was near enough at hand to act against the grosser abuses of navigational rights. The City of London had nominal jurisdiction over the upper reaches, but through the Middle Ages these were too remote to be of much concern. With the mercantile expansion of the Tudors, and the growth of Oxford, the situation changed. Sea-coal became an important commodity, and it was shipped up-river in barges by London coal merchants, and sold from the wharves in the riverside towns. Both London and local merchants, and, indeed, the more substantial householders who could afford to buy coal, were at one in wanting coal to move freely. Coal was not, of course, the only trade to which the river was important. There was a substantial increase in mercantile activity generally, and with the growth of London the grain and cheeses from the Upper Thames meant food for the populace and money for the London shopkeepers.

In the sixteenth century the Thames was reasonably navigable to Burcot Wharf (Dorchester), and again from Oxford to well above Lechlade. But the stretch from Burcot to Oxford via Clifton Hampden, Sutton Courtenay and Abingdon was full of shallows and extremely bad: so bad that cargoes from Oxford had frequently to be unloaded at Burcot and taken on by cart, a difficult journey by sixteenth-century roads, adding substantially to the cost of goods in Oxford. The troubles of this stretch of river were partly natural, partly brought about by the fiddling with the river's course by the monks of Abingdon in the eleventh century. The natural hazard is the rock bed of the Thames at Clifton, the only place in its whole length where the river flows over hard rock and not over gravel or mud. The eleventh-century engineering at Abingdon divided the stream into two branches, weakening the scouring force of the natural river and causing extensive silting.

In 1605 mercantile interests secured an Act for the improvement of this stretch of river. The Act created a body of Commissioners to see to the improvements, but neglected to give them any powers. In 1623 it was repealed, and replaced by a much more sensible Act. This instructed the Lord Chancellor to appoint four representatives of the University of Oxford and four from the City of Oxford to form a Commission to make the river navigable. The Commissioners were specifically empowered to construct locks, to provide a towpath, and to instal winches or other engines at such places as they might deem expedient. The works were to be financed by levies on the University and City of Oxford, and the Commissioners were also given powers to make by-laws and to fix freight rates.

The Commissioners took their job seriously. The University had just been left a legacy of 2,000 marks, and it was decided to apply this money at once to river improvements, recovering it from wharfage dues. (The mark, which was still used in seventeenth-century book-keeping, was two-thirds of a pound sterling, or 13s. 4d. It is impossible to make any exact comparison between the value of money in the seventeenth century and today's value but the purchasing power of the University's 2,000 marks then would be not less than that of £50,000 in 1969, possibly more.) The first use the Commissioners made of their money was to build three locks, at Iffley, Sandford and Abingdon. These were the first modern locks, pound-locks as distinct from flash-locks, on the Thames.*

The pound-lock is one of the most ingenious works of man. It does not seem to have been known to the Romans, though it does seem to have made its first appearance in Europe in Italy: the Chinese are believed to have had it centuries before it came to Europe. It is a simple and extremely efficient way of enabling boats to go uphill, or to go downhill without difficulty or danger. Instead of releasing a head of water by a 'flash' and allowing it to dissipate itself over a whole river, the pound-lock merely impounds enough water to enable a boat to float level with the river above the lock-gates. Going upstream (uphill) a boat enters

---

* But not the first in England. John Trew constructed a pound-lock on the Exeter Ship Canal in 1564.

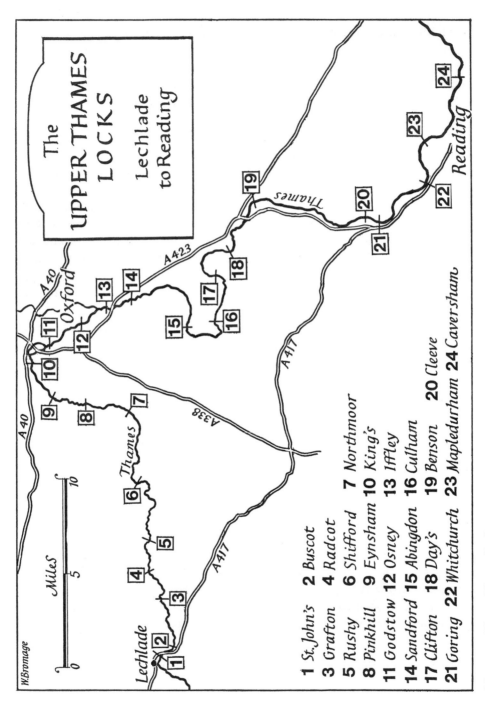

The
UPPER THAMES
LOCKS
Lechlade
to Reading

W.Bromage

Miles
0   5   10

Lechlade

Thames

Oxford
A40
A423
A40
A338
A417
A417

Thames

Reading

1 St.John's 2 Buscot
3 Grafton 4 Radcot
5 Rushy 6 Shifford 7 Northmoor
8 Pinkhill 9 Eynsham 10 King's
11 Godstow 12 Osney 13 Iffley
14 Sandford 15 Abingdon 16 Culham
17 Clifton 18 Day's 19 Benson 20 Cleeve
21 Goring 22 Whitchurch 23 Mapledurham 24 Caversham

Map 12 *Upper Thames Locks.*

the lock, and gates are closed behind it. Similar stout gates at the up-river end of the lock are already closed, holding back the head of water from the upper river. When the boat has been made fast in the lock, an aperture in the up-river gates is opened by withdrawing a paddle, and water, held by the closed gates at the downstream end of the lock, flows in to raise the level to that of the upper river. The boat rises vertically with the water. When the lock is full, and there is no difference in level between the water in the lock and that above the up-river gates, the gates themselves are swung open, and the boat proceeds at the level of the upper river. Going downstream the procedure is reversed. A boat enters the full lock, the up-river gates are closed, and the water let off through paddles in the lower gates. The boat falls gently in the lock, and when its level is equal to that of the lower river, the lower gates are opened and it goes on its way downstream. This process is vastly more efficient than allowing a boat to be hurled through a weir by a 'flash', and it is economical with water: unlike the flash, which releases water impounded across the whole river, the pound-lock need be no wider than of convenient size for boats using the river, and it requires only a small fraction of the flow of the stream to fill it. Moreover, having been filled to enable a boat to go upstream it can be kept full, and the same water used to assist a boat to descend. Outside the lock, the weir or retaining wall built across the river to control the level can be left free to act as a waterfall, the stream simply lapping over it, with no waste of water, and no interference with the volume of water entering the lower section of river. Modern weirs beside locks are in fact a bit more complex than this, for they are used to control the flow of the stream itself, so that if the upper reaches are in spate their flow can be checked at the weirs, reducing the risk of downstream flooding. But no water is wasted, and the flow can be controlled to ensure that there is always adequate water for navigation in the lower reaches.

The Commissioners' work at Abingdon is particularly interesting, for they abandoned the navigational channel dug by the monks in the eleventh century, and restored the original course of the Thames along what had come to be called the Swift Ditch. This leaves the present stream a little below Nuneham railway bridge, and rejoins it at Culham, making an island of Andersey on the way. The Commissioners' lock was in the Swift Ditch, not on the site of the present Abingdon lock. Abingdon made no objection to this diversion of river traffic away from the town, for the stream below Abingdon bridge, where the town wharves were, was always navigable from Culham, kept so by the inflow of water from the tributary Ock. The re-opening of the Swift Ditch meant merely that Abingdon's wharves were on a branch stream a mile or so from Culham, and the improvement to navigation generally outweighed this slight inconvenience. The burgesses of Abingdon were, no doubt, also content that Oxford should pay for the improvements.

Charles I succeeded his father in 1625, and of all English sovereigns he had the keenest appreciation of the value of the Thames as a national waterway. He had a real love for the river, and in his happier days spent much time on it. He provided timber from his royal woods at Shotover, near Oxford, to assist the Commissioners with their improvements, and generally stimulated their activities. Until the Civil War the difficult Oxford–Burcot stretch of navigation was in better shape than it had ever been, and the whole length of the Thames more navigable than at any time in the past. The impetus did not survive the war. For the next 100 years the record of navigation on the Thames is a repetition of all the old complaints of obstruction by millers and landowners. The Oxford-Burcot Commission remained in being, but apart from collecting tolls over its stretch of river, or farming them out to be collected, it accomplished next to nothing, and its original works fell gradually into disrepair.

Its trouble was lack of power to enforce by-laws and regulations. The Act of 1623 gave the Commissioners authority to construct locks and towpaths over the limited stretch of river in their control, but it left the question of ownership of riparian rights untouched. Thus the Commission might own a lock, but the neighbouring weir remained in private hands, and the millers who owned or rented the weirs to serve their mills continued to use the flow of water as they pleased. The Commission made hopeful by-laws to prohibit millers from drawing off water to the obstruction of navigation, and it tried to fix rates of payment to the millers for the water needed to work the locks, but the millers held the whiphand. They grounded barges as they felt like it, and made them pay heavily for the water to re-float. In the spring of 1655, after a dry winter, Anthony Wood records the old complaint that boats could not get through from Oxford to Burcot, and that cargoes had to be taken overland to or from Burcot.

In spite of obstruction river traffic grew, and although in a dry season a barge might be grounded for as long as a month on a shallow patch, it was still worth sending goods by water: indeed, for really heavy loads late seventeenth- and early eighteenth-century roads were all-but useless, and there was no practicable alternative to the river. Burford stone for the building of St Paul's cathedral went by the Thames from Radcot Bridge to London, and timber from the woods of Oxfordshire was shipped to the naval yards at Deptford. The Admiralty's complaints about delays to its timber supplies added to the growing public pressure for real improvements to the navigation.

186

In 1695 an Act was passed 'to prevent exactions of the occupiers of locks and weirs upon the river of Thames'. This may have had some moral effect, but its practical value was negligible. It was re-enacted in 1730, with a virtuous pre-amble denouncing both exactions at weirs and charges imposed for the use of towpaths. This Act, like its predecessor, lacked machinery for enforcement, with the result that no one who was in a position to make bargemen pay bothered much about the legal rights or wrongs of his charges: you paid what the miller demanded, or your barge was stuck. At last, in 1751, Parliament was compelled to take more serious notice of the growing volume of complaint and an Act was passed setting up for the first time a Commission to exercise general authority over the whole river westward of the limit of the City of London's jurisdiction at Staines. The Commission was an extraordinary affair – more like a public meeting than an administrative body. Every landowner worth more than £100 a year in the counties bordering the upper river – Middlesex, Surrey, Buckinghamshire, Berkshire, Oxfordshire, Gloucestershire and Wiltshire – was entitled to be a member, together with the Mayors of all towns along the Thames and representatives of the University of Oxford. This army of Commissioners, many of them directly, or indirectly through their tenants, responsible for the very abuses they were charged to prevent, appears never to have met – indeed it could not, for a full meeting would have required a building with the capacity of the Albert Hall, not then built; there were few secular buildings then capable of accommodating a gathering of such size, and nobody seems to have suggested an assembly in St Paul's Cathedral, though that would have been quite appropriate. The Commissioners had few powers. They could fix tolls, but had no practical means of checking the rates actually charged and paid. They could report abuses to the local justices – but many of them were the local justices. They had no powers to build locks or to make or improve towpaths. Nevertheless, the Commission was not a wholly futile body. Any three Commissioners were entitled to inspect weirs or other river works, and such inspections did serve to correct some abuses. More important, the existence of the Commission, with at least nominal authority over the whole of the upper river, established the idea of having a general Thames Authority. And among the Commissioners were men who saw what immense benefits could be brought to the river if they had powers to bring them into being.

These ideas worked through public and Parliamentary opinion, and produced a much more effective River Thames Act in 1770. This began oddly by increasing the already vast Army of Commissioners by adding all Members of Parliament in the riverside counties, the Corporation of the City of London, the clergy from all riverside parishes, the recorders as well as the mayors of Oxford, Abingdon,

Wallingford, Reading, Henley, Maidenhead and Windsor, the proprietors of the Wey navigation, and numerous others: the new Commission would have needed not a building but an open space about the size of Trafalgar Square to meet. But this enormous establishment for the Commission was no more than public relations, to soothe landowning prickles. The rest of the Act was meant to work. For all the thousands of nominal Commissioners, a meeting to do business required only a quorum of eleven. And this new Commission had powers: it could construct and maintain towpaths, acquiring land if necessary by compulsory purchase, it was empowered to make pound-locks, and to buy up the old weirs and flash-locks if it wanted to. These were real powers, and they were used. Of course there had to be compromises. Ever tender to vested interests, Parliament insisted that when the proprietor of a weir or flash-lock lost revenue from the construction of a pound-lock he had to be compensated, which meant in effect that barges using the new locks had to pay twice. But compensation was based on the official tolls, and it was cheaper as well as more efficient to use the new locks and pay compensation than to be held to ransom by the millers. And this burden was gradually reduced as the Commission bought out the old lock-owners.

The City of London was always a good friend to the Thames, and a powerful influence towards improvement. The Lord Mayor and Corporation never formally surrendered their vague medieval rights over the whole river, but in practice they limited the exercise of their rights to the river below Staines. The Commission accepted the jurisdiction of the City up to Staines, and the two bodies on the whole co-operated well. There was occasional friction when the City sent a boatload of aldermen to 'inspect' the upper river, and some pained correspondence when the Commission charged lock-tolls for the aldermanic barge. But such little quarrels were settled amicably, and the City became a staunch ally of the Commission, helping it in all sorts of ways to get on with improvements, and, perhaps most useful of all, using its influence to see that money was forthcoming for the bonds, secured on river tolls, issued by the Commission to finance its work.

The last quarter of the eighteenth and the first quarter of the nineteenth centuries was the Golden Age of Canals, and a navigable Thames was vital to the profitable use of most of the major canals of Southern England. The Thames and Severn Canal linking the Thames at Inglesham, near Lechlade, with Stroud, and, via the Stroudwater Canal, with the Severn at Framilode, was opened in 1789; the Oxford Canal, providing a waterway from the Thames at Oxford to Birmingham and the Midlands, in 1790; the Basingstoke Canal, from Basingstoke to the

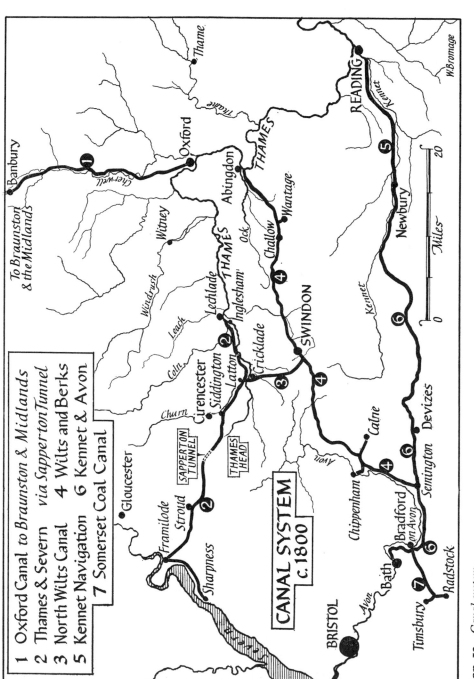

CANAL SYSTEM c.1800

1 Oxford Canal to Braunston & Midlands
2 Thames & Severn via Sapperton Tunnel
3 North Wilts Canal
4 Wilts and Berks
5 Kennet Navigation
6 Kennet & Avon
7 Somerset Coal Canal

Map 13 *Canal system.*

Wey and so to the Thames in 1796; the Kennet and Avon in 1810 and the Wilts and Berks in the same year. (These are the dates on which the canals were opened to traffic along their whole length. Some of their river sections had long been navigable. The Wey was made navigable to Guildford in 1653 and to Godalming in 1762; the Kennet was made navigable from Reading to Newbury in 1723.) The Thames Commissioners were stimulated to get on with the job of improving the Thames by various schemes to build canals to by-pass stretches of the river where navigation was particularly difficult. Most of these schemes never came off, but their threat was generally enough to keep the Commissioners alert. It was not always enough. Had the Thames as a whole been kept in better shape for navigation its one real rival as a waterway, the Grand Junction Canal from Braunston via Aylesbury to Brentford and Paddington, would never have been built. As it was, Midlands coal-owners and manufacturers sending goods to London so distrusted the Thames from Oxford that the Grand Junction was promoted and opened in 1805. An enormous tonnage of goods from the Midlands that might have come to London via the Oxford Canal and the Thames was then lost to the river.

Another Thames Act in 1795 gave the Commissioners more powers for the compulsory purchase of land to provide horse towing-paths along the river, but again it was an Act tender to propertied interests, for the powers were qualified by a prohibition on taking land where there was a house close to the bank, or which was in use for gardens or orchards. These limitations severely restricted the practical value of the Act. A nuisance against which little or nothing was done until late in the nineteenth century was pollution of the river by sewage. A big river can safely dispose of sewage from small communities, but the growth of riverside towns produced appalling problems of pollution. The national habit of using rivers as main drains because they are cheaper than sewage farms was not really tackled until this century. The Thames now is clean among English rivers, but it is fortunate in that it does not flow through any heavily industrialized locality: the condition of rivers in industrial areas is still a national shame.

In spite of complaints, the Thames in the early nineteenth century was kept reasonably fit for navigation. It was the most important inland waterway in England, contributing materially to the nation's economic life. Barges of 140 tons could get up to Wallingford, of 100 tons to Oxford, and of 70 tons to Lechlade, and fleets of barges were in regular use. A joint delegation representing the City of London and the Thames Commissioners made a voyage of inspection from Lechlade to London in 1811, and reported 'We cannot but admire the general nature and state of navigation of this noble river.' The inspectors were not complacent: they made a number of detailed criticisms, the chief of which was the 'very great want of a substantial and uninterrupted horse towing-path'; in general, however, they could feel that the river was being looked after responsibly and well. Their main criticism was never met: there has never been an uninterrupted towing-path along the Thames, and it is still not possible to walk along the river bank for its whole length.

The brave work of Thames Commissioners and City of London alike came to a miserable end. The Commissioners were put out of business by the railways, the City of London was deprived of all its ancient rights on the Thames as the result of an extraordinary wrangle with the Crown. Railway mania affected waterways on two fronts: as soon as a stretch of railway line was built it began taking traffic from any neighbouring waterway: and the scramble to buy shares in railway companies denied the waterways all hope of raising money for the improvements which might have enabled them to compete more effectively with the railways. This double pressure inflicted mortal wounds on the Thames Commissioners. In 1850 they reduced the interest to their bondholders from 5 per cent to 4 per cent; in 1854 to 2 per cent; in 1857 to 1 per cent; in 1863 to one-half of 1 per cent. They were near the end. In 1866 their £100 bonds could be had for two shillings. Speculators who bought at this price did pretty well, for by an Act of August 1866 the old Commission was replaced by a new Conservancy, and bondholders were paid 3½ per cent on their money. Anyone who loyally held on to the Commissioners' bonds did disastrously: in 1895 the bonds were extinguished in exchange for Thames Conservancy stock at one-twentieth of their face value – a £100 bond was reduced to £5. Times change. When the railways, in their turn moribund, were taken over by the State, the shareholders all received compensation. On the other hand the holders of War Loan, like the original Thames Bonds a largely patriotic investment, have fared almost as badly as the Commissioners' bondholders.

The Corporation of London did not run out of money, and up to the last was prepared to do its duty by the Thames. In 1840, however, it fell foul of the Crown over the proposal to build the Victoria Embankment. At this distance the dispute seems incomprehensible: it did not affect the actual building of the embankment, but concerned the legal ownership of the foreshore covered by the tidal river. The Crown's lawyers said peremptorily that the tidal Thames was not a river but 'an arm of the sea', and that therefore the foreshore belonged to the Crown. The Corporation, relying on its ancient charters, disputed the claim. It was willing to give permission for the embankment works to proceed, but this did not satisfy the Crown, which did not want the City's permission, but to go ahead in its own right. The dispute dragged on for years, the Crown pursuing the City with what seems bewildering vindictiveness. While Crown and City argued over who was responsible for what, the Thames itself was sadly neglected. Matters came to a head in 1855 when £30,000 had to be found for urgently needed maintenance work. The Common Council of the City refused to vote the money without an undertaking that it would be repaid if the Crown took away its rights. The Crown, through the Government, declined to give any such undertaking. Continuing the offensive, the Board of Works, the forerunner of the Ministry of Works, issued a statement warning people against carrying out any works on the Thames on the authority of the Corporation. It was an impossible situation, and in 1856 the City gave in, withdrawing all claim to the bed of the tidal river and accepting that it belonged to the Crown. Even this victory was not enough for the Crown. The City humbly suggested that nearly 700 years of jurisdiction over the river should be respected by the grant of a new charter, restoring its old rights in return for a rent which would acknowledge the superior rights of the Crown. The Crown (or the Government) would have none of it. The City had to be finally dispossessed, and in 1857 an Act was passed creating a new body, called the Thames Conservancy, to exercise jurisdiction over the river from Staines to Yantlet Creek. As a kind of afterthought of generosity, the Lord Mayor, two aldermen and four people nominated by the Common Council of the City were to be members of the Conservancy, the other members being nominated by the Lord High Admiral, the Privy Council, and Trinity House. Why the City of London, whose stewardship of the river over seven centuries had been both creditable and just, had to be flung out in such a fashion remains a mystery. Queen Victoria is supposed to have had a hand in things. She may have felt that the City's original resistance to the Crown's claims amounted to a kind of *lèse-majesté*: the Queen was sensitive on such matters. On the other hand Queen Victoria had a sense of history, and it seems unlikely that she would really want to set aside charters going back to Richard Coeur de Lion. More probably, obsequious officials interpreted what they imagined to be the Queen's wish and pursued the Corporation to a point at which they could not give way without loss of face. It was a sad and bewildering affair.

The Thames Conservancy Act of 1857 dealt with the river from Staines to Yantlet Creek: on the Upper Thames it left the Commissioners to carry on their hopeless struggle against the railways and the consequent financial decline of waterways. With all their difficulties, defects in the constitution of the Commission became apparent. It had never become a body corporate, and its members began to be afraid that they might be held personally liable for the Commission's

33. *Aerial view of Oxford.*

34a. *The remains of the seventeenth century lock on the old navigable channel of the Thames by-passing Abingdon via what was called 'the Swift Ditch'. This channel went out of use in the eighteenth century.*

34b. *Boats waiting to enter Abingdon lock.*

35. *Almshouses at Abingdon, Berkshire. The front (a) faces the Church, and the rear (b) the River Ock.*

36. *Regional crafts.*
a. *Saddle making at East Ilsley.*

b. *Basket making at Wallingford.*

debts. In 1866 another Act put the Commissioners out of their misery: they were done away with, and an enlarged Conservancy was made responsible for the entire river from Cricklade to Yantlet. It did not do much for the river above Staines: improving the Thames was no longer regarded as a good investment, there were heavy debts to be serviced, there was no money for engineering and little enough to pay staff. Most of the locks were in bad condition from lack of maintenance, landowners returned to their old encroachments, and the river, particularly above Abingdon, became full of weeds. Nevertheless, navigation continued, and bargemen contrived somehow to work their boats through. In the 1870s and early 1880s shooting wildfowl on the Thames became a great nuisance and considerable danger to other users of the river. This was stopped by the Thames Preservation Act of 1885, which also re-stated the fact that 'the Thames is a navigable highway', and re-enacted the right of the public to use the river for travel or recreation. This was a useful re-statement of public rights, but, apart from prohibiting shooting, it did not do much to improve the river, and all the old complaints went on: most of them were justified. In 1894 the various bits of piecemeal legislation affecting the Thames were consolidated in a new Act, the Conservators were reconstituted, and the burden of old debts reduced largely by writing them off: it was this Act that wrote down the old Thames Bonds to one-twentieth of their original value. In 1908 the Port of London Authority was formed to control the port and tidal river, and the Conservancy handed over its powers relating to the lower Thames, inherited from the City of London, to the P L A. That is the constitutional position today. The Port of London Authority controls the tidal Thames from an imaginary line some 265 yards below Teddington lock to the estuary, and the Thames Conservancy has jurisdiction over the whole non-tidal river from its source to Teddington. Various Acts since 1908 have enlarged both the powers and the duties of the Conservancy. The Land Drainage Act of 1930 made it the Drainage Board for the whole catchment area of the Thames, giving it jurisdiction over tributaries as well as the Thames itself, in all some 2,402 miles of river. The Rivers (Prevention of Pollution) Acts of 1951 and 1961 conferred useful new powers to prevent defilement.

Eight centuries of legislation have left the Thames better looked-after than any other river in the world. Cricklade remains the nominal head of navigation, though the barges that once got there would be hard put to it to arrive today: above Lechlade the tradition of navigation no longer holds. For 124 miles downstream from Lechlade to Teddington the Thames is more thoroughly navigable now than at any time in its history: it is a sad reflection on our use of natural resources that the Thames should have become a splendid highway for barges after the barges are gone. The barges have been replaced, however, by fleets of river cruisers and other small craft, and although it is a wry thought that those who use the river for pleasure should enjoy conditions that those who looked to it for their livelihoods never knew, it is a great national gain that such good conditions now exist. They have been brought about mainly in the past 50 years, thanks to two things – increased administrative efficiency in getting legislation carried out, and increased national interest in small boats. When river navigation was confined to commercial traffic only the narrow world of bargemen really knew what conditions on the river were, and suffered from deficiencies of control. When tens of thousands of spare time sailors and holidaymakers turned to the Thames for recreation, first-hand knowledge of conditions spread through a wide range of society. This has helped to keep authority alert, and revenues from tolls and registration fees for pleasure boats has helped to provide the money for maintenance.

There are 45 lock stations on the navigable river, all manned, and most now equipped with hydraulic power to work the locks. The lock system will admit boats up to 120 ft long and of 17 ft beam up to Abingdon, 110 ft long and 17 ft beam to Oxford and 100 ft long and 14 ft beam to Lechlade. The navigable channel, well buoyed, provides 6 ft 6 in draught from Teddington to Staines, 5 ft 6 in from Staines to Windsor, 4 ft 6 ins from Windsor to Reading, 4 ft from Reading to Oxford, and 3 ft from Oxford to Lechlade. This is enough water for six- and eight-berth cruisers to get up to Lechlade: few normal river craft draw more than 3 ft. A limit to navigation above Oxford is the low clearance under Osney Bridge: at the normal level of the river in summer there is headroom of only 7 ft 7 ins. Recruitment of heavy passers-by to stand on a boat's deck and sink her lower in the water may gain an inch or two for passing the bridge, but vessels with elaborate top hamper cannot get above Osney. Osney Bridge is not wholly to be deplored: at least it keeps the more garish kind of cocktail-bar cruisers from the lovely winding reaches of the higher river. When the Conservancy's plans for the river above Lechlade have been completed small cruisers at any rate should be able to reach Cricklade.

When the railway companies came to kill inland water transport in England the waterway system based on the Thames was just beginning to reach really effective development, turning to steam tugs in place of men and horses. The waterways were put out of business before steampower (let alone diesel power) had a chance to show what it could do: when one reflects on what was achieved by water in the eighteenth and early nineteenth centuries in England it is necessary to remember that this was done almost wholly by muscle-power – man and horse. Sail was used a little here and there: the seagoing Thames barge, with her mast stepped in a tabernacle for lowering under bridges, occasionally came up-river. But sail could not be used to any great extent on the upper Thames: there are too many bridges, and the river winds so much that a fair wind in one reach will be foul round the next bend.

Cheese, corn, flour, timber, hides and (in earlier centuries) wool were the chief downstream cargoes on the Thames, some for local markets in the riverside towns, but mainly for London. Cotswold building stone was brought down-river when it was wanted for some important building project in Oxford or London, but Oxford had nearer quarries of its own at Headington (though the stone is less beautiful than Burford's and also less hard-wearing), and London could get Portland stone so easily by sea that there was no regular stone-carrying trade on the Thames. The main up-stream trade was coal, brought by sea from the Tyne and sent up-river by barge. With the opening of the Thames and Severn Canal in 1789 and the Oxford Canal in 1790, coal from the Forest of Dean and from the Midlands competed with sea coal from London for regional markets, and when the Wilts and Berks canal joined the Thames in 1810 Somerset coal also came on the market. The result was a remarkable fall in the price of coal. This is well illustrated by some figures from Oxford. In December 1789 'sea coal' from London was selling in Oxford at 2s. 2d. per cwt. In January 1790, when Warwickshire coal began to come via the Oxford Canal, the price dropped to 1s. 1d. per cwt.* There was an even more dramatic price change in the winter of 1794–5 when the canal was frozen for ten weeks, from mid-December to the beginning of March. The price of coal in Oxford rose to 4s. per cwt. On 4 March a coal boat got through the canal, and the price dropped to 1s 8d. per cwt.†

Coal, grain, cheese, timber and hides were the staples of river-borne trade, but general merchandise was important, too. Manufactured goods of all sorts came up-river from London, and the Thames and its associated canals helped to make possible the coming into being of small factories and engineering works at Abingdon, Newbury, Wantage and elsewhere in the region.

Passengers also travelled by river. The *Carriers Cosmographie* by John Taylor, printed in 1637, records a weekly service from Queenhithe to Reading, and there were probably more or less regular services long before this. At Reading (though

---

* Kingsley Belsten and H. Compton, articles in the *Oxford Times*, 26 March, 1964, 22 May, 1964, 29 May, 1964.
† Ibid.

it might be necessary to wait a few days) there would be local boats to be had going upstream to Abingdon, and (after the improvements of the Oxford–Burcot Commissioners) to Oxford. More important – or more moneyed – travellers could hire a boat and crew of watermen to go to any of the riverside towns. By the middle of the eighteenth century there were weekly boats from Queenhithe to Abingdon, Reading and Newbury (from Reading via the Kennet, made navigable to Newbury in 1723). By twentieth-century standards river travel was scarcely fast. At the end of the eighteenth century it was reckoned to take six days for a boat to go upstream from London to Oxford, five days to Wallingford, and four days to Reading. The downstream voyage was naturally quicker, roughly a day less for each stage. There was not much in the way of accommodation: these river boats were primarily designed for carrying goods, and passengers had to make do as they could. But there were plenty of riverside inns, and in summer the river voyage could be enjoyed for itself. Even in winter it might be preferable to the roads, and for anyone used to roughing it a place on a barge was probably cheaper than any other form of transport save walking.

Passenger steamers made no regular appearance on the Thames until late in the nineteenth century: their hey-day was just before the First World War. In the years before the railways the development of passenger services was hindered by the lack of a continuous towpath: where there was no path for towing horses, boats had to be poled or manhandled to the next stretch of river where there was a path, a laborious and sometimes difficult process. Owing to ancient landowning rights, the path – where there was a path – changed frequently from one bank of the river to the other. This meant unharnassing horses and taking them across the river by ferry, or, if there was no horseferry, walking them to the nearest bridge, which might mean a round trip of several miles. On the canals, where, of course, there was a continuous towpath, light boats, called flyboats, pulled by relatively fast horses, were used for passengers. In the 1830s there was a regular flyboat service from Abingdon by the Wilts and Berks canal to Melksham, where it connected with another flyboat service to Bristol. There was a more elaborate service, also via Abingdon, from London to Gloucester. This went up the Thames to Abingdon, then by the Wilts and Berks Canal to Swindon, by the North Wilts Canal to Latton, near Cricklade, on the Thames and Severn Canal, and thence to Gloucester via the Stroudwater and the Gloucester and Berkeley Canals.* It was enterprising, but the Thames part of the voyage alone took five days, which was disproportionately long, and there must have been maddening

* Charles Hadfield, *Canals of Southern England.*

delays. In 1815 a passenger service by flyboat from Oxford to Banbury and Birmingham via the Oxford Canal was introduced. It was quite popular and ran twice weekly, but it had to be abandoned because of damage to the canal banks by the wash.

Trade is said sometimes to follow missionaries: on the Thames the missionaries appeared with developing trade. In 1822 'The Society for Promoting Religion and Morality amongst Watermen, Bargemen and Rivermen' was formed in London. In 1839 an Oxford barge owner equipped a barge as a floating chapel for watermen. It was moored to the towpath near Hythe Bridge, and services were held regularly on Sundays and Wednesdays. Its end was sad. After serving the watermen for many years its timbers became badly decayed. One day it sank and the wreck had to be broken up.

Sunday was supposed to be a day of rest on the Thames as elsewhere, but barge crews were as reluctant to lose good water as seamen to miss a favourable tide: if the going was good, they wanted to get on. The Puritan Parliament of 1650 forbade the use of any 'boat, wherry, lighter or barge' on Sundays, except to make a special journey to church or, in emergencies, by permission of a Justice of the Peace. In the flush of Puritan enthusiasm, troops were stationed on the Thames to see that the law was enforced. Commonwealth Acts of Parliament fell automatically with the Restoration, but the ban on using the Thames on Sundays was re-enacted and remained nominally in force until 1827, when it was repealed. This left the situation rather confused. The Watermen's Act of 1827 expressly permitted *travel* by boat on Sundays, but it did not make clear whether *locks* on the Upper Thames might be *worked* on Sundays. In 1842 The Thames Commissioners came down on the side of the Sabbatarians by making a by-law prohibiting the passage of locks between 06.00 and midnight on Sundays. In 1849 they were challenged by one Charles Clark, master of the barge *Susanna*, who forced his boat through a number of locks on a Sunday, declaring that the Thames was a public highway and that he could not be stopped from using it whenever he wanted to. The City of London, which had not then lost its authority, supported him. The Commissioners were on dubious legal ground in making their by-law, and they appear to have been prodded into it by a strong Sabbatarian lobby. After the *Susanna* case the legal rights of Sunday voyaging was established.

It is easy to smile at the 'do goodery' and strict Sabbatarianism of our forbears, but they lived before strong trade unions came into being to protect working men. Barge crews had a hard job, sometimes brutally hard, and the various efforts of the Mission to Rivermen and the Sunday Observers undoubtedly did something to help them. It may be noted that the word 'bargee' is never used, and never has been used, in true river society. River mariners are bargemen, watermen, boatmen, or rivermen, never 'bargees'.

It is as idle to cry over spilt water as spilt milk. Our Victorian great-grand-parents who scrambled to invest in railway shares (many of them to their sorrow) did not consider that they were thereby damaging beyond repair a system of waterways that was a major national asset. The cost of railways to British life has never been calculated – and it is not yet paid. They quickened the pace of industrialization and made a great deal of money for some people. But they took such a large slice of the nation's savings and investment capital that we are paying still for the 'get rich quick' mania of railway building. The railways helped to increase concentrations of wealth in London and in the regions of heavy industry: indeed, they largely shaped those regions which modern national policy is trying to disperse. Where there were bulk loads (of goods or passengers) to be delivered from terminal to terminal, the railways did well: the rest of the countryside they crossed as quickly as they could, fertilizing nothing, and draining people into the great industrial towns. They killed the waterways, which provided a transport system that was an integral part of its countryside, instead of a system that merely passes over it. From the First World War, when the severe limitations of railway transport began to be felt, all the political power of railway interests, reflecting the vast capital invested in them, was used to hinder the development of roads: the railway companies would have killed road transport as they killed canals, had they been able to. After the Second World War nationalization came to the financial rescue of an obsolete railway system, transferring its debts to the taxpayer. That load of railway debt has to be carried still.

One can be angry at the wanton destruction of canals by railway companies, which bought them up in order to put them out of business, but one can too easily be over-sentimental about canals. The tragedy of England's inland waterways was not that the railways came, but that they came when they did. By 1830 there was the nucleus of a magnificent system of inland waterways based on the Thames, linking the Bristol Channel to the North Sea, and the Midlands to Southern England. But it was no more than a nucleus, and its working capacity was already obsolete. Centuries of tenderness to landowning interests on the Upper Thames prevented the navigable potentialities of the river from being developed to anything like their full extent, and the canals that met the river were designed for eighteenth-century traffic, not nineteenth-century needs. Five days to cover the 85 river miles from London to Abingdon was poor going even for 1830. The Upper Thames can take wide barges, relatively big ships: with a dredged channel, sea-going coasters could get up to Oxford. Apart from the Kennet and Avon, which, with foresight, was built as a broad canal, most of the linking canals were narrow waterways, with locks limiting barges to a beam of about 7 ft. This meant either wasting the capacity of the river by sending through cargoes in narrow boats, or wasting time and labour costs on trans-shipment. Magnificent in principle, the inland waterway system was just not good enough in practice to compete with railways. Nevertheless, it was on the way to becoming good enough. For all the delays to navigation, the Upper Thames was carrying well over half a million tons of freight a year by 1800. With the opening of the Kennet and Avon and the Wilts and Berks canals in 1810 the river and its related waterways carried all the coal and most of the goods over the whole area between Bristol, Gloucester, the Midlands and London. In the 1830s the Kennet and Avon canal alone was carrying some 300,000 tons of freight a year, and the Wilts and Berks, serving a thinly populated countryside, nearly 70,000 tons. Passenger services existed, and were on the edge of great development. Given another 20 years of confidence and capital investment the Thames and its waterway system would have been transformed. Instead, almost overnight money and engineering enterprise were diverted to the railways, which touched both the imagination and the greed of early Victorian businessmen. In the coal-carrying trade, where canals could have competed successfully with the early railways, they were not allowed to compete: they were bought up by railway companies and more or less put out of business. As statutory waterways they could not be abandoned without Parliamentary sanction, but a policy of

> Thou shalt not kill, but need'st not strive
> Officiously to keep alive

proved as effective as abandonment, and far less troublesome. Starved of maintenance, and with most of their traffic diverted to railways, the canals soon became weed-grown, and their locks fell into disrepair. The Upper Thames suffered with them. Nevertheless, canal and river carrying took a long time to die. In spite of neglect, water transport, with its small demands on manpower needed to work barges, and the long life of the barges themselves, has inherent advantages. The Kennet and Avon lingered as a working canal until about 1910, the Thames and Severn until about the same time, and the Wilts and Berks until 1905–6. The Wilts and Berks was simply left to decay out of existence: it was not sufficiently important as a competitor for the Great Western Railway to want to buy it. By 1906 it had become unusable, and in 1914 an Act of Parliament authorized its formal abandonment. The Kennet and Avon was bought by the Great Western in 1852, and had become more or less unnavigable by 1910. The Thames and Severn canal, or rather, its bed, almost became a railway, but efforts to turn it into a railway failed to get Parliamentary sanction. In 1882 control of the canal company was bought by the Great Western, which was suspicious of attempts to promote new railways in what it regarded as Great Western territory. The railway company did nothing with the canal and in 1895 permitted it to be taken over by a trust, on condition that it was never to be converted into a line of railway. The trust failed to restore the canal, and in 1901 the Gloucestershire County Council tried to come to the rescue in the hope – advanced social thinking at the time – that the canal could at least be preserved as an amenity. It was a gallant effort but it came to nothing, for the cost of keeping the canal open for such traffic as there was proved a financial burden that (in those days) was considered too heavy for the ratepayers to be expected to bear. Traffic was at an end by 1911 and the canal was formally abandoned after the First World War.

The Oxford Canal put up a tougher fight for life. Leicestershire coal brought to Oxford by canal remained substantially cheaper than rail-borne coal, particularly if whole barge loads were delivered under contract. The University's paper mill at Wolvercote, electricity works at Osney, and a brewery went on getting coal by canal into the 1950s. During the Second World War the canal was a valuable transport link between Oxford and the Midlands, and played a useful part in the industrial war effort. Remarkable as it was for the Oxford Canal to keep going for half a century after the other Upper Thames canals had died, the last three decades of its life were but an Indian Summer. In 1937 its main wharf was sold as the site for Nuffield College (built after the war) and apart from a few coal contracts much of its carrying trade was gone. The war restored temporarily the canal's importance, but with the end of the war trade fell off quickly. In 1948 only 51 commercial boats came to Oxford, in 1951 there were 19; in 1954 they dwindled to 10. The brewery went on getting coal by canal until 1961, but as a commercial waterway it had all but ceased to exist. Two things have saved the Oxford canal from the fate of the Thames and Severn and the Wilts and Berks: the sensitivity of post-war Parliaments and public opinion to the need to preserve amenity, and the immense growth in holiday cruising traffic. The canal flows through a beautiful quiet countryside, away from main roads, by remote villages that have changed little since the eighteenth century. The canal that once brought coal to Oxford now brings recreation to city-dwellers, sailing their own or hired cruisers. Navigation is slightly more adventurous than on the wider Thames, with its fine hydraulic locks, but canal cruising offers a splendid change from the roads and pressures of everyday urban life. It has come to stay as a holiday and weekend activity, and the Oxford canal is a particularly lovely stretch to cruise.

The Inland Waterways Association, representing a great body of inland sailors and people who believe in the economic value of water transport, has done much to preserve such canals as are still navigable, and voluntary effort has even managed to restore to navigation some stretches of derelict canal. An outstanding achievement here was the restoration of the Stratford-on-Avon canal, a work in which the Home Office, showing rare imagination, allowed volunteers from prison to assist. The Wilts and Berks and the Thames and Severn canals have passed into history, but one day, perhaps, the Kennet and Avon may be navigable again from Reading to Bristol: this would not only be of benefit to inland yachts-men, but a national insurance policy should other transport systems ever be seriously interrupted.

Because the railways came when they did, the Thames and its network of canals were never developed as inland water transport has been developed in France, Holland, Germany and many other countries. It is usual to dismiss canals as belonging to the past in England, or useful nowadays only for pleasure boating. But the facts of geography do not change. The Thames is navigable to Lechlade still, and could be made navigable at least to Cricklade: the navigable Thames helped to create modern England, and the fact that the Thames is a navigable river may, perhaps, re-fashion the England of our grandchildren, taking an immense burden from the roads, and much of the roar of traffic from our ears.* That is a dream, maybe: but the potential reality is a geo-physical fact.

* Lord St Davids has pointed out that the effort which goes into carrying 2cwt is enough to pull 1,400 cwt on water, a proportion of 1–700. He observes (*Inland Cruising*) 'to pull a camping punt fully loaded with people and stores weighing rather under a ton costs the same effort as to carry a shopping bag weighing three pounds.'

10

Regional life

It is convenient to think in terms of past and present, but the life of a region as of a man is a continuum: we are what we are because of what we were. The past *is* the present, any dividing line between them purely theoretical. Nevertheless, in considering relatively long periods of human history, certain sharp turns may be observed. The Upper Thames flows through and forms a region of Britain, and the major influences on life within the region have been those that affected the nation as a whole: Roman and Saxon conquest, Danish wars, Norman conquest, the opening of the world beyond the seas, the growth of industry, successive World Wars. Within the national pattern, however, the region has always had a life of its own, local influences modifying the effect of national events. This is most noticeable in the delayed effect of the so-called Industrial Revolution beginning roughly in the middle of the eighteenth century, which brought such swift and profound changes to many other parts of Britain. The Upper Thames region has no coal, and its rivers, although capable of driving water mills, have not the fall of the rivers of Derbyshire, for instance, which powered the early textile factories. Apart from the blanket trade in Witney, plush-making in Banbury, small-scale agricultural engineering works at Newbury and Wantage, the biscuit factories at Reading and the railway workshops at Swindon (both really outside the region) the Upper Thames area had virtually no industry until after the First World War. Its life outside Oxford, which was a world in miniature of its own, was wholly agricultural and pastoral, bound up with grain and sheep and pigs. In 1913, life in many of the villages of the Vale of the White Horse, of the Windrush and Evenlode valleys, and on the banks of the Upper Thames itself, was probably nearer to the life of 1713, or even of 1613, than almost anywhere else in Britain.

With no competition for labour from mines or factories, farm wages in the region were low. There was severe suffering from high food prices during the Napoleonic wars, and it was the Berkshire magistrates, meeting at Speenhamland, Newbury, in 1795, who invented the notorious 'Speenhamland system' of subsidizing wages out of the parish rates. This evil system, widely adopted in other counties, made farm labourers paupers even when they were in work, compelling them to rely on 'outdoor relief' from the parish because wages were too low to live on. It viciously affected the smallholder who employed no labour, because his rates rose to subsidise the wages of those who worked for richer farmers. To twentieth-century social thinking the Speenhamland system seems a nightmare, but it reflects the social conscience of its time. The Berkshire magistrates who devised it were not evil men: they saw men hungry because of war-time inflation, and to them no doubt it seemed humane to use parish rates for relief. It was at least a swift and fairly certain method of relief: to have fixed higher wages, which was within their power, and which to our thinking would have been the right thing to do, might have led to widespread dismissals, and much trouble in getting obstinate farmers to pay. There were then no trade unions, and the idea that employers have a collective responsibility to those who work for them was not yet part of national thinking. The evils that were to flow from Speenhamland were not apparent that May day in 1795. The system lasted nearly 40 years, and the thinking behind it longer still. Farm wages in the region remained low. Towards the close of the nineteenth century, when a farmworker in Yorkshire was getting around 14s. a week, the countryman of the Upper Thames had to make do on 7s. Up to the Second World War, Oxfordshire, with Norfolk and Dorset, paid the lowest farm wages in England. Berkshire wages were generally slightly better.

Attempts by farmworkers to combine for higher wages were bitterly resisted. As late as 1873 there was an instance of this at Ascott-under-Wychwood. Two men who had joined Joseph Arch's Agricultural Workers Union were sacked by the farmer who employed them, and their jobs given to two men from the neighbouring village of Ramsden. A group of enraged Ascott women went to the Ramsden men, explained why they had got their jobs, and asked them to leave. The Ramsden men, who had no idea that they were replacing sacked trade unionists, and whose sympathies were with the union, at once walked off. The farmer summoned sixteen women for interfering with his trade. They appeared before the justices at Chipping Norton, were convicted, *and sent to gaol*, some for seven days, some for ten. For fear of a riot in the countryside when news of the convictions spread the women were taken to Oxford gaol in the middle of the night. They came home in triumph, to a great welcome on the village green and, a presentation of £5 apiece from funds which had been collected for them throughout the district. The nearness of this almost medieval persecution is brought home by the fact that at least one of those women was still living in the 1930s.

This is the dark side of the picture. There was plenty of light. If the country-side suffered from low wages, men lived with the river and the sky and were not huddled into the dreariness of mean streets and Blake's 'dark Satanic mills'. Moreover wages were only one element in the defences of living. Every cottage had a pig, a few hens, a garden and a vegetable patch, sometimes part of the garden, sometimes an allotment from a strip of land saved for common use when other common land was enclosed. This is well illustrated at Bloxham, near Banbury, where the Feoffees, a body still in existence, saw that every man had two chains of allotment after the enclosures; later the ration was increased to five chains. Men looked after the vegetables, and women grew flowers – the flower part of a cottage garden was traditionally the woman's domain. Then there were rabbits, pigeons, and from time to time a pheasant, or, in Wychwood, even a deer, with no questions asked. Common rights 'to lop and top' for firewood were usually respected, as were rights of gleaning after harvest. Bees could be kept, and goats were often tethered along roadside verges. In a countryside criss-crossed by rivers and streams a fishing-rod could usually produce something for the pot, and in the marshes of the Vale of the White Horse there were wild duck to be had in winter. Around Woodstock and Charlbury, and in the Wychwood villages, there was out-work for the gloving industry, and women might make pillow-lace to add to family income. Manufactured goods might be few, and one suit of Sunday clothes might have to last the best part of a lifetime, but for most people life was worth living. With little in the way of outside entertainment people made their own. Every village had its annual 'Feast', usually on the day of the Saint to which the parish church was dedicated. Many of these 'Feasts' are held still, though they have degenerated from the rollicking occasions before the First World War to the more sedate gatherings that are commonly described as 'fêtes' in modern England. For a glimpse of the Great World it was worth walking ten miles to Abingdon or Newbury Fair, and rolling home again, or, with better organization, being rolled home in a farm cart.

If there was next to no industry in the region, there were plenty of local crafts. The blacksmith survived in all villages up to the First World War, and in some places through the 1930s, although from 1920 onwards the tendency for the smithy to become the local garage was apparent. The wheelwright, the joiner and the hurdlemaker were important men in their localities. Before the motor-car brought easy access to multiple stores in market towns, rural communities had to be more or less self-supporting, and quite small villages could support a tailor and shoemaker. Gardner's *Directory of the County of Oxford* for 1852 lists a remarkable number of independent local craftsmen. Culham, a small village near Abingdon, supported two blacksmiths, a tailor, a carpenter and a mason – this with a population of 404. Clifton Hampden, with a population of only 297, had a blacksmith, a mason, a shoemaker and a carpenter. Dorchester, rather larger, with a population of just over 1,000, had three shoemakers, three wheel-wrights, two masons, two blacksmiths and two plumbers and glaziers. These are typical figures for the region as a whole, Many crafts were carried on as part-time jobs. In Dorchester, for instance, one blacksmith was also a publican, and in Clifton Hampden the carpenter not only kept an inn but was also sub-postmaster. Every village had its baker, sometimes two or three. The baker would make cakes and buns as well as bread, and this trade was often part-time, worked in con-junction with a small grocer's shop, or someone who had a cottage with a good baking oven built into the chimney by the fireplace would do the baking for his neighbours. This pattern of life changed little up to the First World War.

In the big houses, the squire's house, the rectory, the houses of the larger farmers, life was comfortable and secure. There was an endless supply of domestic staff, for village girls expected to go into service until they married. Service in a pleasant country house should not be confused with the bitterness of being a 'slavey' in a drab London terrace. There were bad mistresses, no doubt, but for the most part these country girls ate well, were not overworked, and had a recognized place in the community. They also acquired a skilled trade in personal domestic service, a skill now nearly obsolete. To our social thinking, the power of a local landowner over his community was more than one human being should have over others, but it would be wrong to think that it was always – or even usually – exercised irresponsibly. Many, perhaps most, of the so-called 'gentry' in the countryside had a deep sense of responsibility towards their people, and discharged it as honourably as they could.

Regional life up to the First World War was, on the whole, clearly stratified, and static. Children acquired reading, writing and elementary arithmetic in the village schools, but often not much else. An exceptionally able boy, with help, maybe, from squire or rector, might go anywhere, but most children followed their parents, boys to the farm, or to the local crafts of blacksmith, carpenter or mason, girls into service and marriage, usually within the village community. For those who found this static country life stultifying, there were escape routes – the

205

Army, the chance of a job in London, or emigration. The Army had much to be said for it. In the days of county regiments enlistment did not cut off a man from his own community: it widened his community, and it meant travel, adventure, and service abroad, usually in India. And on leaving the Army the ex-soldier still had a place in his village, if he wanted to return to it. Going off to London or some other big city in search of a job was more chancy: it meant heartbreak perhaps more often than success; for girls it could be disastrous. Emigration, to Canada, Australia, New Zealand or South Africa, offered probably the best chance of real advancement in life. It was a big step: in the days before aircraft had shrunk the world, emigration had to be considered as all-but irrevocable. But it took you clean out of stratified English society, and left you free to make what you could of life. For those who could face years of hard work, emigration usually turned out well: the older countries of the Commonwealth are dotted with names recalling the Upper Thames, and the descendants of village lads who emigrated before the First World War are among their countries' leading citizens.

The war of 1914–18 was the most decisive influence on the regions since the Saxon invasion. The old, static regional life was shattered, the effects of political and social change were revolutionary, and the war left major industry established in Oxford. The two decades of uneasy peace before the Second World War of 1939 were merely a continuation of unsettlement: the changes that began after the First World War accelerated after the Second.

The immediate and direct effect of the war of 1914–18 was an appalling loss of male population. The county regiments of the Regular Army and their Territorial batallions, the Royal Berkshires and the Oxfordshire and Buckinghamshire Light Infantry, could be mobilized quickly, and they endured the grim warfare of the Western Front from the start. A few brief figures must suffice to tell the story of the whole. The 1st Battalion of the Royal Berkshires was at Aldershot in 1914, and nine days after the declaration of war on 4 August it was in France. In two days, 15 and 16 May, 1915, it lost 9 officers and 414 men. The 2nd Battalion was in India at the outbreak of war, but was in France by November 1914. On 1 July, 1916 it lost 20 officers and 437 men, ending up under the command of a Second Lieutenant. On the Aisne on 27 May, 1918 the reformed battalion lost 24 officers and 706 men. The 4th (Territorial) Battalion came back from camp on 3 August, 1914 and was mobilized the next day. By April 1916 it had lost 12 officers and 400 men. The 8th Battalion, originally a Service Battalion, went to France in 1915 and on 25/26 September at Loos lost 17 officers and 500 men. It was reformed quickly and back in action within a few days, and by 14

October of that same year it had suffered another 166 casualties. Between August 1915 and November 1918 the battalion suffered a total of 3,600 casualties.* These are the figures for a few battalions of *one* regiment: the sombre pattern was repeated in almost every unit drawn from the region. The dreadful figures are no worse than those for regiments from the great towns and industrial areas, but the effect of such casualties on the relatively thinly populated countryside was more marked. The war memorials on village greens record the scale of calamity – communities of not more than two or three hundred people lost eight, ten, twelve or more of their able-bodied men, sometimes almost every man between 18 and 40. All the menfolk of whole families were sometimes wiped out: a war memorial in Childrey church records the deaths of *two* sets of *four* brothers, and such tragedies were repeated sadly often.

In the towns and industrial areas there was at least some degree of social mobility: the dead could not be replaced, but manpower could be made up. In the isolated villages of the countryside, when hardly anyone possessed a motor-car, the loss of men upset the whole balance of life. Women who had little hope of marrying outside the village were condemned to lifelong spinsterhood. The old pattern of agricultural and village life could not be restored.

In the context of national changes brought by the war, probably it could not have been restored, anyway. Incomes from land which had sufficed for a comfortable living in 1914 were reduced by taxation and post-war inflation to a point at which the smaller squires were hard put to it to make ends meet. The maidservants departed, and so did many of the owners of big houses, who could no longer sustain them. 'Berkshire lands are skittish, and shed their owners', runs an old saying. Many were shed after 1919, and gradually a new pattern of land ownership emerged: old families which had lived by and from the land, were replaced by new men who bought land as an investment, using expenditure on land to offset taxation from other business interests. In the long run, and particularly after the Second World War, the land benefited.

No generalization can be wholly true, and although many estates changed in this way, some did not. The Eystons at East Hendred maintain still land that they have held for 500 years, the Harcourts hold Stanton Harcourt, and the Fiennes (who hold the barony of Saye and Sele) still live at Broughton Castle, near Banbury, which has been their home for centuries. Other ancient families survive in the region: their modern representatives may sometimes live in cottages rather than great houses, but they ensure that continuity is unbroken.

---

* Frederick Myatt, *The Royal Berkshire Regiment.*

The meaning of such continuity is indefinable. Some would dismiss it as having no meaning in a twentieth-century context, but it can also be held that it is just such continuity that gives reality to regional life, defining it, and ensuring that against all pressures from uniformity the regions of Britain remain distinct within the national whole.

There are checks and balances in life. The war of 1914–18, and the social changes brought by it, which made the old pattern of regional life impossible, also brought new ways of living. The most important change was the introduction of major industry.

William R. Morris, an Oxfordshire man, sprung from a family of yeoman farmers settled in the county at least from the seventeenth century, opened his bicycle shop in Oxford in 1893. He produced his first motor-car in 1912. Morris's vision and drive were such that he would almost certainly have created a motor industry in Oxford without the war, but the war hastened the process. During the war he took on engineering contracts for the Admiralty. His works were a going concern when the war ended, and in the brief boom that followed the war he was able to establish his cars. His form of manufacturing was essentially an assembly-line: he bought components made to his specifications from other engineering firms, and assembled them at Cowley, thus setting a pattern for the British motor industry which has lasted to this day: that it is still fundamentally an assembly industry is to be seen whenever a labour dispute in one of the firms making components quickly threatens a stoppage of almost the whole industry. By assembling rather than making, Morris could turn out cars at what, for the early 1920s, was a remarkable rate of production; and they were good cars. While the post-war boom lasted, all was well, but in the slump that followed Morris almost went out of business. He was saved by the confidence of a local Oxford banker, William Gillett. Gillett's bank, an old institution in Oxford and the surrounding region, had merged with Barclay's. Morris had banked with Gillett from his bicycle-shop days, and Gillett had sufficient influence with Barclay's to ensure that Morris got the overdraft he needed. It is an interesting reflection that but for a local Oxford banker's personal judgment of a local Oxford man, the Morris car might have been – probably would have been – no more than a footnote in motoring history, with the Clyno, the Star, the Arrol-Johnston, the Argyll, and a host of other ghosts from the years between the wars. But Morris did survive, to become Lord Nuffield, a princely benefactor of Oxford and of many national causes, and a founding father of the British Motor Corporation, now merged with Leyland in the British Leyland Motor Corporation.

37. *A wide sweep of the Thames approaching Abingdon.*

38a. *The source of the Thames at Trewsbury Mead, near Cirencester. The statue of Father Thames was once at the Crystal Palace, London.*

38b. *Thames head in the eighteenth century. The round structure (now gone) was a pumping-station to raise water for the Thames and Severn Canal.*

By the middle of the 1930s Oxford was securely established as a major centre of the motor industry and its related enterprises in sheet steel. Banbury was also undergoing industrial development – Northern Aluminium (Alcan) came there in 1931. The region outside the towns remained predominantly agricultural, but it was a changing agriculture – tractors and farm machinery replaced men. This inevitable process was made less bitter by the decline in the rural male population, and by the growth of industry to provide alternative jobs. Country bus services made it possible for people living in the villages to travel to and from Oxford, Banbury and Reading for work. In spite of heavy unemployment in most of Britain, there were not enough men to go round in the Upper Thames region: a survey carried out in 1936 showed that 43 per cent of the male insured population in Oxford were recent immigrants.

The war of 1939–45 accentuated all these changes. Although the region remains one of the important agricultural areas of Britain, the jobs provided by agriculture have declined dramatically. The Department of Employment and Productivity generously carried out for me a survey of how people were earning their livings at the end of 1967 in the districts covered by its local offices at Oxford, Abingdon, Wantage, Didcot, Banbury, Bicester, Cirencester and Reading. This showed that 34·4 per cent of the men in the region were employed in manufacturing industry, and only 4·3 per cent in agriculture. Only in Wantage and Bicester, serving the most rural parts of the region, were there more agricultural than industrial workers – in Wantage 402 against 394, and in Bicester 248 against 186. In neither Wantage nor Bicester, however, was agriculture the main source of work for men: the building trades in Wantage provided just over 500 jobs for men, and in Bicester 1,300. Shops, transport, administrative and other services in both areas combined to provide more jobs than agriculture.

Another major change in the structure of living has been in the extent to which women now go out to work. Unlike the industrial areas of Britain, the region has no long tradition of women's going out to jobs outside their homes. Domestic service was traditional for women, but for most that was an interlude between childhood and marriage: after marriage a woman expected (and was expected) to devote herself to her family. In the Witney blanket industry there was some work for women, in the gloving districts around Woodstock and Charlbury women undertook out-work, and there were traditional tasks for women in gleaning after harvest, but for the most part a woman's life was bound up with her home. In the days before packeted prepared foods and mass produced clothing a countrywoman had a whole time job to feed and clothe her family. Now women, before and after marriage, go out to work as a matter of course, although the proportion of married women who go out to work is still lower than in more heavily industrialized areas. Nearly 100,000 women in the districts covered by the Department of Employment and Productivity's survey had jobs outside their homes in 1967, and this number will grow as more light industries providing work for women are established in the region. Manufacturing industry already provides a good deal of work for women – over 5,000 jobs in Oxford (between 2–3,000 in the motor industry), over 7,000 in Reading, 3–4,000 in Banbury, 600 in Abingdon and several hundreds of jobs in the smaller places. But the bulk of work for women is in shops and offices. For office work, particularly for skilled work such as shorthand and typing, the region is already short of womanpower, and is a net exporter of skilled staff: girls who have acquired office skills are attracted to London and the great towns of the Midlands. This has its effect on regional life, for such girls are likely to marry and settle down outside the region – good, no doubt, for the cross-fertilization of the nation as a whole, but weakening the distinctive character of regional life.

A major new industry brought to the region after the Second World War was atomic energy. The idea of setting up an atomic energy research centre in England after the war was first mooted among a group of British scientists working in the United States in 1944. Immediately after the war the late Sir John Cockcroft, the first head of the Atomic Energy Research Establishment (A E R E) and a number of the men who were to be his colleagues worked out what they regarded as the first things to be looked for in choosing a location for the establishment.* These, they decided, were:

(i) reasonable proximity to London
(ii) ease of access to a major university
(iii) a countryside pleasant to live in.

The late Lord Cherwell, relating these qualities to sites that it might be possible to get hold of quickly suggested that they might find what they wanted in some R A F airfields that would not be needed after the war. Several airfields were looked at, but all were rejected for a reason that did not figure in the scientists' first list of desirable qualities – water. Enormous quantities of water were going to be needed to cool an atomic reactor, and most of the places that fitted in with the other considerations had nothing like enough. In the end the R A F airfield at Harwell, on the edge of the Berkshire Downs some five miles south of Abingdon, was found to meet just about every requirement. It was a lovely countryside, barely a dozen miles from Oxford and within easy reach of

* J. M. Turney, 'AERE Harwell, a Geographical Appraisal,' AERE magazine *Harlequin,* 1966.

London. The Thames, three miles away at Sutton Courtenay, could provide all the water that was likely to be needed, and there was a subsidiary source of water near at hand from boreholes in the chalk. The chalk bed of the downs would provide a good firm base for heavy machinery. Moreover, this part of North Berkshire was underpopulated, and an influx of scientific workers and their families would be welcome.

So Harwell was chosen, and in 1946 the pioneers of Britain's atomic energy industry moved in. Between theoretical geographical suitability and practical use for research into nuclear energy there were a host of problems to be solved. The R A F station had huts and a few married quarters: the community at Harwell was going to need houses and schools. Water from the Thames could be pumped readily enough from Sutton Courtenay, and it could be put back in the river after use: but what if it went back radioactive? This possibility worried both the Thames Conservancy and the Metropolitan Water Board, for roughly two-thirds of London's water comes from the Thames. Elaborate precautions against radioactive contamination of the river were devised, and they have worked well. Slightly contaminated water undergoes the most careful decontamination treatment until it is safe to discharge back into the Thames, and a constant check is kept on the water in the river to see that it never reaches a level of radioactivity which could do any harm. More seriously contaminated water is kept in decay tanks until radioactivity has gone, and anything that cannot be treated in this way is put into steel drums, taken far out to sea, and sent to the bottom of the deepest part of the Atlantic.

Abingdon, Wantage, Wallingford and Didcot all co-operated in providing houses, finding sites for the A E R E to build, and making some council houses available. By 1951 the A E R E had 462 houses in Abingdon and 30 in Didcot, this latter figure rising to over 130. As time went on it acquired 120 houses at Wallingford, 76 in Wantage, and another 60–70 in Abingdon. By 1958 there were some 900 A E R E-owned houses in the locality, and A E R E people were occupying about 500 local authority houses. The A E R E has helped its people to buy their own homes, so that the new population has put down roots in the countryside.

This influx of mostly young, well-educated people has helped to improve the quality of life in the region as a whole. Scientists may become local councillors, Harwell people and their wives support local dramatic and operatic societies, and a host of other local activities which benefit from their membership. Their coming has been a major social as well as economic gain.

Atomic energy has not so much re-populated as populated the wedge of the

Downs reaching into the Thames valley south of Abingdon. It has always been a remote and lonely countryside, known (to anyone who did know it) mainly for the cherry orchards around Harwell, and for racehorse training gallops on the Downs. The factory-like atomic energy buildings spreading over a shoulder of the Downs have not improved the landscape, but it has suffered less than might be feared, because the scale of the Downs is big enough to take the buildings. The effect on landscape of the new power station at Didcot is far more harsh than that of atomic energy buildings on the Downs, for the flat, gentle countryside between Didcot and the Thames winces under the towering concrete masses of the power station. The Downs are rounded, but they are also hard. They can sustain a visual shock that the gentler land cannot.

The new life at Harwell has fertilized the human communities of Abingdon, Wantage, Wallingford, Didcot and the villages between them. It has provided some 6,000 jobs: reckoning in the transport and other services required to sustain Harwell, and the shops to provide goods for Harwell families, about 30,000 people in the region now depend at least to some extent on the A E R E. About one-quarter of the present population of Abingdon live in the town because they or their breadwinners work at Harwell, or at its offshoot at Culham, to which some of Harwell's work has been transferred.

Transport for getting to and from Harwell was a major problem from the start, and remains so. The private motor-car has had an effect on country bus services even more catastrophic than on public transport in towns: some villages are reduced to only one or two buses *a week*. But the private car cannot yet wholly solve the rural transport problem. If a man uses the family car to go to work, his wife is left without transport for shopping, for getting children to and from school, for her own social needs. Moreover, a wife may also need to get to work, and she may not work in the same place as her husband. Village families often strain their financial resources to maintain two cars, but for many people the ownership of two cars – sometimes the possession of one – is an economic impossibility. And not everyone wants to, or can, drive. So an industry in the countryside on the scale of atomic energy at Harwell can be manned only by the provision of extensive private bus services. The A E R E has a fleet of something like 100 buses, some chartered, some A E R E owned, which run morning and evening on about 40 routes in the area between Oxford, Newbury, Reading and Swindon, collecting people for work and taking them home. Over 4,000 employees at Harwell use these services daily. But not even a private bus service can run to every hamlet. Those who cannot get to a works' bus must depend either on their own transport, or on complex arrangements for car sharing.

Other industries which move from congested towns into the countryside must also face this problem. In 1950, Smiths Industries, a large concern making instruments and accessories for the motor trade, decided to establish a new factory on the outskirts of Witney. Geographically, Witney is well placed to serve the motor industry in Oxford and the Midlands, instrument manufacture is clean light engineering, and the employment offered by the factory both for men and women was needed in the locality. But valuable as this new industry is to the region, it could not be established without running private bus services, and the company provides transport to collect and take home employees from Stanford-in-the-Vale, Eynsham, Chipping Norton, Blockley, Northleach and Fairford, and the villages in between. The coming of Smiths' Industries to the region is another example of double-fertilization, from an influx of *new* people and from the provision of new jobs for *existing* populations. The newcomers needed houses, so in co-operation with the local authority the company created a new community of 470 houses in the Windrush Valley on the Western side of Witney. This is not merely another housing estate, but an attempt to create a *real* new community, with its own church, shopping centre and pub.

Transport needs are relative. Up to the First World War each village in the region was largely a self-contained community, living on its own produce, and importing little save cloth, salt, sugar, coal and a few manufactured goods. Furniture was made by the local carpenter: pots and pans and china were expected to last a lifetime: if a pan had a hole in it, it would be set aside to be mended next time a tinker came round, a broken plate would similarly be riveted. The carrier's cart would bring what was needed from Abingdon, Wantage, Wallingford, or the nearest market town. Coal was brought round by dray, from river or canal wharf, and later from railway yards where branch lines served the local towns. Outside the bigger houses, coal, although used, was precious, and used as little as possible: brushwood was the major fuel in the villages; it had merits in addition to being had for the effort of getting it – it certainly baked the best bread. Shopping in the sense that it is now understood was a rare excursion: there were annual visits to the fairs, and a very occasional trip to a town by cart. Farmers and their drovers would take cattle to market in the towns, and do such shopping as they needed then. Their wives, and most of their neighbours, might not stir outside their village for a twelvemonth: whole families were born and lived and died within ten miles of where they were born.

Railways did little for *local* transport. In the early years of railway development, much of the region was suspicious of railways and would have preferred to have nothing to do with them. Oxford and Abingdon successfully opposed

Railway Bills, with the result that they were left off the Great Western's original railway map: the line ran from Paddington to Reading and Didcot, then to Steventon and across the Vale of the White Horse to Swindon, and so to Bath and Bristol. The line from London to Steventon was opened in 1840 and to Bristol in 1841. Trains no longer stop at Steventon and the station has been demolished, but for a time it had an important place in railway history as the operating headquarters of the G W R. Board meetings were held there until January 1843, when it was decided that Paddington was more convenient.

When it became apparent that railways had come to stay, and that they were killing transport by river and canal, both Oxford and Abingdon regretted their hostility. Steventon was the nearest station for both, four miles from Abingdon and ten from Oxford. Stage coaches ran to connect with trains, but the journey was irritating. Oxford got a branch line from Didcot in 1844, but Abingdon had to wait until 1856, when a single-track broad-gauge line from Abingdon to Radley on the Didcot–Oxford branch was opened. This line was worked by the G W R, but it was promoted and constructed by the Abingdon Railway Company, and remained its property until 1904, when the Great Western took it over.

The main line ran across the region, missing most of the market towns, which were gradually connected by a series of little branch lines – Faringdon to Uffington in 1864, Wallingford to Moulsford in 1866, Wantage to Wantage Road by its own steam tram in 1875. All these lines are now closed – there is no station on the main line now between Didcot and Swindon.

Oxford, always on a branch line as far as the Great Western was concerned, ultimately became a minor metropolis in the bewildering pattern of mid-nineteenth-century railway development. It gave its own name to the Oxford, Worcester and Wolverhampton Railway, opened in 1853. This was not a distinguished line, its initials O W W being commonly interpreted as standing for 'Old Worse and Worse'. It was taken over by the Great Western in 1861. Oxford got a line to Bletchley in 1850 and to Witney in 1861. In the railway wars of those times Oxford was on the frontier between the Great Western and its allies, using the broad gauge of 7 ft $0\frac{1}{4}$ in. and the London and North Western complex using the standard gauge of 4 ft $8\frac{1}{2}$ in. There were broad gauge, standard gauge and 'mixed gauge' lines, the mixed gauge having a third rail that in theory made it capable of taking trains of either gauge: it was expensive to construct, did not work very well, and it was not a solution to the problem of differing gauges. The 'battle of the gauges' complicated every phase of railway development in this part of the region, and was not ended until 1892, when the broad gauge was abolished. By that time the great age of railway promotion was over

214

and the network of routes established, to the bewilderment of travellers anywhere off main lines until competition from road transport after the Second World War sent most branch lines into oblivion.

The heyday of the country bus was in the 1920s and early 1930s, before ownership of the small 'family car' became widespread. The change in the pattern of regional life after 1919 coincided with the coming of the country bus, and public transport was just adequate to enable those who lived in the villages to get to work in the growing industries of Oxford, Banbury and Reading. But it was never more than barely adequate, and lack of transport led to considerable emigration between the wars from the countryside into the larger towns. This was offset to some extent by the spread of manufacturing industry into smaller towns, where there was less competition for labour. In 1929, for instance, the section of the Morris works making sports cars – the famous M G cars – was transferred from Oxford to Abingdon.

Change in regional life since the Second World War has been more than a continuation of the changes that begun after the First. All these have continued – the decline in employment on the land as agriculture has become more and more mechanized, the growth of industry in the towns, the dying-out of individual craftsmen as mass production has replaced them, or technological innovation rendered the crafts themselves obsolete. The rushes that sealed beer barrels are not needed for steel drums, the wheelwright's skill with a spokeshave has no place in car and lorry wheels, clothes and shoes come from factories, not from village tailors and shoemakers. But the pace of change since 1945, and the emphasis on social planning, with restrictions on building in towns and in the 'green belts' surrounding them, have combined to change the structure of regional life itself, as distinct from changing the regional pattern of living. This reflects, of course, the vast social changes in Britain as a whole since 1945, but their impact on the region has been sometimes sharpened, sometimes noticeably modified by local conditions. Up to 1939, although people were tending to work outside their village or home town, few travelled more than 10 or 15 miles to work: the special importance of industrial development in Oxford and Banbury was that it provided work for a countryside that came to their boundaries without much in the way of suburbs. Migration into the region's chief towns between the wars produced some suburban building, but nothing comparable to the surge of new building after 1945. Kidlington, Botley, North and South Hinksey, Little-more, and other villages round Oxford that were once distinct communities are now all but merged into one Oxford conurbation: so with Abingdon, where

Sunningwell, Shippon, Drayton are now virtually part of Abingdon; and so with Newbury, Wantage, Didcot, Wallingford, Woodstock, Banbury, Witney, and all the other regional towns, which have started to absorb their neighbouring countryside. With this growth in the size of towns has come a tendency for people to work ever farther from their homes, a paradox to be explained by the post-war rise in urban house prices. House prices in London and its nearer suburbs have sent thousands of people who work in London to live as far away as Didcot, Oxford and their neighbouring villages: they face three or four hours of commuting to and from work daily. This is travel to work far beyond the region. Within the region, a similar tendency to accept much longer work-journeys is apparent: people who work in Oxford may live 40 or 50 miles away, a man may travel daily from Cirencester to Abingdon, from Abingdon to Reading, or from Woodstock to Newbury. The routes covered by the private bus services of the A E R E at Harwell and Smiths Industries at Witney show the range of distances for journeying to work that are now considered normal.

With restrictions on building development in towns and their immediate environment, the towns are spilling back into the villages: country cottages which could have been had for a song between the wars now fetch thousands of pounds for conversion into modern houses, and almost every village has its 'estate' of new houses. Not one in a hundred of immigrants to the country villages expects to work in the countryside. This is the structural change in regional life: it is no longer self-contained, and becomes more and more dependent on national policy.

That policy in relation to regional development has strange fluctuations. There are no areas of worn-out heavy industry in the Upper Thames region such as there are in the North, to which all post-war Governments have tried to bring new life. The question in the Upper Thames region is *where* major new developments should take place: Newbury, Bicester, Swindon, Didcot, have all at times been suggested as the nuclei of large new urban development, but fashions in planning change as planners retire and are promoted. There is general agreement that the villages which are the glory of the region should not be permitted to sprawl: what is called 'in-filling', where a garden or orchard within a village may have room for a house, may be allowed, but building beyond the existing edges of most villages is now normally refused planning consent. This is a good planning concept, but for how long it can withstand the pressure for building land awaits the future.

The chief agent of mobility and social change in a long placid region is the motor-car. It has created as many problems as it has solved. Oxford, which has contributed so greatly to the British motor industry, has suffered grievously from its own product: the appalling congestion of Oxford's traffic and controversy over Oxford's roads have been of national concern for thirty years. Abingdon, once one of the most beautiful medieval towns in Europe, has in some sense suffered more than Oxford: it is much smaller, its medieval streets fewer and more compact; its beauty is fragile and more easily hurt. The hurt is not Abingdon's fault. In this world you get what you pay for, you lose what you do not pay for. The nation has preferred to let the main road from Birmingham and the Midlands to Southampton – A34 – cut through the heart of a town that is a priceless heritage, rather than spend money on an adequate by-pass. Southampton docks have had their cargoes from the Midlands, Abingdon has been maimed. The profit and loss in national accountancy will be determined by our children, but a note in the accounts may be written now – a medieval town destroyed is lost for ever. The Birmingham–Southampton road used also to go through the middle of Oxford, and so did the London–Oxford–Gloucester road, A40. After much harm was done by-passes were at last built to carry these huge streams of traffic round instead of through Oxford, as Abingdon will be by-passed one day: by then it may be too late to bother much from the point of view of Abingdon, though it will be of advantage to traffic not to have to thread its way through twisting streets. But through traffic is only one aspect of the problem of the motor-car in towns: no town has yet found a way of living comfortably with its *own* cars. Abingdon's tortured streets are an example: they are littered with parked cars where parking is permitted; shops in places where parking is forbidden can scarcely be reached for the stream of moving cars and lorries. To solve the problem of access to shops, old buildings have been pulled down to make a new shopping centre: one is safe there on foot, but one might as well be shopping in a new suburb of Manchester or Birmingham – the character and atmosphere of the old town are gone.

Oxford is to have a motorway – M40 – from London, and, the old Bath Road, skirting the South of the Upper Thames region – A4 – is being replaced by the motorway M4. This is already in use to just beyond Maidenhead. It will run south of Reading, and then by Theale to the north of Newbury, and by Wickham and Poughley to skirt the southern edge of Swindon. It will scarcely touch the Upper Thames region, but will influence profoundly life in the Kennet and Ock valleys by making road travel to London, Bath and Bristol vastly easier.

The villages of the Upper Thames, of its tributary river valleys, and of the

Downland country of North Berkshire have, on the whole, benefited from the motor-car, without so far suffering much from its contamination. The car has made possible a widening of village life that would have seemed unbelievable a generation ago: you can live in the Vale of the White Horse and work in London, and go to a theatre in Oxford without elaborate planning. Yet the touch of death that the car can also bring is not wholly absent. By crippling public transport it has made villages for those who have no car more isolated than they were half a century ago. It has concentrated shops, services and entertainment in the towns – convenient enough for those who can get there, difficult and frustrating for those who cannot. It has both extended and limited opportunities of employment and training. If a youth or girl has transport – parent's, friends', or their own – the scope of jobs available, and of training for jobs, is greater than the villages have ever known. If there is no car or motor-bicycle, the village offers nothing. The land, which once took everybody, now offers work to four or five in a hundred. Even big houses are servantless, or at best offer a few hours of domestic work a week. A village boy or girl without private transport has either to leave home to find a job or to get training, or is restricted to work, such as at Harwell, which provides private bus services to work. The bicycle, which once largely met the need for cheap transport up to twenty miles or so a day, becomes less practical as motor traffic becomes heavier on the roads. Moreover, the bicycle has suffered from general social change: a generation which thought little of cycling ten miles to work because it had no alternative has been succeeded by one which knows the convenience and comfort of the car.

The car has helped to destroy the capacity for self entertainment in village communities. When the village was self-contained, it had to produce its own recreation: the 'feast', to which people looked forward for months, lantern lectures in the parish hall, barn dances – as their name suggests, dances originally held in a kindly farmer's barn, to music provided by anybody who could play a bit on the piano, fiddle, or accordion. With professional entertainment available in the towns and on television, the attraction of these amateur efforts has faded, and the impulse to produce them waned. To some extent television offsets isolation, but it is a dangerous drug. Life with nothing to do but watch television night after night is dispiriting. The minority who live in rural isolation have excuse for feeling that they are the forgotten ones in an increasingly urban nation.

Yet no one who has really lived by the headwaters of the Thames, in the valleys of Windrush, Evenlode, Glyme or Ock, by the spring-line of the Downs, would want to change. The landscape has been modified and smoothed by a thousand generations of man, but the bones of the land are as firm and good as when the first explorer of the Old Stone Age poled his log up-river. The Thames sustains, and in large measure, controls life still, as it has sustained and controlled life in its countryside before man found his way there. Its light fills the sky, a light uniquely clear, reflected from the water of the winding river, giving the whole landscape a clarity of purpose as well as vision. It is misty often in the lowlands by the river (the best forecast of a fine day is an early mist) but even the mists have a luminous quality, softening the harsher outlines of the modern works of man. Didcot Power Station, one of the new citadels of technological strength, rises from the meadows between Didcot and Sutton Courtenay like some gaunt prison of the spirit. In a light Thames mist it can appear as a fairy castle.

Our engineers are better than our architects: something went wrong with English architecture when architects lost the tradition of the medieval master mason of being able to work with stone as well as with paper. The chief threat to the beauty of the region comes from the uniform ugliness of so much of modern housing. The glory of the village and of the medieval town was that they grew out of the ground to serve the needs of men and women: everything was natural because men had to use the materials that nature gave them. Carpenters and masons in antiquity learned by trial and error roughly what sort of building would stand and what would not, and this knowledge was handed down from father to son. They used local materials because there was nothing else, and from generations of experience acquired great skill in their use. In stone country, the Cotswolds and Oxfordshire, everything from manor to cottage was built in stone: stone was easier to come by than timber, and you will often find an old cottage with a stone staircase. In the Vale of the White Horse, where there is some clay and some ragstone to be dug out of islands in the marsh, there is a nice blending of two traditions, and the typical building is of stone – more or less rubble stone – with brickwork for the quoins, window and door surrounds. In stone country, roofs were of stone slates, elsewhere commonly of thatch. Both are lovely materials, stone weathering to soft brown, green and grey, thatch neat, warm and welcoming.

These once homely materials have all but gone out of use: they demanded patient labour and manual skills, once to be found as naturally as the materials themselves, now rare and hard to come by. The machine and the factory can turn out building blocks far more cheaply than the patient hands of man. People want houses quickly – and it is the inside of a house you live in; you do not spend much time looking at the sad contrast between the weathered local stone of a group of old cottages and the garish new housing estate.

There is no virtue in age for its own sake: new materials and new methods are there to be used, to make if possible a better life for man. The pity is that they are used so often without imagination, without any feeling for the past they must combine with, that they make for a duller, uglier life. Again, every generalization must be wrong in individual cases. There is some good new building, of houses that harmonize beautifully with their local landscape, which will grow old gracefully to match their older neighbours. But uniformity is cheap, and while no two old cottages, built of local materials as they came, are ever exactly alike, a hundred or a thousand new 'semis' have the sameness of processed peas in a tin.

One must try to be fair. People want houses, and nearly everybody needs to acquire a house as cheaply as may be, whether that house is built by a council or a private developer. To return to traditional materials and methods of building can be prohibitively expensive. Planning authorities sometimes insist that new buildings must be in natural stone, but to require this on any scale would be impracticable, and unfair to individuals or ratepayers. It is not the new materials that should be condemned: there are forms of processed stone that can be used beautifully, and in time may weather beautifully; modern brick can also be used beautifully, and equally may weather well. It is not the materials – it is the urban conception of their use, alien to the individual subtleties of the countryside, that is to be deplored.

But a beautiful face is not much marred by a small scar. The scars on the beautiful region of the Upper Thames are so far small, and the noble sweep of landscape can endure them. Nevertheless, it is right to give warning; the landscape of this ancient heart of England is an irreplaceable heritage, but it is not indestructible. It is a false assumption that to let the bulldozers move in to destroy beauty makes for convenience: it may destroy those subtle ingredients and trace elements in the soil that make life possible. Man does not live by bread alone, nor, given all the bread in the world, can he live in brick boxes alone.

Rivers unite and divide. The Thames gives unity to the heart of England, infusing a common culture in the land through which it flows, whose pre-history it has shaped, whose history it has helped to form. But the Thames has been – and is – a boundary. It was the boundary between Wessex and Mercia, between Saxon and Dane, and is the boundary between modern counties, Gloucestershire and Wiltshire below Cricklade, Oxfordshire and Berkshire for the rest of its upper course. So with its tributaries: all unite with the main stream of the Thames, but each is lord, as it were, of its own feudal territory on the way to the main stream, uniting in its valley a common way of life, dividing parishes and properties within its valley. The unity of a river system is stronger than the divisive use that man has made of rivers, though the divisions may sometimes cloud the underlying unity. The unity of the Upper Thames and its tributaries was fundamental to the political expansion of Wessex into the Kingdom of England: it has been at the core of the 'Englishness' of English life ever since. This is part-real, part folk-myth. The England that exiles dream about (exiles in industrial towns as well as overseas), of thatched cottages nestling under great elms, with a duckpond on the village green, *is* the landscape of the Upper Thames. It is also a folk-myth of what an English landscape *ought* to be. It is not less real for being also partly mythical: indeed, the reality lives in the myth. The Thames and its countryside have influenced the lives and thinking of millions who have never seen them.

II

River cruise

At normal summer levels the stream of the Thames is gentle: anywhere above Teddington you have no tides to reckon with, and a boat needs little power to handle easily. I am writing here mainly of powered boats, because although there are good sailing reaches on the Upper Thames, and flourishing dinghy clubs, cruising for any distance under sail can be hard work, and demand more time than one commonly has to spare: there are too many bridges at which the mast has to come down, and the river winds so much, and has so many wind-shadows from trees or banks, that at one moment you may be running, the next beating into a headwind, with little room to go about. I should add that for many years I have kept a small sailing cruiser on the Upper Thames, and enjoyed her greatly; but if I go off for a few days the mast normally comes down and stays ashore, and I use an outboard engine.

The powered cruiser of two berths upwards is nowadays the standard craft for voyaging on the Thames, and there are admirable facilities for hiring such cruisers, and for launching and maintaining privately-owned boats. Cruising voyages can, of course, be made by punt, skiff or canoe, and fine adventures such voyages can be. But for most river-cruising now the small engine, inboard or outboard, is the chosen form of propulsion. And enjoyable as canoe or punt camping may be, the self-contained cruiser, with bunks, galley and living accommodation on board, offers independence and weather protection that are worth having.

It is said that the pleasure you get from a boat is in inverse ratio to her size. Although the locks on the Thames can take pretty large craft (up to 100 ft long the whole way to Lechlade) I would counsel voyagers to use boats of modest size.

222

You can find remarkable comfort in an 18 ft boat, and luxury in one of 30 ft. With such dimensions you will not need to worry about water; you will get in almost anywhere, you will have room to manœuvre, and you will not hog the river to the irritation of others. Moreover, since tolls are based on length, you will save money with a modest craft.

The Thames Conservancy is sometimes criticized for its tolls, but to my view these are reasonable, and surely justified by the care it takes of the river. All locks on the Thames are manned, from 9 a.m. to sunset in summer, and to one hour before sunset in winter. Most locks are now hydraulic, and all are kept in good shape. The bargemen who hauled and struggled over shoals would think themselves navigating an Elysian river if they returned to the Thames now. The channel is well-buoyed, and obstructions marked with red can buoys to be left to port and black diamond buoys to be left to starboard.

Remember that by the traditions of navigation a river is entered from the sea, so that the port (left) and starboard (right) banks are the banks as encountered going *upstream*; proceeding downstream, red can and black diamond buoys are to be left on the opposite hand.

If a fork at an island or a shoal is marked by a black and red spherical buoy it may be passed on either hand. The Thames buoyage system is simple and easily followed, and a clear little chart is published in the Conservancy's *Launch Digest*, issued on registration to every boatowner.

The first step to taking your own boat on the Thames is to apply to the Thames Conservancy (Burdett House, 15 Buckingham Street, London W.C.2), for a licence. This must be renewed annually (or triennially), and once a boat has been licensed she is free to use locks on the river without further payment. There is provision for obtaining short-term licences for boats visiting the Thames from the sea, or other inland waterways. If you wish to hire a cruiser you have a choice of numerous boatyards operating charter fleets, and such boats are already registered and licensed. Boat hire charges, like those for hotels at holiday resorts, normally vary with the season, being cheapest in early spring and late summer, highest at the peak of the holiday period. Most hire-cruisers are 4-berth boats, but some smaller 2-berth craft, and large vessels sleeping up to ten are also available. Again like booking for holiday resorts, it is wise to book in January or February, but if you feel like a Thames cruise on the spur of the moment, it is worth trying for a boat, for a charter fleet may have a cancelled booking, and a cruiser may be obtainable at short notice, though she may be bigger or smaller than you would choose for preference.

223

Charters are normally by the week, from Saturday to Saturday, and the fee usually includes everything necessary for a cruise, covering boat, bedding and saloon furniture, galley and cooking equipment, crockery, cutlery and the like. Blankets are generally provided, but charterers may be asked to bring their own sheets and towels. Food and fuel are the only additional costs on top of the charter-fee, and since these are determined by what you eat and where you go, the cost of a Thames cruise can be estimated pretty well in advance. In making estimates, don't try to calculate fuel costs by miles per gallon: how far a boat travels in any given time is determined by wind and current as well as fuel consumption. The relevant figures are fuel consumption per hour. At ordinary summer levels the stream of the Thames will not make much material difference to passage times from one place to another, but a strong wind can have a marked effect on a river cruiser with considerable top hamper. Speed on the Upper Thames is restricted by the Conservancy to a maximum of 7 knots (8 m.p.h.), and you will often find that a speed of 4–5 knots is both more economical and more pleasant. In any case, there will be many occasions on a cruise when 7 knots is far too fast for prudent navigation. At such a speed even a small boat makes a considerable wash, which can be perilous to a canoe or rowing boat, and make moored craft surge and knock into one another. To cause such disturbance is bad manners, as well as a possible offence of careless navigation under the Thames by-laws.

From Teddington to Lechlade the Thames offers 124 miles of navigable waterway, with access at Oxford to the Oxford Canal, and thence to the still usable canals of the Midlands and their branches that reach across Britain from Llangollen to the Humber. The Thames alone is a cruising ground enough for a meditative lifetime, but it is worth remembering that if you contract on the Thames a pleasant fever for inland cruising, you are not limited to the river, for you can extend your range to the canals as well. One caveat applies if you contemplate buying a boat. Thames locks are wide, and even in the highest reaches of the river will take a boat with a beam up to 14 ft. Many canal locks are much narrower, and if you plan to range from the Thames to the canal system you must limit yourself to a boat with a beam not exceeding 6 ft 10 in. This, however, is ample for a comfortable small cruiser.

The Upper Thames above Reading is navigable for some eighty miles, and, apart from a rather dreary stretch by the gasworks of Oxford, every reach is beautiful. Always, even on a dull day, there is the incomparable, faintly luminous Thames light, and the riverscape changes subtly from one moment to the next:

39a. *One of the oldest bridges across the Thames at Radcot.*

39b. *The Thames spanned by a telegraph pole bridge at Cricklade.*

40a and b. *The excavated Roman villa at Chedworth, Gloucestershire. The site is beautifully maintained, and there is an excellent museum.*

you can sail the same stretch of river a hundred times, and it never seems quite the same.

Let us embark at Abingdon, where there is a boatyard with a good slip, on a late afternoon, with a few days freedom ahead of us. I choose late afternoon for embarking on this voyage, for I don't want to go far before mooring for the first night, and I do want to go to what to my mind is among the loveliest retreats on the whole river. My boat is small, just over 17 ft long, but she will sleep two comfortably, three fairly comfortably, and four at a pinch, though one of the four has to be a child. As I have said, she is really a sailing boat, but for this trip her mast is left ashore.

I am going to voyage upstream to Lechlade, but for this first night I am going a couple of miles downstream, to moor just above the weirs at Sutton Courtenay. This reach of the Thames is now really a backwater, for the navigable channel goes by a lock-cut to Culham, rejoining the river below Sutton Courtenay. It is partly because it is a backwater that the Sutton Courtenay reach is so attractive.

The Thames is legally a navigation, and a boat on passage has a general right to anchor or moor in the river for a 'reasonable' time in the course of navigation. 'Reasonable' in this context is defined by the Thames Conservancy as 'for a period not exceeding 24 hours at any particular place'. Every boat on passage should carry an anchor, for in an emergency it may be necessary to bring up quickly, but to anchor in the stream requires a dinghy if one wants to go ashore, and normally it is preferable to moor to a bank. Wherever there is a towpath it is permissible to moor, though one must be intelligent about it, and not leave ropes lying across a place where people are likely to walk – or even unlikely to walk, for it is the unlikely mishap that leads to claims for damages. Private rights must also be respected: most of the land through which the river flows is privately owned, and if a landowner puts up a notice prohibiting mooring, the prohibition should be accepted. In practice, there is little difficulty. Those inhospitable notices saying 'No Mooring' or 'Keep Off' that are common to the riverside suburbia of the Lower Thames are scarce along the upper river; the water-meadows are quiet and remote, with often not a building in sight. You harm no one by driving a peg into a bank, or tying to an overhanging willow, and if you go quietly about your own affairs, no one will bother you. If you want to moor to the garden of an inn, or to land obviously belonging to someone's house, you should, of course, ask permission first. Mostly it will be given. The innkeeper will welcome your custom but it is not fair to occupy mooring space belonging to a riverside inn, and go off to have a meal or a drink elsewhere; you are keeping someone else away, and if you do so you are asking for unpleasantness. And there is no need to risk unpleasantness, for the Thames has plenty of room.

My outboard engine pushes my boat along at 4–5 m.p.h. – I want to go no faster. The built-up area of Abingdon falls away in a few minutes, and the broad Culham Reach opens up ahead of us. This is one of the finest sailing reaches on the Thames, and a covey of dinghies from the local Sailing Club are under sail. I am a little ashamed (quite illogically) of not being under sail myself, and I remember that with my outboard I am under power, and must therefore give way to the dinghies. They are well-handled, and we have no trouble. The river here flows almost due south. The silver water is fringed with the pale green of willows, and in the distance, beyond the willows, rises the clean line of the Downs.

The cut to Culham Lock goes off to port – strictly, it is the starboard bank, but we are going downstream. We stand on into the wide reach that looks (and once was) the main river. Soon there is the noise of falling water from the weirs, and warning notices to avoid them. We turn through 360 degrees (there is plenty of room) and make for the bank, to moor bows on to the stream. With thirty yards or so to go I shut off the outboard and we carry our way, the stream helping to check it, just to the bank, where there is a tree that I have known for many years. I jump ashore, and moor bow and stern, bows to the tree, and a stern line carried to a convenient thorn bush, prickly, but with a stem amply strong enough to hold us. Although there is no tide to bother about, mooring warps must be slack enough to allow for a sudden rise or fall in the level of the river: if there is torrential rain, the river may rise by two or three feet in a matter of hours, or some emergency may require work at a weir which makes a stretch of river fall. The river may seem tame compared with the sea, but a living river is never really tamed, and the Thames carries a formidable volume of water.

It is time for supper. We cook in my small galley on a two-burner stove fuelled by bottled gas. It is connected to its cylinder in a moment, but I never leave it connected: the cylinder of gas, disconnected and screwed down, lives outside the cabin in an after locker, for safety. After supper we tidy up, make our bunks for the night, and sit in the cockpit for a quiet smoke. It is utterly remote. We are moored, in fact, to an island of farmland, a mile or so long, formed by the cut leading to Culham Lock. Only a footpath crosses it; there is no road anywhere near, and no sound of traffic. Sutton Courtenay village is about half a mile away, reached by a pleasant walk, first along the bank, and then across the bridges of the weirs. The weirs maintain a constant music of falling water, not quite near enough to be loud, but near enough to be present always. If we feel like a drink before turning in, we can stroll into the village – a delightful village, where Mr Asquith (the first Lord Oxford and Asquith) once lived. This first night we do not feel like the urbanity of even a village pub: we are content with the utter peace of nightfall on the river.

My boat has few mod. cons. Lighting is by a brass lifeboat lantern, of an ancient Board of Trade pattern: I have never known it blow out, but it does not give much light. This is no great matter: it is better to turn in early, and wake early, to enjoy the dawn and have a leisurely breakfast before getting under way for the opening of the locks at 09.00. I wake at first light, pull on some clothes and go into the cockpit. The awakening of the river is a daily miracle, fascinating always, different always. This morning there is a light mist, a good sign, for early mist on the river generally means a fine day. The mist prevents a sparkling dawn: daylight comes with a gently-spreading luminosity, at first without definition, then, imperceptibly, becoming sharper. A flash of blue in midstream brings back colour suddenly, to the world. A kingfisher lives in this reach; he is shy by day and the early morning is the best time to see him. I cannot honestly say that I have ever seen *him*, because all you see is his *flight* – a streak of blue so vivid that it seems incandescent and physically glowing in the air.

In the reeds a few yards above our mooring a pair of swans have nested. I am careful to ignore them, for a nesting swan is fierce in defence of her brood. The male swan is a good father, constantly on patrol, alert to the slightest sign of possible interference with his family. It is dangerous to provoke him, for he is a powerful bird, and a blow with his wing can break a man's arm. I throw him some bread, which he takes, but not, at first, for himself: the first piece he takes back to his mate.

Swans on the Thames are commonly supposed to belong to the Crown, or rather, to the monarch personally. This was true once, but it has not been wholly true for the past 600 years. The swan figured early in legislation, originally for economic reasons. I have never eaten swan's meat, but some who have tell me that it is coarse, and disappointing. In the Middle Ages, however, it was much esteemed, as much, perhaps, for quantity as for quality, for a grown swan has plenty of meals on him. With hordes of retainers to feed, the Crown kept a sharp eye on swans, as it did on forest game. But the Crown could give as well as grasp, and the grant of a right to keep swans might be bestowed on people whom the King wished to honour (or placate). At some time in the fifteenth century,*

---

* I am indebted to Mr G. E. Walker, for many years Secretary to the Thames Conservancy, for information on the legal status of swans on the Thames.

probably in the reign of Edward IV, grants of 'a game of swans', and of the right to a 'swanmark', were made to two City livery companies, the Vintners and the Dyers. This conferred the privilege of owning and marking swans, the 'swanmark' being important to identify ownership. Swans are marked by small nicks cut in the upper bill, and a 'mark' consists of a given number of nicks. The Vintners' swans have two nicks, the Dyers' one. The inn sign 'The Swan with two necks' derives from the Vintners' swanmark: properly it is 'The Swan with two *nicks*', nick having been corrupted to 'neck' over the centuries.

Crown birds are not marked, so that all unmarked swans belong to the Crown. The Dyers are entitled to 65 grown swans, the Vintners to 45, and the Crown's swan population on the Thames is reckoned at about 500. An annual count, and marking of new birds, takes place in July or August each year, at a ceremony known as 'Swan-Upping'. The Crown, the Dyers and the Vintners all have official swankeepers, who are responsible for swans on the Thames, and for seeing that ownership is maintained in the established proportions.

Swans are among the most beautiful of birds, though not always the best-tempered, and if you are walking by the river, or in a canoe or small boat, it is well to give them a fair berth. The swan is sometimes accused of destroying fish by devouring spawn, but in fact the swan is no great enemy of fish. He does sometimes eat spawn, but by accident rather than choice, for the swan is by nature a vegetarian, feeding on water plants (and bread and biscuits, when he is given them). He eats spawn only when it has been caught by the stems of water plants. He is, however, both inquisitive and greedy, and if you are fishing and cast a line too near a swan he may sometimes take your bait, and the hook with it. This can lead to a nasty situation, for the hook may be caught in his bill, or perhaps in his throat. Unless you are skilled at handling swans, it is wiser not to attempt to free the bird yourself: he will not know that you are trying to help him, and he may thrash out and injure you. R S P C A officers in Thames-side towns have much experience of dealing with swans, and if you can get someone to telephone the R S P C A, or the police, while you keep an eye on the swan to identify him when help comes, skilled help will usually be forthcoming.

From Sutton Courtenay to Abingdon Lock (the first lock going upstream) at our speed is about half an hour's run. We breakfast and tidy up, and leave a few minutes before nine. The mist has all but gone, and there is lovely early morning sunshine: the river gleams, and the new green of the willows is an enchantment. The visual approach to Abingdon upstream is marred by a new housing estate, but it falls away quickly, and the reach to Abingdon Bridge opens up. This is sheer beauty: on the left bank (going upstream) rises the spire of St Helen's Church, surrounded by gracious old almshouses, and seventeenth- or eighteenth-century town houses, with lovely gardens running to the river. On the right are water meadows and a line of poplars. There is an island (Nag's Head Island) in midstream at Abingdon, but the navigable channel is well marked and leads to the navigation arch of the bridge. Respect the marked channel here, and do not be tempted by what looks like good water on the town side of the island: it shallows as it nears the bridge, the arches here are narrow, and in anything much bigger than a skiff you will get into trouble.

The lock is about a quarter of a mile above the bridge. The lock is against us as we approach, which means tying up to a mooring post outside it while boats coming downstream are put through. We wait until the lock-gates open, and the downstream traffic is clear; then we cast off our mooring and enter the lock, making for the side to which the lock-keeper beckons, and timing things so that we have lost all way as we reach the stone steps leading up the wall of the lock. It is necessary to go ashore here, to take our lines to the top of the lock, to control our boat as the lock fills. There are bollards for making fast, but while you want your boat held as you go through a lock her lines must not be tied, but free to move as she rises (or falls) in the water. The best thing is to put one turn round a bollard and hold the line, so that the strain is taken on the bollard, and you can let out the line as needed. You must have both bow and stern lines, but except with a very big boat one man ashore can easily handle both lines. A word of advice here – make sure that you have good long lines, at least 30 ft both bow and stern. You also need good fend-offs, to hang between your boat's side and the lock wall, so that your paintwork does not suffer if she surges against the wall. But don't leave fend-offs hanging overboard when you leave the lock, for this is slovenly seamanship.

Just above Abingdon Lock, with its own landing stage, is one of the sanitary stations maintained by the Conservancy for the disposal of sewage and other refuse. No sewage or refuse may be discharged into the Thames; if a seagoing boat fitted with a marine water-closet comes into the non-tidal river the closet must not be used, and the outlet should be sealed. The only lavatories permitted on river boats must be of the self-contained chemical type, and these, of course, require emptying from time to time. This can be done at any of the Conservancy's sanitary stations, which, unlike some lay-bys on main roads, are well equipped and decently looked after. Above Reading they are to be found at Whitchurch, Day's Lock, near Dorchester, Abingdon, Eynsham and Radcot.

It is possible to get from Abingdon, or even lower down the river, to Lechlade in a day, but unless one has some special cause for hurry it seems to me to forego much of what the river gives to drive oneself or one's boat too quickly. To my mind many river holidays are spoiled because people attempt to do too much in too short a time: better a day spent leisurely in going a few miles, with time off for exploring ashore, than to spend hour after hour at the wheel or tiller of a boat as if it were a car. For this voyage I plan to get no farther than Newbridge, to spend the night moored to the garden of The Rose Revived, and probably to have dinner ashore in the hotel.

The river above Abingdon is wide and gentle, making a great curve from Sandford, below Oxford, to flow through a park-like countryside of woods and meadows. The land on both banks rises gently, on the Berkshire bank to the Cumnor hills, on the Oxfordshire bank to the ridge that divides the valleys of Thames and Thame. The railway bridge that carries the Western Region line to Oxford is the only obvious sign of man's contrivances, but the whole of this park-like landscape reflects man's patient handiwork over ten thousand years. Above the railway bridge the Oxfordshire bank is indeed a park, the 1,200 acres of the grounds laid out in the eighteenth century for the mansion at Nuneham Cour-tenay built by the first Earl Harcourt. Across the river is Radley College, a keen rowing school, and one may expect to meet a crew from the college practising on the river. The shell of a rowing eight looks sliver-thin, but remember that the oars extend far on each side, and give it a safe berth.

The next lock is Sandford, with a pleasant riverside inn, the King's Arms, almost adjoining the lock. It is a question here of what to do. Above Sandford comes the rather dreary stretch through Oxford, with the locks at Iffley and Osney to be got through before one comes to peaceful countryside again. The question for us is whether to press on through Oxford for a late lunch or early tea at Godstow, or whether to take time off at Sandford and have a leisurely lunch there first. We decide to stay at Sandford, where there is good mooring to the towpath just above the lock, the inn to be visited, and the village to stroll through. Fortified by lunch we approach Oxford.

The passage of Oxford by river has simply to be endured. The medieval river, washing the castle and the walls of Osney Abbey, with St Frideswide's church, and the charming huddle of buildings that made the town rising from its banks, must have been lovely. It must have been lovely still in the eighteenth century. Victorian Oxford let it all go, finding the river plain a cheap site for working-class dwellings and for the location of gasworks and railway sidings. The reach by Christ Church Meadow, where the college barges used to be, and where there are now a number of college boathouses, is at least tidy, but it is the tidiness of a municipal park: if the river here were grass, one would expect notices instructing the public not to walk upon it.

Navigation by Folly Bridge calls for alert pilotage, and careful attention to the signs marking the channel; nevertheless, this is the most interesting part of the voyage through the city, with a brief hint of magic behind ancient walls – the only touch of magic in riverside Oxford. (I exclude the Cherwell: not navigable by cruiser, but attractive water for punt or canoe, the Cherwell still has a quality of dream about it.)

Above Folly Bridge is a dreary stretch leading to the rather nice little lock at Osney, and the tricky passage of Osney Bridge. This is an exceptionally low, exceptionally ugly bridge, and although it is a road bridge it was built to serve the railway station. There is a theory that it was deliberately built low in order to interfere as much as possible with barge traffic, so reducing competition for the railway. Whether such tawdry thinking had any influence in its design I do not know, but the bridge is certainly a dangerous obstruction to boats. It is the lowest bridge on the whole of the navigable Thames, with headroom of only 7 ft 7 ins at ordinary river level: if the river is high, the headroom is, of course, reduced. Windscreens, dodgers and deck-gear of all sorts may have to be removed to enable a boat to pass.

For our small boat, with her low cabin-top, designed for stability at sea rather than for the more luxurious accommodation of the river, Osney Bridge is no hazard, though we take down the jack staff for our ensign, and instinctively duck our heads as we pass under the bridge. The worst of Oxford is now over, and the river soon broadens to a fine reach skirting the great field of Port Meadow. The next lock is Godstow, with the scant remaining ruins of the once-great nunnery, at once romantic and pathetic, on one bank, and the Trout Inn, fashionable and with peacocks on its terrace, on the other. There is good mooring on the Berkshire bank just above the lock.

We are approaching the most northerly point of Berkshire, at Wytham, where the Thames, having made its sudden turn to the north to get round the Cumnor heights, turns back to the south. Hydrologically, this is an interesting bit of river, and hydrological complexity is expressed by four locks in five miles – going upstream, Godstow, King's, Eynsham and Pinkhill. This means work for the crew, but well rewarded, for apart from the road bridge at Eynsham, neither road nor railway comes near the river, and the landscape has the charm of eighteenth-century paintings of country scenes. This, indeed, holds true of the whole river above Godstow: main roads and railways have mostly gone elsewhere, and even riverside villages are far between. It is a remote and lovely country, with the glory of Wytham Great Wood a piece of visible history, reminding us of the dense forest that once covered the land.

You must match supplies to the chart in those parts, for if you run out of bread or matches or fuel you may have a long walk to find any. If by accident you do run short of anything, don't curse too much. It was a quest for tobacco that first led me many years ago through the enchanting lanes that run to Stanton Harcourt.

Once through Pinkhill there is a placid stretch of four miles or so to North-moor. This is Matthew Arnold country, not much changed since he knew and loved it, and you would not be at all surprised to catch a glimpse of his shy Scholar Gipsy

Crossing the stripling Thames at Bablockhithe

We pass Bablockhithe, where there has been a ferry for centuries (but if you want to cross by road from Cumnor to Stanton Harcourt, inquire first if it is working). I doubt if Matthew Arnold's word 'stripling' is quite right. It implies to me a river not much more than a brook, whereas the Thames here is a wide stream, needing a ferry. But I forgive Matthew Arnold his 'stripling' for his splendid denunciation of our generation as much as his, as

> Light half-believers of our casual creeds
> Who never deeply felt, nor clearly will'd,
> Whose insight never has born fruit in deeds,
> Whose vague resolves never have been fulfilled;
> For whom each year we see
> Brings new beginnings, disappointments new;
> Who hesitate and falter life away,
> And lose tomorrow the ground won today . . .

That was written a hundred years ago, but there could be no more percipient description of the moral and economic mess of the twentieth century.

A voyage on the Thames will not cure this diseased century, but it may help individuals to a refreshment of spirit, and at least to a more detached view of the affairs to which after a few days of truancy we must return.

At Northmoor Lock we are within a couple of miles of our mooring for the night at Newbridge. We have taken a day to cover twenty-five miles, about six hours actually under way, but with long intervals for lunch and a walk ashore at Godstow, and a good deal of time spent in going through locks. I have made this voyage several times, and although reason tells me that I have sat at the tiller in oilskins, with the chill rain of an English summer day at its worst lashing my face, in retrospect I remember only the glint of sun on water and meadows, and a warm, soft breeze on my arms with rolled-up shirtsleeves. My river is like the sundial that tells only of sunny hours. Perhaps it does. Of course it sometimes rains, and of course an English summer can be vile, but somehow on the river one is *in* the weather, part of it, and not just scurrying away from it. This is something that a boat gives – you are so sensitive to weather that it is part of your ambient world, and you notice small changes in rain or wind that you would miss on shore. Perhaps this makes even rain more interesting, so that you resent it less.

We reach The Rose Revived in the early evening. It is a nice old inn, with lawns and flower beds coming to the waterside, and good water right up to the bank. Newbridge consists of its medieval bridge, The Rose at the Oxfordshire end of the bridge, and another nice inn, The Maybush, at the Berkshire end. There is nothing else. You can walk two miles to Kingston Bagpuize in Berkshire, or a mile and a half to Standlake in Oxfordshire, or you can stay where you are and enjoy things.

After making fast to the bank below The Rose I go up to the inn to ask if I may moor for the night. I expect no difficulty, for the landlord here is a friend, but it is still polite to ask: it is his property, and he is entitled, if he wishes, to make a charge for mooring.

The Windrush joins the Thames at Newbridge, and the Oxfordshire span of the old bridge crosses the mouth of the Windrush before it gets to the Thames. The navigation arch is narrow, and the stream of the Windrush added to the stream of the Thames calls for careful pilotage here, especially if there is any wind. Two and a half miles above the bridge is Shifford lock. The channel is a cut that avoids the shallows that make the ford at Duxford, which now leads only to an island formed by the cut and the old stream. But a footbridge crosses the cut, and a footpath leads to the ford. It is a good place to go ashore for a stroll, to see this ancient ford by which our prehistoric ancestors crossed the river. Another three miles brings us to Tadpole Bridge, with another pleasant inn (The Trout). If you need stores, or just feel like another walk, it is only a couple of miles from Tadpole Bridge on the Oxfordshire bank to Bampton, well worth a visit.

There are three locks in the next five miles, Rushey, Radcot and Grafton, so it is leisurely travelling on this stretch. And so it should be, for each bend of the stream opens a new reach flowing between quiet meadows, the colouring all pastel shades of green and bluish-brown divided by the silver line of water, every reach subtly different from the next.

233

Two miles above Grafton Lock, on the Oxfordshire bank but now very near the Gloucestershire border, is Kelmscot, an exquisite small village surrounding Kelmscot Manor, which was the home of William Morris from 1871 until his death in 1896: Morris is buried in Kelmscot churchyard.

Kelmscot is a fairy-story manor house, small, and built of the kind of stone that seems to grow out of the ground it stands on – as, in a sense, it does, for it is local stone. Morris described it in a letter to a friend in 1871

> I have been looking about for a house for the wife and kids, and whither do you guess my eye is turned now? Kelmscot(t), a little village about two miles above Radcot(t) bridge – a heaven on earth; an old stone Elizabethan house . . . and such a garden! close down on the river, a boat house, and all things handy . . .*

The main part of the house was built about 1570, with additions in the seventeenth century. Morris originally took a joint tenancy of Kelmscot with Dante Gabriel Rossetti, but in 1874 Rossetti departed, after much strain concerning Morris's wife Jane. Rossetti painted some haunting portraits of Jane Morris, and he was certainly in love with her. Whether she was in love with him is less clear: the mystery that still shrouds their relationship may be explained, at least to some extent, in 1989, when letters between them, now in the British Museum, will become open to readers. These letters were left to the Museum by Morris's daughter, Miss Mary (May) Morris, who died in 1938, on condition that they were not to be inspected for fifty years after her death. Whatever may be the truth about the relations between D. G. Rossetti and Jane Morris, it was a situation that caused much unhappiness to Rossetti, Jane and her husband, although after the crisis of 1874 the Morris household seems to have regained at least stability. Kelmscot was held by William Morris on lease: his family continued to live there after his death, and the freehold was bought by his widow in 1913, a year before she died.

When I was twenty-two or thereabouts I knocked on the door of Kelmscot to ask if I might see the house. Miss May Morris, who was then over seventy (she was Morris's younger daughter, born in 1862), received me with great kindness, and herself took me from room to room, showing me all her treasures. The memory of that visit is yet vivid: if it was not exactly 'seeing Shelley plain', it was a direct and personal link with one of my heroes.

* A. R. Dufty, 'William Morris and the Kelmscot Estate', *The Antiquaries Journal,* Vol. XLIII, 1963.

Miss May Morris left Kelmscot to the University of Oxford to be maintained as far as possible unchanged as a memorial to her father, and to be used 'as a rest house for artists, men of letters, scholars, and men of science'. The university accepted the bequest, but with inflation after the war the income from the Kelmscot estate was not sufficient to maintain the house and to carry out the terms of the will. In 1962 the university took the matter to court: the bequest to the university, and the by-then onerous trust that went with it, were set aside, and Kelmscot passed to The Society of Antiquaries, as residuary legatees of Miss Morris's estate. The Society now maintains the house and lets it as a private residence. It is open to the public on certain days each year, and I visited Kelmscot again on one of those days in 1968. Miss Morris would have approved of the Society's custodianship: the house is lovingly looked after, furnished with the Morris family's belongings, and with carpets, tapestries, and wallpaper of Morris's own design. The four-poster bed in Morris's bedroom has the hangings he knew, with his poem 'For the Bed at Kelmscot (t)' embroidered on them by Miss May Morris, with the assistance, it is believed, of Lily Yeats, sister of W. B. Yeats.

> The wind's on the wold
> And the night is a-cold,
> And Thames runs chill
> Twixt mead and hill
> But kind and dear
> Is the old house here . . .

The words are sharp in the exquisite embroidery. Whatever unhappiness Morris may have known in his earlier days at Kelmscot, the house and the river certainly gave him peace.

It is not far now to Lechlade, five miles of river and only two more locks, Buscot and St John's, the highest lock on the Thames. We have come only about 17 miles from Newbridge, but there have been six locks, and we have taken a good deal of time off. Lechlade is a good place to spend the night before starting the return voyage, the river as serenely beautiful as ever if you just want to sit and look at it, the town at hand if, you feel like a drink or a meal ashore.

I have written of the voyage upstream from Sutton Courtenay because, if one must attempt to classify, I think this passage the loveliest on the whole Thames. But this is a private preference, and must not prejudice the river below Culham:

235

there are many who prefer the rather broader stream, and the riverside towns – Dorchester, with its ancient abbey and fine old coaching inns, Wallingford, as old as the history of the Thames, Goring, Pangbourne, and – below Reading, and therefore outside the scope of this book – Henley, Marlow, Maidenhead and Windsor. Just below Culham, Clifton Hampden and the Wittenhams – Long and Little – are a charming group of villages, with much thatch, and a noble bridge. Sail up the backwater to Long Wittenham, and walk across the meadows to Little Wittenham. There you will find the most poignant of all village memorials to the dead of the First World War – a cross that commemorates one man, who was perhaps the only man of fighting age in the tiny hamlet that was his home. To regain perspective climb the Wittenham Clumps, prehistoric earthworks still with a slight sense of mystery about them, and a magnificent view of Dorchester and the whole of this stretch of the Thames Valley. The approach to Wallingford from the river is made memorable by the 'cheeky' spire of its church – and seeing this delicate stone wedding-cake in its river setting you will perhaps feel as I do that it is not an architectural folly but a most imaginative and completely successful work of art.

Many people charter cruisers at yards near London, and their approach to the Upper Thames is the voyage upstream, from below Maidenhead or Windsor. It is the historical approach, the route of early man, of Saxon and Viking invaders. If you start so far downstream it is a mistake, I think, unless you have at least a fortnight, to attempt to go farther than Abingdon or, at most, Oxford. The boat has to be returned, and although some firms now have arrangements whereby a cruiser can be hired at one point on the river and returned to another, you must reckon the time it will take to get from whatever place you may make for on the river to the returning point. If, as most of us are, you are limited in time, sail one stretch of the river one year, one the next. All good voyages should have some purposes of exploration in them, and the Thames offers much to explore. Particularly if you sail with children, it makes everybody happier if you include a good expedition ashore in every sailing day, and for myself I like to have at least one meal ashore each day, if this be no more than bread and cheese in a pub: it makes a break from the galley for your wife, or for yourself if you are doing the cooking.

And may I here air a theory which I try to practise in my own sailing life? If you sail with a woman who cooks for you on fifty weeks of the year, let her do the navigation and yourself take over the galley. Take over everything to do with the galley, the listing and getting of stores, the preparation and cooking of meals. I think that many women who would otherwise enjoy cruising are deterred by the thought that for them it means merely transferring housekeeping to cramped quarters. I know one splendid Scandinavian small boat sailor who declares firmly, 'I won't have a woman in my galley'. That is, perhaps, a point of view that is slightly too austere, but it is a good approach.

It is not customary to sail by night on the Thames. It is quite proper to do so, and a night passage has a beauty of its own, but your vessel must be fully equipped with navigation lights – the bicolour red and green lights in one housing that are often used on small boats are not permitted. And you must work the locks with your own crew, for the lock keepers go off duty at sunset (in winter an hour before sunset). A few years ago, when locks on the upper river were all manual, it was easy enough to put a boat through a lock yourself. Now the locks are mostly electro-hydraulic, and although there is provision for manual operation, it is a tedious process. In general, therefore, it is customary to moor for the night. You do not need lights on a vessel if she is moored to a bank, but if for some reason you lie at anchor, you should, of course, display an anchor light. With bankside mooring readily available it is normally unnecessary for a boat, unless she is exceptionally big, to lie at anchor.

The Thames is a gentle river, but in midstream it is usually quite deep, and if people who can't swim go overboard they are in immediate danger of drowning. To manœuvre a boat to recover somebody who has fallen overboard is a harder task than is sometimes realized: throw an empty carton overboard, and see how long it takes to pick it up. Moreover, when you have brought your boat to the right place, it may prove difficult to haul a non-swimmer back on board. It is imperative, therefore, to ensure that those who can't swim do not fall overboard, and that if by any chance they do, they are wearing life jackets. For young children the best precaution is a safety harness, with a line and a snap shackle that can be fastened to a handrail, or some other strong point on the boat: the line permits them to move about, and if they do go over, at least they are tied on. But the Thames is not the sea, and the discipline of safety harness for everyone on deck in rough weather is not necessary. For older children, and for grown ups who can't swim and have a working place in the crew, a life jacket worn at all times on deck is a wise precaution. There are lifejackets and lifejackets: *use only lifejackets that meet the full British Standard specification.* If you are offered some cheaper buoyancy aid, reflect that if your son or daughter needs a lifejacket, your sole thought in that emergency will be of the lifesaving and not the money-saving quality of what he or she may be wearing.

Fishing rights in the Upper Thames and its tributaries are privately, or sometimes municipally, owned, and permission to fish any given stretch of water should be obtained beforehand. It is sometimes believed that while fishing from a bank is restricted to the owner of the rights (or his licensees), fishing from a boat is free for all. This is not so – all fishing is legally reserved to the owners of fishing rights. One quite often sees a fishing line dangling from a cruiser: even if permission from all the manifold owners of rights in the waters over which she passes has been obtained (which is improbable), line-fishing from a moving boat is unlikely to catch anything: and the practice is dangerous, because the line may foul a swimmer, or another boat. For serious fishing there are many angling clubs from which advice may be sought. Extensive fishing rights round Abingdon are vested in the borough, and licences may be obtained from the council offices.

Canals are extensions of rivers, but canal cruising has an atmosphere quite different from river navigation. It is not simply that the river is natural and a canal man-made: after a hundred years or so, a canal seems as much part of the landscape as any river. The scale of most English canals is much smaller than even the higher reaches of the Thames, and canal cruising has about it a curious intimacy as if boat, crew, canal and fields were all part of a model landscape. As a method of retreat from the world a still navigable canal, long abandoned by commercial traffic, has few rivals. It is not wholly contemplative retreat, though you can make time for contemplation: canal cruising is harder work than navigation on the Thames, for mostly you have to work locks with your own crew. But the rewards are real, for you see an England that has been forgotten by this century, and you voyage in time as well as in space. The Oxford Canal, although it is never more than a mile or two from the Oxford–Banbury road, traverses a different world: once beyond Kidlington you are as remote from the scatter of twentieth-century life as you might be on the headwaters of the Orinoco. You will be wise to allow at least two days for the journey to Banbury that you would do by road in an hour, but they will be memorable days. From the canal you have a wonderful choice of walks to villages that go back to Saxon, and here and there, to Roman England, all within a couple of miles of your mooring – Kirtlington, where Sir Christopher Wren's father is buried, Somerton, Fritwell, Souldern, Aynho, and several more delightful goals for a brief expedition. This is frontier country, once disputed between Mercia and Wessex, now the borderland between Oxfordshire and Northamptonshire. Souldern is in Oxfordshire, Aynho, a mile and a half away, is in Northamptonshire. At Kirtlington you meet the Roman Akeman Street that led to the once-important, long-forgotten, Roman post at Alchester, near Bicester. A mile and a half to the north of Akeman Street there is an interesting old earthwork known as Ash Bank or Aves Ditch. Its original purpose is obscure. It may be an early Saxon fortification to defend a crossing of the Cherwell, but it is probably much older. How they dug, those remote ancestors of ours!

Navigation on the Oxford Canal is controlled by the British Waterways Board, which has a boat station at Oxford and a new (in 1970) cruising-craft centre at Banbury. North of Banbury the Oxford Canal will take you to Napton Junction and the canal system of the Midlands. The British Waterways Board maintains a fleet of hire craft, and there are a number of private firms chartering boats for canal cruising – a list may be obtained from the Waterways Board.

So this book ends, as it began, with the water that formed, bounded, and has held together the region of the Upper Thames. When I was invited by my publisher to write the book we discussed what it should include. One suggestion was that there ought to be a chapter on the Upper Thames in literature. It was a good suggestion, but I have sat at my window night after night, watching the reflected moon wax and wane in one of the tributaries of the Thames, wondering how to do it. And in the end I cannot. From the compiling of the *Anglo-Saxon Chronicle* to the latest learned work from Oxford, the Thames has flowed with English literature, influencing countless writers. Where begin? Where stop? With Matthew Arnold:

> Runs it not here, the track by Childsworth Farm
> Up past the wood, to where the elm tree crowns
> The hill beyond whose ridge the sunset flames?
> The signal-elm that looks on Ilsley Downs,
> The Vale, the three lone weirs, the youthful Thames?

With Richard Jefferies, on the faint marks of so-called Celtic fields still traceable on the downs above the Vale of the White Horse?

> It is easy to pass almost over them without observing the nearly obliterated marks – the faint lines left on the surface by the implements of men in the days when the first Caesar was yet a living memory . . .

With Samuel Pepys's visit to Oxford, and his description of it as 'a very sweet place?' With Pope translating Homer at Stanton Harcourt, or writing about Miss Blount at Mapledurham? With that cantankerous but vivid seventeenth-century historian of Oxford, Anthony Wood (whose name is current as the pseudonym of

239

the diarist in the 'Oxford Mail', one of the best columns of its kind in modern journalism)? With Shelley's being sent down from Oxford? With Churchill's meditating history at Blenheim? With Kenneth Grahame at Pangbourne? With John Masefield at Clifton Hampden?

I do not know. Let that North Berkshire man Thomas Hughes, of *Tom Brown's Schooldays* sum up:

> I was born and bred, thank God, a Wessex man, a citizen of the noblest Saxon Kingdom of Wessex, a regular 'Angular Saxon' . . . There's nothing like the old countryside for me, and no music like the twang of the real old Saxon tongue as one gets it fresh from the veritable chaw in the White Horse Vale.

That 'old Saxon tongue' may be modified now (but in the remoter villages not much) by the voices of television and the B B C but the sturdiness that transformed the old Kingdom of Wessex into the Kingdom of England lives on. It is a good country.

Gazetteer

This gazetteer lists almost all places other than isolated single farmsteads in the region of the Upper Thames and of its tributaries, and attempts a derivation, or at least an explanation, of their names. It is a compilation, not a work of original research, to which I make no claim. In my study of place-names I have mostly followed the experts, notably Dr Eilert Ekwall, whose noble scholarship in his *Dictionary of English Place Names* (O U P) has added a new dimension to history, and Professor Kenneth Cameron (*English Place Names*, Batsford). Here and there I have drawn on the records, in the possession of my mother, of my own Le Blount, Croke, Fettiplace and Unton forbears, to clear up a puzzling point, or to add an explanatory note. I have translated from Anglo-Saxon or Old English roots rather more freely than severe scholarship would approve: but my aim has been to interpret the social rather than the strictly philological setting of old words, and I hope that I have nowhere exceeded the licence I have allowed myself. It should be understood, however, that while I have drawn heavily on the scholarship of Dr Ekwall and others, the interpretations are my own, and I must accept full responsibility for them.

In the body of this book I have tried to depict the unity of this region of England, deriving from a coherent Saxon settlement that absorbed conquered, and later, conquerors alike. The place names of the region are perhaps the strongest evidence of the continuing reality of this unity. Overwhelmingly they embody the Old English speech deriving from the tongue of our Saxon ancestors. Market town, village, hamlet, meadow and woodland bear today the names given to them by Saxon settlers from about the sixth century onwards. The Normans tagged on family names to distinguish one holding from another in neighbouring settlements, but village, parish or hillside retained its Saxon description. For all the fierce, continued efforts of the Danish Vikings to drive back the Saxons from the Thames, there is scarcely a Viking name in the region south or west of the Upper Thames. The river-line held. Where a Norse name does occur (as at East Garston, a corruption of Esgar's-tun) it is so rare that it can be explained only by the defection of some Norse chieftain to the Saxon side, or by the peaceful acceptance in the countryside of a particular Norse family, probably in the period from Cnut to Edward the Confessor. In the heartland of Wessex south and west of the Upper Thames the Vikings could get no land without Saxon consent. The Normans could take land, but they had to go on using Saxon names for it.

The conservative instinct is strong in human affairs, and an established name normally has a good chance of resisting change. No doubt this helped the Saxon tongue to defeat Norman-French in the matter of place names. But although it may have been expected to, conservatism has preserved relatively few pre-Saxon names in the region. Rivers are the chief exception here, and it is natural that they should be. A river is older than the oldest settlement on its banks; moreover, even a little river or a brook crosses many individual landholdings. It would be inconvenient to call a river by a different name for every mile or so of its course, so it is reasonable that the oldest name should stick. Often it has. The derivations of Thames and Churn and Cherwell (at least the Cher- part of it) and of many other river-names are obscure, and seem older than any known Celtic tongue of ancient Britons. In the course of 2,000 years some river-names have changed, the Berkshire Churn to Ock, Bladon to Evenlode, for example. But the persistence of ancient river-names is such that settlements on river banks may still reflect the older name, as in Charney on the Ock and the place-name Bladon on the Evenlode.

What has happened to all the other pre-Saxon names? Sometimes, of course, there were none: the Saxon settlement that gave its name to a village that grew round it may have been the first human settlement there. But this is likely to have occurred less frequently than first thoughts might suggest; the more we learn of our past the more it becomes evident that continuity of human settlement persists from very early times – as at Widford on the Windrush, where a Saxon building had a Roman floor, used again in the chancel of a Norman church. Bronze Age, Neolithic, Palaeolithic peoples all had speech: what has become of their place-names? They had speech but no writing, and if a settlement were depopulated for a generation, newcomers would have no idea of its name – this helps to explain the persistence of river-names, for while isolated wooden farmsteads might fall down or burn down and their families depart, a river-valley is unlikely ever to be wholly depopulated. Even so, absolute depopulation of communities larger than single homesteads was probably rare: Belgic and later Saxon invaders may have slaughtered menfolk, but women were more likely to be kept as slaves and concubines, and children would usually have been kept, as slaves, or to be absorbed into the tribe. So it is puzzling that so many of the old pre-Saxon names that must have been in use for a long time should apparently have disappeared. I write 'apparently', for while many of the Old English derivations of modern scholarship are certain, others are at best a little dubious. Pre-Conquest Saxon scribes and later Norman clerks may have done their best to write down what they thought a name was – which was what it sounded like to them – but their writing may unconsciously have embodied older, far older, words. Take Wantage, for example. Dr Ekwall has found the little river there (the Letcombe Brook) recorded in the ninth century as *Waneting*, and says 'probably derived from O E wanian, "to decrease", and meaning "intermittent stream".' This is ingenious scholarship, really beautiful scholarship, but as a place name 'intermittent stream' seems to me rather questionable. True, many of these downland streams are intermittent, running flush in winter or after heavy rainfall, in drier weather tending to disappear in runnels in the chalk. If I wanted to explain to someone where I lived, I don't think I should say, 'By the intermittent stream.' It would not be precise enough: how would a stranger know that it was intermittent if it were flowing briskly when he came? There are similar uncertainties with other names. The O E derivation *may* be right, and usually it will be the best derivation that can be suggested. But the place-name as it has come down to us may merely *seem* to embody an O E word, and it may in fact come from a far older tongue with a meaning quite unknown. In some cases I am sure that this is so.

But only in some cases: for the most part, the O E derivation of place-names in the region is assuredly right, reflecting both the dominance of Anglo-Saxon settlement in its early days, and its persistence through the centuries. And what a vivid picture of social life in the region a thousand and more years ago these place-names can still give us! They show us farms and steadings, and our forbears going about their daily tasks, growing barley, taking cattle to the water-meadows, pasturing their horses, dipping sheep, collecting firewood. As we might call our homes Ash Cottage or Pear Tree Farm, so did they. 'Ford' occurs over and over again in place-names, reflecting the importance of river-crossings in people's everyday lives before the brooks and streams that criss-cross the country-side were culverted or bridged. It is an interesting exercise to count the culverts and little bridges that you cross in any road journey of five miles. Before there were metalled roads and county highway authorities, the traveller was constantly being diverted in order to cross a brook – it was vital to know just where each brook could be forded, on foot, on horseback, with a haycart. Our place names reflect all these things.

They reflect, too, the personal names of many of our ancestors – Eadburg, Cuda or Cutha, Babba, Becca, and a host of others, the many-times-great-grandparents of men and women living in the region now. Where Anglo-Saxon place-names have persisted so strongly, it seems a little odd that the personal names should have gone out of use. Here Norman-French and Latin Christianity were certainly triumphant, replacing Anglo-Saxon names with William and Henry and James and John. It is, I think, understandable. When Anglo-Saxon mothers bore children to Norman soldiers, the fathers doubtless had some say in the choice of name. And the Normans were the bosses: even today it is not uncommon for a child to be named after some big man in his parents' lives, or after a general, or queen or princess. I think there was another reason, too. After the Conquest, the priests who christened children were educated in Latin and Norman-French, and Anglo-Saxon names Latinize badly. I think this is probably the main reason why these old names have continued out of fashion: when written, they look uncouth and ugly. With kindlier spellings they might be living still.

Any gazetteer must be a compromise between the information one wants to convey and the space available to convey it. I have restricted myself severely to the barest facts about each place, and an explanation of its name. I am not good on architecture: it is not that I am unmoved by beauty in stone or brick but that my personal human chemistry reacts more readily to the records of the people who built and lived in places than to the buildings they put up. To have attempted to describe the finer points of church or domestic architecture would have meant relying too much on seeing through other men's eyes. And there have been so many splendid books on buildings, above all Professor Nikolaus Pevsner's great series *The Buildings of England*. So I have confined myself almost wholly to dates, again relying on the experts in published sources. But dates, particularly of parish churches, are far from simple to unravel. Our parish churches have lived and grown (and sometimes died) with the communities they have served, and most of them are a palimpsest of masonry over the centuries. I have tried, therefore, to select what I feel to be the major date (or dates) for each entry, so that anyone with a particular interest in the church architecture of a particular period may have at least a brief guide to what the region holds for his interest. I hope it is not asking too much to invite readers to use this gazetteer in conjunction with the relevant sheets of the one-inch Ordnance Survey – these sheets are Nos 144, 145, 157, 158 and 159. Our English Survey is unique – its maps are the finest in the world. Most readers of this book will know them well. If I can convey my own lifelong love of maps to even one newcomer, I shall be happy.

Key to Gazetteer

The letter in brackets after each entry gives the county: B = Berkshire, Bu = Buckinghamshire, G = Gloucestershire, N = Northamptonshire, O = Oxfordshire, W = Wiltshire. Where a place is mentioned particularly in the body of the book, the page-numbers (P) indicate the reference. More general references to places are recorded in the index following the gazetteer. See maps 9 and 11 on pages 140–1 and 163–4.

The six-figure reference to the national grid, preceded by two grid letters, makes each grid reference unique and locates every place listed within 100 metres. The figures in brackets after the grid reference give the number of the Ordnance Survey sheet on which the entry will be found. When used in conjunction with the One-inch maps of the Ordnance Survey the grid letters can be ignored. They are required to ensure absolute precision, for the figures alone repeat every 100 kilometres. Given the OS sheet number the letters are unnecessary, for there can be no repetition on one sheet. Where two or three places are listed under one main entry (Upper Swell, Lower Swell, East Hanney, West Hanney and the like) grid letters and sheet number are omitted after the first entry.

C = parish church. (Note: these churches were built to serve parishes, but nowadays many smaller parishes may be combined.) The figures after C give the century or centuries of the major building that went into it. Thus C 13 indicates that a church was built more or less as it stands in the thirteenth century, but in almost every church there is also work of other periods. There was much rebuilding of old churches in the nineteenth century, and where this has had a major effect on the church it is indicated.

In the text of entries 17 c means seventeenth century.

The final sentence in each entry suggests a derivation or an explanation of the place-name. O E indicates an Old English word or root. The commoner O E endings to place-names are not always easy to translate, for they may have a variety of meanings, usually similar, but by no means the same. Where a variety of meanings is possible that given is the one that seems most likely in relation to the physical setting or the known history of a place. A general guide to some of the commoner place-name endings suggests:

–dun (en, on, own) = hill.

–ham = homestead or meadow.

–lea (ey, eigh) = wood or woodland glade.

–mar (er, ere, ore) = lake or pond (mere).

–mor (ore, oor) = moor, or sometimes marshy land or fen.

–stow (e, ock, oke) = place, but a place with something special about it, often a sacred or holy place, such as the location of a hermit's cell, but also used for an out-lying field or steading belonging to a farm or village some distance away.

–ton = settlement, but the word may imply many different types of settlement, such as farm, enclosure, or even village.

–thorp (e, rop, rup(p)) = farm.

–worth = enclosure

For personal names I have followed *The Oxford Dictionary of English Place Names* (Eilert Ekwall), occasionally slightly simplifying a spelling where this has seemed possible without brutality to the OE habit.

ABINGDON (B) SU 495975 (158) P. 115–32. Settlement from prehistoric times and medieval heart of present town among most ancient in Britain. Abingdon retained its medieval shape almost intact until after Second World War, much affected since by motor-car and new building. Still medieval beauty to be found. East St Helen's Street perhaps most beautiful town street in England; shape of street intact and old houses stand. County Hall (C. Kempster with assistance from Wren) a glory of late 17 c architecture (now Town Hall, since Abingdon was demoted from being county town of Berkshire mid-19 c owing rise of population Reading). C (St Helen) 13 re-built 15–16, lovely setting by R. Thames (St Nicholas) 12 onwards with gatehouse ancient Benedictine Abbey adjoining. Particularly fine Nonconformist chapels Baptist 1841 Methodist 1845 Congregationalist 1862. Some genuine remains Abbey, Chequer (Exchequer) building 13 c with remarkable chimney, Long Gallery late 15 c. St Helen's churchyard unique cloister of almshouses 15 c and 18 c buildings. Old gaol (1805) now corn-store. Good mooring, good port of call for river cruisers. Settlement belonging to a woman called Aebbe (OE).

ADDERBURY (O) East SP 475355 (145) and West 465355. Two halves of one village divided by the Oxford–Banbury road. Possesses one of the three churches once regarded as landmarks for travellers:

> Bloxham for length
> Adderbury for strength
> King's Sutton for beauty

Adderbury C 14, part 13, is magnificent, and worth stopping the car for. The Restora-ation poet, John Wilmot, 2nd Earl of Rochester, lived at Adderbury House. Eadburg's fort (OE).

ADLESTROP (G) SP 244270 (144). Evenlode village, worthy of Edward Thomas's poem. C 14–15. Tatel's farm (OE).

ADWELL (O) SU 695995 (159). Hamlet in the hills between Thame and Thames. C rebuilt 19, parts 13. Edda's spring (OE).

ALBURY (O) SP 655051 (159). Village on the Thame. Queen Elizabeth I stayed here at Rycote Park as a prisoner before she came to the throne. Her gaoler–host was that curious Tudor character Lord Williams of Thame, whose tactful handling of his prisoner brought dividends when she became Queen. C 19 but attractive Norman font. Old fort (OE).

ALCHESTER (O) SP 572202 (145). Not much more than a map reference now, but once important Roman settlement where road north from Silchester, crossing the Thames at Dorchester, met road west to Cirencester. Remnants of population (if any) after Roman departure transferred to Bicester. Name apparently from fort on brook once called Alne.

ALDERMASTON (B) SU 592652 (158). Townlet Kennet valley. C 13. Atomic Energy Authority centre prominent in Campaign for Nuclear Disarmament protests. Alderman's place (OE).

ALDERMASTON WHARF (B) SU 602672 (158). Once busy wharf on Kennet and Avon canal. Picturesque place for meditation.

ALDSWORTH (G) SP 156101 (157). Meditative village watershed between rivers Leach and Windrush. C 12, wonderful medieval carvings. Old homestead (OE).

ALDWORTH (B) SU 555793 (158). High downland village. C 14, de la Beche monuments. Famous yew tree already old in 1760. Somebody's old enclosed homestead (OE).

ALVESCOT (O) SP 273043 (157). In water meadows between Shil Brook and Langhat Ditch, tributaries R. Thames near Oxfordshire–Gloucestershire border. C 13–15. Aelfheah's cottage (OE).

AMBROSDEN (O) SP 605195 (145). Ray valley village, once part of estate of Richard of Cornwall, King of the Romans (brother of Henry III). C 13. Ambrose's hill (OE).

AMPNEY BROOK Tributary of R. Churn. Rises NE Cirencester and joins Churn near Cricklade. Amma's stream (OE).

AMPNEY CRUCIS (G) SP 066017 (157). One of cluster of charming villages on Ampney Brook. C 15 and beautiful 15 c cross. Ampney St Mary 088020, C 13. Ampney St Peter 083014, C Saxon origins. Ancient earthwork Ranbury Ring. Down Ampney SU 102973. Last of the cluster of Ampneys and lowest on Ampney Brook. Birthplace of Vaughan Williams, composer. Amma's Brook (OE).

ANDOVERSFORD (G) SP 025197 (144). Crossing place for tidal streams of traffic on A40 and A436. Lovely Cotswold country off main roads. Ford on a brook once called Ann. (The 'dover' is from Celtic word for water.)

APPLEFORD (B) SU 536936 (158). Hamlet in winding lanes between Thames and

Didcot. C 13 much restored. New housing estates. Ford (across Thames) marked by apple trees (OE).

APPLETON (B) SP 442013 (158). In the bend of the Thames where it turns north. C 12 onwards. Part of 12 c manor, once home of Fettiplaces, described by Prof Pevsner 'an amazing survival'. Orchard settlement (OE).

ARDINGTON (B) SU 432882 (158). Village by Portway out of Wantage. C mostly 19 but bits 13. Settlement of Aethelred's folk (OE).

ARDLEY (O) SP 543274 (145). Village set in park-like countryside Oxfordshire–Northamptonshire border. C 13–14. Once formidable Norman castle, now contemplative green mound with moat. Eardwulf's wood (OE).

ARNCOTT, Upper (O) SP 613173 (145). and Lower SP 610181. Once possessions of Osney Priory (Upper) and Bicester Priory (Lower). Now mostly big Ordnance Depot. The cottages of Earn's folk (OE).

ASCOTT–UNDER–WYCHWOOD (O) SP 301185 (145). Evenlode village lovely weathered stone. C 13 (chancel) 14 (font) and 15 (stone priest's seats). Ascott D'Oyley 306188, Ascott Earl 298183, east and west ends of Ascott-u-Wychwood. Cottage in the East (OE).

ASHBURY (B) SU 264853 (157). Exquisite village near Ridgeway. C 13, fine brasses. Wayland's Smithy chambered barrow tomb in grove. Aese's fort (OE).

ASHAMPSTEAD (B) SU 565770 (158). Downs village, C 13. Dwelling by ash-tree (OE).

ASTHALL (O) SP 288113 (145). Windrush village, C 12. Roman-British settlement. Somebody's east hall, or possibly place of the East Hall people (OE).

ASTON, North (O) SP 478290 (145). Middle 477270 and Steeple 477260. Pleasant villages secluded between Oxford–Banbury road A423 and river Cherwell. The eastern settlements, presumably east of track to Banbury (OE).

ASTON BAMPTON (O) SP 341030 (158). Ancient Saxon settlement 2m E of Bampton. Interesting history of common lands controlled by 'grass stewards'. Eastern settlement (OE) (E from Bampton.)

ASTON BLANK (G) SP 128198 (144). W of Fosse Way in hill country of little springs feeding Cotswold tributaries of R Thames. C 12 Saxon foundations. Place sometimes known as Cold Aston. Eastern settlement (OE) (perhaps E from brook). Blank or cold probably signifies exposed hillside.

ASTON ROWANT (O) SU 727990 (159). Oxfordshire Chilterns. C 14 Chiltern flint. Eastern settlement, probably to distinguish it from Weston, a mile and a half to the west (OE).

ASTON TIRROLD (B) SU 557860 (158). and ASTON UPTHORPE 553864. Adjoining villages in dreamlike country between Wantage–Reading road A417 and Thames. Two C, Saxon foundations and at Aston T. surviving Saxon work. King Aethelred said to have heard mass at Aston U. before battle of Ashdown, but (if fact) it was mass in tent rather than existing church. Earthworks on Blewburton hill above villages. Eastern settlements, perhaps E from Blewburton Fort (OE).

AYNHO (N) SP 514333 (145). Considered among most beautiful villages in England by great editor of *The Manchester Guardian* A. P. Wadsworth. C 18 very pleasing. Aega's hill (OE).

BABLOCKHYTHE (B) SP5 43542 (158). Ferry that crosses Matthew Arnold's 'stripling Thames'. Reached by remote and winding lanes from Cumnor. Hythe (OE landing place) on Babba's river. Presumably one Babba held land on the Thames here.

BALDON, TOOT (O) SP 578008 (158), BALDON ROW 577002, MARSH BALDON SU 565995. Hamlets on ridge S of Oxford dividing Thames from Thame. Toot (B) C 14, Marsh (B) C 13–14, good glass. Toot = tot = look-out hill. Baldon = Bealda's hill (OE).

BALDON BROOK. Rivulet feeding R. Thame near Marsh Baldon.

BAMPTON (O) SP 315032 (158). Ancient market town with most attractive small market hall. Magnificent C 13–14–15–16. Tradition of Morris dancing maintained by probably oldest company of Morris dancers in England. Settlement around wooden building (bam = beam) (OE).

BANBURY (O) SP 455405 (145). P. 156–8. Early Saxon settlement (6 c) brisk modern town, major cattle market, important industries food processing, automotive and agricultural engineering, aluminium. Frontier town between what was Wessex and modern industrial Midlands. C 18 unusual many-sided tower. Banbury Cross not original of nursery rhyme but replacement erected 1859 to commemorate marriage Queen Victoria's eldest daughter to Prince Frederick of Prussia. Bana's fortified place (OE).

BARFORD ST JOHN (O) SP 438332 (145), ST MICHAEL 438325. Villages N and S of River Swere, tributary of Cherwell. St John C 13, St Michael (slightly bigger) C 12. Barley ford, perhaps from crossing of Swere used by grain carts (OE).

BARNSLEY (G) SP 076062 (157). Cotswolds between Coln and Churn. Roman settlement. C 15–16, earlier Norman parts. Beornmod's wood (OE).

BARRINGTON, GREAT (G) SP 210137 (144), LITTLE 206127. Enchanting Windrush villages. Great C 15, Roman settlement, Little (across river) C 14–15. Settlement of Beorn's people (OE).

BARTON (O) SP 552080 (158). Suburb of Oxford N of Headington. Barley-farm (OE).

BARTON (O) WESTCOTT SP 430256 (145), MIDDLE 439256 and STEEPLE 447250. Charming villages on River Dorn, tributary of Glyme. Westcott C 13–15, Steeple C 14–15. Barton = barley farm (OE).

BASILDON (B) SU 610787 (158). Roman settlement on Thames between Streatley and Pangbourne. C 13 tower 17. Basildon Park (1776) 'most splendid Georgian mansion of Berkshire' (Pevsner). Upper Basildon in woods 2 m. SSW 598762. Beorhtel's hill (OE).

BAULKING (B) SU 318906 (158). White Horse country village, big green, C 13. Near source of Ock and may reflect old local name for river (ing = stream), (OE).

BAYWORTH (B) SP 501012 (158). Village on Foxcombe Hill 1 m SE Boar's Hill. Baega's enclosure (OE).

BECKLEY (O) SP 565112 (145). Roman post or settlement on the road from Dorchester to Alchester, just before it enters the strange marsh of Otmoor. C 14 and older. Becca's wood (OE).

BEEDON (B) SU 483782 (158). Under Beedon Hill, in high valley of the downs. C 13. Byden = shallow trough or valley (OE).

BEENHAM (B) SU 592688 (158). In woods between Pang and Kennet. C 19. Douai Abbey and School founded 1903 by Benedictine monks expelled from France where they had taken refuge after dissolution of Bury St Edmunds Abbey 1539. Douai thus claims continuity with medieval Benedictine community of Bury St Edmunds. Enclosure where beans grew (OE).

BEGBROKE (O) SP 467138 (145). Between Cherwell and Evenlode NW Oxford. C 14. Becca's brook (OE).

BENSON (O) SU 620918 (158). Airfield, village. Site of battle 777 in which Mercia defeated Wessex and pushed back Wessex frontier to Berkshire bank of Thames. Earlier form Bensington, settlement of Bencsa's people (OE).

BERINSFIELD (O) SU 570965 (158). New housing on Roman road out of Dorchester, and half a mile from prehistoric earthworks. Possibly barley field (OE).

BERRICK SALOME (O) SU 622939 (158), BRITWELL SALOME 672932. Oxfordshire Chilterns. Berrick S. C 15 restored 19, interesting timbering 17–18. Britwell S. C 15, earlier Norman work. Beautiful daffodils in spring on roadside B4009 past Britwell Salome. Salome not biblical but from OE 'sulh' (plough), also used for furrow or valley. Berrick = Barley farm, Britwell clear or bright spring (OE).

BESSELSLEIGH (B) SP 459019 (158). Home of Bessels (or Besils family, of whom Sir Peter (d. 1434) gave stone for building Abingdon bridge. Fettiplaces acquired estate by marriage, sold to William Lenthall, Speaker of Long Parliament. C 13–17. Bessels' wood.

BIBURY (G) SP 113066 (157) William Morris's 'most beautiful village in England'. Disputable claim, but certainly very lovely, on River Coln, with wonderful old stone cottages (Arlington Row, belonging National Trust). C 15 Saxon foundation. Beage's fortified enclosure (OE).

BICESTER (O) SP 585225 (145) Successor town to Roman Alchester, brisk, busy market town. C 13 some Saxon work. Fort by the burial ground (OE).

BINSEY (O) SP 493077 (158). Settlement in maze of streams (Seacourt Stream, R. Thames and backwaters) S of Godstow. Byni's island (OE).

BISHOPSTONE (W) SU 246837 (157). On Wiltshire border White Horse escarpment. Roman settlement SE. Bishop's manor (OE).

BLACK BOURTON (O) SP 285040 (158). In water meadows, once marsh country, between Windrush and Thames. C 13, wonderful wall paintings. Origin of place name obscure. Bourton is a fortified settlement, but why Black? Possibly from dark water of one of many streamlets, or from colour of earth.

BLACKTHORN (O) SP 620195 (145). Small village on R. Ray near Oxfordshire–Buckinghamshire border. Congregationalist chapel – congregationalists did much good work after outbreak of cholera 1832. Blackthorn (OE).

BLADON (O) SP 448146 (145). On R. Glyme as it leaves Blenheim Great Park to join Evenlode. Long village with C 19 in churchyard of which Sir Winston Churchill is buried. From old name for Evenlode.

BLADON, RIVER. Obsolete name. See Evenlode.

BLEDINGTON (G) SP 245227 (144). On Evenlode. C 13, medieval wall paintings. Settlement on the Bladon (old name of Evenlode).

BLENHEIM PALACE (O) SP 442161 (145). Reached from Woodstock. Stately home of Dukes of Marlborough, birthplace of Sir Winston Churchill. Woodstock estate given to John Churchill, First Duke of Marlborough, by Queen Anne together with some £240,000 towards building of palace, as reward for his victories. Palace built 1705–22 mostly by Sir John Vanbrugh, although after many rows with Sarah, Duchess of Marlborough, he was dismissed as architect before it was quite finished. Lake, formed by river Glyme, in park first planned by Vanbrugh, extended and much improved in 1764 by Lancelot (Capability) Brown. Palace, full of treasures, open to public most days from Easter to October, but in spring and autumn may be closed certain days, so if planning visits advisable to check. Guided tours take about an hour. Park (though private not public park) open to walkers throughout year. Called after Marlborough's victory at Blenheim in 1704.

BLETCHINGDON (O) SP 503176 (145). Pleasant walk from Oxford canal, fine view of Otmoor. Wren married Faith Coghill of Bletchingdon in C 15–17. Blecci's hill (OE).

BLEWBURY (B) SU 534860 (158). Once enchanting village, now A417 runs through it. Still lovely off main road, and starting place for fine downland walks. Name means 'coloured fortress' (OE) from Blewburton Hill Fort 1 m. NE.

BLOWING STONE (B) SU 324871 (158). Outside cottage on Blowing Stone Hill. Sarsen stone with holes which, at some expenditure of breath, can be made to produce horn-like note.

BLOXHAM (O) SP 430360 (145). Most interesting small town four miles S of Banbury. 12 o'clock bell still rung every day except Sunday, originally angelus bell, later to tell farmworkers of dinner time. Bell ringing paid for by Feoffees, body of sixteen established by Act of Elizabeth I originally to inquire into misemployment of land and money left to charity, later given powers to administer charities. Carried out many functions of local government long before there was any effective local government. Bloxham feoffees still sturdily independent. In rhyme about Oxfordshire church spires Bloxham's stood for length. C 14 has tower and spire reaching some 200 ft. Window by William Morris and Edward Burne-Jones. Blocc or Blocca's home (OE).

BOAR'S HILL (B) SP 486022 (158). Oxford's bigger suburban houses on ridge of Cumnor Hills. Hill of the boar.

BOARSTALL (Bu) SP 625143 (145). On Buckinghamshire edge of region. Moat and gatehouse of massive castle survive (National Trust). C 19. Fortress (O E).

BOTLEY (B) SP 486062 (158). Once first village on the road west out of Oxford, now built up part of Oxford. Possibly a wood in which there were rights of gathering fire-wood. (O E) bot = wood for fuel.

BOURNE, RIVER. Tributary of R. Pang, S of Bradfield. Name is simply river (O E).

BOURTON (B) SU 232870 (157). Village W end White Horse vale. C 19. Settlement by a fort (O E).

BOURTON-ON-THE-WATER (G) SP 167206 (144). Windrush setting. Cotswold stone houses, miniature Italianate bridges crossing river in mid-village, tourists' delight. Roman post, Saxon settlement. Fortified place (crossing of the Windrush).

BOWER BROOK. Tributary of R. Cole. Perhaps brook by a cottage (O E).

BOXFORD (B) SU 428715 (158). On Lambourn under Hoar Hill. Roman settlement. C 19 tower late 17. River bank under box trees (old versions of the name suggest that it was not called after a ford, but from another word meaning bank (O E).

BRADFIELD (B) SU 605725 (158). Wooded valley of the Pang. C mostly 19 but tower 16. Bradfield College founded 1850. Broad field.

BRADFORD'S BROOK. Stream near Wallingford.

BRIGHTHAMPTON (O) SP 385035 (158). Hamlet in Windrush valley near junction with Thames. Beorhthelm's settlement.

BRIGHTWALTON (B) SU 430793 (158). High chalk downs C 19. Settlement of Boerhtweald's folk (O E).

BRIGHTWELL (B) SU 578908 (158). At foot of Brightwell Barrow, high point continu-ing Sinodun Hills (or Wallingford Clumps). C 13. Sparkling spring (O E).

BRIGHTWELL BALDWIN (O) SU 654950 (159), UPPERTON 656943, GROVE 656930. Cluster of hamlets in Oxfordshire Chilterns, remote and lovely. Brightwell B. C 14, interesting old glass. Clear spring (O E). Brightwell B. belonged to Baldwin de Berford in 14 c.

BRIZE NORTON (O) SP 300075 (158). Village with big airfield Windrush valley. C 13, believed only church in England dedicated to St Brice, pupil of St Martin. Norton = North settlement, Brize from St Brice.

BROADWELL BROOK. Tributary of R. Thames near Radcot. Broad stream (O E).

BROADWELL (O) SP 205275 (144). Oxfordshire Cotswold village between Evenlode and River Dikler (tributary of Windrush). C 13, fine tower. Broad stream or brook (O E).

BROUGHTON (O) SP 424384 (145). Manor of Broughton was bought by William of Wykeham, Bishop of Winchester, and founder of Winchester College and New Col-lege, Oxford. From him it passed to his sister, and from her to her great-grand-daughter who married Sir William Fiennes. Broughton Castle is still the home of the

Fiennes family (Lords Saye and Sele). Before purchase by William of Wykeham Broughton was held by family called Broughton. Place name seems to mean brook-settlement (OE).

BROUGHTON POGGS (O) SP 236040 (158). Near Oxfordshire–Gloucestershire border on Broadwell Brook tributary of R. Thames. C 12 onwards. Brook settlement (OE) Poggs family name.

BUCKLAND (B) SU 345980 (158). Lovely village on ridge between rivers Thames and Ock. C 12 onwards. Buckland House built 1757 for Throckmortons 'most splendid of smaller Georgian houses in the county' (Pevsner). Boc = book land was held by charter as distinct from folk-land held by customary right in return for services.

BUCKLEBURY (B) SU 552708 (158), UPPER BUCKLEBURY 545685, BUCKLEBURY COMMON 555687. Settlements in Pang valley and on rising ground separating Pang from Kennet. Bucklebury C 13 and every century to 19. Glass by Brangwyn. Common 5 miles of glade between woods, oaks planted to commemorate Trafalgar. Parish said to have more footpaths than any other in England. Burghild's fortified place (OE).

BUCKNELL (O) SP 560255 (145) Village on Oxfordshire–Northamptonshire border. C 13–15. Bucca's hill (OE).

BURCOT (O) SU 562960 (158). Hamlet (new houses now) on Thames near Dorchester, once busy wharf for transhipment barge cargoes by road to Oxford when river had too many shallows for navigation. Home of John Masefield, Poet Laureate. Bride's cottage, perhaps once someone's dowry (OE).

BURFORD (O) SP 252122 (144) P. 146–8. Ford by the hill. (OE).

BURGHFIELD (B) SU 665685 (158), BURGHFIELD COMMON 655665. Villages (Burghfield C. much modern housing) S of Kennet. Ex-gravel pits with boating. Hill field (beorg = hill), (OE).

BURROWAY BROOK. Tributary or backwater of R. Thames in low meadows S of Bampton. Name obscure.

BUSCOT (B) SU 232975 (157) Once busy cheese wharf on Thames. Now quiet hamlet. C 13 onwards. Buscot Park c. 1770. Burgweard's cottage (OE).

BYDEMILL BROOK. Wiltshire tributary of R. Thames above Inglesham. Perhaps mill brook.

CALCOT ROW (B) SU 665720 (158). Village N of Kennet 2 m. W of Reading. Pleasant open country suburb of Reading. Cold cottage, possibly one originally without much shelter (OE).

CASSINGTON (O) SP 456107 (145). At junction of Evenlode and Thames. C 12–14. Apparently a settlement where watercress was to be had (OE).

CASTLE EATON (W) SP 147958 (157). Pleasing village on Wiltshire bank of Thames below Cricklade. Site of Castle to NE. Eaton — island or riverside settlement (OE).

CATMORE (B) SU 454802 (158). Entrancing hamlet lost in the high downs. C some

Norman work but mostly 19. Name goes back to countryside of less docile fauna than now, for it means lake (or pond) of the wild cat (OE).

CAULCOTT (O) SP 508244 (145). Pleasant walk from Oxford canal at Lower Heyford. Near ancient earthwork called Ash Bank or Aves Ditch. Cold cottage (OE).

CERNEY (G) NORTH SP 020080 (157), SOUTH SU 048970, WICK 076963. Settlements on R. Churn N and S of Cirencester. North C 13–15 beautiful rectory (Queen Anne) South C Saxon onwards. Islands in the Churn (OE).

CHADDLEWORTH (B) SU 415772 (158). Lambourn Downs. C 13 but much 19 rebuilding. Poughley Farmhouse has remnants of 12 c Poughley Priory, a community of Austin canons. Ceadela's farm or enclosure (OE).

CHADLINGTON (O) SP 331219 (145). Stone village N of Evenlode. C 13–14. Hawk Stone (strange standing stone) 1 m NNE. Birth place (1810) of Sir Henry Rawlinson, decipherer of Old Persian cuneiform script. Settlement of Ceadela's folk (OE).

CHALFORD, OLD (O) SP 345258 (145) and CHALFORD GREEN 342247. Settlements N and S of headwaters of river Glyme. Chalk ford (OE).

CHALGROVE (O) SU 635970 (159). Gentle countryside between Thame and Thames. C 12 onwards, wall paintings. CHALGROVE FIELD 645972 site of skirmish with Prince Rupert's cavalry in 1643 in which John Hampden received wounds from which he died. Hampden monument in field. Chalk pits (OE).

CHALLOW (B) EAST SU 380880 (158) WEST 367885. Villages on (extinct) Wilts and Berks Canal. East C 13 restored 19, West C 14 nice bellcote. Roman settlement. Ceawa's burial-place (OE).

CHAPEL ROW (B) SU 572698 (158). Hamlet at E end of Bucklebury Common.

CHARLBURY (O) SP 355195 (145). Town of steep little streets on Evenlode. Gloving centre. C 13–15 and Friends' Meeting House 1779. P. 154. The fortified place of Ceorl's folk (OE).

CHARNEY BASSETT (B) SU 380945 (158). On river Ock, once grange of Abingdon Abbey. C 13 possibly Saxon foundation interesting medieval carvings. Manor House (properly grange) part 13 c maintained by Society of Friends as meeting house and conference centre. Island on the Charn or Churn, old name of river Ock. Bassett from Ralph Basset (d. 1127) Justiciar of England, whose son gave land to Abingdon Abbey. Abbey in fact already claimed land, but earlier charters may have been forged or inaccurately copied.

CHARLTON-ON-OTMOOR (O) SP 562157 (145). On river Ray, on edge of marsh of Otmoor. C 13–14. Churl's (freeborn peasant's) settlement (OE).

CHASTLETON (O) SP 248293 (144). On Oxfordshire–Gloucestershire border overlooking R. Evenlode. Ancient settlement, prehistoric barrow 1m SE. C 12 onwards. Settlement by cairn of stones OE (from nearby barrow).

CHAZEY HEATH (O) SU 695775 (159), CHAZEY WOOD 687760. Charming places in backlands from Thames near Mapledurham. Family name de Chauseia who held manor 12 c.

CHECKENDON (O) SU 664830 (159). Lovely wooded Chilterns, C 13 onwards, medieval painting. Ceacca's hill (OE).

CHEDWORTH (G) SP 055115 (144). Deep in Cotswold woods on tributary of Coln. C 13. Prehistoric settlement, splendidly excavated Roman villa 070115 and good museum. Cedda's enclosure (OE).

CHESTERTON (O) SP 562212 (145), LITTLE CHESTERTON 558202 village and hamlet near the all-but vanished Roman town of Alchester, just across the Oxford–Bicester road (A421). C13–14, tower 15. Name derived from Roman remains – settlements near *ceaster* (Roman fort) (OE).

CHERBURY CAMP (B) SU 375963 (158). Near Charney Bassett. Particularly interesting prehistoric earthwork because it has pattern of hill forts but lies in flat marshland. Probably constructed on island of firm ground to defend crossing of Thames at Duxford, 2 miles N. Charn or Churn fort (OE).

CHERWELL, RIVER. Tributary of the Thames, rising in Northamptonshire and flowing generally S to Oxford via Banbury. Well in name is OE stream, Cher is obscure, may be Celtic (British) word also meaning river, or some prehistoric word meaning something entirely different.

CHIEVELEY (B) SU 476738 (158). Downland village N of Newbury. C 13, some 19. Hill fort in Bussock Wood, 1 m SSW of village. Cefa's wood (OE).

CHIL BROOK. Rivulet feeding R. Thames near Eynsham. (OE) spring.

CHILDREY BROOK. Tributary of R. Ock. Cilla's stream (OE).

CHILDREY (B) SU 362875 (158). On Icknield Way, home of the Fettiplaces for five centuries to 1811. C early 13 on site of Saxon church, fine brasses, rare leaden font. Fettiplace school endowed 1529 for teaching children in English probably first village school in England. Nice duck pond on green. From Childrey Brook, which runs through village, Cilla's stream (OE).

CHILSON (O) SP 319195 (145) Hamlet in Wychwood S of Evenlode. Heir's settlement (Like Chilton) (OE).

CHILTON (B) SU 490857 (158). On Downs between Ridgeway and Portway. C 13. Heir's land or settlement OE, that is, provision for the maintenance of someone's heir.

CHILTON (Bu) SP 688115 (159). Thame country, home of the Crokc family (originally Le Blount) from 1529–1700. C 13–16, remarkable monument to Sir John Croke (1530–1608) and wife Elizabeth Unton (of Faringdon) showing them and their eleven children sculptured to represent what they became in life, babes who died in infancy, in marble swaddling clothes. Two were judges Sir John (d. 1619) and Sir George (d. 1641). Sir George C. delivered minority judgment in John Hampden (ship money) case declaring royal attempt to levy taxes by prerogative illegal, which was sensation at time. Child's settlement (probably some heir's land in late Saxon times).

CHILTON FOLIAT (B) SU 322703 (158). On Kennet on Wiltshire border of region. Heir's settlement, land left by Foliat family 13 c.

CHIMNEY (O) SP 358008 (158). Hamlet on Oxfordshire bank of Thames by crossing at Duxford. Ceomma's island (island of firm ground in marshy country) (OE).

CHIPPING NORTON (O) SP 315270 (145). Highest town in Oxfordshire (650 ft), centre for Oxfordshire Cotswolds. C 14–15. Market Norton (North settlement) (OE). Chipping same root as in London's Cheapside.

CHISLEHAMPTON (O) SU 594998 (158). On Thame, crossed by interesting long bridge. C rebuilt 18. Gravelly settlement (OE).

CHOLSEY (B) SU 597805 (158). Where the Downs fall to the Thames just above the Goring Gap. Very ancient settlement, abbey founded by Ethelred the Unready 986, destroyed by Danes, lands later given to Reading Abbey. C 12–13 on Saxon foundation, and perhaps some Saxon work remaining. Ceol's island (OE).

CHRISTMAS COMMON (O) SU 715933 (159). High Chilterns, enchanting country on Oxford–Buckinghamshire border. Name obscure, but why not from somebody who enjoyed the place in the cold clean air some sparkling Christmas Day?

CHURCHILL (O) SP 283243 (145) Oxfordshire Cotswolds. C 19. Birth place of Warren Hastings and William Smith, founder of modern systematic geology. Church on a hill.

CHURN, RIVER, Berkshire. Obsolete name. See Ock.

CHURN, RIVER, Gloucestershire tributary of the Thames held by some to be head-waters of the Thames itself above Cricklade, this making Seven Springs, source of the Churn, the source of the Thames. History against this claim, for river from Seven Springs has been called Churn from earliest times. With some other river names may reflect prehistoric language spoken in district.

CIRENCESTER (G) SP 025020. P. 50–2, 139. Fort by the Churn.

CLANFIELD (O) SP 285020 (158). Bridging Sharney Brook minor tributary of Thames. C 14. Clean field (OE).

CLAPTON (G) SP 164180 (144). W of Windrush just below its junction with Dikler. C 13. Hill settlement (OE).

CLEVELEY (O) SP 392238 (145). Hamlet on steeply wooded Glyme. Cliff wood (OE).

CLIFTON (O) SP 490318 (145). Pleasantly lost world between Oxford–Banbury road and Cherwell (Oxford canal). Settlement on a hillside (OE).

CLIFTON HAMPDEN (O) SU 557956 (158). Thatched cottages (to some tastes rather too perfect). C 12 restored 19 on cliff above lovely reach of Thames. Attractive 19 c brick bridge. Cliff settlement (OE), Hampden family name.

COBERLEY (G) SO 966158 (144). Source of Churn (disputed source of Thames) at Seven Springs just NNE of village. C 14 chapel 15 tower mostly 19. Upper Coberley 978157 E across main road A435. Cuthbert's Wood (OE).

COCKLEY BROOK. Tributary of R. Dorn, which it joins at Middle Barton. Brook of the wild birds (OE).

COGGES (O) SP 363096 (158). Village on E bank of Windrush across river from main part of Witney. C 12–13–14, founded by monks from Fécamp. A hill standing up like the cog of a wheel (OE).

R

COKETHORPE PARK (O) SP 365065 (158). Windrush country. C 15. Mansion in park built by Lord Harcourt early 18 c. Probably a farm (thorp) belonging to the monks of Cogges, q.v.

COLD ASH (B) SU 513695 (158). Lovely views over Kennet C 19. Presumably from an ash tree in an exposed and windy place.

COLE, RIVER. Wiltshire and Berkshire tributary of Thames, rising near Swindon and joining Thames at St John's Bridge, just below Lechlade. Origin of name dubious, but may derive from Celtic (ancient British) word meaning hazel.

COLESBOURNE (G) SO 991129 (144). In deep combe of Churn. C 13–15. Col's burn or stream.

COLESHILL (B) SU 236938 (157). Charming village on Cole. C 13 onwards. Great park of Coleshill House (destroyed by fire 1952) now National Trust. Badbury Hill 260950 Iron Age fort. Hill on the river Cole.

COLN, RIVER. Gloucestershire tributary of Thames which it joins at Lechlade. Origin of name obscure, may embody speech of prehistoric folk.

COLN ST DENNIS (G) SP 087109 (144) COLN ROGERS 086095 (157), COLN ST ALDWYN'S 144053 (157). Villages in Coln Valley. St Dennis C 13–15, Rogers C 13–15 some Saxon work at St Aldwyn's C 13–15. John Keble was curate to his father at Coln St A. From river, with family and church names.

COMBE (O) SP 412158 (145). Exquisite setting on Evenlode. C 15 on earlier foundation, wall paintings. Combe or narrow valley (OE).

COMPTON (B) SU 520800 (158). Downland village under Penborough Castle (Iron Age earthwork). C mostly 19 tower 13 and Norman font. Race training country. Settlement in a combe (OE).

COMPTON ABDALE (G) SP 064168. Exquisite Cotswold village N of Coln. C 15. Roman settlement to SW. Combe or valley settlement (OE).

COMPTON BEAUCHAMP (B) SU 282871 (158). Under White Horse Hill C 13, beautifully wooded parkland round 17 c mansion. Settlement in a combe (OE). Beauchamp family name.

COOKLEY GREEN (O) SU 698902 (159) Woods and hills above Henley. Cucca's wood (OE).

CORNWELL (O) SP 271271 (144). In hill country above R. Evenlode. C 12 small and particularly beautiful. Spring of the cranes (OE).

COTE (O) SP 352032 (158). Hamlet in water meadows between Windrush and Thames. 17 c Baptist chapel, among oldest in England. Cottage (OE).

COTHILL (B) SU 465996 (158). Village NW Abingdon. Ruskin Reserve, $4\frac{1}{2}$ acres marshy woodland leased by National Trust to Nature Conservancy and maintained as original wild marsh country. Marsh orchid (Dactylorchis Incarnata) may be found there, and other rare plants. Cottage on a hillside (presumably firm ground rising from marsh) (OE).

COWLEY (G) SO 965147 (144). Pretty village on Churn. C 13–14–15. Cow's wood or glade (OE).

COWLEY (O) SP 545040 (158) Home of Morris Motors, now part of British Leyland complex. Excellent shopping centre. C 12 onwards Cufa's wood (OE). Old spellings indicate Oxford's Cowley has this different meaning from Cowley (G).

COXWELL (B) GREAT SU 269935 (157), LITTLE SU 282934 (158). Great C 13, magnificent 13 c. barn once belonging to Beaulieu Abbey (although called 'Tithe Barn' on notices was not for tithes but for storing produce of Beaulieu Abbey's land). Little C 13, Iron Age fort on Furze Hill. Wild birds' spring (OE).

CRAWLEY (O) SP 341120 (145). On N bank of Windrush above Witney. Wood of the Crows (OE).

CRICKLADE (W) SU 101935 (157) P. 66, 82. Two C, St Mary's and St Sampson's, both interesting. Passage or crossing (of the Thames) by a hill (Horsey Down W of town) (OE).

CROWELL (O) SU 744997 (159). On Icknield Way below escarpment of the Chilterns. C 13. Birth place Thomas Ellwood, Quaker and friend of Milton. Spring of the crow (OE).

CROWMARSH GIFFORD (O) SU 617893 (158). On Oxford bank of crossing by Wallingford Bridge. C 12, still marks of cannon balls from Civil War siege of Wallingford. Crowmarsh Battle 616906 Preston Crowmarsh 617908 adjoining villages N. Marsh of the crows (OE). Gifford land belonging to Gifford family in 11 c. Battle land belonging to Battle Abbey, Preston land for the maintenance of the priest.

CUDDESDON BROOK. Tributary of R. Thame at Cuddesdon. From village.

CUDDESDON (O) SP 600030 (158). Home of Bishops of Oxford, modest palace replacing more princely one burned down. Theological college. C 12–13 onwards. Cuthen's hill (OE).

CULHAM (O) SU 505950 (158). Village on old course of Thames where it joins present mainstream below Abingdon. C 19 tower 18. 13 c. manor house. Cula's homestead (OE).

CUMNOR (B) SP 462038 (158). Matthew Arnold country, now prosperous Oxford suburb, but still much open country. C 13 onwards. Amy Robsart, wife of Robert Dudley, Earl of Leicester, tragic third party in her husband's affair with Queen Elizabeth I died at Cumnor Hall after mysterious fall downstairs, having let all servants go to Abingdon Fair. House demolished 1810. Cumma's hillside, perhaps from an 8 c. Abbot of Abingdon called Cumma (OE).

CURBRIDGE (O) SP 334086 (158). Outskirts of Witney. Creoda's bridge (OE).

CUTTLE BROOK. Tributary of R. Thame rising Buckinghamshire and joining river near Thame. Perhaps Cuda's brook.

CUTTS END (B) SP 456039 (158). Hamlet W of Cumnor. Cuda's end of Cumnor, perhaps to distinguish it from Cumma's land (OE).

CUXHAM (O) SU 666953 (159). Nice village with stream. C rebuilt 18 out of old materials. Cuc's meadow (OE).

DANES BROOK. Oxfordshire tributary of R. Thame S of Studley. Reflects some struggle with, or settlement by, Danes.

DAYLESFORD (G) SP 243258 (144). On Evenlode, home of Warren Hastings's forbears, bought back by him. He is buried here. C not the one Hastings restored but rebuilt again since. Daegil's ford (OE).

DEDDINGTON (O) SP 467315 (145). Traffic on Oxford–Banbury road pours through it, but bits either side are attractive still. C 14 tower 17, replacing one which collapsed. Settlement of Daeda's folk (OE).

DENCHWORTH (B) SU 382918 (158). Nice Vale of White Horse village. C from 13 restored 19. Denic's enclosure (OE).

DERRY BROOK. Wiltshire tributary of R. Thames, joining it above Waterhay Bridge. Perhaps deer brook (OE).

DIDCOT (B) SU 525900 (158). Railway promoters did not promote beautiful towns, and Didcot is a railway town. Now dominated by huge power station. But pleasant flat countryside all round. All Saints C of many different periods but 13 c. memorial, St Peter late 19. Dudda's home or cottage (OE).

DIKLER, River. Tributary of the Windrush, joining it below Bourton on the Water. Rushy river (OE).

DONNINGTON (B) SU 468688 (158). Suburb of Newbury Castle gallantly held for Charles I in Civil War. There was a Roman road in the vicinity, and possibly similar derivation to Donnington (G), otherwise obscure.

DONNINGTON (G) SP 193283 (144). On Fosse Way (now A429) between headwaters of Evenlode and Dikler. Roman settlement. Origins of name a fine piece of detective work by Ekwall. He traces name to old form Dunnestreatun, which would mean 'settlement on the street (Fosse Way) belonging to Dunne', a nun to whom Aethelbald gave land in 736.

DORCHESTER (O) SU 588944 (158). P. 133–4 Settlement from antiquity, prehistoric earthworks, Roman frontier post to guard crossing of R. Thames, Saxon bishopric. Site of introduction of Christianity to Wessex by St Birinus 635. C magnificent 12–15, cathedral-like church of medieval Dorchester Abbey. Pre-Saxon Celtic root may mean 'good place' plus OE ceaster from fortifications.

DORN RIVER. Tributary of the Glyme, which it joins above Woodstock. Name obscure, but may mean hidden or secluded river.

DRAYTON (B) SU 476941 (158). Once attractive village murdered by traffic on main road from Midlands to S coast, A34, which cuts it in two. May recover when new road built. C 19 but some very old bits. Name implies a place where goods could be hauled or dragged (doubtless to and from Rs Thames and Ock) (OE).

DRAYTON ST LEONARD (O) SU 598962 (158). On the Thame above Dorchester. C 13–14. Thame could be forded here, which explains name (see above).

DRIFFIELD (G) SU 075997 (157). Village ½m W of Ampney Brook, on small feeder to brook. C rebuilt 18 again 19 some old bits. Muddy or dirty field (OE).

DRY SANDFORD (B) 467003 (158). Hamlet NNW of Abingdon. Name implies sandy ford and there is a Sandford Brook which feeds the Ock. Apparently the ford was usually dry.

DUCKLINGTON (O) SP 356078 (158). Nice straggling village with fine duck pond. C 13–15. Name regrettably not derived from ducks, but seems to mean settlement of Ducca's folk (OE).

DUXFORD (B) SU 368999 (158). Prehistoric crossing of the Thames, still a ford, although navigable river now follows a cut which has to be crossed by a bridge. Countryside infinitely peaceful and remote. Duduc's ford (OE).

EASINGTON (O) SP 688102 (159) Hamlet open rolling country N of River Thame. C 13. Hill of Esa's folk.

EAST GARSTON (B) SU 365768 (158). Pretty village on R. Lambourn. C 14 much rebuilt 19. Original name Esgarston, corrupted to East Garston. Interesting name because Esgar is old Danish or Viking name and land here was apparently granted to Norse nobleman by Edward the Confessor.

EASTBURY (B) SU 348771 (158). Another pretty village on R. Lambourn. C 19. Eastern fortified place (OE) – east perhaps from village of Lambourn, although it is really SE.

EASTLEACH MARTIN (G) SU 203054 (157) and Turville 198054, villages E and W of River Leach, joined by a bridge. Martin C 13–14, Turville C 13–14. John Keble preached in both villages when he was vicar of Southrop, 1 m S. Leach from OE word simply meaning stream. Martin from church, Turville family holding land there 13 c.

EATON (B) SP 448032 (158). Hamlet in lovely remote countryside between Cumnor and Thames. Island or river settlement (OE).

EATON HASTINGS (B) SU 264982 (157). Scarcely anything there now but the lovely little church (late 12–13) on hill above the Thames below Buscot. Island settlement plus family name.

EDDINGTON (B) SU 344690 (158). Just across Kennet from Hungerford. C 19. Settlement belonging to a woman called Eadgifu (OE).

ELKSTONE (G) SO 968124 (144). High Cotswolds S of Churn. C 13–14. Roman villa SSE. Eanlac's settlement (OE).

ELSFIELD (O) SP 540102 (145). Quiet, pretty village E of Cherwell near Oxford. C 13. John Buchan (Lord Tweedsmuir) lived here. He died in Canada but his ashes were brought to Elsfield churchyard. Elesa's (medieval name) field.

ENBORNE (B) SU 438659 (158). On Enborne river near Newbury. C 12 on Saxon foundation, some 19 work. From river.

ENBORNE, RIVER. Southern tributary of the Kennet, which it joins just W of Newbury. Stream with alders, or perhaps duck stream (OE).

ENGLEFIELD (B) SU 625720 (158). N of Kennet near Reading. C 13 much rebuilt 19. Site of skirmish in 871 between Danes who held Reading and West Saxons, Danes driven back to Reading. Land (field) granted to Angles who settled in Saxon country (OE).

ENSTONE (O) SP 375245 (145), CHURCH ENSTONE 380250, NEAT ENSTONE 380242. Cluster of villages (really one scattered village) on steep N and S banks of River Glyme. C 14 on Saxon foundation. Hoar Stone just S of Neat Enstone marks ancient burial ground. Enna's stone, perhaps relating to Hoar Stone. Neat = OE cattle – part of village where cattle kept.

EVENLODE (G) SP 222292 (144). Village near headwaters of River.

EVENLODE. C 14. From river.

EVENLODE, RIVER. Tributary of the Thames rising in Gloucestershire and joining Thames near Cassington, above Oxford. Old name of river was Bladon, origin obscure.

EWELME (O) SU 646916 (159). Lovely old village Oxfordshire Chilterns. C 14–15, nice almshouses. Many royals and great have lived at Ewelme, including Prince Rupert, Margaret of Anjou (as a prisoner), Elizabeth I, William de la Pole, Duke of Suffolk, and Alice Duchess of Suffolk, granddaughter of Geoffrey Chaucer. OE name means spring or source of river.

EWEN (G) SP 005975 (157). First bridge over the infant Thames is on road from Kemble to Ewen. This small settlement in meadows S of Fosse Way (A429) was apparently once considered to be at the source of the Thames, for name means spring or source of river (OE). Actually Thames rises N of Fosse Way, flowing under the road through a culvert, but there may be little or no water here for much of the year. At Ewen it is a proper streamlet.

EYNSHAM (O) SP 430100 (158). Saxon town near prehistoric settlement. Fine C 14–15, wall paintings. Toll bridge over Thames. Egone's homestead or enclosure (OE).

FAIRFORD (G) SP 155010 (157). Old stone town on Coln. P. 142–3. Clean-water ford (OE).

FARINGDON (B) SU 285955 (158). P. 88–90. Old settlement at meeting-place of trackways (now modern roads) running N to R Thames at Radcot, NW to river at Lechlade, E to Abingdon, SE to Wantage and SW to Swindon. Important in early Kingdom of Wessex, whose kings had a palace (probably group of wooden buildings) there. C 12–13, beautiful setting, central tower which once had a spire, destroyed by cannon fire during siege of Faringdon House in Civil War. Society of Friends Meeting House 18c. Nice 17 c market hall in what was once charming market place. Ferny hill (OE).

FARINGDON, LITTLE (O) SU 225015 (157). Pretty village on Leach, a little off main road A361. C 12–14. Ferny hill (OE).

FARMINGTON (G) SP 135155 (144). High village near headwaters of Sherborne Brook, tributary of Windrush. C 14. Pump House with roof presented by Farmington, Conn, in 1935 to commemorate 300th anniversary of founding of State of Connecticut. Earthwork (Norbury Camp) NW. Old name Thormerton, settlement by a pond with thorn trees (OE).

FARMOOR (BO) SP 455065 (158). Large reservoir on Berkshire bank of Thames much used for dinghy sailing. Perhaps ferny mere, from old pond long before modern reservoir in marshy district.

FARNBOROUGH (B) SU 435820 (158). 700 ft up on the Downs. C part 13. Ferny hill (OE).

FAWLER (O) SP 373170 (145). Across Evenlode from Finstock. Roman settlement, which gives place its name from OE word for flooring or (Roman) pavement.

FAWLEY (B) SU 393813 (158), SOUTH FAWLEY 390802. Ancient settlements S of Ridgeway on Berkshire Downs. North has C 19. Countryside of Hardy's 'Jude the Obscure'. Clearing in a wood (OE).

FENCOTT (O) SP 575161 (145). Small village on Ray, on edge of Otmoor. Cottage in a fen or marsh (OE).

FERNHAM (B) SU 292920 (158). White Horse village near source of Ock. C 19. Ferny homestead (OE).

FIFIELD (O) SP 241188 (144). Delightful Wychwood village ½ m safely E of A424. C 14. Saxon nobleman's (thegn's) holding of five hides of land (OE).

FILKINS (O) SP 238044 (157). On Oxfordshire-Gloucestershire border near headwaters of Broadwell Brook tributary of R. Thames. Home of Sir Stafford Cripps who established interesting museum of local history. Name obscure.

FINSTOCK (O) SP 362165 (145). Wychwood village on Evenlode. Hermit's cell in a place with woodpeckers (OE), or perhaps simply place of the woodpeckers.

FLAGHAM BROOK. Wiltshire tributary of infant R. Thames above Ashton Keynes. Perhaps peaty brook (OE).

FOREST HILL (O) SP 585078 (158). E Oxford ½ m N of A40. C 12–13, where Milton married his first wife, who came from Forest Hill. Probably not forest but OE for frost, cold or exposed hill.

FREELAND (O) SP 415126 (145) In wooded country, once Wychwood, in bend of Evenlode before it joins the Thames. Perhaps part of Wychwood with common rights.

FRILFORD (B) SU 442972 (158). Prehistoric, Roman and Saxon religious settlement and burial place. Frithda's ford, across Ock or brook tributary of Ock (OE).

FRILSHAM (B) SU 546732 (158). Upper Pang valley. C 12 some 19. Frithel's settlement (OE).

FRITWELL (O) SP 525295 (145). Ancient settlement E of Cherwell, once on boundary between Wessex and Mercia. C 13–14 on Saxon foundation, interesting dedication to St Olave (Norse Olaf) suggesting Christian Viking settlement. Wishing well (OE).

FULBROOK (O) SP 260130 (144). Main road A361 runs through it to cross the Windrush at Burford, but off the road the water meadows rise to coppices that hint still of Wychwood. C 12–13–14. Muddy or dirty (foul) brook (OE).

FYFIELD (B) SU 433988 (158). Possesses elm (actually at Tubney ½ m E) to which Matthew Arnold's maidens came 'To dance around the Fyfield elm in May'. Tree struck by lightning but some growth survives. C 13 rebuilt with old stone after fire 1893. Lady Catherine Gordon ('White Rose of Scotland') once wife of Perkin Warbeck buried in church. She had four husbands, last Christopher Ashfield of Fyfield. Estate of five hides (see Fifield).

FYFIELD WICK (B) SU 414967 (158). S of Fyfield, important pig-breeding farm. Wick (OE wic from latin vicus) often used to distinguish parts of village or parish. May mean several things, from cluster of cottages to dairy farm, usually dairy. May sometimes mean Wych elm, i.e. part of village where such a tree stood.

GAGTE BROOK. Oxfordshire tributary of R. Ray, W of Bicester. Perhaps friends or relation's brook (OE).

GALLOS BROOK. Oxfordshire tributary of R. Ray, E of Kirtlington. Name obscure, gallows?

GARFORD (B) SU 428962 (158). On River Ock, settlement from prehistoric times, Roman temple on site of Iron Age shrine, Anglo-Saxon cemetery. Charming C 13 reached through farmyard. Gara's ford (across Ock) (OE).

GARSINGTON (O) SP 581022 (158). SE outskirts Oxford, nice open Chiltern country. C 13–15. Grassy hill (OE).

GINGE BROOK (B) Stream flowing S of R Ock to join Thames via network of other brooks near Sutton Courtenay. Perhaps twisting brook (OE).

GINGE, EAST (B) SU 448866 (158), WEST 445869. Hamlets at headwaters of Ginge brook. From brook.

GLYME, RIVER. Tributary of the Evenlode, which it joins at Bladon, just before the Evenlode itself joins the Thames. Most beautiful river flowing through beautiful country. Name seems to mean gleaming water (OE).

GLYMPTON (O) SP 426215 (145). Old cottages in beautiful Glyme valley. C 13, Norman font. From river name.

GODSTOW (O) SP 478093 (158). On Thames N of Oxford, site of nunnery. P. 100–1, 231. God's place (from nunnery) (OE).

GOOSEY (B) SU 358920 (158). Nice White Horse village, round enormous village green. C much restored 19, some early work. Goose island (in marsh that covered much of Ock valley) (OE).

GORING (O) SU 600810 (158). On Thames, where river cuts 'Goring Gap' through ridge of chalk. Prosperous Thames townlet, much commuting. C 13. (Place where) Gara's folk (lived) (OE).

GOZZARD'S FORD (B) SU 469985 (158). On Sandford Brook tributary of Ock. Ford of the geese (?)

GROVE (B) SU 403902 (158). Once pretty village N of Wantage, with Letcombe Brook flowing through it. Now subject great housing development. Interesting modern church. From OE word for grove or wood.

GUITING, TEMPLE (G) SP 092278 (144), POWER 095247. Lovely Cotswolds near headwaters of Windrush. Temple G (once held by Knights Templars) C 16 and early Norman work. Power C 13–15. From OE word meaning flood, no doubt young Windrush in spate.

HAGBOURNE, EAST (B) SU 532883 (158) WEST 513877. Pair of Berkshire Downland villages. C is at East 13 onwards. Pretty houses. West near Icknield way, Bronze Age axe found. Hacca's stream (present Mill Brook).

HAMPNETT (G) SP 100157 (144). Off Fosse Way (A429) near headwaters Rivers Leach and Windrush. C 12–15. High settlement (OE).

HAMPSTEAD NORRIS (B) SU 527764 (158). Upper Pang valley, Roman settlement. C 13 and 17, 19. Homestead (manor held by Norreys family in 15 c.)

HAMPTON GAY (O) SP 488165 (145) Poyle 504155. Villages on Cherwell (Oxford Canal) N of Kidlington. Hampton Gay C 19 parts 15. H Poyle C 13–14. Settlement in meadows OE. Gay, Poyle family names, de la Puiles held Hampton P in 13 c.

HAMSTEAD (sometimes Hampstead) MARSHALL (B) SU 412658 (158). Pretty country S of Kennet. C 14 tower 18. Homestead (once held by Lord Marshall officer later called Earl Marshall) under Henry I.

HANBOROUGH, CHURCH (O) SP 427128 (145) LONG 428143 Wychwood villages in bend of Evenlode. Church H. C 13–14–15. Perhaps hill of the wild birds (OE).

HANNEY, EAST (B) SU 420930 (158), WEST 405930. Pleasant villages (West prettier) on brooks running into R. Ock. West has old church (St James) 12–13, interesting memorial to lady who d. 1715 aged 124. Island (in Ock marshes) of wild birds, or perhaps where hens were kept (OE).

HANNINGTON (W) SU 175933 (157). Village on Wiltshire bank of Thames. Hill of the wild birds (OE).

HARNHILL (G) SP 070004 (157). Small village 1m W of Ampney Brook. C 12 onwards. Hill of the hares (OE).

HARWELL (B) SU 490890 (158). Once famous for cherries (still fine cherries) now known for Atomic Energy Research Establishment P. 210–11. C v. old, 12 perhaps some 11. Stream from the grey hill (OE).

HASELEY, GREAT (O) SP 640018 (158), Little 643005. Pleasant villages in bend of R. Thame. C 14. John Leland, whose journeyings through England 1534–43 are basis much English social history was rector of Haseley. Hazel wood (OE).

HASELEY BROOK. Tributary of R. Thame. Hazel wood brook (OE).

HATFORD (B) SU 338948 (158). Vale of White Horse. Original C (St George) 12–13 now shell, new C 19. Ford (on brook running into Ock) at the foot of a hill (OE).

HATHEROP (G) SP 156053 (157). Near Coln St Aldwyn's on R. Coln. C 13–15. High farm (OE).

HAZELFORD BROOK. Tributary of R. Windrush, which it joins at Taynton. Ford by the hazel tree(s). This brook was once known as the Tegn (see Taynton.)

HAZLETON (G) SP 080180 (144). High Cotswold hamlet W of Fosse Way (A429). C 12–15. Settlement by the hazel trees (OE).

HEADINGTON (O) SP 545075 (158). Suburb of Oxford, source of Headington stone used for many Oxford buildings. C 15. Hedena's hill (OE).

HEMPTON (O) SP 436318 (145). Hamlet in high country W of Oxford–Banbury road. High settlement (OE).

HENDRED EAST (B) SU 460890 (158) WEST 450887. Spring-line villages on downs E Wantage, attractive thatched, half-timbered houses and cottages. East H C (St Augustine) 19 some 14, Jesus Chapel (wayside) built by Carthusian monks 15 c., Roman Catholic Church (St Mary) 19. Hendred House, with 13 c. chapel, still in possession Roman Catholic Eyston family after 500 years. Relics of English Martyrs St Thomas More and St John Fisher. West H C 14, Methodist Chapel 1830. Brook of the wild birds (OE) (brook is Ginge Brook q.v., which does not mean wild bird brook. Presumably birds haunted brook at Hendreds.)

HENSINGTON (O) SP 450150 (145). Hamlet on the edge of Blenheim Great Park. Probably place where hens were kept (OE).

HERMITAGE (B) SU 510732 (158). Roman villa, prehistoric settlement, lovely country W of R. Pang and N of R. Kennet. C 19. Name explains itself.

HEYFORD UPPER (O) SP 498260 (145) LOWER 488248. Villages E of Cherwell (Oxford Canal). Upper C 19 tower 15, Lower C 14. Upper has large airfield used by USAF. Ford (across Cherwell) used by haycarts.

HEYTHROP (O) SP 352278 (145). Oxfordshire Cotswolds. Fine park with mansion used as Jesuit college until seminary transferred London 1969. Since then staff training centre for bank.

HIGHMOOR BROOK. Oxfordshire tributary of R. Thames, rising N of Bampton and joining Thames via network of brooks and watercourses in low meadows above Newbridge. High moor (rising ground N Bampton).

HIGHWORTH (W) SU 200925 (157). Small town on a hill dominating rather flat country on Wiltshire bank of Thames, near Gloucestershire, Berkshire borders. C 16, memorial to First World War VC (Sub. Lt. Warneford RN) who destroyed Zeppelin. High enclosure (OE).

HINKSEY STREAM. Tributary of R. Thames at Hinksey.

HINKSEY NORTH (B) SP 490055 (158) SOUTH 509040. Very ancient settlements by cattle crossing (oxen-ford) of Thames, now suburb Oxford. North C 13, South C 13 and 18. Interesting name suggests Hengest's island, from early Saxon leader.

HINTON, LITTLE (W) SU 233832 (157). Just below Ridgeway W end of White Horse escarpment. Monks' settlement OE. Little perhaps in contrast to Bishop's manor (Bishopstone) 1 m E.

HINTON WALDRIST (B) SU 378992 (158). Old settlement near ford across Thames at Duxford. Earthwork probably related to Cherbury Camp (q.v.) 1½ m S, as defences for ford. C 13. Name here means high settlement, perhaps from earthwork. Waldrist corruption of St Valery family which held land 12 c.

HOLTON (O) SP 601068 (158). By Holton Brook, tributary of R. Thame. C 14, some earlier. Moat in Holton Park. Settlement in a valley (OE).

HOLWELL (O) SP 244087 (157). On Akeman Street (here minor road crossing A361) N of Lechlade. C 19. Holy spring (OE).

HOLYWELL BROOK. Rivulet feeding R. Ock near Stanford in the Vale.

HORSPATH (O) SP 572048 (158). Suburb and trading estate E of Oxford. C 13. Horse-track (OE).

HUNGERFORD (B) SU 335685 (158). On R. Kennet, Wiltshire border of region. Beautiful old town, held by John of Gaunt, Duke of Lancaster. Red rose (of Lancaster) still presented to reigning monarch visiting town, given Queen Elizabeth II on visit 1952. C 19. Congregational church 1840. Grim name means ford (across Kennet) where people suffered from hunger, presumably in some Saxon war (OE).

ICKFORD (Bu) SP 659074 (159) and Little Ickford 655071. Adjoining villages on R. Thame. C 13 some earlier work. Ica's ford (across Thame) (OE).

ICKNIELD WAY. Prehistoric route roughly following line of the Ridgeway (q.v.) but lower on the Downs, with access to water at spring level. A later route than The Ridgeway, when danger from wild animals became less acute, and it was safe to travel nearer to water.

ICOMB (G) SP 215226 (144). Grand Cotswold country by Westcote brook, high tributary of R. Evenlode. C 13 tower 17. Earthwork on Icomb hill. Ica's combe (OE).

IDBURY (O) SP 235200 (144). Above Evenlode. C 13. Earthwork SW. Ida's fortified place (OE).

IFFLEY (O) SP 526036 (158). Suburb S Oxford. Iffley lock, one of first three pound locks built on Thames. Plover's wood (OE).

IGHT, RIVER. Obsolete (Celtic) name for R. Ray.

ILSLEY, EAST (B) SU 494812 (158) WEST 474835. Racing country on Berkshire Downs. East C 13 rebuilt 19, West C 19. (H)ild's wood (OE).

INGLESHAM (W) SU 205985 (157). On Wiltshire Thames 1 m above Lechlade. Thames terminal of Thames and Severn Canal. C 13–14. Upper Inglesham hamlet 1½ m S. Inga's meadowland (OE).

IPSDEN (O) SU 631852 (159). Oxfordshire Chilterns. C 13–14. Charles Reade b. 1814. Hill place (OE).

ISIS, RIVER. Factitious name for R. Thames above Oxford, never used save in some pedantic writing. And the pedants are wrong, for the word is a wholly artificial concoction, and relatively late at that. Should be removed from Ordnance Survey.

ISLIP (O) SP 526140 (145). At junction Rivers Ray and Cherwell. Site of Saxon palace, where Edward the Confessor was born 1004. Medieval village. C bits 13 much rebuilt. Ight was ancient name of River Ray. Slip from OE word probably relating to place where carts could be dragged into the river, like modern slipway.

KELMSCOT (t) (O) SU 251991 (157). Home of William Morris P. 234–5 C 13 onwards. Cenhelm's cottage (OE).

KEMBLE (G) SO 988975 (157). Across infant Thames from Ewen, first settlement below source of river at Thames Head. C 13. Appears to derive from name of Ancient British god Camulos.

KEMPSFORD (G) SP 156970 (157). On Thames between Cricklade and Lechlade. Saxon outpost guarding river crossing. Lands later held by John of Gaunt and House of Lancaster. C 12–13–14. Cynemaer's ford (OE).

KENCOT (O) SP 256046 (157). Lovely corner of Oxfordshire–Gloucestershire border, countryside of meadows and streamlets feeding R. Thames. C 12–15. Cena's cottage (OE).

KENNINGTON (B) SP 520025 (158). Now suburb Oxford but saved from complete domination main roads by Bagley Wood. New C 20. Settlement of Cena's folk (OE).

KEY, RIVER. Wiltshire tributary of R. Thames near Cricklade. Perhaps from OE word meaning cow, river where cows stand.

KEYNES, ASHTON (W) SU 046940 (157), Poole (G) 000954 Somerford (G) 020951. Wiltshire and Gloucestershire boundaries much mixed up here. Three charming villages on young Thames, held by powerful Norman Kaynes or Keynes family 12 c. Somerford K. C part Saxon, v. interesting Saxon doorway. Ashton settlement by ash tree, Poole by pool in river, Somerford by ford good in dry weather (OE).

KIBBLE DITCH. One of network small streams feeding R. Thames near Wallingford. Probably Cybbel's ditch (OE).

KIDDINGTON (O) SP 415228 (145), OVER KIDDINGTON 410220. In R. Glyme valley. C 12–14. Settlement of Cuda's folk (OE).

KIDLINGTON (O) SP 495145 (145) Old village by R. Cherwell and Oxford Canal, expanded to suburb of modern Oxford. C 13–14. Another place of Cuda's folk (OE).

KIDMORE END (O) SU 698793 (159). Settlement in wooded hills above Mapledurham. Somebody's mere or pond, perhaps Cuda (OE).

KINGHAM (O) SP 260240 (144). East bank R. Evenlode, Western Region station 1 m. S of village serves wide area. C 14. Not king, but probably settlement of Caega's folk (OE).

KING'S SUTTON (N) SP 498363 (145). On Cherwell–Oxford Canal, E of Oxford–Banbury road, actually in Northamptonshire. Third church in old rhyme 'King's

Sutton for beauty'. C 15 certainly lovely. South settlement, perhaps from Banbury, relating to Roman–British settlement ½ m. N of present village. King's signifies once Crown land.

KINGSTON BAGPUIZE (B) SU 408982 (158) LISLE 325875. Berkshire villages. Bagpuize first settlement on Berkshire bank of Thames after crossing at Newbridge. C late 18–19. Lisle near Blowing Stone (q.v.) under White Horse Hill. C early 13. Crown manors granted to Norman families, Bagpuize to de Bachepuz, Lisle to de l'Isle.

KINGSTON BLOUNT (O) SU 739995 (159). Village Oxfordshire Chilterns by Icknield way. Crown manor granted to Le Blount family (William Le Blount was in charge of ships for William the Conqueror at invasion 1066.)

KINTBURY (B) SU 385668 (158). Settlement from antiquity on R. Kennet E of Hungerford. C 19 some 11 bits. Jane Austen quite often stayed at Kintbury. Name from Kennet.

KIRTLINGTON (O) SP 500195 (145). On R. Cherwell–Oxford Canal. Saxon settlement. C 12–13, perhaps Saxon foundations. Settlement of Cyrtla's folk (OE).

LAMBOURN, RIVER. Tributary of R. Kennet. Stream for dipping lambs (OE).

LAMBOURN (B) SU 326790 (158). Village on R. Lambourn in superb downland. Inhabited from earliest times. Seven Barrows (actually 24) and Long Barrow prehistoric burial sites 2½ m. N of village. C 12–13. Upper Lambourn 315804. Natural reservoir (deep pools) near source of river ensuring summer flow.

LANGFORD (O) SP 248028 (157). Ancient settlement on Broadwell Brook near Oxfordshire–Gloucestershire border. C 12 Saxon foundations and interesting Saxon carving. Long ford (OE).

LANGHAT DITCH. Tributary of Broadwell Brook, which tributary of R. Thames near Radcot. Difficult name, perhaps long hill ditch (OE).

LATCHFORD (O) SP 660015 (159) Hamlet by Haseley Brook, tributary of R. Thame. Ford over brook (OE).

LATTON (W) SU 094957 (157). Hamlet near Cricklade. Place for growing leeks (OE).

LEACH, RIVER Gloucestershire tributary of the Thames, which it joins just below Lechlade. Name from OE word simply meaning river.

LEAFIELD (O) SP 320154 (145) Wychwood village between Rivers Evenlode and Windrush, ancient settlement, earthworks and barrows. C 19. Field or clearing (in Wychwood). Mixture of OE feld and Norman–French Le = the, The Field.

LECHLADE (G) SU 215995 (157) P 82–4. River crossing (of the Thames) by the Leach (river) (OE).

LECKHAMPSTEAD (B) SU 439760 (158). On Downs above lower Lambourn valley. C 19. Homestead or settlement where leeks were grown (OE).

LEDWELL (O) SP 420282 (145). Hamlet by Cockley Brook, tributary of R. Dorn, which tributary of R. Glyme. Loud (rushing water) stream.

LETCOMBE BASSETT (B) SU 373851 (158) REGIS 382866. Downland villages inhabited from prehistoric times. Fine hill fort enclosing some 26 acres on Segsbury Down 1 m. SE Letcombe B. Letcombe brook, tributary of R. Ock via Childrey Brook, notable for water-cress. 'Bassett Cress' was 18 c. street cry in London. 'Cresscombe' in Hardy's *Jude the Obscure* based on Letcombe B. Swift stayed at Letcombe B. rectory. Letcombe B. C 12–13, Letcombe R. C 13–15. King John had hunting lodge at Letcombe R. Racing country, training stables. Origin name obscure, perhaps ledged combe or valley (OE). Bassett family held land 12 c. given to Abingdon Abbey. Regis Crown manor.

LEW (O) SP 325064 (158). Tiny village on little rise in Windrush meadows. Hill (OE).

LEWKNOR (O) SU 715975 (159). Village under Beacon Hill overlooking Thame valley. C 12–14. Leofeca's hillside (OE).

LIDSTONE (O) SP 356246 (145). Tiny hamlet exquisite Glyme valley. Near Enstone and name also seems to come from the nearby standing stone (Hoar Stone).

LIMB BROOK Tributary of R. Thames S. of Eynsham. Perhaps lime tree brook (OE).

LITTLEMORE (O) SP 550027 (158). A village now suburb SE Oxford. C 19. Cardinal Newman was vicar of Littlemore before he joined Roman church. Little moor.

LITTLEWORTH (B) SU 312972 (158). Small village Thames end of White Horse vale. C 19. Small enclosure (as distinct from Longworth, not far away) (OE).

LOCKINGE, EAST (B) SU 425874 (158) and West 423877. Villages on Downs W outskirts Wantage, with brook flowing into Ginge Brook. East L. was built as 'model village' in 1860. C (in park between two villages) 14, tower 16, enlarged 19. From OE word meaning stream.

LONG CRENDON (Bu) SP 695090 (159). Attractive village N of Thame. C 13. Courthouse 14 c. once staple hall for wool merchants now National Trust. Creoda's hill.

LONGCOT (B) SU 275907 (157). White Horse country. C 13, tower 18. Long cottage(s) (OE).

LONGBOROUGH (G) SP 179296 (144). High Cotswolds, above source of R. Dikler, tributary of Windrush. C 12–14. Long hill (OE).

LONGWORTH (B) SU 390994 (158). Nice old village Vale of White Horse near Thames. C 13–15. Long enclosure (OE).

LYFORD (B) SU 393945 (158). Hamlet on R. Ock. C 13–15. At Lyford Grange Edmund Campion, Jesuit martyr, was arrested 1581. Ford (over Ock) where flax grew (OE).

LYNEHAM (O) SP 279204 (144). On E bank R. Evenlode, once site of Norman Abbey, now tiny village. Place for growing flax (OE).

MAPLEDURHAM (O) SU 672770 (158). Between woods and river just above Reading. Great house (home of Blount family) fine example Tudor building. Martha Blount attracted devotion of Alexander Pope. C part 14 interesting and attractive. Settlement by a maple tree or trees (OE).

MARCHAM (B) SU 455965 (158). Village on R. Ock. C 19 some 13 bits. Denman College, pleasant early 19 c. house, training centre for Federation of Women's Institutes, beautiful examples handwork, country crafts. Curious salt spring near village, with interesting flora. Meadows growing wild celery (OE).

MAUGERSBURY HILL (G) SP 205237 (144) and Maugersbury village 201252. High Cotswolds, watershed between Rivers Dikler and Evenlode. Maethelgar's strong place (OE).

MARSTON (O) SP 528088 (158). Village N Oxford now Oxford suburb. Was HQ Parliament troops under Fairfax in Civil War siege of Oxford. C 14–15. Marsh settlement OE (in R. Cherwell marshes).

MERTON (O) SP 576177 (145). Village N of R. Ray near Otmoor. Once held by Knights Templars. C 14. Lakeside (flooded Otmoor) settlement (OE).

MEYSEY HAMPTON (G) SP 120999 (157) and MARSTON MEYSEY (W) 128974. Picture postcard villages between (and safely off) main roads A417 and A419 in gentle Upper Thames country on Gloucestershire–Wiltshire border. Meysey Hampton C 13, fine old glass. Lands held by de Meysi family 13 c.

MIDDLETON STONEY (O) SP 535235 (145). Saxon settlement E of earthwork Ash Bank or Aves Ditch. Mound of Norman castle. C 12 onwards. Middleton Park home of Earls of Jersey 1736–1946 now Managers' Conference Centre National-Westminster Bank. Middle settlement OE perhaps between Ash bank and Akeman Street to the S. Stoney explains itself.

MIDGHAM (B) SU 555672 (158). Settlement on N bank R. Kennet. Name does imply midges, no doubt from river (OE).

MILCOMBE (O) SP 413347 (145). Oxfordshire Cotswolds 1 m SW Bloxham. C 13–14. Middle combe (OE).

MILTON (B) SU 487923 (158). Originally small village on Mill Brook SW of Thames at Sutton Courtenay. C 18–19. Oil Company (Esso) Research Centre with beautifully maintained lawns and gardens–object lesson on how industry should look after countryside. Large area of district taken over by Government for depot during 1939–45 war, unwanted after war, object lesson how not to treat countryside. Mill settlement.

MILTON (O) SP 452351 (145). Village S. Banbury. Middle settlement, perhaps between Bloxham and Adderbury (OE).

MILTON, GREAT (O) SP 630030 (158) and LITTLE 620006. Villages E of River Thame. Great M. C 13–14. Little on main road B4013 now considerably larger than Great, pleasantly off main road, but Great's distinction as place of origin John Milton's family cannot diminish. Another middle settlement, perhaps between Thame and Haseley Brook.

MILTON-UNDER-WYCHWOOD (O) SP 265183 (144). Wychwood village C 19. Middle settlement (OE).

MINSTER LOVELL (O) SP 318112 (145). Exquisite village on Windrush. Peaceful ruins of great house (well cared for by Ministry of Works) with river lapping lawns. C 15, beautiful setting. Site of priory (giving name Minster) on land held by Lovells.

MORETON NORTH (B) S U 562896 (158) SOUTH 560882. Villages between Didcot and R. Thames. N C 13–14 some earlier bits S C 11 onwards some 19. Marsh settlement O E (in marshes of Kibble Ditch and streamlets feeding R. Thames).

MORETON-IN-MARSH (G) SP 207326 (144). Old town near Cotswold headwaters of R. Evenlode. Name is interesting often assumed to signify Moreton (moorland settlement) on March, or frontier because near Gloucestershire–Oxfordshire border. But old name was Moreton in Hennemarsh, which clearly means boggy or marshy land where wild birds were to be had (O E).

MOULSFORD (B) S U 592836 (158) Thames-side village. C 19. Puzzling name. Appears to mean (O E) mule's ford: Ekwall suggests it may be somebody's nickname.

MURCOTT (O) SP 585158 (145). Hamlet on edge of Otmoor. Cottages in fen or marsh (OE).

NAUNTON (G) SP 115234 (144) Lovely village on Upper Windrush. C 15, perhaps Saxon origins. Name obscure, possibly corruption of New Town, but new about 1200 years ago.

NETHERCOTT (O) SP 483205 (145). On W bank R. Cherwell–Oxford Canal. Lower cottage(s) (O E).

NETHERTON (B) S U 420993 (158). Hamlet N of A420 in lanes running down to R. Thames. Lower settlement (O E).

NETTLEBED (O) S U 700868 (159). On main Oxford–Henley road A423. Fine common. Ground covered with nettles (OE).

NEWBRIDGE (O,B) SP 404015 (158). Medieval bridge across Thames from Standlake (O) to Kingston Bagpuize (B), but villages each bank a couple of miles away from bridge P 151–2, 233. Was 'new' in 13 c.

NEWBURY (E) S U 470670 (158) P 161–8. New borough (new from older settlement at Speen).

NEWINGTON (O) S U 610967 (158). Pretty village on R. Thame. C 12–15. New settlement (O E).

NOKE (O) SP 545132 (145). Remote little village W of Roman road across Otmoor. C 13. Name from corruption of (O E) word meaning settlement by an oak tree.

NOR BROOK. Tributary of R. Ock near Marcham. Presumably North brook (N of Childrey Brook).

NORTH STOKE (O) S U 610864 (158). Oxfordshire bank R. Thames below Wallingford. C 14, wall paintings. (North) hermit's cell or holy place (O E).

NORTHBROOK (O) SP 493220 (145). 1 m W Aves Ditch earthwork, on E bank R. Cherwell–Oxford Canal. Explains itself.

NORTHFIELD BROOK Part of network small streams feeding R. Thames S of Oxford.

NORTHLEACH (G) SP 115146 (144). Very old settlement at headwaters of R. Leach. Cotswold stone small town, C 15 of exceptional grandeur, reflecting prosperity of medieval wool trade from Cotswold sheep. From river.

NORTH LEIGH (O) SP 385130 (145). Hilltop village Wychwood country between Rivers Evenlode and Windrush. Settlement of great antiquity. Important Roman villa at East End in bend of Windrush 2 m N (395154). C 12–15 and Saxon. (North) wood or glade (OE).

NORTHMOOR (O) SP 422029 (158). Peaceful water meadows between R. Thames and Windrush. C 13–15. Once marsh country, North fen (OE).

NORTON DITCH. Brook feeding Highmoor Brook N of Bampton, near Brize Norton.

NOTGROVE (G) SP 108202 (144). Settlement from antiquity high Cotswolds over headwaters R. Windrush. Glorious hill country. Prehistoric long barrow, Roman tomb, probably Saxon foundations Norman church. Rest of C 14–15 some 19 rebuilding. Grave in a thicket (probably from nearby barrow) (OE).

NUFFIELD (O) SU 668873 (159). High Oxfordshire Chilterns, just off main road A423. Settlement from antiquity. C 12–13. Home of William Morris, founder of Morris Motors, who took his title Lord Nuffield from place. Corruption of OE word meaning hill-field.

NUNEHAM COURTENAY (O) Su 552992 (158). Beautifully placed on ridge rising gently from R. Thames on Oxfordshire bank between Oxford and Abingdon. Mansion 18c. by first Earl Harcourt, who rebuilt C. Corruption of (OE) new homestead, land held by Courtenay family 13 c.

OAKLEY (Bu) SP 638122 (145). Village in Chiltern valley by headwaters of brooks feeding R. Thame. Oak wood (OE).

OCK, RIVER. Berkshire tributary of R. Thames. Rises S of Faringdon and joins Thames at Abingdon. Ock valley forms Vale of the White Horse. Once a good salmon river, and name derives from old (Celtic) word for salmon. Still older name of R. Ock was R. Churn.

ODDINGTON (G) SP 230259 (144). On R. Evenlode near Oxfordshire border. Two C, one modern, one 12 restored, fine medieval wall paintings. Oda's settlement (OE).

ODDINGTON (O) SP 554148 (145). Village on edge of Otmoor. Ota's settlement.

OSNEY (O) SP 500060 (158). Islanded in R. Thames backwaters and tributaries, now part of Central Oxford. Site of Osney Abbey P 97, 105. Osa's island (OE).

OTMOOR (O) Strange area of fenland in Ray valley W of Chilterns. R. Ray exceptionally sluggish and Otmoor fen seems all but undrainable. Roman engineers drove road to Alchester across Otmoor on faggots, a remarkable engineering feat. Ota's moor or fen.

OVER NORTON (O) SP 315283 (145). N of Chipping Norton. Higher (up hillside) Norton.

OXFORD (O) SP 510070 (158). P 91–114 Power-house and treasure-house of Western civilization through eight centuries. Possibly rivalled by Prague as the finest example of a living medieval city in Europe. One of the greatest universities and homes of learning in the world. County town of Oxfordshire, natural capital of Upper Thames Region. Habitat late Lord Nuffield (William R. Morris) founding-father of British mass-production motor industry. From his works at Cowley (now part of British Leyland complex) Oxford has become a major manufacturing centre and added large-scale industry to learning. Two do not always mix happily and those who wish contemplative life inevitably regret roar of traffic and bustle of chain-stores. Yet none should regret vigorous life. Modern Oxford tingles with life and has pumped new economic fertility into wide area of region. Major shopping centre, bookshops particularly (new and secondhand) in and around Broad Street maintaining real distinction. Blackwell's shop deservedly world-famous still practises art of bookselling rare in twentieth century. Cowley Shopping Centre ingenious and largely successful attempt to come to terms with motor-car. Elsewhere car, source of Oxford's industrial wealth, is cause also of much discomfort and ugliness. Behind walls and under skin of traffic much medieval beauty remains. Tourists lose sadly from attempts to 'do' Oxford in one day: like attempt condense Shakespeare into single gramophone record, won't work. If only single day available select one special interest (cathedral, one particular museum, individual college, bookshops) and concentrate on that. COLLEGES and HALLS (with dates of foundation). University 1249 (but first statutes 1280). Balliol 1263. Merton 1264. (Univ. Balliol Merton all have claim to be considered oldest college in Oxford but which claim best justified is matter of interpretation or choice.) St Edmund Hall (about) 1270. Exeter 1314. Oriel 1326. Queen's 1341. New 1379. Lincoln 1427. All Souls 1438. Magdalen 1458. Christ Church (founded as Cardinal College by Wolsey 1525 refounded Henry VIII 1532). Brasenose 1509. Corpus Christi 1517. St John's 1555. Trinity 1555. Jesus 1571. Wadham 1610. Pembroke 1624. Worcester 1714. Keble 1868. Hertford 1874 (but as Hart Hall 1301). St Peter's 1928. Nuffield 1937. St Antony's 1948. Greyfriars (Franciscan hall) – Franciscans deeply involved Oxford from 13c but their institutions dissolved 1538. Order returned to Oxford 1910, present status as Hall 1957. Campion Hall (Society of Jesus) 1896 status as Hall 1918. St Benet's Hall (Benedictine) 1897 as Hall 1918. St Catherine's (as Society for Non-Collegiate Members of the University 1868, as college 1962). Linacre House 1962. Mansfield (Congregational) founded Birmingham 1838 moved Oxford 1886 became Hall 1957. Regent's Park (Baptist) founded London 1810 became Hall 1957. Manchester (Nonconformist, originally mainly Unitarian) founded Manchester 1786 moved Oxford 1888. Ruskin (founded to enable working men to study at Oxford) 1899. Wolfson College, established with grants for the Wolfson and Ford Foundations, 1966. WOMEN'S COLLEGES. Lady Margaret Hall 1878. Somerville 1879. St Hugh's 1886. St Hilda's 1893. St Anne's (as Women's Society of Oxford Home Students 1879) 1952. CATHEDRAL. A place of haunting beauty enriched by every century from 12 c onwards. Lovely Shrine of St Frideswide. Tombs and memorials reflect 800 years of history, moving reminders of past wars, of those who fell fighting for Charles I, of the Oxfordshire and Buckinghamshire Light Infantry in two world wars. Some 14 c glass, Jacobean pulpit. BODLEIAN LIBRARY, among world's greatest collection of books, treasures include first book printed in England by Caxton 1477, Shakespeare's first published work Venus and Adonis. ASHMOLEAN MUSEUM, magnificent collection paintings, silver, musical instruments, antiquities, oriental art. BOTANIC GARDEN, exquisite garden cultivated since 1621, originally as Physik Garden growing herbs for Faculty of Medicine. DIVINITY SCHOOL 15 c architecture of great beauty. CONVOCATION HOUSE 1634. PAINTED ROOM (3, Cornmarket) room in which Shakespeare probably slept on visits to Oxford. EXAMINATION SCHOOLS, Elizabethan in style but built 1882 to design by Sir Thomas Jackson. Note carvings over entrance showing candidates undergoing ordeal. UNIVERSITY MUSEUM (1855) primarily scientific collections PITT-RIVERS MUSEUM of ETHNOLOGY and PRE-HISTORY, unique collection of anthropological exhibits, including material brought back from the South Seas by Captain Cook. MARTYRS MEMORIAL, designed by Sir Gilbert Scott, commemorating English martyrs Latimer, Ridley and Cranmer burned to death by Mary Tudor for supporting the reformed Church of England. The memorial, erected 1841, is in St Giles, but the burnings took place in Broad Street. MODERN ARCHITECTURE. Plumbing has certainly improved since the 18 c but 19 c and 20 c building in general compares ill with the masterpieces of medieval masons and the stone harmonies of even the lesser disciples of Wren. Nevertheless there is some good, even exciting 20 c architecture in Oxford. St Catherine's College by Arne Jacobsen is an interesting example of entrusting one man of vision with the design of a complete college and everything in it including the cutlery. See also the Blue Boar Quad and Picture Gallery at Christ Church by Powell and Moya, and the same architects' ingenious work at Brasenose and Corpus Christi; the beehive-shaped building at St John's by Architects' Co-Partnership; the graduate block at Somerville in Little Clarendon Street by Philip Dowson of Ove Arup and Partners; the Manor Road building for the Law Library, Institute of Statistics and English Faculty Library by Sir Leslie Martin; the new HQ for the British Council in Beaumont Place by John Fryman of Architects' Design Partnership; and the residential blocks at St Anne's by Howell, Killick, Partridge and Amis. SEEING OXFORD. The special beauty of Oxford is the concentration within an area of less than one square mile of the (mostly) devoted building work of eight centuries, domes, pinnacles and spires combining to form a frieze upon the skyline unmatched anywhere in the world. Matthew Arnold's happy phrase about Oxford's 'dreaming spires' was precise. Alas, the water-meadows and line of silver river that were once the setting for this wonderful tracery of stone have been smothered by acres of railway lines and gasworks and an environment of brick suburbs. But the river is still kind to Oxford. Approach from Abingdon or Boar's Hill on a September morning when mist covers all the low-lying land and you will see Oxford's half-magical half-mystical skyline rising above the mist, as beautiful as it was when Arnold wrote about it. In the city itself it is worth getting up at first light on a June morning (preferably a Sunday) and walking through the medieval streets before the owners of motor-cars have stirred. The quality and subtle colouring of the stonework, becomes alive again. It is all there – only you must choose your time to see it. TOURIST NOTE. Most of the colleges and University institutions are open to the public at normal times, but in term-time some of the colleges may be open to visitors only in the afternoons. The inquiry office in Carfax is a friendly place, and it is worth planning a visit beforehand by asking there to make sure that what you want to see is open when you go to see it. OXFORD'S NAME. Attempts are made from time to time to find elaborate and recondite explanations for the name Oxford, but there is no reason to doubt its straightforward derivation from Oxenford, a cattle-crossing of the Thames (OE).

PADWORTH (B) SU 614663 (158). Beautiful small village in woods S of R. Kennet. C12 particularly fine example, wall paintings. Peada's enclosure (OE).

PANG, RIVER. Berkshire tributary of R. Thames, joining it at Pangbourne. River of Paega's tribe or folk (OE).

PANGBOURNE (B) SU 635766 (159). On one of most beautiful reaches of R. Thames. Settlement from antiquity, now considerable commuting town. C 18, replacing 12. Pangbourne College, formerly Nautical College. Kenneth Grahame (*Wind in the Willows*) lived at Church Cottage. From river Pang.

PEASEMORE (B) SU 458771 (158). Lovely remote downs. C 18–19. Pond by the peas.

POSTCOMBE (O) SU 709996 (159). Village in foothills of Chilterns on A40 S of Thame. Combe is valley, derivation post obscure. Possibly corruption OE word meaning wooden building, making it combe of the wooden hut.

POULTON (G) SP 100009 (157). Village N of R. Churn, in countryside of brooks feeding river. C modern, some stonework from old 14 c. church. Settlement by a pond or pool (OE).

PRESTON (G) SP 047008 (157). E of R churn near Cirencester. C 12 onwards. Priest's holding (OE).

PRESTON CROWMARSH, see Crowmarsh.

PURLEY (B) SU 658763 (159). Rather straggling, on reach of R. Thames below Pangbourne. C mostly 19 but parts old. Warren Hastings lived at Purley Hall for a time during his trial. Memorial Hall built by voluntary labour as memorial 1939–45 war interesting example co-operative effort, and of great value to community. Heron (or bittern) wood (OE).

PUSEY (B) SU 356967 (158). Legendary Canute country, White Horse Vale. Tiny village with C 18 and mansion 18 c. P 69. Island (in valley marshes) where peas were grown (OE).

PYRTON (O) Su 688960 (159). Pretty village below Icknield Way Oxfordshire Chilterns. C 12 onwards. John Hampden married to Elizabeth Symeon in C 1619.

QUENINGTON (G) SP 145044 (157). On R. Coln above Fairford. C 12–15, medieval carvings. OE settlement of women, perhaps some heiresses' land.

RACK END (O) SP 402032 (158). E end of Standlake village on Windrush. Interesting name meaning bed of river OE, and here one of diversions of Windrush rejoins main stream.

RADCOT BRIDGE (B) SU 285995 (158). Fine medieval bridge across R. Thames. P 84–6. Probably reed cottage (OE).

RADFORD (O) SP 409239 (145). Bridge 403236. Bridge over R. Glyme and hamlet reached by gated road from A34. Exquisite countryside. Appears to mean ford to be crossed on horseback (OE).

RADLEY (B) SU 525988 (158). On R. Thames above Abingdon. C 15–16. Radley College. Reed wood (OE).

RAMSDEN (O) SP 356152 (145). Wychwood settlement from pre-history. C 19. Valley of the ram, or perhaps wild garlic, two rather confusing OE words, either of which makes sense.

RAY, RIVER. Oxfordshire tributary of R. Cherwell. Rises Buckinghamshire Chilterns and flows sluggishly across Otmoor to join Cherwell at Islip. From OE word apparently meaning river.

RAY, RIVER. Wiltshire tributary of R. Thames, rising W of Swindon and joining Thames 1 m below Cricklade. As Oxfordshire river.

READING (B). County town of Berkshire, University, manufacturing centre. S limit Upper Thames Region, not covered here. Name means place of tribe called, Readda's folk (OE).

RENDCOMBE (G) SP 020098 (157). Ancient settlement on wonderful hill site upper Churn valley. C 16. Valley of the rapids (OE).

RIDGEWAY, THE. Prehistoric trackway running over the high chalk downs to cross R. Thames at Streatley (Goring Gap). With linked trackways provided routes from English and Bristol Channels to the Wash. Track still clearly defined on Downs and offers magnificent walking.

RISSINGTON, Great (G) SP 198173 (144) LITTLE 192198. WICK 190215. Cluster of Cotswold villages overlooking Rivers Dikler and Windrush. Great C 15, Little C 13–15, Wick C 12–13. Remarkable maze in rectory garden at Wick R, constructed by rector in 1950 after vivid dream, to illustrate life's pilgrimage. Brushwood hill (OE). Wick, see Fyfield Wick.

ROLLRIGHT, GREAT (O) SP 323313 (145) LITTLE 295300 STONES 296308. Villages and Great Stone circle standing stones high Oxfordshire Cotswolds. Great C 12 onwards Little C 15 Rollright Stones remarkable prehistoric monument or place of worship. Name obscure, possibly OE Rolla's land, perhaps much more ancient name from prehistoric tongue.

ROUSHAM (O) SP 476242 (145). Village on R. Cherwell. C 12 onwards. Grounds of

Rousham House nice example work of William Kent 18 c landscape gardener. Rowulf's settlement (OE).

RYCOTE (O) SP 667047 (159). Hamlet S of R. Thame. Rye cottage (OE).

SALFORD (O) SP 288280 (145). Village NW Chipping Norton. C 13, 14, perhaps older foundations. Ford (across brook, tributary of R. Evenlode) where salt traders passed (OE).

SALPERTON (G) SP 078204 (144). High Cotswold hamlet near headwaters of stream feeding R. Windrush. C (in Salperton Park) 12–15, wall paintings. Brook by the willow trees (OE).

SANDFORD-ON-THAMES (O) SP 535018 (158). Riverside village, lock, S outskirts Oxford. C 12, restored 17. Sandy ford (OE).

SANDFORD ST MARTIN (O) SP 420266 (145). On headwaters R. Dorn. C 12 onwards. Sandy ford (across R. Dorn.)

SANDLEIGH (B) SP 476010 (158). Hamlet S Cumnor. Sandy wood (OE).

SARS BROOK Oxfordshire tributary of R. Evenlode, which it joins near Lyneham. Name obscure, perhaps prehistoric language.

SARSDEN (O) SP 288230 (145). Charming hamlet on Sars Brook. Something valley, but what is obscure.

SEACOURT STREAM One of network of rivulets joining R. Thames near Osney. Seofeca's stream (OE).

SEGSBURY CAMP or CASTLE (B) SU 385845 (158). Impressive hill fort enclosing some 26 acres. Magnificent view over Downs. Name obscure, perhaps from prehistoric language plus burg OE fort.

SEVEN SPRINGS (G) SO 969171 (144). Source of R. Churn and disputed source of R. Thames.

SEVENHAMPTON (G) SU 206904 (157). Gloucestershire edge of R. Cole country. C 13. OE word for seven, but seven of what is unclear.

SHABBINGTON (Bu) SP 667070 (159). Small village on R. Thame W of Thame. C 12 onwards. Place of Sceobba's folk (OE).

SHARE DITCH. Wiltshire tributary of R. Thames joining it 1 m E of Castle Eaton. Name obscure.

SHARNEY BROOK Oxfordshire tributary of R. Thames SW Bampton. Perhaps muddy brook (OE).

SHEFFORD, EAST (B) SU 389746 (158) GREAT 384753. Ancient settlements both banks of R. Lambourn. East C 15–16, bits earlier Great C 12–13. East S. was early home of Fettiplace family. Sheep ford (over Lambourn) (OE).

SHELLINGFORD (B) SU 320935 (158). White Horse vale, on Holywell Brook tributary R. Ock. C 12 spire 17. Ford held by Saxon tribe Scoringes.

SHERBORNE BROOK. Gloucestershire tributary to R. Windrush, joining it just above Windrush village. Pure stream (OE).

SHERBORNE (G) SP 177146 (144). Attractive village on Sherborne Brook. C rebuilt 19. From brook.

SHIFFORD (O) SP 374020 (158). Hamlet on Oxfordshire bank of R. Thames across river from Duxford. Sheep ford (OE).

SHILL BROOK Small tributary of R. Thames on Oxfordshire–Gloucestershire border. Dubious, possibly noisy (shrill) brook.

SHILLINGFORD (O) SU 598927 (158). Ancient crossing of R. Thames above Wallingford. One of earliest wooden bridges on Thames, present bridge 19 c. Perhaps ford held by Saxon tribe of Scillingas (OE).

SHILTON (O) SP 266085 (157). Village on Shil Brook tributary of R. Thames. C 12 onwards. Name from brook.

SHIPTON OLIFFE (G). SP 036185 (144) Solers SP 033185. Enchanting villages headwaters of R. Coln. O. C 12–13, S. C 13. Sheep farm OE. Held by Olyve and de Solers families 14 c.

SHIPPON (B) SU 479982 (158). Hamlet 1 m. NW Abingdon, now almost part of Abingdon. C 19. Cow-byre (OE).

SHIPTON-ON-CHERWELL (O) SP 480168 (145). C rebuilt 19 on Norman remains. Sheep farm on C. (OE).

SHIPTON-UNDER-WYCHWOOD (O) SP 278177 (144). Nice Wychwood village. C 13, 15. Sheepfarm in Wychwood (OE).

SHIRBURN (O) SU 698960 (159). Small village on brook at foot of Oxfordshire Chilterns. Pure stream (OE).

SHORTHAMPTON (O) SP 328201 (145). Remote Evenlode Hamlet, lovely country. C 12–15, wall paintings. Short steading or farm enclosure (OE).

SHOTOVER HILL (O) SP 565062 (158). E outskirts Oxford. Steep hill (OE).

SHRIVENHAM (B) SU 235890 (157). NW end Vale of White Horse. C early 15 enlarged 17. Royal Military College of Science. Name puzzling, appears to relate to receiving absolution after confession (shrive), perhaps place where some penance was performed.

SIDDINGTON (G) SU 035998 (157). Ancient settlement on R. Churn S Cirencester. Roman tombstone. C 12, 13, 14, fine carvings, tower modern. Southern settlement (OE) (presumably S from Cirencester).

SLAUGHTER, Upper (G) SP 155233 Lower 165226. On brook tributary to R. Dikler. Upper C 12, 15 Lower C 12 rebuilt 19. Lower S often called 'most beautiful village in England', and has some claim to title. Name has in fact nothing to do with slaughter, but from (OE) word meaning morass or mud, no doubt from brook in early times.

SOMERTON (O) SP 498286 (145). On R. Cherwell–Oxford Canal, near Northampton border, once border Wessex-Mercia. C 12, 14. Summer settlement, probably summer grazing ground for cattle (OE).

SONNING COMMON (O) SU 705805 (159). Pleasantly wooded area Oxfordshire bank of Thames N of Caversham (Reading). Now considerably built up. Some 5 m. from Sonning (B) on R. Thames below Reading. Place of Sunna's folk (O E).

SOR BROOK. Oxfordshire tributary of R. Cherwell S of Banbury. Perhaps narrow brook (O E).

SOTWELL (B) SU 589909 (158). Small village NW Wallingford. C 19 replacing Norman. Name obscure, possibly corruption of South Stream or brook (O E) (south from Thames).

SOULDERN (O) SP 524315 (145). E of R. Cherwell, near Northamptonshire border. Pleasant village, C 12 onwards. 'Dern' corruption OE word for thorn, so thorn-thicket in valley.

SOUTH LEIGH (O) SP 392087 (158). In Windrush water meadows SE Witney. C 13–14, wall paintings. South wood (O E).

SOUTH MARSTON (W) SU 193880 (157). On brook tributary of R. Cole. Marsh settlement (O E).

SOUTH NEWINGTON (O) SP 407332 (145). Nice village on R. Swere. C 12–14, wall paintings. Southern new settlement (new about 1,200 years ago – S of river.)

SOUTH WESTON (O) SU 702982 (159). Hamlet by Icknield Way foot of Oxfordshire Chilterns. Western settlement (O E) (W perhaps from Beacon Hill) and S of somewhere (perhaps Postcombe).

SOUTHMOOR (B) SU 395980 (158). Hamlet now much new housing Kingston Bagpuize-Faringdon road A420. South marsh, S from R. Thames (O E).

SOUTHROP (G) SU 200035 (157). On R. Leach. C part 11. John Keble was vicar. Southern farm OE (S perhaps from Eastleach settlements just to N).

SPARSHOLT (B) SU 347876 (158). Village just below Ridgeway on beautiful high Downs. C 12–13, stone with markings for medieval game Nine Men's Morris. Spear wood (perhaps where men got spear shafts) (O E).

SPEEN (B) SU 463682 (158). Very old settlement NE Newbury, now part of Newbury. C 19. Fine old houses. Romans knew the place as Spinae (thorn bushes) and modern name derives from latin.

SPELSBURY (O) SP 350216 (145). Nice old cottages Evenlode valley. C 19 but Norman origins. Ditchley Park, mansion and Roman villa 2 m. E. Appears to mean look-out hill or something of the sort (O E).

STADHAMPTON (O) SU 602985 (158). On R. Thame, NE Dorchester. C 15. Horse meadow (O E).

STANDLAKE (O) SP 398032 (158). Pleasant Windrush village near junction with R. Thames. C 12–14. River with stones (O E).

STANFORD DINGLEY (B) SU 575715 (158). Charming village middle Pang valley. C 12–13 and later work. Strong ford (over Pang) (O E). Held by Dyngley or Dyneley family 15 c.

STANFORD-IN-THE-VALE (B) SU 343935 (158). Biggish straggling village, metropolis of Upper Ock valley. Otherwise remote. Interesting village long held by small freeholders, no dominant landlord. C 12–13–14. Stony ford (across Ock) (OE).

STANTON FITZWARREN (W) SU 178903 (157). Nice village on Bydemill Brook, little Wiltshire tributary of R. Thames. Roman settlement, stones of which probably give village its (OE) name. Fitzwarren, son of one Warinus, who held land 12 c.

STANTON HARCOURT (O) SP 415057 (158). Settlement from prehistory. Village about 1½ miles W from R. Thames at Bablockhythe, same distance E from Windrush, in network backwaters and ponds. C 13. Manor still in possession Harcourts from 12 c. Pope's Tower of Harcourt mansion where Alexander Pope translated Iliad. Name from standing stones plus Harcourt.

STANTON ST JOHN (O) SP 577094 (158). Nice village off main road W outskirts Oxford. C 12 onwards. Oxford Crematorium, set in flowers and trees on beautiful open hillside is near by. Stony settlement (OE).

STERT, RIVER. Berkshire tributary of R. Thames, rising near Boar's Hill and joining Thames at Abingdon. Now culverted under Stert Street, Abingdon. Stream from the spur of a hill (OE).

STEVENTON (B) SU 472920 (158). Exceptionally fine village green, now bisected A34. C 14. Settlement of Stif's folk (OE).

STOKE ROW (O) SU 685840 (159). Village in woods, one row of cottages, S of Oxford–Henley road. C 19. Maharajah's Well ½m. W well and well-house given to village by Maharajah of Benares 19 c. in recognition kindness of Englishman whose home was here. British have given many irrigation schemes to India: this is perhaps only well given by India to England. Stoke implies hermit's cell, or holy place.

STOKE, SOUTH (O) SU 600835 (158) NORTH 610862. Pleasant Thames-side villages Oxfordshire bank S Wallingford. S. C 13 tower, 15, N. C 14 wall paintings. N. and S. hermit's cells or holy places (OE).

STOKE TALMAGE (O) SU 678993 (159). Hamlet S of Haseley Brook. C 19 but some much older work. Hermit's cell or holy place (OE), land held by Talmache family 13 c.

STONESFIELD (O) SP 395175 (145). Village near R. Evenlode, remarkable quarries for building stone, particularly stone slates, worked from Roman times. C 13. From quarries.

STOW-ON-THE-WOLD (G) SP 193256 (144). Small town high Cotswolds where springs feed R. Thames tributaries. Great prosperity medieval wool trade. C 12–13 onwards, 17 c. picture of Crucifixion by Craeyer of Antwerp. Holy place on Wold (OE).

STOWELL (G) SP 090130 (144). Small village by Fosse Way (A429) near R. Coln. C 12 onwards, wall paintings. Stony spring (OE).

STREATLEY (B) SU 592807 (158). Berkshire bank of R. Thames where it cuts through chalk ridge at Goring Gap. Settlement from antiquity. C 19 tower 15–16. Wood on the road (ancient track from Downs to Goring Gap) (OE).

STUDLEY (O) SP 596124 (145). Eastern edge of Otmoor. Studley Priory bought at dissolution by John Croke of Chilton 1539 for £1,187 7s. 11d., bought from elder branch of Croke family in 1621 by Judge Sir George Croke for £1,800, plus some other land. Home of Crokes for next two centuries. Horse wood, or maybe grazing land in wood (OE).

STUTFIELD BROOK. Tributary of R. Ock above Charney Bassett. Possibly gnat-ridden brook (OE).

SULHAM (B) SU 645742 (158). In beautiful woods S Pangbourne. C 19. Meadow or homestead in valley (OE).

SULHAMSTEAD (B) Su 632688 (158) ABBOTS 648678. Villages S bank of Kennet near Reading. S. C 20 (1914), Abbots c 12. Has nice 16 c. brass warning visitors to shun the damnable wiles of women. Meadowland in valley.

SUNNINGWELL (B) SP 496005 (158). Village N Abingdon, pleasantly off Abingdon–Oxford roads. C 15–16, earlier bits. Spring of the Saxon Sunninga tribe (OE).

SUTTON COURTENAY (B) SU 502939 (158). Settlement from antiquity. Charming village with green on exquisite backwater R. Thames, once main stream now by-passed by Culham lock cut. C 13–14. Home of 1st Lord Oxford and Asquith, who buried in churchyard (d. 1928). South settlement, S from Abingdon OE. Held by Courtenays 12 c.

SUTTON GREEN (O) SP 416066 (158). Hamlet in lanes N of Stanton Harcourt. South settlement, presumably S from ancient settlement at Eynsham.

SWELL, UPPER (G) SP 178268 (144) Lower 176256. Settlements from antiquity on R. Dikler. Prehistoric barrows $\frac{1}{2}$ m W of villages, Roman settlement. Upper C 12–15, Lower C 12–15 on site Roman burial place. Fold in the hills (OE).

SWERE, RIVER. Tributary R. Cherwell, rising Oxfordshire Cotswolds near Chipping Norton, joining Cherwell on W bank SE of Adderbury. From OE word meaning neck, perhaps narrow river.

SWERFORD (O) SP 372311 (145). On headwaters R. Swere. C 13 onwards. Ford (across Swere).

SWILL BROOK. Wiltshire tributary of R. Thames, joining it near Ashton Keynes. Floodwater (OE).

SWINBROOK (O) SP 281122 (145). Oxfordshire home of Fettiplaces, later acquired by Redesdales, on Windrush. C from 11 onwards, restored 1864. Bunks of stone Fetti-places from 1613. Pulpit hanging made from dress of Anne Pytts (née Fettiplace) d 1716. Swine brook (OE).

TACKLEY (O) SP 476205 (145). On W bank R. Cherwell (Oxford Canal). C 12–15. Sheep pasture (OE).

TADPOLE BRIDGE (O–B) SP 334004 (158). Pleasantly in the middle of nowhere, bridge across R. Thames (once important for coal traffic) between Bampton (O) and Buckland (B). 2 m. away from both. Bridge late 18 c., to serve coal wharf. Presumably tadpoles once numerous here.

TAYNTON (O) SP 234136 (144). By Windrush 1$\frac{1}{2}$ m. NW Burford. C 13–15. Taynton quarries are the source of stone for many noble buildings, including St Paul's Cathedral. Brook in village now called Hazelford Brook was once called the Tegn, from Celtic word meaning stream. Taynton gets its name from this.

TETSWORTH (O) SP 687017 (159). On main road A40 N of Haseley Brook. Taetel's enclosure (OE).

TEW, GREAT (O) SP 397293 (145), LITTLE 385285, DUNS TEW 457283. Three charming villages Oxfordshire Cotswolds SW of Banbury. Great C 12 onwards, grave of Lucius Cary, 2nd Viscount Falkland, killed at Battle of Newbury 1643. P 167. Whole village park-like, landscaped by early 19 c. landscape gardener John Loudon. Wonderful thatch. Duns Tew C 13 onwards. Name obscure. Ekwall suggests may be related to (OE) word meaning 'long', applied to long ridge on which the Tews stand. But why not ancient pagan cult of worship of God Tue? Dun from family called Dunn who held land.

THAME (O) SP 705060 (159). On R. Thame, splendid old market town, with magnificently wide main street. P 158–60. C 13 onwards, considerable grandeur. From river.

THAME, RIVER. Tributary of R. Thames, rising in Buckinghamshire and joining Thames at Dorchester. Waters fertile valley of its own. Ancient river name, perhaps from Celtic, but more likely prehistoric.

THAMES, RIVER. Rises in Gloucestershire, waters Wiltshire, Oxfordshire, Berkshire, Buckinghamshire, London, Essex and Kent on way to the North Sea. Once tributary of R. Rhine. The 'h' in spelling of Thames is an intrusive pedantry of no merit and would be better omitted. Romans found it called *Tems*, which they latinized to Tamesis. Much speculation on origin of name, even to Sanskrit root *Tamasa*, meaning *dark*. No one knows, and name undoubtedly derives from prehistoric tongue (which might well embody Sanskrit root).

THATCHAM (B) SU 520674 (158). On R. Kennet, $2\frac{1}{2}$ m. E of Newbury. Mesolithic settlement of great interest. C 19, older bits. Thatched house.

THEALE (B) SU 643713 (158). Settlement from antiquity on R. Kennet. C 19. From OE word for plank, implying wooden bridge (across Kennet).

THRUPP (O) SP 480158 (145). Nice little village, on R. Cherwell–Oxford Canal. Farm (OE).

TIDDINGTON (O) SP 650047 (159). Small village S of R. Thame, just off Oxford-Thame road. Tytta's hill (OE).

TIDMARSH (B) SU 635748 (158). In woods on R. Pang above Pangbourne. C 12 onwards. Tydda's marsh (OE).

TILEHURST (B) SU 675735 (158). Suburb of Reading, C 12 onwards. Place where tiles were made.

TOKER'S GREEN (O) SU 700775 (159). In wooded country N of Caversham (Reading). Obscure. Perhaps from OE personal name Tocga.

TREWSBURY MEAD (G) SO 983995 (157). Source of R. Thames, near Cirencester. P 80–82. Name probably means strong place or fort by trees.

TUBNEY (B) SU 436987 (158). Matthew Arnold's Fyfield Elm is actually at Tubney. C 19. Tubba's island (in Ock marshes) (OE).

TURKDEAN (G) 108175 (144). Nice Cotswold village W of Fosse Way (A429) near headwaters of brooks feeding R. Windrush. C 11–12 onwards. Valley of the boar (Celtic, not OE, word for boar.)

TYLE MILL LOCK (B) SU 637693 (158). On R. Kennet. Limit of practical navigation of Kennet from Reading.

UFFINGTON (B) SU 305894 (158). Delightful village under White Horse Hill. C 13, 18 additions. Uffington Castle, Iron Age hill fort, marvellous views. Dragon Hill, on which traditionally St George killed his dragon. Settlement of Uffa's folk OE).

UFTON NERVET (B) SU 635675 (158). Village S of R. Kennet. C 19, with some old monuments. Settlement of Uffa's folk (OE). Nervet from Neyrnut family who held land 13 c.

UPTON (O) SP 243124 (144). On Windrush ½ m. W Burford. Quarries for Cotswold building stone. Home of Christopher Kempster (d. 1714) Wren's master mason for St Paul's. Home of C. E. Montague (author of *Disenchantment, Fiery Particles*). Upper settlement (OE) (above Burford).

UPTON (B) SU 513867 (158). Downland village under Ridgeway as track makes for the Thames at Streatley (Goring Gap). Very old settlement. C 12, probably Saxon foundations. Upper settlement (above the Hagbournes).

WALLINGFORD (B) SU 605895 (158). P 134–8. Very ancient settlement at crossing of R. Thames, fortified by Saxons, Norman castle played important part wars Stephen and Matilda, Civil War. Nice old town, good port for river cruisers. C (St Leonard) 12 rebuilt 19 (St Peter) 18, attractive 'wedding cake' spire (St Mary) 19 older tower. Meeting House Society of Friends 18 c. Ford held by Saxon tribe called Walingas or Wealh's folk (OE).

WANTAGE (B) SU 400800 (158). P 172–7. Settlement from antiquity, birthplace of King Alfred. Market town for S parts of White Horse Vale. C 13 restored 19. Home of Anglican Order of Wantage Sisters, whose boarding-school for girls, St Mary's, Wantage, is well known. Perhaps from river name meaning stream of 'waning' water (i.e. sometimes dry) OE, perhaps from much older tongue.

WARBOROUGH (O) SU 599936 (158). Picturesque village E Dorchester. C 13 onwards. Watch hill OE (lookout covering approaches to Dorchester from N and E).

WATCHFIELD (B) SU 255905 (157). Vale of White Horse, near Shrivenham. C 19, but some old bits. Wacca's field (OE).

WATER EATON (O) SP 515120 (145) WOOD EATON 535120. Old settlements each bank of R. Cherwell NE Oxford. Water C 15–16, Wood C 13, wall paintings. Roman settlement and temple. Island settlements OE (in Cherwell and backwaters).

WATERHAY BRIDGE (G) SU 060934 (157). Bridge across infant Thames near Ashton

Keynes. Though it seems improbable now, barges used to get up to Waterhay, which served as coal wharf for surrounding villages. Not a very old bridge, (built for 18 c. coal trade, later rebuilt) but there was probably a ford where hay carts could cross the river, and name from that.

WATERPERRY (O) SP 628065 (158). Old settlement on R. Thame. Pleasant village. C 13 on Saxon foundation. Pear tree by the river (OE).

WATERSTOCK (O) SP 638058 (158). Just below and across R. Thame from Waterperry. C 15 onwards. Place (perhaps holy place) by the river (OE).

WATLINGTON (O) SU 685945 (159). Big village or small town under Watlington Hill, Oxfordshire Chilterns. Ancient settlement on Icknield Way. C 12–15, rebuilt 19. Settlement of Waccol's folk (OE).

WAYLAND'S SMITHY (B) Su 283856 (158). Just N of Ridgeway 1¼ m. SW of White Horse Hill. Chambered long barrow built over earlier barrow tomb. About 2,800 B.C. P. 46.

WEALD (O) SP 308022 (158). Hamlet on outskirts of Bampton. Wooded area (OE).

WENDLEBURY (O) SP 569197 (145). Just off Oxford–Bicester road, near site of Roman town of Alchester. C 18, medieval bits. Wendel's strong place (OE).

WESTCOT (B) SU 340874 (158). Tiny Downland village below Ridgeway 2½ m. NE of White Horse Hill.

WESTCOTE BROOK. Tributary of R. Evenlode, fed by many little streams from Cotswold escarpment between Icomb Hill and Westcote Hill. Joins Evenlode near Bledington. Name from settlement.

WESTCOTE (G) SP 220206 (144), NETHER WESTCOTE 226203. Villages on upper reaches of Westcote Brook. Cottage in the west (OE).

WESTON-ON-THE-GREEN (O) SP 534187 (145). On Oxford–Northampton road. Pleasant green C 18 (rebuilt after fire), Norman tower. West settlement OE (perhaps W from Wendelbury or Alchester).

WESTWELL (O) SP 226099 (157). N of Akeman Street 3 m NE R. Leach. C 12–14. Western spring OE (W of Holwell q v).

WHEATFIELD (O) SU 690992 (159). Tiny village near headwaters of Haseley Brook, tributary of R. Thame. C 15. Name explains itself.

WHEATLEY (O) SP 596047 (158). Large village now almost suburb Oxford on W bank R. Thame where river turns S on meeting high ground E of Oxford. Ford across R. Thame now bridge carrying A40. C 19. Woodland wheatfield (OE).

WHITCHURCH (O) SU 636775 (159). Oxfordshire bank of R. Thames opposite Pangbourne. Birthplace of architect Sir John Soane, founder of Soane Museum in London. C 14 onwards, much older foundation. White church (OE). Ekwall suggests white church means stone church, distinction from wooden churches which were much more common Saxon times, and this certainly seems probable.

WHITE HORSE HILL (B) SU 302866 (158). Magnificent white horse 360 ft long by 130 ft high cut in chalk below Uffington Castle hill fort. Commonly assigned 1c.

because horse used on coins that period but evidence thin and figure may be much older. Gives name to Vale of the White Horse. Now in care Ministry of Public Building and Works.

WHITTANDITCH (B) SU 290723 (158). Small village on brook flowing into R. Kennet, 3 m. NW Hungerford. Perhaps white ditch, perhaps Witta's ditch (OE).

WICKHAM (B) SU 395717 (158). Very old settlement on Roman road (to Cirencester) NW Newbury. C Saxon, restored 19. Dairy farm (OE).

WIDFORD (O) SP 271120 (144). Tiny hamlet on R. Windrush near Burford. Settlement in continuous occupation certainly from Roman times, probably earlier. Remarkable C with remains floor of Roman villa in chancel. Norman building on Roman foundations, probably with Saxon intervening. Exceptionally lovely site. Ford by the willow trees (OE) – the name might be given to it today.

WIGGINTON (O) SP 388334 (145). Village headwaters R. Swere. Roman settlement ½ m E. C 13–15. Wicga's settlement (OE).

WILCOTE (O) SP 374155 (145). Wychwood hamlet lovely setting on bank R. Evenlode. C 14 restored. Wifel's cottage.

WINDRUSH, RIVER. Tributary of R. Thames, rising in Gloucestershire Cotswolds, joining Thames at Newbridge, 6 m. SSE Witney (O). Beautiful name might well stand for itself, but philologists say ancient Celtic river name meaning something like white marsh.

WINDRUSH (G) SP 193132 (144). Delightful village on R. Windrush. C 12 onwards. From river.

WINSON (G) SP 091087 (157). Village on R. Coln. C 12 onwards. Wine's settlement (man's, or perhaps woman's name, not drink) (OE).

WINTERBOURNE (B) SU 455723 (158). Village lovely country above R. Lambourn. Roman settlement 1 m. W.C 18 restored 19. Brook flowing in winter (OE).

WITHINGTON (G) SP 032155 (144). Ancient settlement on upper reaches of R. Coln, S Andoversford. Roman settlement, site of Saxon monastery. C 12 onwards. Hill of legendary Saxon hero Widsith (OE).

WITNEY (O) SP 359103 (157). Centre of blanket weaving, market town lower Windrush valley. C 12–15. P. 149–51. Witta's island (OE) (in what were Windrush marshes).

WITTENHAM, LITTLE (B) SU 564932 (158), LONG 545936. Villages on R. Thames under Wittenham Clumps, across river from Dorchester. Settlements from antiquity P. 56, 134, 236. Long, the bigger of the two, is now on quiet backwater since, navigable channel goes by cut to Clifton (Hampden) Lock. Pendon Museum, exquisite scale models of countryside, thatch reproduced from human hair, also museum of railway history. C 12 onwards. Little C 19, but old bits and some old monuments. War (1914–18) memorial on small enclosed green commemorating one man, perhaps Little Wittenham's total manpower of military age. Witta's meadows or settlement (OE).

WOLVERCOTE (O) SP 490097 (158). On R. Thames N Oxford. University's paper mill. C ancient foundation, rebuilt. Wulfgar's cottage (OE).

WOODCOTE (O) SU 645820 (158). Village in woods above Goring. Cottage in woods.

WOODHILL BROOK. Downland stream feeding Childrey Brook NW Wantage.

WOODSTOCK (O) SP 452168 (145). Beautiful stone town, very old. Hunting lodge of Norman kings, birthplace of Black Prince. C 12 onwards, tower 18. Blenheim palace. Splendidly run Oxfordshire museum P. 155–6. Place (possibly hermit's cell or holy place) in woods (Wychwood).

WOOLHAMPTON (B) SU 572668 (158). Village on R. Kennet in beautiful woodlands. C 19. Douai Abbey and School (partly in parish of Beenham, q.v.). Settlement of Wulflaf's folk (OE).

WOOLSTONE (B) SU 294878 (158). Fairy story village hidden in fold of Downs below White Horse Hill. Thomas Hughes (*Tom Brown's Schooldays*) country. C 13–14. Wulfric's settlement (OE).

WOOTON (O) SP 438198 (145). On R. Glyme, near junction with R. Dorn. C 13–15. Settlement in a wood (OE).

WOOTTON (B) SP 478018 (158). Village NNW Abingdon on S side of Boar's Hill, now extension of Boar's Hill suburb of Oxford. Settlement in woods (OE).

WORLD'S END (B) SU 488766 (158). Hamlet on Downs S of East Ilsley. Now on busy main road A34. Once what its name implies.

WORMINGHALL (Bu) SP 644083 (159). Village N of R. Thame. C 12–15. Meadow where snakes were likely to be found (OE).

WORTON, NETHER (O) SP 426302 (145), OVER 432292. Little villages in lovely Oxfordshire Cotswolds S. Banbury. Nether C 13, tower 17. Hillside settlement, lower and upper (OE).

WORTON (O) SP 462114 (145). Hamlet near Cassington. This Worton is from a different OE root and perhaps means settlement in a garden.

WYTHAM (B) SP 476089 (158). At the N tip of the great bend made by the Thames above Oxford. Beautiful woods. C early 19, incorporating much older bits. Curving meadow (from bend in the river) (OE).

YANWORTH (G) SP 079139 (144). In woods, upper reaches of R. Coln. Roman settlement across river. C 12. Geana's enclosure (OE).

YARNTON (O) SP 476120 (145). Just off Oxford-Woodstock road A34. NW Oxford. Pleasant old village C 12 onwards. Settlement of Earda's folk (OE).

YATTENDON (B) SU 554745 (158). In wooded hills overlooking upper reaches of R. Pang. C 15 rebuilt 19. Grave of Robert Bridges, poet laureate (d. 1930). Gave name to Yattendon Hymnal compiled Robert Bridges and H. E. Wooldridge. Valley of the Geatingas or Geat's folk (OE).

Bibliographical notes

Regional history tends to be either a part of national history, or intensely detailed study of a very small area, perhaps a single house. It is difficult to compile a reading list which is neither too general, nor too detailed. I list here those works which I have found particularly helpful in my own study.

The Oxford Region, being papers prepared for the meeting of the British Association at Oxford in 1954, edited by A. F. Martin and R. W. Steel (Oxford, 1954). These papers are:

Geology and physiography – J. M. Edmonds.
River development – K. S. Sandford.
Geomorphology – R. P. Beckinsale.
Climate – C. G. Smith.
Soils – G. R. Clarke.
Vegetation and flora – E. F. Warburg.
Forestry – E. W. Jones.
Fauna – B. M. Hornby, H. N. Southern, M. H. Williamson.
The Prehistoric period – H. J. Case.
The Roman period – M. V. Taylor.
The Anglo-Saxon period – J. N. L. Myres.
The Medieval period – W. G. Hoskins and E. M. Jope.
The seventeenth, eighteenth and nineteenth centuries – J. N. L. Baker and Audrey M. Lambert.
Agriculture – Sir E. John Russell.
Industries – J. M. Houston.
Communications – C. F. W. R. Gullick.
Population and settlements – R. W. Steel and E. Paget.
The Growth of the City of Oxford – E. W. Gilbert.

т

The Growth of the University of Oxford – I. G. Philip.
The University today (1954) – Sir Douglas Veale.
Museums – D. B. Harden.
Libraries – J. N. L. Myres.
The University Science Area – S. G. P. Plant.

Geological structure and pre-history

STAMP DUDLEY L., *Britain's Structure and Scenery* (Collins, 1966).

MANLEY GORDON, *Climate and the British Scene* (Collins, 1955).

HAWKES JACQUETTA, *A Land* (Pelican 1959).

COON CARLETON S., *The History of Man* (Pelican, 1967), *The Origin of Races* (Cape, 1963).

HOWELLS WILLIAM, *Mankind in the Making* (Pelican, 1967).

FOWLER PETER, *The Archaeology of Wessex* (Heinemann, 1967).

WINBOLT S. E., *Britain B.C.* (Pelican 1943). This is a useful little book, but since the eclipse of Piltdown Man some of it is out of date.

Romans, Saxons and Normans

RICHMOND I. A., *Roman Britain* (Cape, 1963).

WINBOLT S. E., *Britain Under The Romans* (Pelican, 1945).

BLAIR PETER HUNTER, *An Introduction to Anglo-Saxon England* (Cambridge, 1966).

WHITELOCK DOROTHY, *The Beginnings of English Society* (Pelican History of England, 1966).

STENTON DORIS MARY, *English Society in the Early Middle Ages* (Pelican History of England, 1965).

BRØNSTED JOHANNES, *The Vikings* (Pelican, 1965).

The River Thames

THACKER F. S., *The Thames Highway*, Vol I *General History* 1914, Vol II *Locks and Weirs* 1920. (Published privately. Republished David and Charles, 1968).

HADFIELD CHARLES, *The Canals of Southern England* (Phoenix, 1955).

WATERS BRIAN, *Thirteen Rivers to the Thames* (Dent, 1964).

HALL MR and MRS S. C., *(sic) The Book of the Thames* (c 1890, J. S. Virtue, Paternoster Row).

PILKINGTON ROGER, *Small Boat on the Thames* (Macmillan, 1966).

Stanford's Chart of the River Thames (Edward Stanford).

The Region Generally

WOOLLEY A. R., *The Clarendon Guide to Oxford* (Oxford, 1963).

CANNAN JOANNA, *Oxfordshire* (Robert Hale).

BRILL EDITH, *Old Cotswold* (David and Charles, 1968).

RYDER T. A., *Portrait of Gloucestershire* (Robert Hale, 1966).

PEVSNER NIKOLAUS, *The Buildings of Britain* (Penguin).

BETJEMAN JOHN and PIPER JOHN, *Architectural Guide to Berkshire* (Murray, 1949).

BRABANT F. G., revised PIEHLER H. A., *Berkshire* (Methuen original edition 1911, revised 1934).

VINCENT J. E., *Highways and Byways in Berkshire* (Macmillan, 1906).

MEE ARTHUR, *The King's England,* volumes on *Oxfordshire, Berkshire, Gloucestershire, Wiltshire, Buckinghamshire* (Hodder and Stoughton).

CROKE SIR ALEXANDER, *The Genealogical History of the Croke Family, originally named Le Blount.* 2 vols, (John Murray, 1823).

MYATT FREDERICK, *The Royal Berkshire Regiment* (Hamish Hamilton, 1968).

BOWEN H. J. M., *The Flora of Berkshire* (Holywell Press, Oxford, 1968).

PHILIP KATHLEEN, *Victorian Wantage* (Published by the Author, 1968).

HAMMOND NIGEL, *Golden Berkshire* (Abbey Press Abingdon, 1967).

PLAISTED ARTHUR H., *The Romance of a Chiltern Village* (The Village Bookshop, Medmenham, 1958).

PLUMMER ALFRED, *The Witney Blanket Industry* (Routledge 1934).

BAKER AGNES C., *Historic Abingdon* (Privately printed, 1955), *Historic Streets of Abingdon* (Abbey Press, 1957).

NICHOLSON ERNEST, and BAKER AGNES, *Guide to Abingdon* (Abingdon Corporation)

GILES THE REV. J. A., *History of the Parish and Town of Bampton* (Printed at the Author's Private Press, 1848).

GROVES MURIEL (ed). The History of Shipton-under-Wychwood (Federation of Women's Institutes, 1935).

COURSE CAPTAIN A. G., *Painted Ports* (Hollis and Carter, 1961). For history of the Nautical College, Pangbourne.

JENNINGS PAUL *The Living Village* (Hodder and Stoughton, 1968).

HAYDEN ELEANOR G., *Islands of The Vale* (Smith, Elder, 1908).

BELSTEN KINGSLEY, and COMPTON H., articles in the *Oxford Times* 26.4.63, 3.5.63, 26.3.64, 22.5.64, 29.5.64.

BUTLER C. A., *The Bloxham Feoffees,* address to Banbury Historical Society, 1961.

NAYLOR L. G. R., *The Malthouse of Joseph Tomkins,* 58–60 East Saint Helen Street, Abingdon (Published privately).

CHAPMAN D. EMERSON, *Is this your first visit to Avebury?* (H M Stationery Office, 1947).

ATKINSON R. J. C., *Stonehenge and Avebury* (H M Stationery Office, 1959).

TAYLOR A. J., *Minster Lovell Hall* (H M Stationery Office, 1958).

GODDARD-FENWICK T. J., *Stanton Harcourt* (Published by the author, 1967).

POCOCK E. A., *The Mystery of White Horse Hill* (Published by the author, 1965).

Charney Manor and Church (Society of Friends).

GIBBON R. G., *The History of Somerford Keynes* (The Vicarage, Somerford Keynes).

HUGHES THOMAS, *Tom Brown's Schooldays* (Blackie).

JEFFERIES RICHARD, *Wild Life in a Southern County* (Nelson).

DUFTY A. R., *William Morris and The Kelmscott Estate* (The Antiquaries' Journal, 1963, vol XLIII pt 1).

TURNEY J. M., *A Geographical Appraisal of the AERE, Harwell* (AERE Journal *Harlequin,* 1968).

OSWALD ARTHUR, *Old Towns Re-visited – Abingdon* (Country Life 1952).

Properties of the National Trust, 1969.

The AA Illustrated Road Book.

Official Guides (obtainable from the relevant local authorities) to Abingdon, Banbury, Bradfield, Bicester, Bullingdon, Cheltenham, Chipping Norton, Cirencester, Faringdon, Hungerford, Newbury, Northleach, Swindon, Thame, Wallingford, Wantage, Witney.

Blenheim Palace (Blenheim Estate Office, Woodstock).

Place Names

EKWALL EILERT, *The Oxford Dictionary of Place Names* (Oxford, revised 1960).

CAMERON KENNETH, *English Place-Names* (Batsford 1961).

General History Relevant to Life in the Region

CLAPHAM SIR JOHN, *A Concise Economic History of Britain* (Cambridge 1949, revised 1957).

TREVELYAN G. M., *English Social History* (Longmans).

The Pelican History of England (*England in the Late Middle Ages,* A. R. Myers; *Tudor England,* S. T. Bindoff; *England in the Seventeenth Century,* Maurice Ashley; *England in the Eighteenth Century,* J. H. Plumb; *England in The Nineteenth Century,* David Thomson; *England in The Twentieth Century,* David Thomson).

GREEN J. R., *A Short History of the English People* (Everyman). Green's *History* was published in 1874, and revised by him 1877–80. It has, of course, dated, but the work is splendid in conception and still worth reading.

Index

Abingdon, 21; Old Stone Age settlement, 33; Neolithic settlement, 40; Abbey, 94, 115 et seq; guilds, 120–1; Abbey riots, 126–7; dissolution of Abbey, 127; titular Abbot of, 128; bun-throwing, 129–30; Charles I at, 130; William of Orange at, 130; 196, 209, 211, 213–14 216–17, 225, 228–30, 236.

Abingdon Bridge, 119 et seq

Acheulian culture, 31–2

Adlestrop, 153

Aethelbald, King of Mercia, 62

Aethelred I, King of Wessex, 64; death of, 65

Aethelred II, King of Wessex, 67–8; restoration of St Frideswide's church, 95

Agriculture, Neolithic, 39; early food grains, 40; in Roman Britain, 53–4; wages 203; modern employment in, 209

Agricultural Workers Union, 203

Alchester, 52, 91, 238

Akeman Street, 52, 238

Aldith of Wallingford, marries Robert D'Oyley, 70; founds Osney Abbey, 97

Alfred the Great, 57; birth at Wantage, 62; succession to crown, 65; struggle with Danes, 64–6, 69, 86, 115; attitude to

Abingdon Abbey, 122; memorial at Wantage, 173

Algar of Mercia, 94

Andersey Island, 77, 118, 122

Angles, 58

Animals, domestication of, 41

Anne, Queen, 155

Antiquaries, Society of, 235

Arch, Joseph, 203

Arnold, Matthew, 232, 239

Arthurian legend, 59

Ascot, 20

Ascott under Wychwood, 145

Ash Bank, 238

Ashampstead, 168

Ashdown, battle of, 64

Ashton Keynes, 82

Aston, 87

Athelstan, King of Wessex, 67; mint at Oxford, 95; at Abingdon, 123

Athelwold, Saint, 115, 117, 124

Atomic Energy Research Establishment, 22, 210 et seq

Atrebates, 22, 50

Augustine, Saint, 61

Avebury, 47, 134, 161

Aylesbury, 20; vale of, 158

Aynho, 238

Churchill, Sir Winston, 155
Churn, River, 25–6, 50, 139, 142
Cirencester, 20, 25, 50, 139, 209
Cissa, founder of Abingdon Abbey, 94
Clarendon, Lord, see Hyde, Edward
Claudius, Emperor, 50
Clifford, Rosamund ("Fair Rosamund"), 100–101
Clifton Hampden, 182, 205, 236, 240
Cnut, 68 et seq; traditional grant of manors in Vale of White Horse, 69; 96, 134, 145
Cockcroft, Sir John, 210
Cole, River, 26
Colesbourne, 142
Coln, River, 139, 142–3
Compton, 168
Cotswold stone, 78; shipped by Thames for building St Pauls, 86
Cotswolds, 26, 152
Cowley, 74, 208
Coxeter, John, 165
Coxwell, Great, barn, 88
Coxwell, Little, 169
Cranmer, Thomas, 113
Crayfish, 180
Cricklade, 26; Saxon defence system, 66; 79, 194
Croke, Sir George, 160
Cromwell, Oliver, 85, 136, 148
Crowmarsh, 31
Cuddesdon, 106
Culham, 74, 115; ford and bridge, 119 et seq; 205, 225–6, 235–6
Cumnor, 127, 131, 169, 230, 232
Cumnor ridge, 26, 231
Cuthwulf, King of Wessex, 60
Cynegils, King of Wessex, 61, 91
Cynric, see Cerdic

Danegeld, 67
Danelaw, 22
Danes, 20; Danish Vikings, 63; invasion of Upper Thames, 64; defeat at Ashdown, 64; Alfred the Great's strategy against, 65; renewed invasion, 67; Oxford burned, 67; Svein Forkbeard on Thames 68; Cnut, 69 et seq; Danish Vikings in Normandy, 69–70; relations with Saxons after conquest, 70–2
Daylesford, 153
Days Lock, 229
Denchworth, manor of, 69
Didcot, 80, 94, 170, 209, 211, 214, 216, 219
Dikler, River, 143
Ditchley, Roman villa at, 53
Dobunni, 22, 50–2, 139
Dominicans at Oxford, 102
Donnington Castle, 167
Dorchester, 49, 52, 56, 62; conversion of Wessex, 61, 91; bishopric, 94, 132; Abbey, 133–4; 205, 236
Downer, Anne, 154
D'Oyley, Robert, marriage to daughter of Wigod, q.v., 70; at Oxford, 96–7
Dragon Hill, 170–1
Drayton, 216
Druids, 50; Roman suppression of, 55
Ducklington, 151
Dudley, Robert Earl of Leicester, 131
Duxford, 53, 86, 233

Eadred, King of Wessex, 67; restoration of Abingdon Abbey 94; 115
Early, Richard, 151
Edington battle of, 65
Edmund, King of Wessex, 67
Edmund Ironside, 68, 124
Edward I, 146
Edward IV, 166, 181
Edward VI, 120–1, 160
Edward VII, 156, 173
Edward the Confessor, 62, 86, 134, 143; charter for Thames, 178
Edward the Elder, King of Wessex and England, 66; death at Faringdon, 88
Egbert, King of Wessex, 63

Iberians, 20
Ice Age, 29, 30
Icknield Way, 59–60, 79, 172
Iffley, 183, 230
Ine, King of Wessex, 62
Inglesham, 82
Inland Waterways Association, 201
Iron tools, 49
Isis, corrupt intrusion of name, 75–6
Islip, 62, 158

James I, 166, 179
James II, 130, 154
Jane, Wantage locomotive, 174
Jefferies, Richard, 239
John, King, 101, 146, 164; Thames in Magna Carta, 179
Jutes, 58

Keble, John, 143
Kelmscot, 234–5
Kemble, 82
Kempster, Christopher, 86, 144
Kempster, William, 144
Kennet River, 20–21, 26, 34; made navigable to Newbury, 76; 91, 161, 165, 168, 196
Kennet and Avon Canal, 76, 190, 199, 200
Kensington, St Mary Abbots, 124
Kidlington, 158, 215, 238
Kingston Bagpuize, 233
Kingston Blount, 71
Kingston Lisle, 71
Kirtlington, 238
Knights Templar, 143

Lambourn River, 161–2
Langland, William, author of Piers Plowman, 127–8
Latimer, Hugh, 113
Leach River, 82

Lechlade, 26, 79, 82–4, 107, 194, 224, 235
Leicester, transference of bishopric to Dorchester, 94
Lenthall, William, Speaker of Long Parliament, 147, 160
Letcombe Bassett, 71, 176, 177
Letcombe Brook, 172
Letcombe Castle, see Segsbury camp
Letcombe Regis, 176–7
Lew, 87
Lincoln, diocese of, 80, 94, 158
Littlemore, 215
Lockhart, Elizabeth, 176
London, 21, 26, 107, 218
London Stone, the, 182
Longbow, 40
Loyd-Lindsay, Col. of Lockinge (Lord Wantage), 173
Lyford, 170

Magdalen College, 104
Maglemosian people, 34
Maidenhead, 236
Mapledurham, 239
Marlow, 21, 236
Mary Tudor, Queen, 120–1, 160
Masefield, John, 239
Mason, Sir John, 120
Matilda, daughter of Henry I; struggle with Stephen of Blois, 99, 136, 145, 165
Matilda of Scotland, 124
Medley, 97
Mercia, 62 et seq, 94
Merton College, 104
Milton-under-Wychwood, 144
Mons Badonicus, battle of, 58
Montague, C. E., 144
More, Saint Thomas, 177
Morris, Miss May, 234–5
Morris, William (of Kelmscot), 234–5
Morris, W. R., Lord Nuffield, 111, 113, 208